ARRIVING AT BOULOGNE

A LONDONER'S HOLIDAY TRIP

J. GULICH

'The Smell of
the Continent'

'The Smell of the Continent'

The British Discover Europe
1814-1914

RICHARD MULLEN
AND JAMES MUNSON

MACMILLAN

First published 2009 by Macmillan
an imprint of Pan Macmillan Ltd
Pan Macmillan, 20 New Wharf Road, London N1 9RR
Basingstoke and Oxford
Associated companies throughout the world
www.panmacmillan.com

ISBN 978-0-230-74190-4

1 3 5 7 9 8 6 4 2

A CIP catalogue record for this book is available
from the British Library.

Typeset by SetSystems Ltd, Saffron Walden, Essex
Printed and bound in the UK by
CPI Mackays, Chatham ME5 8TD

To all those who have travelled with us

Contents

Introduction

'I remember being much amused last year, when landing at Calais,' wrote Frances Trollope in her travel book, *Paris and the Parisians in 1835*, 'at the answer made by an old traveller to a novice . . . making his first voyage. "What a dreadful smell!" said the uninitiated stranger . . . "it is the smell of the continent, sir!" replied the man of experience. And so it was.'

Smell is the most immediate of the senses, the one we are least able to control. Whether it is the aroma of good food or the smell of roses on a summer's day, or, conversely, of bad drains or damp rooms, its impact is immediate and its influence is long lasting. Mrs Trollope, a well-travelled woman, spent her last decades on the Continent and she well knew its various smells, pleasant and unpleasant. In this book we go beyond the smells to describe why, how, and where the British travelled in Europe in the hundred years from the fall of Napoleon to the outbreak of the First World War. For the first time in history people in their hundreds of thousands set out to discover Europe. For the first time in history, people in Europe came face to face with the British at a time when the 'Island Race' was at the height of its power.

The story begins on a summer's day in 1814 when a small ship hove into sight of the French coast at Dieppe after an eighteen-hour journey from Brighton. A rowing boat approached, collected the British passengers and took them to the empty beach. Among them were the young artists Benjamin Haydon and David Wilkie, and a friend who jumped out and waded ashore. 'The French looked on us,' Haydon wrote, 'as if we had dropped out of the moon . . . everything was new and fresh. We had thought of France from youth . . . as the abode of the enemies of our country. It was extraordinary. They absolutely had houses, churches, streets, fields and children!' In April Napoleon had abdicated as emperor and sailed for Elba. For the first time in twenty-five years Europe was free of bloody revolution and war. France, 'that remarkable country . . . in which refinement and filth, murder and revolution, blasphemy and heroism . . . alternately reigned triumphant', was once again open to the victorious British. Now travellers could see the works of art that Napoleon had stolen from collections throughout Europe.[1] Now they could see the very spots on which dynasties had fallen and the Terror had reigned.

In Rouen the young men were impressed by the beauty of High Mass in the cathedral and by the performance of a Beaumarchais play at the theatre, but not by their room at the inn. This was 'a perfect illustration of French character. Elegant satin sofas and a greasy floor; beautiful curtains and a dirty bed.' The landlady had 'filthy hands' and close to the kitchen was 'the dung of six horses – the accumulation of many months'. When the three of them set out on their way to a Paris occupied by victorious allied troops, they had perhaps had a little too much wine, which had 'a visible effect on all of us'. Haydon shouted, 'Let us give 'em "God save the King."' As their carriage left Rouen they spotted a Frenchman and 'two elegant women' who looked on amused as once more the patriotic trio burst into the National Anthem at which the Frenchman simply shrugged his shoulders.[2]

Once the men were in Paris, Haydon was overwhelmed by the recollection of what had happened there since 1789: 'its murders in the name of liberty, and its imperial despotism'. At the Louvre they were surprised by the sight of other tourists. When Wilkie was asked how he could distinguish the British from the others, he replied, 'Dear, dear, they just look as if they had a balance at their bankers.' The local inhabitants were themselves somewhat over-whelmed. A bemused Prince Metternich, noting that 600 English-man a day were arriving in Paris, protested, 'it is raining Englishmen.' The Austrian diplomat wryly added that the prosti-tutes in the Palais Royal were doing tremendous business. Napo-leon's brief return during the Hundred Days in 1815 stemmed the tide of travel, and tourists were 'all running' for home: 'Hurry-scurry is the word'. However, after the decisive victory of Waterloo, travellers hurried to the Continent in even greater numbers.[3]

Almost six decades later, in the summer of 1872, an open carriage was slowly conveying two middle-aged ladies up a steep, narrow road through the pine forests of the Dolomites. The carriage was packed with the usual impedimenta of middle-class travel: bags, shawls, rugs, books, sketching equipment, stools, easels, baskets of food and the essential Etna stove for tea. Suddenly the road came to an end. Ahead some 200 Italian peasants were breaking stones for a new road. They ceased work and stared at the two well-dressed ladies, as if 'we were creatures from another world'. 'You are the first travellers who have come up this way,' said the man in charge, adding in words that were heard round the Continent from 1814 to 1914, 'You must be *Inglese.*' Amelia Edwards and her companion, Lucy Renshawe, were most definitely British. Amelia was tall and dignified, the daughter of a prosperous banker and she had been publishing novels since her twenties. Like so many other writers she then turned to travel books, and by the time she was exploring the Dolomites she was an established member of that select group, the 'intrepid travellers'.[4]

Having reached a favourable spot, Amelia sat down, like a proper Victorian lady, to sketch a distant mountain peak. An aged peasant woman hobbled out of a nearby cottage, anxious to discover why this exotic being was sitting outside her home with a large sheet of paper on her lap, staring at a mountain. She asked the visitor, 'Where do you come from?' The English woman answered, 'From a country you have no doubt heard of many a time. From England.'

However, moderate arrogance was about to be vanquished by impenetrable ignorance: *'Gesù Maria*! From England! And where is England? Is it near Milan?'[5]

Forty-two years later on a night in early August 1914 while Europe was within days of a terrible war, a ship was setting out from Dover to Calais. In the distance the search-lights of German ships were sweeping the skies, and behind the steamer loomed the comforting presence of British warships. On board a journalist noticed a group of young Frenchmen called back to join the colours. As sirens hooted and chains rattled, the Frenchmen waved farewell to England and burst into the 'Marseillaise', mingled with cries of 'Vive l'Angleterre!'. A lone voice on the quayside shouted back 'Vive la France!'. Down below in the bar a group of Manchester lads, setting out on a short holiday 'excursion' to Paris, were 'drinking themselves fuddled'. A travel agent had 'promised them a "good time". There were plenty of pretty girls in Paris.'[6]

The new era of travel began with the end of one great war and ended with the beginning of an even greater one. Haydon and his friends were a new breed of traveller, having little in common with those who had gone on the eighteenth century's Grand Tour. This had been undertaken mainly by wealthy, young and usually aristocratic men whose years after university were often pleasantly filled by long visits to France and Italy. There they were supposed to cultivate their minds and widen their cultural horizons, though the reality could be rather different. One young man, writing to his father back in Dorset for more money, added that he was 'in good health. Champagne agrees with most constitutions.' Once in Paris there was another request for funds: 'Silks are the only thing a man can appear in in France so you must not wonder if I get another light suit . . . You must not think I have a mind to turn fop.'[7]

In the years immediately after 1814, while there was still a sprinkling of young aristocrats going abroad with their tutors, travel to the Continent entered a new era. Of the young men who now set out, most were as interested in recent events and the developing

Romantic movement as in contemplating Roman ruins or flirting with ageing countesses. Haydon and Wilkie were self-made men of the middle class who were establishing themselves as artists and were anxious to see the world. British travel was no longer the preserve of young *milordi*, even if the term lingered. For the first time, family groups and women would travel in significant numbers. Nor did these new travellers expect to have just one visit, however lengthy. Continental travel had once been an interlude in a young man's life; it was about to become an oft-repeated pleasure for the expanding ranks of the middle class.

Between 1814 and the outbreak of the First World War, Europe adapted to an ever-increasing number of British travellers, the bulk of whom believed that their country was the most important in history: its balanced constitution, reformed Church, thriving economy and expanding empire were, or should be, the envy of the world. Self-confidence was the Victorians' chief characteristic.* That belief affected the conduct of British tourists, whether they went for serious study or for 'fun', and sometimes it meant that they, like their descendants today, left resentment in their wake.

British travellers also believed in 'comfort' as a prerogative of their success and as an essential ingredient of civilization. They insisted that those whom they patronized with their custom should raise themselves to British levels if they wanted British gold. The greatest single improvement when it came to comfort was brought by the railways, which so accelerated the increase in travel that by mid-century the Swiss were already using the term *die Fremdenindustrie*, or tourist industry, one created to cope with the Victorians in their restless wanderings about the Continent. Railway companies soon realized that there were people who would travel if helped. Some were content with 'excursion tickets' for a long weekend in Boulogne. Others wanted shorter 'holidays', a demand that was met

---

* The term 'Victorian' will be used to cover the whole period because this self-confidence came with victory over the French and marked all generations from then to the outbreak of war in 1914.

by travel agencies offering 'all-in' packages and guided tours. The most famous of these was, of course, Thomas Cook & Son. While never underestimating the importance of travel agents we do want to put their achievements into perspective. All these developments created not just a new 'industry' but a new phenomenon, mass tourism as the numbers increased from a few thousand in 1814 to over one million in 1914. This phenomenal growth created a world in which those of us who book holidays in Europe, travel through the Channel Tunnel or fly on budget airlines are only following where they led.

For the first time in European history armies set out each year, not to kill or destroy, but to see and, in seeing, to enjoy. There was a conquest of sorts, but it was a peaceful one. Instead of cannons and cavalry the troops were armed with umbrellas, teapots and bonnets. How did this happen? To answer this overriding question we shall ask several smaller ones. Why did people travel? Who travelled? Where did they go and what did they look at? How did they do it? What was the role of railways and tourist agencies? What did travellers have to cope with? What did they read? What and how did they eat? Where did they stay? What was the effect of all this travel on continental life? What did tourists wear? How did they cope with foreign languages, luggage, money and continental Catholicism? What was the role of sport? How did they keep in touch with home and with their memories once they returned? What did they think of Europe and what did Europeans think of them?

We shall concentrate on those countries that were most visited, those most affected by travel and those that most influenced the British view of Europe: France, Germany, Italy, Switzerland and, to a lesser degree, the Austrian Empire. Spain, Portugal, Greece, Russia and Norway were visited, but the numbers were really quite small and did not contribute much to the development of mass travel in the nineteenth century – and books, like rivers, must have boundaries lest they overflow. While we shall generally use the term 'British', continentals used 'English' to apply to anyone from the British Isles. So universal was this term that in parts of Italy all foreigners were called *Inglese*. In addition, many travellers from Scotland, Wales and Ireland were quite happy to describe themselves as 'English', however annoying this might be to their descendants. We shall also concentrate on individuals, for this is very much a story of individual people. Many were noble-minded, intelligent and civilized and returned from their trips with a deepened understanding of life and a heightened appreciation of other cultures. Some were stupid, narrow-minded and philistine when they left and the same when they returned. Readers will find that many aspects of travel between 1814 and 1914 are unfamiliar, but they will also discover how much our own travels still have in common with those undertaken well over a century ago.

The story of Victorian travel is one of invention and discovery, of progress and destruction, of the extraordinary and the commonplace, of occasional tragedy and of frequent humour. Between Benjamin Haydon in 1814 and the unnamed Manchester lads in 1914 travel had been transformed. Long before 1914, older visitors to Europe were bemoaning that 'Travellers are things of the past; in the present day we have only tourists . . . The majority of us go in order to hurry as quickly from one place to another as steam can carry us.'[8] This lament – still heard today – summarizes the tremendous changes that occurred between 1814 and 1914. For good or ill, mass tourism must be included among the 'great British inventions', and it is this invention that we wish to describe in all its fascinating aspects in the pages that follow.

The research for this book began more than three decades ago when we were both doing research for doctorates in history at Oxford, one of us concentrating on the first half of the century, the other on the second. Both had become fascinated with how Victorians increasingly travelled and how important this became. We began to scribble down references to European travel in the back of biographies, diaries and novels. Other notes were put on index cards, the then approved tool of research. While writing books on the First World War, Queen Victoria, the Trollope family, Thackeray, Victorian religion or while preparing just under one hundred BBC documentaries we carried on compiling notes. Similarly, while looking at Victorian magazines in dusty second-hand book shops, risking one's sight reading the bound volumes of *The Times*, or examining manuscripts up and down the country, we jotted down interesting anecdotes and revealing stories. In time the index cards gave way to word processors and then to PCs – which now contain 115 separate files.

The authors are indebted to the hundreds of writers of travel books, articles, diaries and letters we have read. Without their exploits and accounts this work would have been impossible. Of equal import-ance are the manuscripts kept in the wonderful network of county record offices whose holdings constitute such a treasure house for historians. We would especially like to thank the librarians in the record offices of Bedfordshire and Luton, Buckinghamshire, Devon, Dorset, Gloucestershire, Hampshire, the Isle of Wight, Hereford-shire, Shropshire and Warwickshire.

We would also like to acknowledge our indebtedness to the librarians and archivists in Duke Humfrey's Library and the Bod-leian Library, Oxford, the Scottish Record Office, the National Libraries of Scotland and Wales, the British Library, Lacock Abbey and the National Trust, the National Archives, the Birmingham City Archives, Clandon House and the National Trust, the Univer-sity of Westminster Library, the University of California at Los Angeles Library, the Harold Acton Library in the British Institute of Florence and the Archivo Storico in the Palazzo Strossi in that same city.

Finally we wish to thank the following people who have helped us in our research: Colin Harris, Superintendent of Duke Humfrey Library, Vera Ryhajlo, Sally Matthews and David Busby in the Upper Reading Room, Bodleian Library, Alyson Pryce of the British Institute of Florence, Mrs Celia Treleaven of Brittany Ferries, M. Nicolas Forint and the staff of Galignani's Bookshop in

Paris, Dr Julia Bolton-Holloway of Florence, Professor J. C. Barnes, Mrs Susan Kennedy, the Very Reverend Robert Byrne of the Oxford Oratory, Magister Thomas Ilming of the Heeresgeschichtliches Museum, Vienna and Frau Doris Schneider-Wegenbichler of the Österreichische Nationalbibliotek, Vienna, Caterina del Vivo and Maria Novella Rossi of the Archivo Storico, Palazzo Strossi, Florence, Stefanie Ambühl, Davos Torismus, Davos, Switzerland, Fr Lawrence McLean of St Mark's English Church, Florence, the late Mrs Betty Nicoll, Anselma Bruce, Martyn and Sue Kelly of Dives-sur-Mer, Peter Shone and Sylvia Dugan, Tony and Sarah Thomas, Dr A. F. Kerr, Sir Peter Morris, Dr Christopher Winearls, our agent, the ever-resourceful Andrew Lownie, and our patient and helpful editor, Georgina Morley.

Richard Mullen
James Munson

A Note on Money

Between 1814 and 1914 the pound or 'sovereign' was divided into 20 shillings (*s*) and each shilling contained 12 pence (*d*). A shilling was therefore worth 5p in today's money and a penny was worth one-twelfth of 5p. In addition, people frequently spoke of a *guinea*, a notional sum that meant 21 shillings. This term was used regularly by tourist agencies for their prices as the extra 5 per cent provided much of their profit.

To find the value of the pound during this period, see www.measuringworth.com. As a rough guide the pound in 1854 was worth £66.50 in 2007 values. To put thing in contemporary perspective: a rural postman in Victorian England earned about 12*s* a week for walking about sixteen miles a day.

Coping with foreign money was, as always, difficult – as explained in Chapter 10. One fact made it easier: from 1814 to 1914 the pound bought about twenty-five French francs. Thus each British shilling was worth 20 per cent more than a franc. After 1870, one German mark was roughly equal to a British shilling.

In today's money, 20p could buy an above-average meal or room in a continental hotel for most of the period and equalled 4 shillings (4*s*), 5 French francs (5FF) or 1 US dollar ($1).

Why Do You Travel?

When the peasant woman asked Amelia Edwards 'Why do you come here at all? Why do you travel?' she was only asking a question that perplexed many in Europe. Why *did* increasing numbers of people leave home, especially in the early decades of the century when doing so was difficult, expensive and sometimes dangerous? The reasons are many and, like the number of travellers, they expanded with the years.

'When peace came . . . when our island prison was opened to us,' wrote an anonymous contributor to the *Westminster Review*, 'it was the paramount wish of every English heart, ever addicted to vagabondizing, to hasten to the Continent.' In 1814, those who had the time and money to travel now had the freedom to do so. They wanted to see where the events that had dominated their lives since 1789 had taken place. The Vicar of Harrow, J. W. Cunningham, cast a somewhat jaundiced eye at these travellers: 'The great bulk . . . are not occupied by any specific object.' Most were 'indolent' or motivated by 'restlessness, by an ill-defined curiosity, by ennui, by the love of dissipation, by a spirit of wandering, by a fancied regard to works of art, by the love of novelty, by the ill-governing consideration that "every body travels", by the superabundance of money' and by the hope that life abroad will be without 'sorrow'. Other observers were more charitable and saw evidence of a national characteristic at work. Samuel Rogers, a banker as well as a poet, wrote that 'Ours is a nation of travellers'. Frances Trollope, who heartily despised the Vicar of Harrow, her vicar, for refusing to bury Byron's illegitimate daughter, agreed: 'There certainly is in the blood of our race a very decided propensity' to visit 'mountains and valleys yet unseen'.[1] Somewhere between Cunningham and Mrs Trollope lies the answer to the question 'why *did* people travel?'

In 1832 a London wine-merchant's son was given a copy of Samuel Rogers's poem *Italy*. As the young boy pored over the book's illustrations, his mother asked, ' "Why should not we go and see some of them in reality?" My father hesitated a little, then with glittering eyes said – "Why not?" ' Within months the Ruskins had set out and young John was laying the foundation of his career as the century's most influential writer on art. This incident must have been repeated in thousands of homes. The desire actually to *see* famous cities, buildings, scenery and works of art was a prime motive for travel. Even today, when we are overwhelmed with television programmes about famous tourist sights, we still travel to see them first-hand. How much greater was the desire between 1814 and 1914 when people had far fewer representations? It was Samuel Rogers again who asked, 'Would he who sat in . . . his library, poring over books and maps, learn more . . . [than] he who . . . is receiving impressions all day long from the things themselves?'[2]

Travellers' diaries were another source of inspiration. As one diarist wrote, 'Travelling in retrospect' is when 'the Traveller looks back only to bright spots and sunny hours: time and distance shed their glow upon remembrance . . . and if a shadow of any pleasurable feelings perchance be communicated by the perusal . . . of these pages my task will have proved doubly useful.' This was the case with the aunt of the travel writer Augustus Hare. When she was a girl of eight a family friend read her selections from her travel journals. 'My first longings to see Rome,' she said, 'came from this source' and after her own tour she made sure that her travel journals and sketches were always available on her table for nephews and visitors to admire. She even took to singing Alpine songs to call in the cows, although this appears neither to have increased their milk yields nor to have influenced her nephew's writing career.³

Many Victorians went to Europe in the belief that they would appreciate their country and its mission better for having been away. By the 1850s Britain had become Europe's first urban and industrialized society. To go to Europe was to visit countries where the pace of life was slower and less 'modern'. As early as 1829 visitors moaned about 'the *procrastination* of the people . . . across the channel'. The British were engaged in a mighty effort to build a new and better world. Life was a struggle and victory was in sight. One reason for going abroad was to give oneself a sense of proportion. One tourist used a military metaphor: 'our short excursion has shown us a map of the field . . . we work . . . with a far clearer understanding of what we are about, when we come "back again."'⁴

Others, especially those who would be influenced by Ruskin's writings, were not so sure that progress was all it was made out to be. Such people developed what might be called a 'Disneyland' approach to the Continent. In 1816 Marianne Thornton wrote that 'France is a Fairy Tale kind of scene', and thirty years later *Blackwood's Magazine* began serializing a novella about tourists who had arrived in Brussels. One of the party regarded English (and even more, Scottish) cathedrals as 'mere architectural monuments, half-deserted, one corner only employed for the modest service of his church'. In the days before the Oxford Movement affected cathedral life, they were places 'for meditating on past times and the middle ages'. But in cities such as Brussels 'those past times . . . have come back again'. The British felt themselves transported back to the Middle Ages when they came across Latin Masses, incense and colourful vestments. The wider application of this view was described by the travel writer Percy Fitzgerald, who went into rhapsodies about his trip to France. Its 'quaint old towers, and town-halls, and marketplaces . . . – all this scenery was "set," – properties and decorations – and the foreign play seemed to open before my eyes and invite me.' Elsewhere Fitzgerald said his visit 'was surely a dream, or like a dream! . . . towers, towns, gateways

... savoury and unsavoury smells.' If not a dream it had been 'a very welcome show or panorama'. Even allowing for a travel writer's exaggeration, the point is clear.[5]

This attitude inevitably meant that many travellers resented the near presence of other British travellers who were intruding into their private 'experience' of Europe. As early as 1819 an English visitor on holiday in Switzerland moaned about 'the introduction of carriages into the mountain districts . . . and . . . the old fogies who used them'. The growing number of tourists was forcing 'the arbitrary, pitiless, Godless wretches' – that is, the local authorities – to cut roads through the mountains so that 'the lover of nature can nowhere find a solitary nook to contemplate her beauties. Yesterday . . . at the break of day, I scaled the most rugged height within my reach; it looked inaccessible; this pleasant delusion was quickly dispelled; I was rudely startled out of a deep reverie by the accursed jarring, jingling, and rumbling of a *calèche*, and harsh voices.'[6] Having vented his spleen, William Wordsworth called for his own *calèche* and was driven away. Consistency has never been a necessary part of denunciation.

Many of the annoyed got their revenge by poking fun at other travellers in their diaries, letters and published works. In 1819, Lord Byron was, like Wordsworth, in Switzerland. He was returning from the Castle of Chillon, surrounded by the Romantic joys of 'rocks – pines – torrent – glaciers . . . and summits of eternal snow' when he met 'an English party in a carriage – a lady in it fast asleep! . . . in the most anti-narcotic spot in the world'. This reminded him of an earlier encounter in France, 'in the very eyes of Mont Blanc – hearing another woman – English also – exclaim to her party "did you ever see anything more *rural*" – as if it was Highgate or Hampstead'. Lady Frederick Cavendish, visiting Switzerland in 1864, asked herself, 'Why does one hate and despise nearly all one's fellow-countrymen abroad?' Five years later Bishop Magee set out to 'do' the Italian lakes. He stopped at Bellagio but 'forty-three Americans and English landing there in a body were too much for my nerves, and I went on to . . . Lago Maggiore.'

Some forty years later an English woman in Paris put it more starkly: 'The Cockney accent necessarily jars more on an English ear than on a foreigner's.'[7] Not that 'foreigners' don't say stupid things; it is just that we don't understand. When stupid things are said by Britons with 'cockney' accents, that is, accents not as polished as our own, we resent them even more.

With every year more sensitive travellers bemoaned that travel 'no longer affords scope for romantic adventure'. J. W. Burgon, writing in 1862, complained that railways 'spin along . . . at . . . twenty miles an hour'. When one comes down Rome's Spanish Steps a man approaches to offer a 'clean cab'. But this same debate, which continues today with different settings, predates the 1860s. In 1768 Laurence Sterne had pronounced that 'an Englishman does not travel to see Englishmen'. In 1819, Thomas Moore asked in his *Rhymes on the Road*:

> *And is there then no earthly place*
> *Where we can rest, in dream Elysian,*
> *Without some cursed, round English face,*
> *Popping up near, to break the vision.*

Related to all this was the use of the words 'traveller' and 'tourist'. In essence this boils down to 'I am a traveller. He is a tourist.' Travellers are said to be independent, resourceful and intelligent while tourists go in guided parties, know little and learn nothing. The distinction is a Victorian one. At the start of our period the terms were interchangeable, but by the 1840s writers started to describe someone who travelled 'too rapidly' and who 'saw more than he could mark' as 'rather a tourist than a traveller'. Ruskin was using the word in this sense in the 1880s when he wrote of a spot as 'a tourist rendezvous'. The new distinction, which was never absolute, is traceable to the century's new travel agencies: Thomas Cook, for example, conducted 'tours' and described its branches as 'tourist' offices. Groups started to become 'tourists' while individuals remained 'travellers' – and it was individuals who wrote travel books.[8]

Between 1814 and 1914 scarcely a year passed in which an article did not appear bemoaning the horrors inflicted both on Europe and on fellow British travellers by the growing numbers of tourists. If we recall Moore's phrases, 'dream Elysian' and 'break the vision' (not 'the view'), we return to our main theme. In earlier decades people went more to see famous buildings, cities and sights. Later, others travelled, as we would say today, to 'experience' the country, to be uplifted by contact with the 'real Italy' or the 'real France'. Like their hero, Byron, they wished to realize a 'vision'. When Jerome K. Jerome visited Germany in the 1890s he made sure he went in to 'one or two of the beer-halls – not into the swell cafés, crowded with tourists . . . but into the . . . cellars where the life of the people is to be seen'. In such places travellers could meet the 'ungenteel people' who were 'so much more interesting than the gentlefolks . . . We gentlefolks only play at living.' But even Jerome admitted that the struggle for 'reality' was more difficult than it had been. He lamented the loss of 'quaint, centuries-old costume' in the face of fashion's 'world-wide crusade against variety and its bitter contest with form and colour'.[9] Dress was important: exchange a peasant's peculiar clothes for corduroys and an open-necked shirt and all one had was an agricultural labourer, the same as in England.

Of course, such comments were based ultimately on double standards, a point made by the Reverend A. N. Cooper who walked from Filey in Yorkshire to Rome in the 1890s:[10]

In England, when a slum is pulled down, and sanitary houses built . . . every one applauds. When in . . . Venice . . . a ghetto is pulled down to make way for better houses, there is an outcry as if it were the business of the Italians to keep their country as a preserve for the hunter after . . . antiquities . . . Yet how should we like to be condemned to live in such a stench if we were Venetians, just to please a number of visitors?

Another reason why British travellers disliked their countrymen was the feeling that to visit Europe, especially France and Italy, was to escape the rules and regulations that governed respectable middle-class life. Increased wealth meant that more people had servants whose presence imposed certain standards of behaviour. The novelist Blanchard Jerrold remembered that his parents went to France in part so that 'the stiff dressing, the conventional laces, of the West End could be cast away'. To go to the south of France or Italy was to visit lands marked by a 'lightness of heart, joined to the lightness of the atmosphere' and this 'produces that open-air festivity and community of enjoyment which makes the taciturn, heavy hypochondriacal man stare'. In other words, in warmer climates people lived more out of doors. This quote, from an 1857 guide-book, was both an analysis and an advertisement. No wonder people avoided their countrymen: to meet them was to re-impose the bonds one had temporarily escaped. One final object from which people sought to escape was expressed by Thackeray in 1840: 'I . . . never landed on Calais pier without feeling that a load of sorrows was left on the other side of the water; and have always fancied that black care stepped on board the steamer . . . at Gravesend, and accompanied one to . . . London – so busy, so dismal, and so vast.'[11]

One of the most important reasons for travel was that 'We do as our neighbours do. Though we don't speak to each other much when we are out a-pleasuring, we take our holiday in common, and go back to our work in gangs.' With each year that passed it became more and more the fashion to travel. In the 1820s Coleridge expressed this in *The Delinquent Travellers*:

> But O, what scores are sick of home,
> Agog for Paris and for Rome!
> Nay! Tho' contented to abide,
> You should prefer your own fireside;
> Yet since grim war has ceased its madding,
> And Peace has set John Bull agadding,
> 'Twould such a vulgar taste betray,
> For very shame you must away!

In mid-century a writer in *Fraser's Magazine* was impressed (or appalled) at the power of fashion. It was 'difficult to determine why the thousands of English who may be tracked annually up the Rhine, and over the Alps and the Pyrenees, go abroad at all'. 'Intelligible purpose,' he declared, 'they have none.' When in 1866 Anthony Trollope wrote a series of essays about travellers, he included those who travel 'because it is the thing to do'. From 1814 there was an increasing number of travel books, guides and articles, while Byron's search for the 'romantic' continued to influence people. Well into the 1860s British travellers were said to go about with their Murray *Handbook* under one arm and Byron's poems under the other. Even in the early years of the twentieth century Italian guides still referred to the poet, and buildings associated with him would be pointed out.[12]

Fashion was as much part of our herding instinct in the 'long nineteenth' century as it is today. Travel very quickly became the fashion for those who could afford it and, with each passing year, more could do so. A household guide for the lower middle classes from the 1880s, for example, was discussing the fashion for 'wedding tours' or honeymoons abroad. It admitted that this custom was 'of questionable advantage or satisfaction, but, since it is the custom, those who do not conform to it are liable to be regarded as not in the fashion'.[13] That would never do. In E. M. Forster's *Where Angels Fear to Tread* (first published in 1905), Miss Abbott said that while 'I am John Bull to the backbone, yet I do want to see Italy, just once. Everybody says it is marvellous, and that one gets no idea of it from books at all.' (Chapter 2)* The operative words were, of course, 'everybody says'.

Many looked upon travel as a form of education, especially art education, because the great collections in Paris or Dresden were then so much better than anything on view in Britain. In an early

---

* Because there are often so many editions of the novels cited in this book, references are by chapter as indicated within brackets in the text.

guide to continental art galleries, a master at Rugby School singled out Dresden because it had not only the 'finest collection in the world' but the 'finest picture in the world'. This was Raphael's *Madonna di San Sisto* or Sistine Madonna. When a nineteen-year-old squire followed this advice and visited the Saxon capital in the 1860s he told his mother, 'To-day I went over a part of the gallery where there are some most lovely pictures, which I have noted down, but do not at present recollect their names.' Despite his lapse of memory he had no doubt that travel '*has really improved my mind immensely*!!'. He then added, 'Will you please, Mama-dear, send me a little more money?' (He got £10 to refinance his learning and improve his memory.)[14] Of equal importance, especially in the earlier years of the century, was the desire to see Roman ruins, so few of which had survived in Britain. This was a particular attraction for men whose education had been based on the Classics.

Samuel Rogers had no doubt that travel would improve the British moral character and would make people more tolerant and less insular. It is a theory that is still expounded. 'Our prejudices,' he wrote, 'leave us, one by one . . . we learn to love, and esteem, and admire beyond them. Our benevolence extends itself with our knowledge. And must we not return better citizens than we went?' To others, travel 'enlarges the mind, and teaches a lesson never forgotten through life; a lesson of universal love, toleration, and doubt of our own exclusive merits. After this an Englishman is much better at home.' On occasion this worked: a Scottish father and son said of their 1867 trip, 'very interesting and instructive: many erroneous impressions and ideas have been removed'. There were also those who saw in travel a means to become 'a missionary in the work of civilization and in the promotion of good fellowship among nations'. In this case one became a 'missionary' by buying a copy of Bradshaw's *Illustrated Travellers' Hand Book in France*, from which this quote is taken.[15]

A yearning for adventure, for 'sights and sensations that are new' because one is 'wearied of every day sounds and sights' was probably as great a reason for travel as was the desire for moral improvement. Indeed, some of these new 'sights and sensations' had very little to do with improved moral character and were encountered even before people arrived in Europe. Frederick Leveson Gower MP was travelling from Dover to Calais when he spotted a well-known barrister, William Ballantine, 'accompanied by a young and pretty girl' whom he introduced as his niece. Leveson Gower again met Ballantine on another crossing and noticed he had yet another 'good-looking young woman as his companion, whom he likewise presented as his niece'. When the MP's son pointed out that this niece was a different woman, Leveson Gower said, 'Yes, he is rather careless. He changes them too often.'[16]

On another crossing in the early 1860s passengers were intrigued by a burgeoning romance between a man and a woman who was noticeable for her short hair. Unknown to the man, she was Henrietta Unwin, who had run away from her husband after a long history of mental illness, cut off her hair (a scandalous thing in itself) and left for France. After landing she and her new friend spent several days in a Parisian hotel. What happened afterwards is not known. These flights to the Continent by estranged husbands or wives were not just the stuff of novel writers. In September 1891, passengers might have noticed a discreet but observant man travelling by himself. This was a detective on his way to France. Once in Le Havre he wired the solicitors who had hired him, 'Have clue – fear suspicions founded – be careful to let nothing transpire but await letter.' The solicitors then wrote to their client, a Mr W. W. W. Bingham, to warn him 'to take great care that *no one* gets any hint of what you know. Otherwise Mrs. B. or her friends might send someone to Havre . . . & we might subsequently find ourselves frustrated.' The detective had found Mr Bingham's wife and her female companion, known as '*les Anglaises*', along with her lover, in a hotel where they had taken 'a suite of adjoining rooms with communicating doors'. The last one hears is a telegram from

Bingham to a friend: 'Will be with you 11.20 for a few minutes am too upset to stay longer will explain when I see you Bingham.'[17]

Once on the Continent men travelling by themselves or with male friends were more than likely to meet an 'adventure' since prostitutes and pimps were a continuing problem, and one discussed in several travel books. People grumbled about the number of English prostitutes who crossed the Channel to 'service' the English 'colonies'. Even worse were the pimps: in Milan in the 1820s 'a young man (a stranger) cannot walk the street in the middle of the day without being continuously accosted by men . . . enquiring if you want a *"bella ragazza."* ' In Venice's St Mark's Square the Hills were shocked to see 'young men and youths' (and even young children) handing out cards for prostitutes to male tourists and speaking 'a few words in a subdued voice'. One Catholic bishop visiting Naples was horrified when he met 'a ruffian who made . . . the most abominable exhibition of himself to me that I have ever witnessed or even supposed human depravity to be capable of. Dr. K. related a similar incident that occurred to himself. He added that immorality of any kind may be practised here with impunity, provided politics are eschewed.' Yet another visitor to Naples, who may or may not have told the truth, claimed that as he left his hotel a well-dressed man asked if he would like to meet 'charming ladies', and when this got little response the man said, 'Ah! the Signor would perhaps like a fine young man.'[18]

Others ventured forth to enjoy those pleasures that only 'change and novelty and excitement afford'. Indeed, one travel article in 1875 defined the tourist as someone who 'is wearied of every day sounds and sights, and hungers . . . for sights and sensations that are new'. The attraction of the unknown and unfamiliar – the 'foreign' – was a constant theme. When a Yorkshireman was told that he could more easily go to Harrogate for the waters than to Vichy he replied, 'I believe it is an excellent place but we shall never go to it – it is so near one's home.'[19] Then there were those who turned to Europe only after they had exhausted Britain: 'What an anxious question this annual holiday is now becoming!' wrote another diarist in the 1860s. 'Everybody has been to Scotland, some of us had done the Land's End, Ireland is not everybody's choice, the International Exhibition [of 1862] had tired us all of London, Scarbro' is only suitable for invalids and children, the Lake District done years ago, and Fleetwood is worse than Scarbro' – where shall we go next?' The answer in this case was Switzerland on a Cook's Tour.

A few people even travelled for the sheer pleasure of travelling itself – James Augustus St John, who was something of a pompous ass, wrote in mid-century that 'travelling is a sort of mechanical happiness to me'.[20]

Others went abroad because their personal circumstances meant they were more comfortable living outside Britain: the divorced, the separated, those who wanted to marry a deceased wife's sister (illegal before 1907), the illegitimate and those living as a couple outside marriage. When the novelist George Eliot and G. H. Lewes visited Germany in the 1850s they were accepted socially and could call on others in a similar position, such as the composer Liszt and his companion, Princess Carolyne Sayn-Wittgenstein. Yet even George Eliot's situation was rather tame when set beside the ducal scandal that swirled round the head of the 5th Duke of Newcastle and fascinated Victorian Britain. In 1848 while still heir to the dukedom, as Lord Lincoln, his wife told him she was going to Germany for medical treatment. In the event she left him and their five children to meet Lord Walpole, who was deserting his wife. The pair travelled round as Mr and Mrs Laurence. Lord Lincoln's friend, William Gladstone, agreed to set out after Lady Lincoln to 'rescue' her. In twenty-seven days the future Prime Minister travelled more than 3,000 miles taking in Paris, Marseilles, Geneva, Milan, Rome, Naples and Lake Como, where he tried to get into the couple's villa. When denied entrance he returned disguised as a troubadour, complete with mandolin, hoping to find out the couple's next port of call. He finally caught up with Lady Lincoln, now heavily pregnant, but she refused to speak to him and he returned home, defeated and presumably without the mandolin. Lady Lincoln eventually tired of Lord Walpole and married a Belgian courier. When this marriage failed, she returned to England to die in poverty.

Thirteen years later scandal once again engulfed the Newcastle family when the next Lord Lincoln ran up racing debts of £230,000 – almost £15 million today – and fled to Paris. There he married the illegitimate daughter of an Anglo-Dutch family on the understanding that his new wife would get a duchess's coronet while he would have his debts settled and his future income secured. The ceremony was attended by Lincoln's sister, who had been cut off without any income by her father, and her husband, another gambler. Lincoln's brother, who lived in France to escape debt collectors, did not attend. As he was said to be a 'cross-dresser' this may have been just as well.[21]

Sometimes people travelled because their work or interests required it. In the 1880s Granville Lloyd Baker, a Gloucestershire landowner, toured Normandy to investigate cheese-making. While he was impressed by the coffee and butter at Isigny he had his doubts about Livarot cheese: 'the taste is strong & the smell so coarse that I do not think English people would buy it.' Architectural students keen on the Gothic Revival naturally wanted to see what Europe had to offer. As early as 1840 the architect Augustus Pugin was writing to Charles Barry, with whom he was working on the new Palace of Westminster, that 'you ought, as a positive duty, to come to these countries'.[22] Before 1869 many set out for the Continent to avoid imprisonment for debt, while throughout the period surprisingly large numbers travelled because they could live in some style more cheaply than in Europe. Likewise, some homosexual men found in France – and more especially Italy – a tolerance they did not enjoy in Britain. When Oscar Wilde was released from Reading Gaol he left that same day for France.

Yet others went to enjoy and learn from the various 'international exhibitions' that followed Britain's pioneering Great Exhibition of 1851. Exhibitions were held in Paris, Vienna, Florence, Munich,

Rome and Berlin. In any year that featured an exhibition the number of travellers soared. The Paris Exhibition of 1889, for example, attracted an extra 107,500 tourists to the city, in part due to Monsieur Eiffel's new tower. Most of these people must have enjoyed their trips because the numbers held up during the years that followed and the same was true with every exhibition during our period.

In some cases parents or teachers took their daughters to 'finish' their education through exposure to European life. Some went to learn foreign languages while after the 1850s others went for sport. The most popular venue was Switzerland because of the new fashions for mountaineering, skiing and tobogganing, all three largely popularized by the British. Normandy and Brittany were popular from the 1890s for cycling.[23]

As travel became easier, quicker and safer the British started going to Europe for specific cultural events. The first was the famous outdoor Passion Play at Oberammergau, performed every ten years with a cast made up of local villagers, with a chorus, orchestra and specially composed music. Interest in the play was such that in 1871 Thomas Cook organized an all-in tour. After that year British visitors were always the majority among foreign spectators, many of whom lodged with the performers. When Charles Oman went for the performance, he stayed in King Herod's house and expected the performance to be 'artificial and exploited'. Instead he found it a 'purely religious experience', while Lord Sandwich was 'immensely impressed by the sanctity of the performance', which lasted from 8 a.m. to 12 and then from 1.30 to 5.20 p.m. The second great cultural attraction, which also took place in Germany, was the annual festival of Wagnerian operas at Bayreuth, which began in 1876. (Tickets for the complete *Ring* could be bought through tourist agencies in London for £4 in the 1890s.)[24]

The search for health far outranked that for art, music or theatre. Some rejected Mrs Trollope's companion's lament about smells and claimed immediate benefit from 'the elasticity of foreign air', while others yearned for a fashionable rest at European spas. The belief in the curative power of water, whether consumed or bathed in, went back millennia and was supported by much medical opinion. Added to this were diets of varying types and mild exercise in pleasant surroundings. For those who could afford it, spas beckoned even if cynics said they contained 'the usual collection of bewigged and washed-out oddities, who assemble in such places in search of a new lease of life'. Each spa had a different appeal: Marienbad in the Austrian Empire was favoured by those who had eaten far too well, which meant that some described it as 'a paradise for fat people'. It also appealed to royalty, from Austria's Franz Joseph to Britain's Edward VII.[25] Tourist agencies provided medical guides at Paris's Gare du Nord to advise passengers about the most appropriate spa while guide-books compared and contrasted various locations. Some publishers such as Murray and Bradshaw even published entire books to help people choose a spa that specialized in their particular complaint.

Vichy was one of the most popular. By 1858 over 10,000 people a year were enjoying its pleasant walks, donkey rides, concerts, reading rooms and balls. A typical lunch consisted of soup followed by three types of meat followed by pastry, cheese, strawberries, grapes, peaches, as well as bread and wine during and absinthe after the meal. Guests were not permitted salads or anything with 'acid'. As Vichy water was alkaline the point seems to have been to attack acidity in the body. In 1894 John Oglander left the Isle of Wight for Vichy while his wife went to Royat for her throat. He was out by 7.30 a.m., drank some water, then went for a walk followed by a twenty-minute bath. At 10.30, after an hour's 'repos' he had breakfast. After breakfast he wrote letters until about 3 p.m., when he went for another walk. Between 4.30 and 5 he drank more water. At six came dinner, after which a friend joined him on his balcony for coffee, and he was in bed soon after nine. His main problem was the 'deaf old Frenchman' who sat next him at dinner: when Oglander asked for the white wine the Frenchman in turn asked if he had '*diarhée*'. 'I answered "no" and considered it was not a subject for dinner table conversation.' The Frenchman then went on to describe how anyone with 'diarrhoea should not drink white wine and to expatiate on his own diarrhoea'. Poor Oglander was put out because 'I hear nothing on all sides, but whether or not my neighbours are "fatiguing" their "astomacs." Still, the bands are very good.'[26]

In 1897, Oglander was once again in Vichy, at the Grand Hôtel des Ambassadeurs:

> I have a very clean little room with a balcony . . . and a dressing closet . . . I was very glad to change my clothes and then went off to the source and after my 2 glasses to the bath, an hour's rest and then dejeuner. At 1, I trotted round to Vilemin [his physician] who has been to examine me today. I don't think he believes my liver is much wrong, but says my heart is inclined to fat and the 'pavoi' is so thick that it is difficult to hear through it. He has ordered a masseur to come tomorrow to massage my tummy and chest and he is to come every day for a fortnight.

While Oglander enjoyed his walks, he wasn't so sure about the massages from 'a nice smart young Swede' who charged ten francs a day. 'It seems a great deal to spend on my poor old tum-tum . . . They say they are going to take my fat off, as if I was an old plank to be shaved down.' He clearly expected some benefit because he told his wife he would make his way back to England via Bourges, Blois, Tours and Caen 'all big places with good hotels'. But almost three weeks later he was becoming slightly fed up with the regime. 'It seems quite ridiculous that my masseur should be able to rub away fat as he professes to do, but I certainly have gone down ½ stone in weight and feel less sleepy and stupid than I did.'[27]

Not everybody who went to a spa did so because of 'indolence and over-indulgence'. In 1835, one English father, whose daughter suffered from rheumatism, wrote that he had heard 'so much of the Baths of Aix en Savoie [Aix-les-Bains] as being beneficial for Rheumatic attacks that we think of going there with Hor[atia]: for

what they call a *Cure* which takes about 3 weeks & – but we have
not yet seen any medical man.' Thirty years later the famous Anglo-
Catholic priest Father Dolling left Poplar for six weeks in Aix-la-
Chapelle. He described his day: 'At 6.45 I drink cups of sulphur
water, and drinking, bathing, douching, etc., goes on till 9.30; then
I have breakfast. In the afternoons, at 2, we start for the forest on
an electric tram' for a six- to seven-mile walk. Restored by tea or
coffee, the walkers took another tram back to the hotel for a rest
and dinner. 'I am in bed before ten.' A lending library supplied
English novels and there was free time for the priest to visit Aix
Cathedral and local churches. Unfortunately, the cure did little
good and within nine months he was dead. He was fifty-one.[28]

People suffering from consumption, as tuberculosis was then
known, or other respiratory illnesses, were advised to escape the
British winter if they could afford to. Thanks to heavy industriali-
zation and the prevalence of coal fires, pollution was far worse in
Britain than in most places on the Continent. The choice of a
winter retreat changed with the fashion: at one time Nice, Cannes
and Menton were favoured, but they were superseded by Switzerland, especially Davos. Pau in south-western France was recommended by Dr Alexander Taylor in 1842 for its altitude. After a
railway line to Paris was opened in 1863 the number of British
visitors to Pau soared. Two bundles of letters written by Frances
Blathwayt, who suffered from asthma, bronchitis, rheumatism and
'problems' with her chest, afford a vivid insight into an invalid's
life. The first batch, written in 1865, shows a young woman whose
spirits and sense of fun have not been broken by bad health. She
writes of a marriage 'which has caused *no end* of talk' between
Colonel Steele, 'something to Ld. Raglan . . . & a Miss Macarthy.
It was a lengthy flirtation & has given great offence to the English
belles here as she is a great flirt and an American!' The colonel had
arrived 'with a delicate little girl *inconsolable* for his first wife, &
the bride elect is said to be pretty empty headed & to spend
£600–0–0 a year on her dress . . . The place was crowded with
carriages all day paying congratulatory visits.' In March she talks of

'a Belgian lady (I should think she weighs 18 stone) who has been spitting blood ever since she was 17 & is now about 60 & quite well to all appearances.'

Three years later the letters resume: 'The gaiety here is tremendous. The Brownlows [the Earl and Countess Brownlow] are out every night & she looks fagged to death . . . Pau has got to that pitch that people must be made of money to even dress for it.' But a month later, in February 1865, disease and scandal arrived. French troops stationed there were 'dying like dogs all winter' from typhoid due to their water being contaminated by drainage from a nearby cemetery. Pau was convulsed with stories of a fancy-dress ball and of 'a fracas which took place owing to young Comte Barotte [?] in his character of [the] Duke of Buckingham having paid a wager with another exquisite that he would kiss the two beautifully displayed shoulders of Madm. S.' Madame S. was so shocked that she went to the local *préfet* who ordered the comte to apologize. 'It served her right for they say she had on a tiger skin & *very little else* except magnificent diamonds. She is a 3rd wife or the husband would hardly have accepted any apology for such an insult but thrashed him there and then.' In March Frances refers for the first time to her own health: 'What a life it is. I wake, eat, & sleep – a nice way of keeping Lent however everyone has a skeleton only sometimes they will come out & shew themselves instead of being reasonable skeletons & staying in their cupboards.'

The summer found Frances Blathwayt at Les Eaux Chaudes, nearer the Spanish border:

This place is very lovely & charming for invalids . . . There are always luxurious [?] seats to be had so I sit out till one if I am up & it is not too hot. Then we dine & abt. 3 go to the Blunts. It's up an awful hill but I spend ½ a franc in a chair, & we sit there and read or work or write till tea. After that chairs & donkeys for two hours & then another sit. Occasionally we club [together] & get a drive. Then home & get a sort of supper tea or soup meal & have Ivanhoe & go to bed.

In August she writes to her sister-in-law with advice about travelling and the next surviving communication, a telegram, is dated 23 February 1869. It is addressed to the Reverend W. T. Blathwayt: 'Fanny breathed her last at six Monday evening.' Her struggle with ill health was over but her enjoyment of life survives in her letters, published here for the first time.[29]

A final reason for foreign holidays, and one that is sadly still prevalent, was that they were often cheaper than holidays in Britain. During 1853 a public debate blew up, one that readers will find all too familiar. In September a Lancashire magistrate wrote to *The Times* to compare a holiday in England with one in France, Italy and Switzerland. The English holiday cost twice as much: 'I cannot afford to travel in England . . . all my future tours shall be on the continent.' The next month *Eliza Cook's Journal* published an article attacking the exorbitant rates charged by British hotels. This, inevitably, drove people 'to foreign countries, where such impositions and tricks . . . are not practised.' The article pointed out that, in Lucerne, by no means a cheap destination, the best hotel could cost as little as nine shillings a day and in Venice, eleven shillings, whereas in 'the principal English hotels . . . the charge averages from 20 to 30 shillings a day. No wonder, therefore, that . . . travellers . . . prefer rushing abroad.' It was better than being 'systematically fleeced'. Eventually the debate produced pamphlets such as *The English Hotel Nuisance* by Albert Smith, famous for popularizing Mt Blanc, and on 3 November 1855 *The Times* pronounced that 'on the continent of Europe these things are better managed'.[30] They still are.

Chapter 2

Epitomes of England

The American writer Washington Irving described a party of Englishmen in their carriage travelling near Rome in the mid-1820s. The Popkins were 'an epitome of England; a little morsel of the old island . . . the ruddy faces gaping out of the windows . . . and then the dickeys loaded with well-dressed servants, beef fed and bluff, looking down . . . with contempt on all the world around; profoundly ignorant of the country and the people, and devoutly certain that every thing not English must be wrong.' Starting with these carriage parties in mind we can begin to answer the question, 'who travelled?'. In time many different types of tourists would come to epitomize Britain, from the well off with their servants to shopkeepers, schoolteachers and even East End basket-makers, people who would take advantage of the changes in travel that were themselves products of the Victorian spirit. Within ten years of Waterloo observers such as Lord Normanby saw what was happening: travel was no longer confined to the 'higher orders'. Now, he wrote, however ungrammatically, 'lesser men with less fortunes' had learned to be 'ashamed of their former backwardness and fears' regarding foreign travel: the 'Jenkinsons and Tomkinsons tumble down the Alps in living avalanches'. As another observer put it, travel was no longer 'confined to persons in the highest rank of life . . . the subordinate classes . . . have also caught the same mania'. In addition, a 'large proportion of our travellers are *females*', whereas 'formerly travelling was almost confined to our own sex'.

What is more, 'a considerable portion . . . are persons in the earlier stages of life'.[1]

In the beginning, however, Normanby's 'higher orders' very much dominated the scene. Lady Fremantle wrote from Paris in 1815: 'It is quite ridiculous the number of English friends we have met now, & the number which are going on to Italy.' Travelling to Florence with her husband and daughter in their own carriage, she complained that 'the expense is immense & it has not cost us less than eight Guineas a day during our sejour'. Because her letters to her son have survived, along with her husband's accounts, we can get an insight into the leisurely pace of aristocratic travellers – though the pace was due as much to the state of the roads and the difficulty of travel as to any leisurely outlook. The Fremantles, like most wealthy travellers in these early years, made their way to Paris and went to Geneva via Dijon. They then crossed the Alps and travelled to Milan, ignoring their daughter's sneer that the city 'is no "great shakes"'. From there they set out for Venice and then on to Florence, Rome and Naples, returning to Rome for the Holy Week and Easter ceremonies. They then retraced their steps back to Florence and Paris. Most people of their class spent several months in Florence, where they took apartments, entertained and were presented to the Grand Duke. Young Emma took lessons in Italian, dancing and drawing while her mother still shuddered over the inns between Rome and Naples: 'dreadful & filthy, nothing to eat, in short we have lived upon Tea, & were perfectly worn out'. For his part Sir Thomas grumbled about the 'hard tooth brushes' and the lack of a decent razor strop.[2]

Among the most distinguished of these early, wealthy travelling families were Lord and Lady Vernon. They went to Italy to retrench after his income fell from £40,000 to a mere £10,000 a year and because his lordship wanted to polish his translation of Dante. Their huge luggage wagon, pulled by four horses, always set out an hour before the rest of the vehicles to arrive at the next destination in time for the servants to make suitable arrangements. Inside were four vast mahogany cases containing the collection of books on

Dante; on top, the family's carpet bags and in front, seats for their French cook and dog. In addition to being a Dante scholar, Lord Vernon was also an excellent marksman and shot at 'every rifle match that takes place in Switzerland'. His many prizes included 'gold watches, flags, teaspoons, teaboards [tea trays] and so forth', all of which were carried about in his carriage. The main procession consisted of a barouche containing some of the children, Lord Vernon's own, large travelling carriage and, finally, Lady Vernon's 'chariot'. It is no wonder local people were impressed with the wealth and grandeur of Britain.[3]

If upper-class family parties such as the Fremantles and Vernons dominated the world of travel in these early years they were never the whole picture. Wealthy individuals travelled on their own: Lord Byron is arguably the most famous. But there were many others including the eccentric Yorkshire sportsman Colonel Thomas Thornton, the beautiful society figure Lady Blessington, with her husband and a French count (whom gossip said was the lover of both), and the young Benjamin Disraeli, who went in his friend's carriage on a three-month tour of Italy in 1826. That same year George Purefoy Jervoise and Thomas Fitz-Gerald went on a four-and–a-half-month tour, during which Jervoise kept detailed accounts. He spent £546 7s 7d, including £208.8s on travel in his own carriage, £18 15s on crossing the Channel, £70 for his servant and £126 10s on wine, which included £18 for thirty-six bottles of Johannisberg, Germany's most famous Rhine wine, at 10s a bottle. (It now sells for not much under £40.)[4] When Robert Parker went to do scholarly research in Paris in 1818 he was entranced by his Parisian washerwoman, Mlle Rosette L'Amour (or so she called herself). When the Earl of Carnarvon visited Turin a few years later he was not so much entranced as fascinated by the lady who paid an extended visit to the Italian Cardinal in the next room.[5]

By the 1830s travel was beginning to move somewhat down the social scale, to 'those persons and families who have no estates of their own to retire to in England [who] have been going down the Rhine, and sojourning during the autumn at Baden'. Yet travel was dominated by families who had sufficient money and time for lengthy trips, the comfortable upper-middle class. The barrister Thomas Noon Talfourd complained that when he first took his daughter to Europe he had only a 'limited holiday', by which he meant seven weeks. Mary Wilson had a successful linen draper's shop in London's New Bond Street with her sister and brother, and by 1847 the three had already made four trips to the Continent. They set out that year for a nine-month visit centred on Dresden. The Galtons, whose son Francis later became the famous scientist, were Birmingham Quakers and bankers. John James Ruskin, whose son's travel books were to influence the tastes of millions, was a wine importer who could afford to take his family to Europe on extensive summer tours. Others preferred to spend the entire summer in one place, often at a spa. One of the most popular was the Bagni di Lucca, north of Lucca, which attracted hundreds of British people each year. One visitor told her son that his sisters were there, and though there was 'no visiting', so dear to Victorian ladies, they did have 'the Faro table, the Balls and riding parties'. She added, it was only the last two that 'I consent to my girls joining'.[6]

The one thing observers in 1815 could not have foreseen was the advent of the railway. London's first railway to a Channel port came in 1840, and within seven years all major Channel ports were linked to the capital by rail. This opened a new chapter in travel, not simply because railways made getting to the ports easier and quicker (though not always cheaper) but because trains fulfilled the Victorian longing for innovation, comfort and speed. 'There is nothing in this levelling world of ours, which so effectually annihilates conventional respectability, as the modern mode of travelling – in which speed and safety are rightly judged to be valuable compensations for state and seclusion.' Time was now something that needed to be 'saved' and travel to Europe was becoming part of the 'modern' way of life. On the other side of the Channel, Belgium had a rail link between Ostend and Brussels by 1838, and by 1849 Calais, Dieppe, Boulogne and Le Havre were all linked to

Paris. The effect on tourism was startling: it is estimated that between 1840 and 1851 the number of travellers arriving in Calais and Boulogne almost trebled. Once people could travel from London to Paris in twelve hours and from London to the Alps in under twenty-four hours they realized that they could have shorter, cheaper trips and the idea of a 'holiday' was born.[7]

By mid-century people were using the new definition of a 'holiday' when they declared that 'an autumn holiday is one of the institutions of Great Britain; so that a hard-worked doctor need little excuse for giving himself three weeks off'. The upper-middle class was increasingly able to afford 'holidays' as breaks from their successful careers. In the summer of 1853 a Welsh clergymen had a two-month trip to France, Switzerland and Florence and spent on average some £3 2s a day, under a half of what the Fremantles had spent thirty-eight years earlier. His expenditure was roughly the same as that of mid-Victorian Britain's most popular poet, Martin Tupper. During his family's three-month tour, accompanied by two servants and a courier, Tupper spent about £40 a week. These travellers did a fair amount of sight-seeing, but they did not have to cram their activities into the hectic schedule adopted by their descendants. They followed the same leisurely pace of life abroad as they followed at home. There was time for writing up one's diary, keeping up one's correspondence and dressing. One example is the six-month tour undertaken by the Liberal MP Edward Horsman and his wife. This included several weeks in Rome. Charlotte Horsman described a typical day: up at eight to dress and study French until breakfast at nine. From ten to 4.30 the couple were out riding or sight-seeing in the carriage they had brought with them. One expedition took them 'to the English burial ground which contains the tombs of Shelley and another English poet who died very young of a broken heart. I forget his name'.[8] (Keats' death was caused by tuberculosis, not by a broken heart.) On their return to the hotel, Charlotte studied Italian and French until six, when they had dinner. At 9.30 they returned to their room, where she devoted herself to letters and her diary.

The arrival of railways led to new enterprises that made travel easier. The first really significant travel business was set up in 1844 by Henry Gaze in Southampton. His 'tourist system' made 'travelling arrangements' and his company later claimed to be 'THE INITIATORS OF THE PRESENT SYSTEM OF POPULAR CONTINENTAL TRAVEL.' In the first year of operation Gaze organized a tour from London to Boulogne and within ten years added tours to Brussels and the battlefield of Waterloo. In 1845 another pioneer, Joseph Crisp, was offering a 'combined ticket' to Paris, which was later expanded into an all-in holiday for seven guineas, a 50 per cent reduction on the standard fare. He was helped by a commission of 5 per cent from the railways plus an advertising allowance. It appears that this offer was not a success.[9] Despite this, a growing number of London agencies were advertising 'combination' tickets, for a fortnight in the French capital.

Despite the burgeoning number of agencies, nothing had been done to tackle the underlying fears of the timid or would-be traveller who still shied away. What was needed was someone who would organize everything, or almost everything. In 1849 Joseph Crisp did just that. He arranged a trip to Paris for 350 supporters of the new French republic who were responding to an earlier visit to England by some 500 members of the French National Guard. Crisp, a 'jolly old Soul' to his clients, arranged transport and a week's bed and breakfast for five guineas, first class, or four guineas, second. He provided his own *Guide Book* and local guides and asked customers to call each morning at his hotel to get 'plans for the day'. The group was received in Boulogne with a twenty-one-gun salute and a civic welcome, while in Paris the new government organized a reception in the Hôtel de Ville. When some of the party found a restaurant that offered '*côtelette de boeuf*' at half the cost of other places they were delighted until, like all Anglo-Saxons, they began to fear that the dish was really '*côtelette de cheval*'. Of one thing the group was in no doubt: 'For the first time in the memory of man, did the *people* of England visit the *people* of France, as members of one family' even at the risk of eating horse-meat.[10]

Where Crisp led, others followed. Reduced fares based on large bookings and group travel, with all bookings made by the 'contractor' who also organized tours and local guides had obvious advantages. Foreign languages, timetables, hotel bookings and foreign currencies would no longer frighten the timid. In the same year in which Crisp's party set out, the Continental Railway Company in London's Regent's Circus offered a week in Paris with full board. There was also free entry to the major tourist attractions 'under the guidance of intelligent cicerones [guides] speaking English' and first-class travel, all for £8, which is what the Fremantles had been spending *per day* thirty years earlier. While this was more expensive than Crisp's offer, it did include local guides and all meals. Within three months the offer had become a 'week of pleasure' in the French capital and the price had risen by £2. In addition, for twelve guineas people could have a fifteen-day all-in excursion on the Rhine.[11] The package holiday had arrived.

Railway companies themselves were also soon selling a new type of discounted offer: half-price 'excursion tickets' for long weekends in Boulogne for £1 7s first class and £1 second. A new phenomenon in British life had also arrived: the short break to France. The idea took root very quickly and soon these 'excursions' were the main traffic out of Newhaven, already the cheapest route to France. Between 1840 and 1855 the number of people arriving in Boulogne trebled and by 1860 excursion tickets made up 40 per cent of all tickets sold. By 1899 the number of 'excursionists' had soared to almost 55,000 a year or just over half of all arrivals in the port. Companies such as Southeastern Railways were advertising 'excursions' to Paris for £3 and £2 4s, exactly the sort of low fares that would appeal to the growing ranks of the middle class. Other companies came up with rival offers. The Chatham & Dover advertised weekend breaks to Calais for £1 return in 1863. These were never as popular as trips to Boulogne, although the Chatham & Dover's family ticket from London to Calais for a month at £2 5s (first class) and £1 15s (second) did sell well.[12]

The range of holidays now possible for independent travellers can be seen in the experiences of three different people. In 1852 'The Roving Englishman' described in the middle-class magazine *Household Words* how he travelled comfortably from May to September for £120. He reckoned that a 'fair travelling allowance' for a single man was £1 a day. A family of four should budget £3 daily. (This assumed they all stayed in first-class hotels and travelled first class.) Yet in the same year, the clergyman and author Charles Kingsley spent under three shillings a day on a walking tour of Germany, solaced by hock at 9d a bottle. Walking tours seem to have been a Cambridge speciality, and eight years later the future novelist Samuel Butler set out on a whirlwind tour of Normandy, Brittany, Paris (one day), Germany, Switzerland and the 'north-west corner of Italy', all in three weeks. Butler and a fellow Cambridge undergraduate left London by train on Tuesday morning and by Thursday were walking in the Alps: it was, he admitted, 'sharpish work, but very satisfactory'.[13] Some readers may recall the 1969 American film *If It's Tuesday It Must Be Belgium*, except in this case 'it' was the French Alps, the tourists were British and the year was 1859.

The next stage lay in convincing those with sufficient money that the advertisements' claims were genuine. Henry Gaze realized this in his *How to See . . .* booklets, which sold for a shilling. On the cover of the Switzerland pamphlet he reassured customers that the author was 'One Who Has Done It (Henry Gaze)'. He knew his market. First he justified the increasingly popularity of 'holidays': 'An annual season of recreation is absolutely necessary to the continuance of mental and physical health.' Second, he knew his customers had, or felt they had, exhausted Britain: 'Doubtless most of my readers have already seen many of the principal spots . . . in Great Britain.' Having once conquered one's fears over visiting Switzerland, customers might well want to consider other locations. Most importantly, he insisted that one really *could* visit Switzerland for ten guineas, Holland and Belgium for seven, Paris for five, north Italy and Venice for fifteen and could sail up the Rhine for seven.

An independent source agreed in 1865 that one could 'do' the Rhine in ten days for £5 but to do so 'comfortably', £8 to £10 would be 'ample'.[14]

Starting in 1864, *Gaze's Tourist Gazette*, published ten times a year, advertised a variety of 'tours'. Unlike Crisp, Gaze was not offering a conducted, all-in trip. Instead he suggested routes, gave practical hints on dress and luggage, provided a detailed breakdown of expenditure and suggested three 'skeleton tours'. Then, in 1866 he began 'conducted tours' for 'select parties' led by 'conductors' who made travellers 'free from all kinds of embarrassment'. He still acted as a booking office for railways and hotels for 'independent travellers' who did not want to travel 'with a party'.[15] By the 1870s Gaze had moved to London and his new offices in the Strand were not so far from the firm that was becoming his main rival, Thomas Cook & Son, at 108, Fleet Street.

Social changes among travellers were noted by an American observer in 1863: '"He is an Englishman, and very wealthy" ... always went together ... [but] the majority of the present race of travelling English are by no means lavish in their expenditure or very wealthy.' Less charitable descriptions came from other travellers: the greatest 'travelling nuisance' was 'the Cockney on a fortnight's tour ... He is donned in a span [*sic*] new travelling suit ... a new Alpen-stock, upon which he gets inscribed the names of the mountains he may ascend ... he has a fresh courier-bag, a flask, and a small telescope slung across his shoulders ... He generally condemns everything, and thinks nothing good can be got out of London ... He is ... as arrogant as he is ignorant.' He 'usually prefers Bass to Burgundy' and worse of all, 'he swallows his food almost as quickly as an American'.[16]

Gaze knew perfectly well what snobbish people were saying and he replied in his *Outline Plan. Holland and Belgium. How To See Them for Seven Guineas*, published in 1864: 'There are some who raise objections because they do not desire to see those for whom these pages are prepared, too freely circulating in the picture galleries and ecclesiastical edifices of Belgium and Holland or too numerously climbing the snowy sides of the Alps.' However he also implicitly conceded the need for improvement in travellers' manners when, in a later booklet, he urged them to be polite to French customs officials and, when visiting churches, to 'walk softly and speak likewise'. They should never turn their backs on an altar or stare at confessionals, a great temptation for those who found these both fascinating and horrifying. Gaze might have taken comfort from an article published as far back as 1837 which pointed out that the English 'raise the cry of vulgarity against any place where they meet each other'. It wasn't just the English who raised the cry. Philip Hone, formerly Mayor of New York, also writing in the 1830s had decided that the English who 'swarm' over the Continent 'are generally vulgar people, without taste, and with their pockets well filled'.[17]

Gaze kept his costs down by booking only third-class tickets and by making bookings at hotels not frequented by the English. He justified this by saying that those who stayed in such hotels returned 'with little more knowledge of the people through whose territory they have passed than if they had never been there'. Despite all that, he admitted that 'a small margin beyond these sums would greatly tend to enhance the pleasure and increase the comforts of the trips'. He carefully set out the costs in his guide to Holland and assured readers they would have 'meat breakfasts', wine with dinner, tea, and 'attendance' in their hotels. In other words, there would be no hidden 'extras'. However, George Bradshaw, another rival to Gaze, estimated in the 1860s that travellers constantly on the move 'may average 16s to 20s a day' when travelling on their own, while almost fifty years later guide-books said a person could travel on about a pound a day plus railway fares. The savings came through cheaper hotels.[18]

Eleven years after Henry Gaze set up shop in Southampton, Thomas Cook sent his first party of tourists to Europe. Cook's influence on travel has become legendary. He was a colourful character and a magnificent self-publicist. His company has survived into the twenty-first century, while most of his rivals have long since vanished – Henry Gaze & Son collapsed in 1903, for example. In time 'Cook's tourists' became a general term for all holiday-makers of a social class beneath one's own. When Leslie Stephen wrote about Switzerland in the 1870s he sneered that the 'real' Switzerland only survived in valleys 'which have not yet bowed the knee to Baal, in the shape of Mr Cook and his tourists'. Three decades later Parisians watching groups of tourists muttered: '*Regardez-moi ces Cooks, ils son drôles, n'est-ce pas?*'[19]

Cook's story has often been told.[20] He started out in the 1840s as a provincial Nonconformist teetotal campaigner promoting cheap railway day-trips for working people. He then took advantage of the expanding railway network to organize trips to Scotland and then to Ireland, which allowed him to appeal to the middle class. It was not until 1855 that he thought of entering the steadily growing European market. He abandoned a planned tour to the Paris Exhibition of that year because he could not arrange reduced fares on Belgian and French trains and made do with holidays to Calais at a return fare of £1 11s. Later that year he organized two 'circular tours' of the Rhine which also took in Antwerp, Brussels, Cologne, Heidelberg, Strasbourg and Paris. His appeal was to the lowest ranks of the middle class, such as one teetotal schoolteacher who noted in her diary that in Antwerp 'Everything looked so foreign.' These were people who were prepared to travel third class and in a somewhat 'haphazard' manner, since Cook spoke neither French nor German. His main value was in 'selecting hotels, arranging with landlords, procuring railway tickets, exchanging money, or learning the times of trains'.[21] Above all, like Gaze, Cook gave travellers the confidence to travel in the first place.

These early tours left Cook out of pocket, and he returned to organizing trips to Scotland, the Lake District and Cornwall. In 1861 he tried Europe again and organized a trip to Paris for a 'demonstration' of working men, similar to the one Crisp had arranged in 1849. He signed up 1,673 people who paid a £1 each for the return journey (third class) for a six-day visit. However, this did not include hotels, meals and so on. When we include all these 'extras', the total cost would have been considerably more. Only the highest paid 'working men' (that is self-employed and skilled craftsmen) could have afforded the time and the expenses. It was only when his trips to Scotland stopped that he really concentrated on the European market.

Then, in 1862, Cook finally reached a deal with the railway serving Newhaven and his outlook brightened. In 1863, he relaunched his Parisian expeditions and began sixteen-day trips to Switzerland with a party of sixty-four people. Although his average total price of £15 12s 7d did not compare favourably with Gaze's ten guineas, he aimed, like Gaze, to appeal to 'ushers [teachers] and governesses, practical people from the provinces, and representatives of the better style of the London mercantile community', people who were 'fulfilling the wishes of a life-time, in a pleasant duty never to be repeated'. Cook publicly described his clients as 'English clergymen, physicians, bankers, civil engineers and merchants'. But this was a great exaggeration and secondly, if such customers did exist they probably only booked their tickets through Cook's, not conducted tours. On this first Swiss trip Cook conducted the group for six of their sixteen days. The tourists, or at least those who left records, were satisfied: 'It is to the Swiss that we look back with the greatest pleasure, apart from the recollection of a pleasant companionship.'[22] These trips tapped into the growing market not just for holidays abroad but for Switzerland in particular, and by September, Cook had taken 2,000 people to Paris and of these 500 had gone on to Switzerland. He soon added Italy, and the European side of his business began to expand.

Finding hotels remained a problem. Gaze's solution for those on tours was simple: book places ahead in one hotel and get a cheaper rate. For those not on his tours he came up with the 'hotel coupon' at 8s 6d plus a small fee. Bought before leaving Britain these could be presented at any hotel in the scheme. Customers were guaranteed a room, attendance, candles, a 'meat breakfast' and a '*déjeuner à la fourchette* [main meal]'. In addition, anyone could buy these coupons without using any other service provided by Gaze. Cook responded three years later with a coupon at 8s. However this had only one 'meat' meal and only people who booked through Cook could buy the coupons. After some fine tuning both sets of coupons were highly successful: within four years, Cook by himself had sold 120,000 sets.[23]

By 1865, Thomas's son, John, had joined the firm and established better business practices, and within years Thomas Cook & Son was flourishing by aiming their advertisements at a more sophisticated audience. The firm had followed Gaze in offering tours to northern Italy and to Rome for the famous Holy Week ceremonies. It was soon dealing with the highest in the land: it arranged a trip to the Riviera for the Archbishop of Canterbury to recover his health and it organized a Catholic pilgrimage led by the Duke of Norfolk to a French shrine. When the Franco-Prussian War erupted in 1870 and Paris was besieged, and then convulsed by the Commune, Cook's arranged alternate routes to avoid the French capital. When the siege was finally lifted in January 1871, John Cook helped organize the delivery of 75 tons of provisions. That same year the Cooks claimed to have arranged travel for no fewer than 105,000 people, of whom some were not British.[24]

The British market for 'arranged' holidays was dominated by these two firms, each of which had been founded by men who mixed idealism with the profit motive: Henry Gaze and Thomas Cook. One 1871 reference work compared the two. Gaze had 'not achieved quite so wide a notoriety [fame]' as Cook but provided 'the intending tourist with the same facilities, both for ordinary expeditions and for those joint stock journeyings known as "personally conducted parties"'. The prices were practically the same, and in most cases identical. In their conducted parties these men offered a safety net, as it were, for those who were not natural travellers. For those who did not go on conducted tours the advantage of using Cook, Gaze, or any other firm was described in an article in which first-time travellers met an experienced traveller, 'Dr Melchisidec':

On our arriving at Calais, no crush, or excitement, and fighting for places. We were met by three courteous, military-looking officials, who talked four languages between them, and ushered us to our 'reserved' places . . . 'You're all right with COOK,' observed Dr MELCHISIDEC. 'He's got a man everywhere, and, if there's any hitch, you've only got to call him in.' . . . I had always hitherto considered Cook's Excursionists as rather a comic institution . . . Nothing of the sort . . . we found his name a perfect tower of strength along the entire route.

Jerome K. Jerome admitted that 'We all of us sneer at Mr. Cook and Mr. Gaze . . . who kindly conduct travellers that cannot conduct themselves properly . . . but . . . most of us appeal, on the quiet, to one or the other of them the moment we want to move abroad.'[25]

Thomas Cook's penchant for self-advertisement drew public attention to the growing number of travellers, and he personally soon came to embody the changes taking place. As we have seen already, there were furious attacks on the new type of travellers from the early 1860s, and in 1864 Dickens asked the gossipy journalist Edmund Yates to interview Cook for an article on the guided tour. Yates noted that the 'ushers and governesses stop at all the principal towns, visiting all the curiosities to be seen in them, and are full of discussion among themselves, proving that they are all thoroughly well up in the subject. Many . . . carry books of reference . . . and nearly all take notes', but these were people who booked through Cook's but travelled without him. For those on the conducted tours, the 'Whitsuntide trip', Yates was scathing. This collection had 'a good deal of the Cockney element in it' – for 'Cockney' read 'common'. It was 'mostly composed of very high-spirited people, whose greatest delight is "having a fling", and who do Paris, and rush through France, and through Switzerland . . . [and] carry London everywhere about them'. Substance is given to this charge

in the surviving diary of one of the tourists who recorded the fun
had on this tour. Take the entry for Lucerne: 'We had but four
hours in Lucerne, and in those four hours a respectable dinner had
to be taken . . . the Cathedral to be done, the gabled frescoes of the
Bridges to be examined, the feudal wall and its four watch towers
to be inspected, and of course Thorwaldsen's Lion would feel
slighted if forgotten.'[26]

After this somewhat mixed review, Cook was savagely attacked
by the Irish-born novelist, Charles Lever, in *Blackwood's Magazine*.
Lever claimed to have met these tourists and 'anything so uncouth
I never saw before, the men, mostly elderly, dreary, sad-looking;
the women, somewhat younger, travel-tossed and crumpled, but
intensely lively, wide-awake, and facetious'. Group travel, he
announced, 'reduces the traveller to the level of his trunk'. Cook
agreed 'to carry [transport] them, to feed them, lodge them, and
amuse them'. They were 'low-bred, vulgar, and ridiculous', people
who would undermine Britain's standing in Europe.[27] He claimed
he had told Italian friends that the tourists were really convicts that
Australia would not take: they were going to be dumped in Italy. If
the criticism was accurate, it was only accurate in part.

Yates had based his article – as the title, 'My Excursion Agent',
hints – on conversations with Cook himself, so his information was
hardly unbiased. In Lever's case we should remember that he lived
in Italy: as none of the tourists described actually visited the
country, one does not quite understand how he witnessed their
'Cockney' antics. Not surprisingly, Cook was furious and attacked
Lever as someone who 'would reserve statue and mountain, painting and lake, historical association and natural beauty, for the
so-called upper classes'. With Lever's time at Germany universities
in mind he referred to 'Irish doctors with German degrees as
choose to be their [the upper classes'] toadies'. Cook saw 'no sin
in introducing natural and artistic wonders to all'. The juggernaut
of progress was rolling and those who wished 'to have the exclusive enjoyment of earth's provision, had better make a tour to
Timbuctoo'. Cook never forgave Lever and five years later, when

the insult still rankled, he petitioned the Foreign Secretary to 'discipline' Lever, who was a British Consul in Italy, though to no effect.[28]

This debate about 'vulgarity' carried on throughout the century, and even the Germans joined in. In Max Nordau's 1896 novel, translated as *The Malady of the Century*, two Germans discuss British tourists: 'They are not the best sort. They are common city people, who even drop their h's but who play at being lords on the Continent' (Chapter 1). Back in Britain, the magazine *Vanity Fair* had a story about the difficulty 'Cecil' faced in 1900 in selecting a place in Europe not overrun by the 'British Bounder'. The 'British Bounder on his native soil is obnoxious,' Cecil moaned, 'but his individual aggressiveness is softened and toned down against the background of the prevalence of his species. On the Continent he is abhorrently conspicuous . . . a staring blot on every landscape . . . And his brother from across the Atlantic is, if possible, a shade more unspeakable.' If France, Germany, Switzerland and Italy were now overrun Cecil had no choice but to go further afield: the Austrian Empire was perhaps still free of 'bounders'.[29]

Such attacks made liberal publications such as the *Illustrated London News* demand that the 'stupid and unjust practice' of sneering at tour parties should end. These people were no different from other travellers 'save they were better behaved and more anxious to acquire information' than the 'Travelling Gentlemen' from the 'stuck up' classes. There was also a spirited defence of the increasing numbers by Thomas Trollope, who lived in Florence. He was a man who seldom claimed to be an egalitarian and normally endorsed the 'good old days' syndrome, in which things were usually described as being better in the past. In 1875 he admitted that British travellers, as well as American, were 'a very motley and heterogeneous crowd' and foreigners 'are apt to sneer on occasion at the unkempt and queer specimens of humanity which often come . . . from the two English-speaking nations'. He then rounded: 'We can well afford to let them stare and smile, well knowing that if a similar amount of prosperity permitted the people of other countries to travel ... in similar numbers, the result would be at the very least an equally – shall I say undrawing-room-like contribution to cosmopolitan society?'[30]

These debates focused on the changes that had been slowly developing since 1814. Increasing prosperity meant that travellers from what Boulogne's Chamber of Commerce described as '*le classe moyenne, la petite bourgeosie de Londres*' were increasingly taking trips of perhaps three to four weeks. Hyppolyte Taine, the best French observer of the British, sat opposite a Newcastle family en route for Venice in the 1860s. They were 'small tradespeople, pretty well dressed and in new clothes'. They travelled third class and like many other people, 'expend all their surplus', about £40 to £50 a year he estimated, on trips to the Continent. 'My three fellow-passengers prepare themselves conscientiously; they have their Murray, a manual of Italian phrases ... What strange visitors to Venice! Nevertheless, they are sensible folks, capable of learning, and who, if they do not appreciate painting, will bring back ... all kinds of information and useful notions.' These were the type of people Henry James observed in 1873. They were rarely 'children of light in any eminent degree' but people 'for whom snow-peaks and glaciers and passes and lakes and chalets and sunsets and a *café complet*, "including honey", as the coupon says, have become prime necessities for six weeks every year.' True, such people 'have rather too few h's to the dozen, but their good-nature is great'.[31]

There were still upper class travellers on extended trips, the leisured classes who had 'an autumn in North Italy, a winter in Rome, [and] a springtide in Sorrento'. One such was Lord William Russell, an army officer, diplomat and brother of the Prime Minister. His domineering wife, who had been brought up on the Continent, was 'bored to death' in England and when there, had 'the fidgets & die to travel'. The Russells and their children wandered round Europe, from Florence to Berne, from Lausanne to Paris. In addition, their income was not enough to live in style at home. Lord William worried about the 'butcher's bills' and when he considered living in Brighton he asked, 'how are we to do it, without getting into debt?'. Even when abroad, he was 'obliged to pinch & screw'. On occasion he was called home because he happened to be MP for Bedford. When his constituents, as much as his ducal family, insisted that he ought to 'come up now & then to town [London] for a vote' he agreed, but Lady William stayed in Europe.[32]

Likewise, comfortably off upper-middle-class people were still going to Europe, often annually. People such as George Mason and his wife (a niece of the former Speaker of the House of Commons) went to Montpellier to get away from 'the cold of the ensuing winter', after which they travelled round Austria. Once settled in their Montpellier hotel, they went out to hire a piano, find the French Protestant Church and locate the English circulating library. Helen Mason described a typical day in her entry for 29 November 1859:[33]

At 8 a.m, we have our cup of Café noir – after which George either goes out or reads till 10, the hour for Dejunner à la forchette then occupy ourselves till 1.30 when we start either for the [Jardin de] Peyron, or some walk in the environs, returning about 3 & at 4 George again sallies forth for his Evening stroll . . . dinner at 5.30 after which, reading, chit chat, & Piano, while away our Evening most happily. Each day, therefore, being so like its predecessor, I shall with very few exceptions, during our stay at Montpellier, merely notice the different walks or drives which we took, at our midday outing.

Younger members of landed families such as Challoner Chute, an Oxford don in his mid-thirties, took a two-month trip to Rome in the early 1870s for 'less than £150', while those being conducted round by Gaze or Cook were enjoying a tour of north Italy and Venice for a tenth of that sum. In 1895 a schoolgirl and her 'auntie' spent at least four months in Freiburg. The unnamed girl's diary, now in the authors' possession, describes her time from May to early September. She and her aunt visited churches and cathedrals, went for long walks in the woods, attended the local Anglican church, exchanged visits with fellow travellers, sketched, and made various day-trips. The schoolgirl read to her aunt from Ruskin, took lessons in German, French, Italian, sketching and music, went canoeing and wrote letters home. She stayed overnight at the top of Feldberg, went up its tower to watch the 'splendid sunrise' and gaze at the Jungfrau in the distance. She also went to dances although she could 'not get on with the waltz' and was shocked to discover that one partner, 'whom I had not liked . . . informed me he was a *kaufman* [tradesman]'. Apart from her commercial partner, all was very proper, restrained and civilized.[34]

The increase in the number of women who were travelling was worrying to some men because, they claimed, women were 'more susceptible of impression than males'. Women might return home too 'Frenchified' or, worse, they might turn Catholic. Such worries fell on deaf ears: women travelled in large numbers as part of family groups. Some insisted on travelling on their own, 'those adventurous English dames, whom we have occasionally met journeying . . . unsquired and unescorted save by their waiting-maids'.[35] These 'unprotected females' were looked at askance, as doing something that was not quite 'proper'. This attitude, which lasted for much of the period, was not just confined to men. It was generally feared that women on their own might be attacked or that they might not stand up to the rigours of travel.

All this was only part of the transformation that occurred in the nineteenth century regarding the position of women. In part the changes were due to numbers: the 1821 census showed there were over 500,000 more women than men. In 1911 the number soared to an excess of 1.3 million.[36] There simply were not enough men to 'protect' them. In addition, women began to have more educational opportunities and often studied subjects such as art and foreign languages that encouraged travel. Middle class women were the driving force in the huge expanse of Victorian charitable work and they were slowly entering the civil service and the medical profession. They always made up the vast bulk of primary schoolteachers and once Board Schools (state schools) started in the 1870s the number of teachers increased significantly. These were the women from whose ranks many 'unprotected' travellers came.

As early as 1814 there were women such as the guide-book writer Mariana Starke, who broke with convention and showed that they could get about successfully and safely on their own. Not infrequently they went on to write the best books about their travels. One such was Mrs Dalkeith Holmes, who rode all the way to Florence in 1838. While she was not quite alone (she took her husband with her), her sense of priorities is reflected in the long poem with which she ends her story:[37]

> *Flowers shall shine and laurels nod*
> *O'er the gay, the bold, the canny;*
> *Larks upsoaring from the sod,*
> *Swell their songs in praise of Fanny*

Fanny was her horse.

Emily Lowe set out in the 1840s with her mother to visit Norway. She wrote with a refreshing sense of humour and without the pomposity so often associated with campaigners. 'Ladies *alone*,' she wrote, 'get on in travelling much better than with gentlemen; they set about things in a quieter manner, and always have their own way; while men are sure to go into passions and make rows if things are not right immediately.'[38] Emily Lowe may have influenced Anthony Trollope because in his 1859 story 'An Unprotected Female at the Pyramids' he defended the 'unprotected female' who 'is becoming an established profession . . . in opposition to the old-world idea that women, like green peas, cannot come to perfection without supporting-sticks'. The short story's 'unprotected female' 'had no idea of being prevented from seeing anything she wished to see because she had neither father, nor husband, nor brother available'.

Of all the 'unprotected females' who became travel writers,

Amelia Edwards, quoted in the Introduction, was one of the most famous. Born into a middle class family in 1831 she established herself as a novelist, poet and advocate of women's suffrage before becoming a travel writer. She began with Belgium and then moved on to the Dolomites (to escape tourist-infected Switzerland) which she visited in the 1870s to write *Untrodden Peaks and Unfrequented Valleys*. She combined travel writing with the yearning for adventure buttressed by a sense of humour and a respect for those through whose lands she roamed. She was also a woman of some strength and warned readers that 'the passes are too long and too fatiguing for ladies on foot, and should not be attempted by any who cannot endure eight and sometimes ten hours of mule-riding'.[39]

For women on their own things remained difficult, as is seen in Alice Ivimy's *A Woman's Guide to Paris*, published in 1909. Amelia Edwards had appealed to women who wanted an 'adventure'. Alice Ivimy appealed to the 'new woman' who did not seek 'adventure' but the chance to do what men did: visit Paris, eat out, go to the races and visit theatres. What held such women back was the residual fear that they would be taken for 'loose' women. She noted with some exaggeration that 'a steadily increasing number of women, both English and American, visit Paris each year, the great majority of them either alone or accompanied by another woman'. However, there were still problems. Guide-books were not written for the 'solitary woman' who was 'hampered at every turn by agonizing doubts and fears' including fear of crime, of eating alone in restaurants or of going to the theatre on her own. To prove her point she described a woman stuck in her hotel room 'seated with a bag of biscuits beside her, flanked by a large slice of *foie gras* . . . with a little fruit by way of dessert' because she was afraid of going to a restaurant and did not want a 'dull dinner' in her hotel. To help women cope she gave practical advice about restaurants, about the 'vexed question of tips' (10 per cent), about theatres ('no lady need hesitate to . . . go alone to the play') and, as important, about public water-closets or 'Châlets de Nécessité' and where these could be found. (She listed five.) She warned that French women 'never smoke in public' even though 'so many American and English women smoke a cigarette after lunch'. It is better not to do so in Paris lest one shock the French.[40]

While many single women might have admired Amelia Edwards or Emily Lowe they did not always imitate them. For such women, conducted tours offered the perfect solution. As we have already noted, group travel lessened fears and on the early tours conducted by Cook himself observers noted that 'unprotected females confide in him'. Of equal importance was the growth of *pensions*. These were important not just for women travellers but also for single ladies who found they simply could not afford to live in Britain. Society made it difficult for such women to work and retain their social position. Others simply wanted to get away. The obvious solution was to spend considerable periods on the Continent. Janet McNair was one such. We know she spent the summer of 1886 in the Tyrol and then went to Florence, which in time she left for Rome where she rented a 'little apartment' that was 'nice and sunny and the landlady is, if anything, too obliging'. She missed the 'lemon trees that we had last winter' and agreed that a six-month lease 'seems a long time to be settled' by herself but it will be better than a *pension* or 'to having an uncongenial companion in lodgings'.[41] She does not say where she will go when her lease is up – perhaps back to the lemon trees, or to the Tyrol or to Florence or somewhere else?

Women without Janet McNair's income were always looking round for places where they could live for that little bit less. They combined relative want with absolute pride. Henry James describes one such in Geneva, in his story 'Pension Beaurepas'. Mrs Church moves about from *pension* to *pension* with her daughter and instead of paying seven francs gets the charge reduced to five and a half. In Piacenza she had found one for four francs and at her next stop, Dresden, her daughter confesses, 'Mamma means to make them give us wine' for the eight francs charged. In essays Vernon Lee wrote in 1897 she referred to that 'mysterious class of dwellers . . . curious beings who migrate . . . from the cheap boarding-house in

Dresden to the cheap boarding-house in Florence . . . A quaint race it is, neither marrying nor giving in marriage, and renewed by natural selection among the poor in purse and poor in spirit.'[42]

Arnold Bennett had observed these 'determined ladies' when staying in a Florentine *pension* where they had obviously lived for months. They were women like the fictitious Mrs Church who followed a regular circuit: so many months in Florence followed by so many months in some other city. When sitting down at the breakfast table, Bennett found them 'calm, angular, ungainly, long-suffering, and morose'. 'They are,' he continued,[43]

> astoundingly gentle with each other, cooing sympathetic inquiries . . . They know by experience the strict observance of a strict code is the price of peace . . . Nevertheless I feel that I am amid loose nitro-glycerine; one jar, and the whole affair might be blown to atoms . . . The danger-points are the jam-pots . . . and the marmalade pots, of which each lady apparently has her own . . . And when one of them says to the maid . . . 'This is not my jam – I had more,' I quake. We talk. We talk to prove our virtuosity in nice conduct.

'In Florence,' he added, 'there are dozens upon dozens of such breakfasts every morning.'

As early as the 1820s, magazines were referring to the new custom of a 'wedding tour' on the Continent in which 'the newly-married pair drive from the church to the packet-boat'. What began as a luxury for the rich became in time the fashion for the middle class and a factor in the growth of travel. The 1884 social guide, quoted earlier, said 'it is a custom peculiar to the English that the bridegroom and bride spend the first month, or so much of such period as can be spared, on a tour amongst strangers'. It agreed that the custom was 'of questionable advantage or satisfaction, but, since it is the custom, those who do not conform to it are liable to be regarded as not in the fashion'.[44] One of the delights of travel lay in spotting newly-weds, people who were, usually, young and easily embarrassed. To lessen this risk, the 1884 household handbook advised newly-weds that 'Good taste and convenience both suggest that conspicuous dress should be avoided during the wedding tour.' In 1822 Lady Blessington watched how 'a new-married pair . . . who entered the packet all smiles and love' coped with sea-sickness:

> The bridegroom had been encouraging the bride, by asserting that *he* was so used to the sea that he heeded it not. He sat by her . . . until an ejaculation of "Take me to the cabin, Henry, Oh! Oh!" broke from the lady. He attempted to assist her . . . but, alas! Before he had moved three paces, he reeled, and crying "Steward, Steward," consigned his bride to the tenderer mercies of that useful person, who, with basin in hand, escorted her below; while her liege lord eased his full breast over the vessel's side.

Even honeymooners themselves joined the game. In 1873 the future Lady Monkswell was 'amused at the distressed behaviour of various brides & bridegrooms; we flatter ourselves we are taken for brother & sister!'.[45]

These honeymoon tours usually began in Paris and moved on through France to Italy via Switzerland. One early tour sadly achieved renown: Thomas Welch Hunt and his new wife, Caroline, were in the south of Italy in 1824. On a December morning they left their inn at Eboli for the temples at Paestum. Their landlord had noticed the husband's silver-backed brushes and silver-mounted cruets and informed a local gang. The Hunts' carriage was stopped by four men with pistols. Mr Hunt drew out his own pistol as his wife threw herself across her husband: a single shot went through both their bodies. The husband died that same evening while his wife lingered for a few days. He was twenty-eight, she twenty-three, and they had been married for ten months. The landlady informed on her husband and he saved his neck by betraying the others. The couple was buried in one grave in Naples and a memorial was erected in their parish church at Wadenhoe in Northamptonshire. The inscription ends with the biblical quotation:[46]

> *They were lovely and pleasant in their lives*
> *And in their death they were not divided.*

A thankfully more typical honeymoon tour was made by Thomas Best and his bride, Louisa, in 1858–9. Best was thirty-one, a wealthy country gentleman, and a veteran traveller. They were accompanied by an aunt, an uncle and several other members of Louisa's family. (Such group honeymoon tours were not unusual.) They set off from Gloucestershire on the day of their wedding for a 190-day tour. The couple visited Paris, Nice, Carrara, Modena, Lucca, Florence, and then went on to Naples, Sorrento, Capri, Amalfi and Rome, after which they retraced their steps back to Paris and then home. They stayed in unpretentious inns that sometimes provided wry amusement, as when they spotted 'the clergyman who preached on Sunday morning' in Genoa. The said clergyman had arrived the night before and 'left just before us in the morning, with two ladies, *we think* his two sisters'.[47]

A second and increasingly popular wedding tour was to visit Switzerland. Leslie Stephen described his honeymoon with 'glorious rambles . . . about the hills gathering edelweiss . . . lying on the grass & smoking (this doesn't apply to Mrs S.) the pipe of peace. They were really of those days that one doesn't forget.'[48] This was also the place selected for the honeymoon for one of the more bizarre marriages of the nineteenth century, that between the Reverend Edward White Benson and Mary Sidgwick. Benson had chosen his second cousin to be his wife when she was eleven and he was twenty-three. When she was twelve he took her on his knee and told her of his love. Six years later, in 1859, the couple were married and set out for Europe that same day. Mary Benson's diary depicts a lively young woman with a sense of humour and adventure as well as a serious side, one for whom religion was understandably important. She began her diary in Rouen and from there they moved on to Rheims, Paris and Strasbourg where she 'bolted into the refreshment room' for food whilst her husband ran for tickets. In Switzerland the newlyweds climbed the Rigi, spent the night at a hotel on the top to watch the sunrise the next morning, hired a guide, bought a St Bernard puppy for ten francs and then made for Lake Lucerne. There they met another honeymooning couple with whom they made a party. They rowed on the lake and bathed in the moonlight and then set off for the St Gotthard Pass. As was the usual arrangement, the gentlemen walked while the ladies rode on mules. Umbrellas were lost, mules misbehaved and Mary walked the whole way down the pass – a feat which took two hours. They climbed mountains, decried the goitres of which some villagers boasted, and visited the famous Reichenbach Falls. In the evenings they read aloud from Charles Kingsley's *Westward Ho!* and Thackeray's *Virginians*. Whenever possible they went to an English church except one Sunday when 'there was no English Church so we went up the side of the hill a little way, and there by the side of a brook under some kind sheltering trees, we had a service by ourselves – & – we felt we had indeed a nobler church than any of man's making ... these things filled our hearts with joy & thanksgiving'.[49]

Looking back seventeen years later Mary Benson painted a very different picture in a series of random notes: 'Ed. coming – fear of him – love? Always a strain'; 'Desire of pleasing E. because of fear of vexing'; 'dreary, helpless ... I see now I *did not* love him – yet he loved me ... most miserable – cry to sleep'; '*childish in understanding*'; 'danced & sang into matrimony with a loving, but exacting spirit ... The nights!'; 'I wd. have died rather than anyone shd. have thought for a moment I wasn't happy.'[50] This retrospective cry of anguish was completely at variance with Mary's original notes, but by 1876 she realized that she was more comfortable with other women than with her overbearing husband, who eventually became Archbishop of Canterbury. Also, it is not at all unlikely that Edward read over her original diary entries. One can only wonder how many women enjoyed similar experiences among the mountains and lakes only to disown them in later years.

As the century wore on, the social range of honeymooners expanded, as with travellers in general. More people could go to Europe, if few could spend as much time as the Bests. In 1874 Thomas Hardy and Emma Gifford were married in Paddington, took the train to Brighton and then crossed over to visit Dieppe, Rouen and Paris, a favourite choice for people like themselves with little time or money. Clutching their Murray's guide-book they enjoyed seeing the Place de la Concorde by moonlight, visited Versailles, stopped in cafes to drink *vin ordinaire* 'like French people', visited Notre-Dame, the Invalides, Père Lachaise, where they picked an ivy leaf from Balzac's grave, and the Morgue where Emma found the bodies on view 'not offensive but repulsive'. While Thomas made architectural observations, Emma noted differences in food and social customs, including the *latrines publique* – 'most strange for English eyes'.[51] Emma was frightened by the number of Catholic priests and in return the French stared at her English dress with its shorter skirt.

Perhaps the most exotic wedding tour was that undertaken by the novelist Edward Bulwer-Lytton and his wife in 1827. The story comes to us through Sir William Fraser. While travelling on a train in Italy he was reading one of Bulwer-Lytton's novels when a fellow passenger, who was Lady Lytton's solicitor, told him about the honeymoon. The Bulwer-Lyttons were being driven in an open carriage along the Italian Riviera. Bulwer-Lytton, who was already known for his flamboyant dress, sat with his wife facing the driver. Opposite them was her maid. As they were passing through a village Bulwer-Lytton noticed that he was being stared at by a 'singularly handsome girl standing at a cottage door'. He mentioned this to his wife who replied that 'if you wear that ridiculous dress no wonder people stare at you'. To this Bulwer-Lytton replied: 'You think that people stare at my dress; and not at me: I will give you the most absolute and convincing proof that your theory has no foundation.' He then ordered the carriage stopped, removed all his clothes with the exception of his hat and boots, told the maid to sit next his wife, and took the maid's seat. The carriage then drove on for ten miles with what results Sir William did not say.[52] Not surprisingly, the couple separated nine years later in one of the most notorious divorce cases of the nineteenth century.

One new feature of organized travel that appeared in the 1880s was the travelling 'club' based on educational institutions. One of the best known was the Polytechnic Touring Association (PTA) from the Regent Street Polytechnic (now the University of Westminster). The PTA began in 1882 and within four years it was sponsoring short trips to Boulogne and longer holidays in Belgium, Switzerland and France. Eventually the Association even bought chalets by Lake Lucerne as study centres. By 1896 it owned its own yacht for cruises of the Norwegian fjords and by 1900 was offering conducted visits to the Rhine and the Passion Play at Oberammergau for twelve and a half guineas. By 1903 some 12,000 people were taking their holidays through the PTA. However, what had started as an adjunct to learning soon became a business in its own right. It survived into the 1960s when it was taken over by Henry Lunn Ltd to become Lunn Poly.[53]

The Polytechnic, like Crisp, Gaze and Cook, all aimed at a market which went to the lowest reaches of the middle class, but no further. The reasons for this were obvious to Victorians: 'The general body of the great unwashed have not . . . the means . . . and even if they had the means and had learned the manner of "doing the Rhine for five pounds" they could not avail themselves of holidays of that kind.' A man who had the money and left his work for a week or fortnight, let alone a month, 'would certainly be "sacked"! And in addition . . . would . . . be regarded by his brethren as . . . a traitor to his class.' True, publications aimed at working-class audiences had featured articles on foreign places as early as 1833. In that year the *Penny Magazine*, published by the Society for the Diffusion of Useful Knowledge, had articles on the Tyrol, Ypres, Cologne and Poland. But these were to spread knowledge, not to enourage travel. At the highest levels in the working class, typesetters, for example, it was not so much a question of money (for their annual wages were well above £150 a year) as lack of education, motivation and free time. At lower levels the need was to survive: in the 1850s, for example, the best-paid postman earned £61 7s 2d a year and this could just about clothe, feed and house his family. There were very few paid holidays and no bank holidays until the 1870s. There was, in short, no time and no money: 'The nearest thing to a holiday the majority were likely to experience would have been the works outing, Sunday school treat or day trip.'[54]

There were, as always, exceptions, but of the handful of working-class people who did travel to Europe, very few left records. Fortunately one exception was a Sheffield man named Jehoida Rhodes who did write up his holiday and offered his account to Anthony Trollope's short-lived magazine, *Saint Pauls*, in 1867. Rhodes, who described himself as a 'workman', got a £1 14s return fare as part of a 'workman's' offer to visit the Paris Exhibition of that year, and set out with a group from Sheffield. He was an acute observer of French life and quite tolerant even if not impressed by Napoleon III's regime or the continental Sunday. He found a hotel for a shilling a night and visited the standard tourist sights. He spent much of his day walking and only once took an omnibus down the Rue de Rivoli. He was intrigued by *café* society in the evening and had to pay for all his meals. Like Crisp's peace activists of 1849, he had the thrill of wondering about the provenance of a 'bifteck' – 'I don't say the steak was not horse; I don't know. But I know it was one of the best steaks I ever ate.'

Rhodes twice visited the Exhibition and admired much of what he saw but felt that French electroplating, a Sheffield speciality, was 'nothing like the goods to be seen in our shops'. For his souvenirs he bought five shillings' worth of grapes and peaches and kept 'every handbill and card offered . . . in veritable French'. He was in no doubt that those who could afford it should have a week's foreign trip. While most of his fellow passengers on the journey home complained of being cheated – two women were returning after only two days because of French 'robbery' – Rhodes had only one occasion where he felt he had been overcharged. He enjoyed his time but 'would not choose to be a Frenchman . . . We may not have so many palace privileges, but then we enjoy more rights . . . So while I remember with pleasure what I have seen . . . I say with a deeper love than ever, "England, with all thy faults, I love thee still." ' His trip cost £3 10s and *Saint Pauls* paid him £7 10s so he was left with a nice profit of £4.[55]

One of Rhodes's reasons for going to Paris had been to examine the quality of French electroplating at the Exhibition. In 1889 increasing competition caused the Lord Mayor and Corporation of London to offer workmen free trips to Paris to see what the French were producing. The corporation arranged second-class rail fare and crossing, a fortnight in a 'good hotel' with a 'meat breakfast', wine, lights in the room and £2 pocket money. If a man wanted to receive a bonus of £1 15s he had to draw up a report of what he had seen. Seventy-six men came forward representing sixty-four different trades including cooks, bakers, bookbinders, lithographic artists, portmanteau-makers, railway servants and carriage-makers. On their return, and having submitted their reports, the group was received at Mansion House.[56] Several provincial towns followed London's example, but the aim was always to improve Britain's competitive edge, not to encourage travel among the working class.

Thomas Okey was a different type of working-class traveller. He was born in 1852 into a Spitalfields family that specialized in basket-making. He left school at twelve to go into the family trade, knowing that if he were lucky he would eventually make about £78 a year. He had an enquiring mind and started attending lectures, including those at the famous Toynbee Hall, established in White-chapel in 1884 and from 1903 the first home for the Workers Educational Association. Even before this, Okey was successful enough to take afternoons off 'for literary work'. He had a gift for foreign languages, especially Italian, and at Toynbee Hall he was a member of the Mazzini Circle, a study group named in honour of the Italian revolutionary nationalist Giuseppe Mazzini. He also joined the Hall's Travellers' Club, which in 1887 made its first trip, to Italy. The club organized everything and got concessions from railway companies. Various supporters put up 'travelling scholarships' to help defray the costs, estimated at £12 to £13 for a seventeen-day trip to Florence, Pisa and Genoa. Prior to departure there were lectures while photographs were passed round and reading lists of books on Italian art and history were drawn up. In March 1888 'eighty-odd travellers', chiefly 'School Board [state school] teachers and the lower grades of civil servants', the majority 'innocent of foreign travel', set out. The Italian government offered free admission to public museums and galleries and, once the group was in Florence it was given special lectures. On their return the travellers were told that the cost had worked out to only £10 6s 7d each.[57]

Okey was a popular member of the club because he spoke Italian and on the return to England he was appointed a lecturer in Italian at Toynbee. By 1892 the club was 'fully established' with 153 members, the majority of whom were women. Okey also joined the Art Workers' Guild, which had also been founded in the 1880s, and was welcomed as someone able to plan their European travels. Starting in 1891 he organized various trips, the first of which was to Venice. One of the party was the struggling writer George Bernard Shaw. The splenetic Irishman, when not complaining about the stupidity of his fellow travellers, complained about Italy. It was 'a humbug', 'a show and nothing else. Neither the Italians nor the trippers on whom they sponge have any part or lot in the fine things they see.' Italian architecture was 'inferior to northern [European] architecture . . . it is not organic . . . the cathedral at Milan disgusted me', St Mark's was 'disappointing' and so on and so on. He also caused poor Okey no end of trouble because of his vegetarianism. Italians simply could not understand why anyone would not eat meat, or even pasta when served with gravy. Okey coped by seeking out the head waiter at their hotels to explain that Signor Shaw was a devout Catholic who had taken a vow to abstain from meat, wine and tobacco.[58] This did the trick and Shaw was spared a lingering death from starvation.

Meanwhile the Toynbee Club grew until it had some 234 members, though there were 'storms' when people were allowed to join who did not wish to study before they set out; the club dissolved itself in 1913. In the meantime a new Workmen's Travelling Club was established in 1902 for people who thought that a week or ten days on the Continent was 'something not for them' because it 'seems to involve too much adventure and money'. The new group sponsored day-trips to Brussels, Antwerp, Paris and Rouen when it could not convince members that the cost of a week abroad was 'probably less than . . . a week at Margate'. They travelled over Easter weekends to take advantage of the Good Friday and Easter Monday holidays.[59]

It is pleasing to note that Okey's visits to Italy spurred his studies of Italian language, history and literature, and in 1919 he became the first holder of Cambridge's chair of Italian Studies. Rhodes, Okey and the clubs remain an inspiring memorial to the Victorian ideal of self-help at its best, even if their numbers were never large.

The final group of travellers we want to look at was servants. In the early decades of the nineteenth century it was often assumed travellers would bring their servants, and so ships offered concessionary rates while guide-books expected that servants would help with Customs and other annoyances. When the Masons arrived at Boulogne Helen Mason noted in her diary that, 'after duly presenting ourselves at the Passport Office, we leave our ser[van]t to struggle through the Douane [Customs] & follow on with the luggage' while they raced for the train. As the social background of travellers broadened, the number with servants diminished, although as late as 1914, large hotels were still providing servants' bedrooms at reduced rates.[60] Because the vast majority of servants were women, we are really talking about maids who looked after luggage, helped their mistresses dress and keep clean and arranged their hair.

Because the vast majority of maids had little education, they were frequently seen as sources of amusement. However, just as frequently they became friends and confidantes. As the pompous actress Fanny Kemble wrote, 'It is a very great blessing to have a comfortable maid, and the next blessing to that is to have an entertaining one – to expect both would be unreasonable, for the creature maid cannot by possibility be both useful and entertaining.' Of course Fanny Kemble's maid might have said the same thing about her. One 'entertainment' came from servants' unwillingness to share their employers' romantic effusions. In the late 1840s Lord and Lady Albert Denison took their servant as they trudged up Vesuvius to peer over the rim. As the couple marvelled at the works of nature Lady Albert's maid simply noted, 'Lor, if it is not for all the world like looking down a London chimney.' One of the most popular source of 'servant jokes' was the Channel crossing. Lady Burton asked rhetorically in the 1850s, 'Why are maids always sick at sea, and have to be waited on, poor things, by their mistresses who are not?'[61]

Another source of humour was servants' traditional dislike of foreigners and foreign travel. Mary Boyle recorded that her mother's manservant, Henry Mansell, actually enjoyed travel and studied Italian. Yet when in Florence he resisted the assertion that in Italy *he* was the foreigner: '"No, ma'am," he used to say, "the Italians are foreigners, but I am an Englishman!"' Henry Mansell was unusual in actually liking foreigners. Far more common was the reaction of an unidentified lady's maid who found herself in Rome. She was 'thoroughly English, and has hearty contempt for foreigners and antiquities. When she sees a ruin she says, "Here is another of their old concerns."' However, difficult as servants might be, life without them was more so. When Lady Frederick Cavendish's maid was taken ill during her employer's honeymoon, Lady Frederick bemoaned '4 days' maidlessness, makeshifts, and packing for oneself'.[62]

Lack of time, desire and, earlier on, literacy, meant that few servants could have kept diaries. Even if they had done so their records were less likely to survive. Fortunately there are three particularly interesting servants' diaries, the first of which was kept by Matthew Todd, a twenty-three-year-old Yorkshireman who travelled with his master between 1814 and 1820. Young Todd met his continental challenges with a matter-of-fact manner and was in many ways his employer's friend. On the whole he took life as he found it. He had a sharp eye (especially for young women) and, unlike most middle class diarists, avoided generalizations and was not judgemental. He also had a nice sense of humour: when he described the killing of a pig outside his window at the inn in Dijon he noted, 'The whole of this job was performed in about 10 minutes. So ended poor Piggy.' His lack of diffidence was confirmed when they visited Geneva: there he met, courted and 'took to myself a wife' in 1816. Was it an example of his dry Yorkshire wit when he wrote that during his honeymoon, 'fishing and shooting was my chief amusement'?[63]

The next servant was John Ruskin's 'man', John Hobbs, who was known as 'George' to avoid confusion with the writer and his father, yet another John. Like Matthew Todd, John Hobbs was as much a friend and occasionally an amanuensis as he was a servant. He also struggled with the heavy photographic equipment which Ruskin needed for his research. He kept diaries of two visits to Europe, the first in 1846 (with the Ruskin family) and the second, in 1849 (with John and his new bride). The diaries show Hobbs to be an intelligent young man, hard-working and a keen observer. He was amused in Avranches at the number of English residents, people who were 'looked upon by the peasantry about them as milors, but then they should not be so big and so elevated and give themselves such airs'. He may have lacked Matthew Todd's humour and love of 'larks' but he valued beautiful scenery and appears to have been devoted to his unstable 'master'. On one occasion Ruskin noted in his diary in 1849, 'I was irrevocably sulky and cross, because *George had not got me butter to my bread at Les Rousses.*'[64] When Ruskin came to write his autobiography he never mentioned Hobbs.

One of the few female servants who left a diary was Alison

Cunningham, a forty-year-old Scot taken by Thomas Stevenson and his wife to look after their tubercular son, Robert Louis, in 1863. 'Cummy' was, again, as much a friend as an employee. She was, like Hobbs, an acute observer of life, noting for example that cows in Menton were fed on lemons and that in Florence the men who carried the coffin in a funeral procession were 'all shrouded in black . . . All wore masks of black linen.' She liked Italy: 'Every new part . . . one visits is always the most beautiful', though papal Rome was 'a poor, priest-ridden city'. Florence was much nicer, in part because it was 'free from smells, which is no small comfort' and Venice was best of all. She wondered, like so many others, if 'the people take the advantage of us foreigners'. Catholics were 'deluded mortals' and the French – 'very nice people too' – were 'under the reign of the man of sin [the Pope]'. She tried to talk to the French chambermaid in Menton about the Bible. 'She pointed up. I asked her about Jesus but she said *non*, so I gave it up . . . I fear she is a Roman Catholic.' When it came to theology Cummy did not have any more luck with her employer whilst driving round Genoa. 'I had a very nice conversation with Mr. S. . . . . The time passed pleasantly and I trust, not unprofitably, while we were talking. Mr. S. is still suffering much from piles.' The Stevensons insisted she dine with them at 'that awful table d'hôte'. 'The dinners are much too grand for my humble taste, and a waiter to wait on you.' On the way home the party stopped in Munich and Cummy had a day on her own, got lost and was desperate to get back to the hotel because 'I was rather in a sad plight for a *wee*.'[65] Her writing is straightforward, amusing and interesting.

Those who did not bring servants could always hire them. When the Jervoise family stopped in Rome in 1838 they hired a manservant for £7 a month, which was not cheap, although this was 'to cover all [his] expenses.' They also employed his wife as a lady's maid for about a quarter of that sum. Mr Jervoise was 'in every respect well satisfied' and noted the servant's address for future reference. When the Horners took on a maid during their long stay in Florence in 1861 they were less fortunate. In November Susan Horner noted in her diary that 'we parted with our maid Luisa, who is dirty and takes snuff'. Whilst we can discover what the English thought of the people who waited on them, it is rare to find out what the servants thought. There is a rare exception in the papers of the writer Lina Duff-Gordon, when she was in Florence. She told a friend that one servant had 'a profound contempt for us Signore who, in her mind, are only good *a mangiare, dormire e scrivere!*' – to eat, sleep and write. When she later wrote up her experiences, Lina Duff-Gordon warned Englishmen, 'Never set your heart upon having a conventional household in Italy; even with "trained servants!" something unusual is sure to happen.' This turned out to be the experience of the Reverend Herbert Jeaffreson and his family when they wintered in Castel Gandolfo in 1893. They employed a married couple known as 'Bat' and 'Bar' or Battista and his wife, Barbara, the cook. Things deteriorated and Jeaffreson asked the couple to leave upon which 'Bat' turned on his employers and in broken English called them 'thieves' and 'dirty English'. Far, far worse, he said they were not grand but merely 'ordinary people'. Then 'Bat' discovered that the wine and the brandy had not been locked away so he got thoroughly drunk and began smashing things. When he eventually collapsed in a drunken stupor Mr Jeaffreson found him 'asleep with a bottle and a glass beside him, and a long, sharp knife'. On waking up 'Bat' re-launched his oral attack: the Jeaffresons were not just *'Brutti bovi inglesi'* or 'ugly English cattle' but 'dirty heretics' and he struck Mrs Jeaffreson. The couple now locked 'Bat' in the dining room and themselves in their bedroom. By 3.30 a.m. Battista had finally stopped raving and they could all get some sleep. The next morning, Bat and Bar, now sober and apologetic, were packed off to Rome and heard of no more.[66]

So far we have been looking at the various types of travellers, but it might be helpful to look at the overall numbers involved and then at the economic changes that made the growth in travel possible. In

Britain, the government simply did not keep records of those leaving the country. When in 1831 the Chancellor of the Exchequer proposed a two-shilling tax on everyone crossing the Channel, he had to admit that he had no idea of the number who did so. There are some records kept by French port authorities and by some British railway companies for certain years. Using what statistics there are, we can estimate that in 1814 fewer than 10,000 people left for the Continent. By the 1820s the number had more than doubled and from then on the numbers grew steadily. One statistic, based on French police returns, claimed that by the 1860s annual arrivals in France had soared to some 250,000 a year. By 1911 *The Times* were reporting that 'about 1,000,000 people go . . . to the Continent in the course of a year' and by 1914 the number would have been even greater because the rate of growth was rapidly increasing.[67]

This growth was based on profound economic changes. The economy was booming because of the growth of railways, technology, manufacturing, the domestic consumer market and exports. This led to the first development that affected travel: the growth of the middle class. Between 1851 and 1911 the number of people in the middle class doubled, from fewer than five in every hundred to just over eleven in every hundred. This growth occurred in two ways. Middle class professions grew considerably: there were more clergymen, physicians, solicitors, barristers, architects, civil servants, bankers, commercial clerks, shopkeepers and teachers with each passing year. For example, in 1861, there were 14,600 physicians and surgeons; in 1901, there were 23,000. Secondly, the middle class expanded because new professions were created: civil engineers, chartered accountants, mechanical engineers, surveyors, financial experts in the City and, after 1870, teachers employed by the state. For example, in 1861 there were 110,300 teachers; by 1901 there were 230,000. Thirdly, the greatest growth in income came not among the highest paid in the middle class, such as barristers, but among the lower echelons such as teachers and shopkeepers, the very people who would take advantage of lower fares and conducted tours. The teachers mentioned above would have earned on average £51 in 1815 compared with £176 in 1911. These salaries were, of course, averages, and the lowest paid would most likely have regarded a week in Paris as beyond their means; but they might have afforded a weekend in Calais for fifteen shillings. The better paid could have put aside, say, two shillings a week and in about a year and a half would have had enough for one of Gaze's or Cook's tours. The more adventurous 'pedestrian of moderate requirements' could have undertaken a walking tour in Austria for six to eight shillings a day.[68]

The middle class also grew richer, that is, it had more disposable income. In 1843, about one million people had incomes above £150 a year. Forty years later the number had grown to 1.4 million. If, like some nineteenth-century sociologists, we define the middle class as those with at least one servant, by 1901 some 4.5 million people belonged in this category. Likewise, as incomes rose prices fell, considerably so between 1800 and 1900.[69] Finally, the birth rate was declining most markedly among the middle class. Fewer children meant fewer expenses, which left more for luxuries such as foreign trips.

By the final decades of the nineteenth century the range of people setting out for Europe had widened to a degree that few in mid-century would have thought possible. In 1877 a party of three enjoyed 115 days in Holland, Germany, Austria, Switzerland and Italy for £214 (or some 12s 4½ d a day), while a married couple took their first trip abroad – three weeks in Germany and Switzerland on less than nine shillings a day each. Alongside these independent travellers were the day-trippers to Calais and Boulogne where, thanks to the growth of new, large hotels, people could have weekend breaks with bed and board starting at 4s 9d a day. There were tours organized by Cook, Gaze, Florian's, Frame's, Lunn's, Dean & Dawson or Pickford's, whose customers must have numbered in the hundreds of thousands: in 1878, Cook by himself had had 75,000 customers going to that year's Paris Exhibition. But most people used the agencies only to get tickets and hotel coupons. They relied on guide-books to plan their holidays. In 1888, the

Chemin-de-fer-du-Nord noted that only about nine in every hundred passengers between Calais and Paris travelled '*à prix reduit*', that is, on special tickets arranged by travel agents. While this is only one year's statistics there is no reason to believe they are not typical.[70]

The range of travel that existed by the 1890s can be illustrated in the case of two travellers. The first is Sibella Bonham Carter who visited Italy in 1894 for five weeks. When not sight-seeing she went for walks, visited other Englishmen, went to the galleries, attended Anglican and Catholic services (for the music), sat for a photograph, shopped and went to a tea party laid on by 'English & American ladies'. She devoted part of each day to reading or letter-writing, while her daughter took Italian lessons. Her visit was very little different from that of any upper-middle-class lady of 1814. What was different was the second traveller, Philip Gibbs, a twenty-one-year-old Londoner who earned £120 a year and was able to have a fortnight in Paris with his young wife in 1898. They followed advice to 'drink native wines and eat the fare of the country'. The man who gave this advice never spent more than eight shillings a day for bed and board. The couple stayed in a cheap hotel, explored the back streets, visited the Louvre, did some window-shopping in the Palais Royal and walked 'hand in hand through the Bois de Boulogne'.[71]

Philip Gibbs and his wife symbolized the massive developments that had taken place in travel during this long period and were heralds of a future when there would be an even greater expansion of foreign holidays for people like them.

Chapter 3

Seeing the Lions

$\mathcal{G}$uide-books always told a traveller 'to sketch out a plan of his tour in advance . . . and to guard against overlooking any place of interest'. The Victorians usually referred to the principal tourist sights as 'lions', and the 'lions' that most tourists hunted were concentrated in six countries. What tourists regarded as worth seeing between 1814 and 1914 was in most cases what many today still regard as worthwhile; but there were some surprising differences: morgues were perhaps the most notable exception. When M. J. Torr was in Munich she went, like many others, to see the laying-out room at the cemetery: 'In a large building adjoining, we saw the dead laid out before burial – decked out with flowers, and each body having a bell-wire in the hand. This is done to prevent the possibility of any being buried alive – but it was rather a ghastly spectacle.'[1]

Brussels, 'the great treasure-house of mediaeval art', was, at least in the early decades of the nineteenth century, one of the most famous 'lions' and was always one of the destinations offered by the new tourist agencies. In 1843 Bishop Hynes praised 'this beautiful city. The Collegiate Church of S. Michael, a Gothic structure, pleases me more than the Cathedrals of Strasbourg or Cologne. The wood carving . . . is magnificent – the stained windows too, are the finest I have ever seen.' The city's *Quartier Léopold* was also known as a place where British expatriates seeking to 'retrench' and to find cheaper education for their children could settle. As early as 1814 one traveller was impressed 'with the *vast numbers* of my fellow subjects' he met. Lord Palmerston was less kind when he said that Brussels 'swarms with rum English'. By the 1880s there were some 6,000 expatriates settled in the city. Nearby Bruges also provided a welcome refuge for the British: Frances Trollope and her family went there when her husband fled England to escape arrest for debt.[2]

It was rare for anyone to visit Brussels without also visiting the battlefield of Waterloo. When the Capel family went there in August 1815, only two months after the battle, they were shocked at 'the mounds of earth covering dead horses, and . . . [the] many caps, broken swords, and knapsacks . . . lying by the roadside'. They also visited the cottage where their uncle, Lord Anglesey ('By God, Sir, I've lost my leg!'), had had his leg amputated. The continuing popularity of Waterloo meant that it was usually one of the 'tours' offered by men such as Gaze or Cook. In the early years of the century one aspect of a visit that was most remembered was the abundance of guides who had been, or who claimed they had been, in the French or British army. When Marianne Thornton visited in 1817 her party were taken round by 'Mons[r] La Coste, le Guide de Bonaparte . . . whether this is the real La Coste, I am such a heretic on these matters I chose to doubt, however if not he does as well, as he knows the Ground perfectly.' More trustworthy was the famous Sergeant Cotton who *had* been in the battle and who could be reached at his 'Hotel du Musee – English Bar' in Waterloo. Visitors could also engage a rival such as Martin Viseur whose 1836 business card claimed that he 'was present to assist the wounded and bury the dead, and has acted as Guide since the Battle'. One should write ahead care of the 'Hôtel Mont St. Jean near the Field, Belgium'. References were provided on request. The greater problem was the gruesome relics: 'Boys were continually offering us bones, pieces of hair, buttons, Bullets etc. etc. . . . but I . . . have no faith in them.' The vendors of bones and hair were still about in the late 1830s and Murray warned against these 'harpies in the shape of guides and relic vendors'. Later visitors were amused to see that the famous statue of a lion, erected on a huge mound on the spot where the Prince of Orange had been wounded, now had a reduced tail: bits had been 'broken off by the French'.[3]

By the closing years of the century travel writers were still insisting that it was 'the first duty of the British tourist . . . to visit the field of Waterloo', and guide-books were still including the site; yet inevitably the number of visitors had declined as the historical memory faded. Because it was normal to go to the battlefield from Brussels, this meant that the battlefield shared the same decline as a tourist destination that affected the Belgian capital and, indeed, Belgium itself. This was due to several factors. The first was the country's success in building Europe's earliest railways: by 1843 tourists could go by rail from Ostend all the way to the Prussian border. While this helped to guarantee the success of the tour down the Rhine it also meant that tourists arrived at Ostend and immediately took the train through 'monotonous Belgium on their way to the Rhine'. This reduced Belgium to 'a kind of enlarged railway platform'. One such through-traveller was Charlotte Horsman, en route to a Rhine trip in the 1840s. It would have been little consolation to the Belgians that she did not find Belgium monotonous. Indeed, she was 'charmed everywhere with the extreme cleanliness and neatness . . . the Inns were Palaces and the whole country a garden . . . seen a great advantage from the railroad most of which is raised on embankments'. But she only saw it 'from the railroad'. Finally, Brussels, Waterloo and Belgium simply could not compete with the evolving pattern of travel which resulted from the growth of Calais and Boulogne, the development of railways in France, and the overwhelming attraction of Paris.[4]

'Almost all educated Englishmen visit Paris at some time in their lives' it was said, and the city was always a place to be 'enjoyed': one of the earliest guides was entitled *How to Enjoy Paris*. From the outset, the British discovered one of the city's great attractions: 'all the public buildings are magnificent' and, what is more, in Paris visitors could see stone's natural colour. As one French guide-book boasted, 'How unlike London . . . [where] every building is blackened with smoke.' Paris never suffered from London's smog and the cleaner air lifted visitors' spirits as well as eased their breathing. In addition, entrance into the Louvre was gratis.[5] One disadvantage, or, to many, a cause of added pleasure was the massive redevelopment that went on in Paris between 1814 and 1914 when so many famous attractions were created. The Arc de Triomphe was completed in 1836 and the land along side the Champs-Élysée was developed after 1828. Most radical of all, Haussmann's network of boulevards, parks and squares starting in 1852 altered the appearance of much of central Paris. The Eiffel Tower was put up in 1889 while both the Grand and Petit Palais were built for the exhibition of 1900.

In addition to the creation of the modern Paris there was the excitement of recent French history. British travellers arriving in the early decades of the century did so in the shadow of the Revolution of 1789 and its subsequent Terror, a history almost all would have known. In addition there was, between 1814 and 1871, a succession of governments, coups and revolutions: Bourbons to Napoleon to Bourbons to Orleans to republic to Napoleon III and back to republic. Three times between 1814 and 1914 Paris was convulsed with revolution – in 1830, 1848 and, more violently, in 1870–1. These upheavals created an interest in and an underlying contempt for French public life. They inevitably reduced tourism at the time but in the years following, the ruined buildings joined the list of things any tourist must see. In 1871 tourists 'drove . . . round the principal parts destroyed . . . saw the ruins of the Vendome Colume, Tuilleries, Louvre, Hôtel de Ville, and other buildings – all much changed'.[6]

Paris was regarded as Europe's most beautiful city, even before Haussmann's redevelopment, and as its centre of art and fashion. In addition to the Louvre, the deserted palace at Versailles was used for many years as an art museum. When Thomas Best and his new bride visited it in 1858 he was honest enough to write: 'I think we saw every picture in the building & were not very sorry when we came to the last.' There was also a considerable desire to attend French theatres, while some wished to study Haussmann's improvements. For many years visitors paid handsomely to see the guillotine, but trips had to be booked to allow time for the machine to be set up. As Robert Parker noted in 1818, 'no doubt but that it is the easiest and speediest Death'. After that he went to see a manufactory of mirrors. While most visited Père Lachaise cemetery and one of the most popular 'lions', the Jardin de Plantes, others were keen to see the city's morgue and slaughter-houses, 'a sight no gentleman should miss altho' not a pleasant one for ladies'.[7] Yet others found time to visit the mental asylum. To be fair, most people now came not to gape but to see the rate of progress being achieved.

If some wished to explore the 'restaurants', some of the men wanted to embrace other aspects of a city with an established reputation for vice. While vice meant different things to different people, sexual profligacy and gambling were always top of the list. Although, according to one Tory author, they were 'the natural result of a successful Revolution', even he admitted that Paris had far less drunkenness than London. Thackeray was one of the few to leave a record of visits to the gambling 'hells' of Paris. Even fewer left records of visits to brothels, although Wilkie Collins seems to have taken Dickens to one, while later in the century Oscar Wilde and A. E. Housman visited similar institutions providing alternative pleasures. Somewhat removed from this form of entertainment was shopping. Paris long had a great reputation for the variety and quality of its goods, especially women's clothes. In the 1840s English women were urged 'as soon as possible . . . [to] apply to M. Hoffman, No. 8, Rue de la Paix, who will fit them in such a light and elegant manner, giving such a *"jolie tournure"* to the foot, that they will scarcely know their own feet again'. In addition, many women, including Queen Victoria, enjoyed window-shopping. So great was Paris's reputation that by 1912 writers could claim that 'the Rue de la Paix is known from end to end of the world as the shopping street par excellent', that is, 'for those fortunate ones who have money'.[8]

In general, Paris was a cheaper city than London to visit and even more as a place to settle. This attracted many Britons who created an 'English colony', which tended to have little to do with the French; in some cases there was positive hostility: Thackeray's step-father named his dog 'Waterloo' so that he could go down the street calling out the word to the annoyance of patriotic Frenchmen. The life of this colony was centred in the area close to the Louvre, and the hotels that enjoyed English custom were in the Rue de Rivoli and the area near the Place Vendôme. Near here, too, was the British Embassy, the English language library, and the English Church, with four services every Sunday. The Latin Quarter's main appeal was to young Britons studying medicine or art, since lodgings on the Left Bank were at least a third cheaper than on the fashionable Right. Young men in the 1850s could live on £4 a month including room and meals with wine at the Hôtel Corneille, provided they could endure the eternal tobacco smoke.[9]

Compared with the present, there was relatively little interest in most of provincial France. Occasionally tourists confided in their diaries that 'above all things I love the air of liveliness which pervades a French town', but to most travellers 'France is but a thoroughfare, with one halting place and bright centre of interest in Paris'. A few provincial cities received some attention: Dijon, for example, was on the regular route to Switzerland, and one guide said the city 'will well repay the traveller who has a day to spend in quiet disengagement from the present'. More common was Lord Fortescue's verdict on one provincial town: 'dirty beyond the average of French towns'. Interest in the provinces only really began at the start of the twentieth century when the desire to see the 'real France' became fashionable. In addition, places such as Lyons set up tourist offices or *Syndicats d'Initiative* to promote their areas while new forms of transport such as bicycles and automobiles made touring the countryside so much easier.[10]

Boulogne and Normandy had long been exceptions to this lack

of interest. Boulogne had a major 'colony' of British debtors and, after the 1840s it became the favoured place for long weekends while Normandy was 'the part of France most commonly explored by . . . tourists'. It attracted visitors because of its connection with English history and its geographic closeness. Likewise, Dieppe was a major port for travellers and Rouen was visited because in the early days of rail one went there to get the train for Paris. Through trains to Paris ended this practice. When cycling became popular, Normandy's appeal was enhanced, especially when cheap hotels were taken into consideration: Norman hotels were charging on average from seven to ten francs a day, which could include meals and wine. Water 'should never be taken except with caution'.[11]

By the early years of the twentieth century the Riviera was, next to Paris, the most popular French destination for British travellers. The principal resorts were Nice, Cannes and Menton. Nizza formed part of the Italian Kingdom of Sardinia until 1860, when the town was transferred to France and became Nice. Since at least the 1730s it had had a steady stream of British travellers. With the sparkling blue Bay of Angels to one side and the snow-capped Alps in the distance, Nice was deservedly popular. As early as 1824 there were placards throughout the town in English advertising houses and provisions because of its fame as 'a cheap place as a permanent residence', and by the 1850s hoteliers had established a form of 'tourist information office' or 'syndicate' to help visitors. In the 1820s one wealthy British visitor, the Reverend Lewis Way, was so concerned about local unemployment that he produced the money to build the Promenade des Anglais to provide jobs for the poor. The promendade remains the most enduring monument of the many humanitarian acts performed by British travellers on the Continent.[12]

Cannes, across the Var River in France, was accidentally 'discovered' by Lord Brougham in 1834, as Elisabeth Feilding described in a letter from Nice. 'Yesterday just as we were sitting down to dinner . . . Estorforth arrived from Cannes with a letter to

Mr. F[eilding] from Lord Brougham who had not heard of the cordon de Santé [quarantine] when he left Paris.' Not surprisingly, the former Lord Chancellor was 'most indignant at learning that he was not suffered to enter Les Etats Sardis [Sardinia] without a Quarantine of 31 days.' Brougham, never a patient man, had hired a 'desperate smuggler' to help him, but to no avail. Then 'Mr. F. immediately went to all the authorities & the governor & President were willing to shorten the Quarantine, but the old Queen Marie Christine . . . who is dreadfully afraid of the cholera would not consent . . . the loss of Lord Brougham is most vexative for even his enemies allow his powers of conversation.' Brougham, forced to stay in France, was so impressed by the beauties of Cannes that he decided to build a villa there. And so the Queen Mother of Sardinia's fear of cholera would lead, indirectly, to one of the Riviera's most famous resorts. Within forty years the town would have about 3,000 British visitors a year.[13]

However, Nice remained the most important spot on the Riviera because of its fame as a place for invalids to winter. For many years British physicians praised its climate for those with chest problems, though by 1860 opinion had changed: the town's 'reputation for the cure of consumption . . . was not founded on fact'. The wind and the summer heat were 'most injurious to invalids, especially those of the pulmonary class'.[14] It is sad to note that one English consumptive in search of health, the Rev Henry Lyte, was among those who came to Nice but who did not leave. Unlike most of those who sought but could not find health he left behind a memorial, a poem that became a hymn that has brought comfort to millions in the English-Speaking World, 'Abide With Me! Fast Falls the Even Tide'. The third line of the second stanza – 'Change and decay in all around I see' – must have been a sad reflection of his plight and of that of so many others.

By 1860 Nice, with over 50,000 inhabitants, was 'now a place of resort for other purposes than the restoration of health'. That year visitors had a golf course, numerous physicians, an English church (with cemetery), a Scottish church (without cemetery), an opera house, a theatre, an English school, hotels, *pensions*, apartments, circulating libraries, sea bathing with bathing-machines, as in England, physicians and a casino that was 'fitted up with taste'. The real breakthrough also came that same decade when the Riviera got a through train from Paris. When Tchaikovsky arrived in 1872 he found Nice 'charming but what is awful is the worldly way of life. All the idle rich from all over the world come here in winter.' In the mid-1880s the Chemin du Fer de Nord noted the connection between the growth of *'le traffic anglaise'* and that of the 'de luxe' trains to the Riviera. Nice also had royal approval: of Queen Victoria's nine visits to the Riviera, five were to Nice with one each to Menton, Cannes, Grasse and Hyères. It is in Cimiez, the elegant suburb that overlooks Nice, that the grateful owner of the Hôtel Excelsior Régina, where Victoria stayed, erected a charming statue of the Queen. This shows her seated and smiling as children hand up garlands during the annual Battle of Flowers, which she so enjoyed.

The statue was erected in front of the Queen's hotel in 1912, the same year in which neighbouring Cannes unveiled a statue to her son, Edward VII, to join that put up to Brougham in 1878. Even with Queen Victoria's presence, it was always Nice that led the way as something of a Mediterranean Brighton. To *The Times* in 1911 it was a 'clean and brilliant' city but one noted for the 'third-rate gaiety which she flaunts'. The paper feared that Cannes would 'try to imitate her gayer, less reputable cousin'. In the event Cannes, described by English visitors as 'a little Paradise', only really caught up in the twentieth century.[15]

Mentone, which nestles between Monaco and the Italian frontier, was one of those resorts that owed its fame to a book by a doctor, in this case Dr James Henry Bennet. The city, which dropped the Italian 'e' after annexation by France in 1861, had an older, Italian section on the hill, and a new section along the coast. It was (and is) far more sedate than Cannes, let alone Nice. Likewise, it was much smaller: the population in 1856 stood at 4,800 and by 1911 had reached 18,000, but this was a long way behind Nice's 150,000.

Its reputation was enhanced by Queen Victoria's 1882 visit when she enjoyed carriage rides round the countryside. Peasants flocked to greet her with cries of 'Bonjour Madame la Reine et votre compagnie'. She avoided Monte Carlo with its 'nasty disreputable looking people' who came for the gambling, which flourished after France outlawed it in 1857. The famous casino sent the Queen a bouquet as a peace offering but she ordered it returned. When Victoria left she referred to 'beloved and beautiful Mentone'. Less sympathetic visitors recalled a local saying: 'Cannes is for living, Monte Carlo is for gambling and Menton is for dying.'[16]

'The Germans are an extremely civil people compared with the French; a traveller is better treated among them, without the perpetual *affectation of superiority*', while their 'passion . . . for *music* is very strong'. This was far better than 'the tiresome recurrence of political discussions, so general in France'.[17] This view, favourable if patronizing, dates from 1815 but it lasted well into the 1860s. It was based on the many dynastic, diplomatic, cultural and religious ties between the British and the Germans, who often referred to each other as cousins, and on a shared wariness of an unstable France. It was also based on the single most popular British holiday of the nineteenth century, a trip up the Rhine.

Anthony Trollope had no doubt that 'men there are bold enough to stay from church on Sundays but where is the man who can tell his wife and daughters that it is quite unnecessary that they should go up the Rhine?'.[18] The Romanticism that the British saw in Germany's medieval cities, ruined castles and sometimes dramatic countryside seemed to be encapsulated on the banks of the Rhine. These sights particularly appealed to a generation rediscovering the medieval past and revelling in Romantic imagining. Byron, who wrote as he travelled, sailed on the river in May 1816 and praised it and its ruins in the Third Canto of *Childe Harold's Pilgrimage*. He was especially taken with the Drachenfels, or Dragon's Rock mountain, and described it and its ruins in verses that would be recited by thousands of tourists after him:

> *The castled crag of Drachenfels*
> *Frowns o'er the wide and winding Rhine,*
> *Whose breast of waters broadly swells*
> *Between the banks which bear the vine,*
> *And hills all rich with blossom'd trees,*
> *And fields which promise corn and wine,*
> *And scatter'd cities crowning these,*
> *Whose far white walls along them shine.*

In the very year that verse was written boats were already taking tourists up the river to see Byron's Drachenfels. Steamers started in 1817, but for two decades one company had the monopoly which kept prices relatively high. Once that monopoly ended it became possible to enjoy a nine-hour cruise from Cologne to Mainz for nine shillings, and passenger numbers soared. In 1827, with the monopoly in place, there were 18,000 passengers. In 1851, after the monopoly had ended, the number soared to a million, but these would have included local people as well. Then, in 1845, a journey up the Rhine received royal approval when Queen Victoria and Prince Albert travelled on the river. What had been a water highway for Germans became the most favoured of all British holiday spots, not just because of the all-in nature of the trip but because it took less time, thereby appealing to the new generation of travellers. The normal route was to travel to Ostend and then across Belgium, but with the spread of railways people could book tickets from London to any of the cities on the river and stop off en route. For example, by the 1850s one could make the trip *and* a tour in Switzerland for £3 7s. So great was the demand that railways began offering special short break fares, leaving London on Sundays at noon and returning on Wednesdays. Fares could be as cheap as 12s 6d for second class.[19]

Cologne was the favourite spot to board the steamers, and if tourists had the time they could get a quick glimpse of St Ursula's Church containing the bones of 11,000 British virgins supposedly martyred in the fourth century. Bones were 'stuck about everywhere – in the walls and in the pavements; skulls are peeping out of nooks and crannies'. Most thought this a 'pious fraud', but even worse were the city's drains. Coleridge expressed this particular 'smell of the continent' in verses somewhat less romantic than Byron's:[20]

> *In Köhln, a town of monks and bones,*
> *And pavements fang'd with murderous stones*
> *And rags, and hags, and hideous wenches;*
> *I counted two and seventy stenches,*

Of course, the city was also famed for a somewhat different scent, its Eau de Cologne, which became a standard souvenir. Almost all guide-books carried advertisements from Johann Maria Farina, whose ancestor had invented the perfume in 1709. It solemnly warned travellers that cabmen and waiters would try to trick them into buying inferior versions, whereas only his shop had the true cologne. Part of its popularity was its price: even Herr Farina's was one-third cheaper than at home.

The Rhineland soon learned the lesson of tourism: if one had a 'lion' one needed to make it even more attractive. Tourists wanted to be entertained as well as to be moved by the scenery. Hotels in Cologne laid on bands to serenade tired tourists in hotel gardens and in 1833 Germany's first funicular railway replaced donkeys to take people to the top of the Drachenfels. Because Rhine tours were booked in England and included accommodation, passage and fees, they were in effect the first modern holiday package. They also led to attributes of tourism still with us: increased facilities, guide-books, souvenirs and overcrowding. By the 1850s the Rhine was 'where Regent Street may be said to be let loose in the summer months'. All along the river new hotels were built, providing omnibuses to take guests to the steamers. The authorities also arranged to fire cannons so that tourists could hear the celebrated echoes. In Koblenz, another favourite stop, an enterprising book-seller named Karl Baedeker advertised that he stocked English guide-books and would be glad to give the British information about the Rhine. As early as the 1830s there were books of Rhine views which served both to 'whet present appetite, and thereafter for a memento'.[21]

From the 1840s a tourist could also buy a small German-made statuette of himself. *'Der englischer Reisender'* – 'The English Traveller' – was a terracotta figure about six inches high. He is shown with his Murray guide-book in one hand, his overnight bag in another, an umbrella under one arm and his courier's bag slung round his neck. He is rosy cheeked, wears a Homburg hat, has a full set of whiskers and is pot-bellied. The caption, in English, reads 'I am starting for a long journey.' A second statuette portrays his wife with shawl, bonnet, hat-box and spaniel and is captioned, 'I am off with him.' The following year yet another poem was written, not about the glories of the Rhine but about the English who travelled on it:

> *Sir Shropshire steigt in Bonn ans Land*
> *Mit seiner Gemahlin an der Hand*
>
> *Sir Shropshire steps ashore in Bonn*
> *With his wife on his arm.*

The poet, Heinrich Hoffmann von Fallersleben, more famous for his poem 'Deutschland über Alles', was here describing a couple who jump off the boat at Bonn, race to see a new statue of Beethoven, look at it for a few seconds and race back, *'ganz gebildet'* ('totally cultured').[22] The slowly developing distinction between 'tourist' and 'traveller' is nowhere better illustrated.

Because the boats were also used by local people the British had a chance to meet Germans face to face, an opportunity many heartily disliked. These 'smoking, drinking Germans . . . swaggered and talked and what was hideous to English eyes kissed one another' noticed one young English couple. When returning from a ramble ashore this same couple were irate to find their seats taken. This led to an argument and Percy Bysshe Shelley knocked the German intruder down, much to the approval of his future wife. However, Mary Shelley also admitted that common but rarely mentioned fact that after a holiday, memory takes 'all the dark shades from the picture', but 'the filthy habit of smoking' remained inerasable. It was worse because men smoked in the presence of ladies. Twenty years later another British tourist sat near 'an old baron, with a name too long to attempt, who . . . puffed away, from morning till night . . . I was glad, however, to observe a notice in the cabin, that neither cigars nor pipes were allowed below deck' where the dining room was located.[23]

By the 1840s the steamers had room for about 200 passengers, who were divided into classes. The after cabin was for 'servants and inferior persons' while the more expensive pavilion, which was smoke free, was preferred by the wealthier British voyagers. From whatever vantage, travellers enjoyed the view: 'the scenery is finer than ever my imagination had designed it' is a typical comment, while the rapid succession of views resembled a 'magic lantern' show. 'Village after village – vineyard, mountain, and ruin – seemed to run by . . . while we, seated at our . . . ease, looked with delight at the wonderful and beauteous panorama. It would be a vain effort to attempt to detail to you even a small portion of what we saw, and of the legends that were narrated to us. You must come and see, and hear, all yourself!'[24]

Yet the steam-driven tourist who was content just to sit would have no conception of the splendours along the river. A serious Victorian traveller expected to work, as we see in one middle class family's trip in 1844 as told by their teenage son. Boarding the steamer at Cologne they scorned the pavilion, 'reserved for those English . . . who will on no account travel without a partition between themselves and their inferiors in wealth'. The boy was delighted to be on the 'majestic river' but regretted that 'English faces met our eye on every side, and our native language proceeded from the mouths of all.' This family did as Murray advised and left the bulk of their luggage on board while they made short trips to Wiesbaden and Heidelberg before finally reaching their goal, Basle. Another tourist had 'never seen anything so beautiful' as the Rhine but wondered if 'it was the Liebfraumilch or a bit of real sentiment . . . after a good dinner'. Most people agreed (with or without the wine) and were delighted with the Rhine, but as always some were disappointed. One man wrote home that while the Drachenfels was wonderful, by the time he reached Baden-Baden he had had enough of Germany and the 'disagreeable guttural language'.[25]

By the 1880s the popularity of the Rhine Tour had begun to decline. The banks now had cement works and quarries which broadcast the united Germany's industrial might. To the British the sights were not only ugly but frightening, as attitudes towards the new, Prussian-dominated Germany changed. Up to the 1860s the Germans, divided into their various kingdoms and duchies, were seen as dreamy, impractical romantics who had splendid cultural achievements but were not a threat. The growth of Prussian power which culminated in unification in 1870 changed all that. With their new wealth Germans themselves began to travel in France and Italy, from where one British traveller wrote, 'The hotel is full of noisy Germans but some are not so bad.' When Lord Sandwich was motoring in France in 1908 he noted that '[i]n old days' travelling, one generally was somewhat oppressed by English fellow-travellers . . . not always of the most attractive type . . . but I found all this changed; there were Germans everywhere, and their loud shouts . . . and the eternal "colossal" were very distracting.' Other visitors left with more reassuring views. Jerome K. Jerome described the Germans in 1891 as a 'simple, earnest, homely, genuine people . . . They look straight before them like a people who see a great future in front of them, and are not afraid to go forward to fulfil it.'[26]

An insight into this 'new' Germany came in 1914 when Captain Francis Grenfell was attending army manoeuvres in Germany. In Dresden he was arrested because his name had been entered in the

hotel register as 'Private' Grenfell and not as an officer. He was
fined the equivalent of £1 5s and told to leave Dresden within
twelve hours. He protested and the next day went to see the police.
There he was told that he had done nothing wrong: 'I had been
suspected of being a spy but could now go where I liked.' He had
already heard of children coming from school to ask for half a Mark
'to help to pay for a fleet to beat the cursed English [and] . . . some
officers talk quite openly about future war with England.' He added
a few days later, 'War with France is bound to come as Germans
wish to assert their superiority.'[27]

Throughout the century British visitors visited Germany's fashionable spas at Baden-Baden, Homburg, Wiesbaden and elsewhere.
The gambling casinos that were part of the complexes were added
attractions to many until the new empire banned them in 1872.
(Gambling only resumed after the Nazis came to power in 1933.)
There was also a host of German cities that were famous for their
art and civilized way of life: Munich, Stuttgart, Koblenz, Augsburg,
Regensburg, Freiburg and Nuremburg. While each had its devotees,
it was Dresden, capital of the Kingdom of Saxony, that 'had a
magnetic attraction for English folk'. This 'Florence of Germany'
had a magnificent setting beside the Elbe with the 'Saxon Switzerland' in the distance. (It is interesting that to people at the time, the
best way to praise Dresden was to compare it to two of the favourite
British destinations, Florence and Switzerland.) At night 'the domes
& steeples of Dresden shone dimly in the moonlight'. To many it
was 'the most attractive town in Germany' with its museums,
palaces, gardens and galleries. The king's art collection was one of
the finest in Europe and was open to the public: it boasted
Raphael's *Madonna di San Sisto*, arguably the most popular painting in the nineteenth century. Dresden may not have had 'the gaiety
of Paris or Vienna' but 'its charms are more solidly German, and
more lasting'. It was also known as 'the Mecca of the musician. For
five shillings . . . you can purchase a stall at the opera house.'
Young Edward Peek listed all its charms in 1870: Dresden had 'the

finest picture gallery in Europe, plenty of first-class music and lovely scenery close at hand. Add to that it is very cheap.' The English who wintered there were 'of a superior class, though often straightened in circumstances'.[28]

Among visitors in the 1840s who were not of 'a superior class' were three London drapers, Mary and Emily Wilson and their brother, John, who spent a month in the city. Like so many others they took German lessons (at 6*d* an hour), attended the English Church and became part of what Mary called 'quiet Dresden'. They frequently went to the opera, attended concerts, crossed the street beside 'Her Saxon Majesty' as she trudged through the snow, visited the porcelain works at Meissen, endured the 'hateful smoking', mounted ponies to tour Saxon Switzerland, listened to military bands, visited the royal *Schatzkammer* (a collection of treasures), went to Catholic churches (for the music) and took numerous daytrips. They were also thrilled to meet a dashing but rather 'silly young English Baronet' who was going on to Berlin to ride in a race against one of the Prussian king's horses. It was also said that he had been flirting with an actress, but this was only a rumour.[29]

'If you would see the glory of God, go to Switzerland', the Reverend Thomas Guthrie rhapsodized in 1872. 'Everybody should, if possible, scrape together sufficient money . . . to go there, before they die'. Go there they did from the moment travel resumed in 1814. Of all European countries, Switzerland became, perhaps even more than Italy, the favoured destination for British travellers. The arrival of railways meant that a new type of traveller, those who were 'stinted for time' and could only come for 'a run' – the very people on Gaze's ten-guinea tours – could see Switzerland. By the 1850s they could travel from London in thirty hours and by 1899 the time had been cut to twenty hours and twenty-five minutes.[30] It is hardly surprising that Thomas Cook's first all-in tour was to Switzerland.

The country remained the perfect destination for holidaymakers who had only a week or two and were interested only in the 'picturesque' such as a visit to Lucerne, the William Tell Chapel and the Reichenbach Falls. Each became a tourist 'lion', and one visitor, Arthur Conan Doyle, was so impressed that he later used the Falls for the struggle between Sherlock Holmes and Professor Moriarty: the ledge from which they fell is marked by a plaque. Perhaps the greatest experience was to go to the top of the Rigi Mountain to watch the sunrise. This was an event which 'forms an epoch in one's life, which can never be forgotten'. So popular did this become that a railway was built which in 1875 was carrying some 110,000 passengers a year and stands were erected on the mountain top to accommodate the crowds. A longer visit would allow time for extensive walks, such as one undertaken by the Torr family in 1863. While walking up one mountain they came across chalets near which children were tending cattle. 'At one we got milk warmed & very nice & went inside the chalet to have it. Everything was as clean & neat as it was possible in such a place where the smoke of the fire had no outlet but the interstices of the planks with which the chalet was roughly built.' On their way back down, the group found 'the woman milking the cows in a shed & had some new milk & rested again ... the view at every point fine & that over the valley ... & the opposite side stretched out ... with its fine slopes pastures waterfall & woods very beautiful.' Others, people such as the Oxford don Chaloner Chute, his sisters and a companion, packed their rucksacks and set off for extended walking tours. While the ladies travelled on mules, Chute and his friend walked up to twenty-five miles a day. At night Chute recorded each day's activities: on 10 September 'Prothero & I ascended the Wildgirt ... with a view over the lake of Neuchatel & even of Zurich. Marvellously beautiful. I saw various avalanches; had two delicious baths in the solitude of a mountain stream.' 'It was a scramble to the top – but we were repaid ... Next day walked to Grindelwald.'[31]

The British quickly developed something of an ambivalent relationship with Switzerland and its people. When Lord Fortescue set out in 1815 he noted the 'wonderful panorama of mountains &

AUGUST. —— "Sic Omnes."

In George Cruickshank's *Comic Almanack for 1838* he portrays, with some exaggeration, the horrors of a Channel crossing. The new steam packets improved matters but did little to prevent sea-sickness and they introduced new horrors: smoke and vibrating engines.

Galignani's *Messenger* provided British news and information for Britons on the Continent. It also carried advertisements for both steam packets and public coaches as this issue of December 1828 shows.

FOUR ROUTES TO PARIS.

CALAIS.

BOULOGNE.

HAVRE.

These illustrations, published in *The Illustrated London News* of 16 August 1856, show the four principle French ports. From the top: Calais, Boulogne, Le Havre and Dieppe. Calais was the most popular for travellers while Boulogne became famous for day-trippers.

The *Invicta*, launched in 1882, was the first steel ship to cross the Channel. At twenty-two knots she crossed from Dover to Calais in one hour and thirteen minutes.

As this illustration from *The Illustrated London News* of 23 August 1884 shows, bunks were not that luxurious. The man on top is obviously going on a walking tour while the dog seems most comfortable of all three. There were no restrictions on taking dogs to the Continent.

Punch's Almanack for 1890 looks back to the *diligences* or European coaches that dominated public transport before trains and forward to a railway bridge that would have spanned the Channel by 1940. While there was talk of a cross-Channel bridge, the idea was less favoured than proposals for a tunnel.

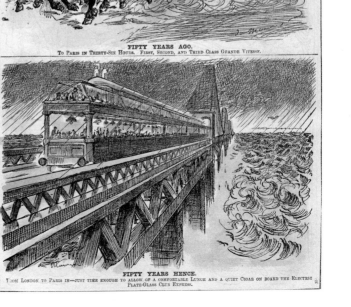

FIFTY YEARS AGO.
To Paris in Thirty-Six Hours, First, Second, and Third Class Grande Vitesse.

FIFTY YEARS HENCE.
From London to Paris in—Just Time Enough to Allow of a Comfortable Lunch and a Quiet Cigar on Board the Electric Plate-Glass Club Express.

7719

We, Henry Charles Keith Petty Fitz-Maurice Marquess of Lansdowne, Earl Wycombe, Viscount Caln and Calnstone and Lord Wycombe, Baron of Chipping Wycombe, Baron Nairne, Earl of Kerry and Earl of Shelburne, Viscount Clanmaurice and Fitzmaurice, Baron of Kerry, Lixnaw and Dunkerron, a Peer of the United Kingdom of Great Britain and Ireland, a Member of His Britannic Majesty's Most Honourable Privy Council, Knight of the Most Noble Order of the Garter &c. &c. &c. His Majesty's Principal Secretary of State for Foreign Affairs.

Request and require in the Name of His Majesty, all those whom it may concern to allow

Mr John Charles Cottam (a British subject)

travelling on the Continent ———

to pass freely without let or hindrance, and to afford him every assistance and protection of which he may stand in need.

Given at the Foreign Office, London, the 29 day of September 1904

Lansdowne

Signature of the Bearer:

John C Cottam

UK Passport. The passport, a large sheet of paper with the Royal Arms and the arms of the Foreign Secretary (here the Conservative peer, Lord Lansdowne), changed little from 1814 to 1914 save that in 1858 French was dropped for English. Travellers hated the bureaucracy surrounding passports that prevailed in most European countries but not in the UK.

In this drawing from *The Illustrated London News* of 16 September 1871 a French official examines an arriving passenger's passport. France had earlier abolished the need to produce passports but reimposed it during the Franco-Prussian War and subsequent unrest. This would have been the first of many inspections.

This drawing, from *The Illustrated London News* of 26 September 1885 portrays an imaginary scene but one which occurred all too frequently in fact. The three Britons, on a walking tour somewhere in Germany or Austria, endure a passport inspection from the local *polizei*, anxious to exert authority and ignorant of the relaxed rules governing passports by the 1880s.

This advert, from *The Queen, The Lady's Newspaper* of 26 September 1891, shows how Victorian manufacturers kept up with the growth in travel and the demand for comfort. In addition to advertisements for trunks and 'dressing bags' there are two versions of a device for making tea while on a train. The device could also be used in hotel rooms.

DREW & SONS

DREWS' PATENT EN ROUTE 5 o'clock TEA BASKET

A HANDSOME AND REALLY USEFUL WEDDING PRESENT!

DREWS' PATENT 'WOOD FIBRE' TRUNK, The Lightest and Strongest Trunk Made.

Prices from 45/-

DRESSING BAGS FOR WEDDING PRESENTS.

DREWS' BASKET TRUNKS.

DREW & SONS' DEPOTS: CITY, 156, LEADENHALL ST., E.C.; WEST END, 33, PICCADILLY CIRCUS, W.

BIRD'S CUSTARD POWDER

Supplies a Daily Luxury—Dainties in Endless Variety. The Choicest Dishes and the Richest Custard.

NO EGGS REQUIRED.

The appetite for continental travel was increased by illustrated publications such as the Anglican *Saturday Magazine*. As it only cost one penny it was affordable for some of the better-off working-classes. The weekly supplement was devoted to some foreign location and usually featured several drawings. Few of the first readers of this issue could have afforded travel but with increasing prosperity and cheaper travel some would have eventually have been able to visit places about which they had only read.

The Vienna Universal Exhibition of 1873 as seen in *The Illustrated London News* of 10 May 1873. International Exhibitions were a great inducement to travel. The Birchalls, a Gloucestershire couple, found this Exhibition a highlight of their wedding tour and were 'more and more charmed with Vienna.'

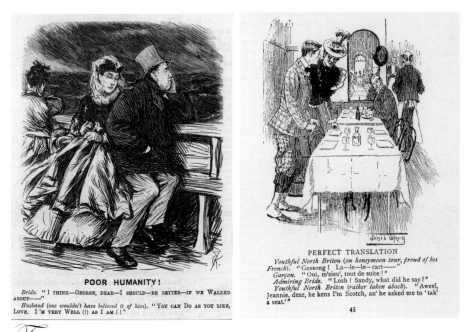

POOR HUMANITY!

Bride. "I THINK—GEORGE, DEAR—I SHOULD—BE BETTER—IF WE WALKED ABOUT——"
Husband (one wouldn't have believed it of him). "YOU CAN DO AS YOU LIKE, LOVE. I 'M VERY WELL (!) AS I AM !!"

PERFECT TRANSLATION

Youthful North Briton (on honeymoon tour, proud of his French). "Gassong! La—le—le—cart——"
Garçon. "Oui, m'sieu', tout de suite!"
Admiring Bride. "Losh! Sandy, what did he say?"
Youthful North Briton (rather taken aback). "Aweel, Jeannie, dear, he kens I'm Scotch, an' he asked me to 'tak' a seat.'"

45

These cartoons from (left) *Punch* of 9 April 1870 and (right) *Punch*'s collection, *On the Continong*, combine three of the favourite topics that travel gave Victorian humorists: seasickness, honeymooners and the difficulties people faced with foreign languages. The young man in the right-hand illustration is wearing the fashionable tourist's checked suit.

A Table d'Hôte at a Prague hotel in the 1850s. This is a good example of the mixed company travellers came across. They sat at a common table or tables which included local residents and officers. The two (presumably) English women on the right avoid looking at the hairy, 'vulgar' local man opposite them. Wine, unless one wanted some special bottle or champagne, was usually included in the cost. Small groups of musicians, as here, sometimes provided entertainment. Prague, not on the main tourist routes, rarely won praise for its hotels. Taken from Richard Doyle's *The Foreign Tour of Messrs Brown Jones and Robinson*, first published in 1854. (The term, 'Brown, Jones and Robinson' was the Victorian equivalent of our 'Tom, Dick and Harry').

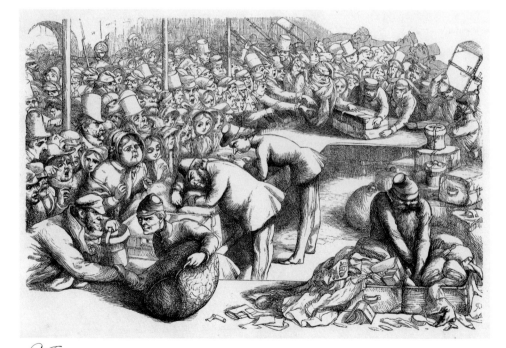

A search of rail passengers' luggage at Cologne, a popular place for Britons to begin their Rhine trips. Prussian customs officials examine bags while frustrated tourists point towards their trunks and hat boxes. A perplexed English woman in a bonnet looks annoyed while one customs man rummages through her bag. Next to her a man bribes an official to hand over his bag unexamined. The contents of a less fortunate Englishman's portmanteau and small dressing case, including his *Murray* guide book, are tumbled about the counter. From Doyle's *Brown Jones and Robinson*.

lakes ... the famed beauty of Swiss scenery', but he also noted the number of 'miserably poor & squalid' places he saw. The combination of natural beauty and widespread rural poverty was a part of this mixed view. Another was the behaviour of the Swiss. The following is a view expressed by many: 'Switzerland every succeeding day looks more beautiful and every day the natives appear less interesting, more brutish and more immoral.' Sometimes the hostility could be quite brutal. The first British Minister to the Swiss Confederation described the people of Berne in 1858 as 'the ugliest race I ever saw and a full century behind the rest of Europe'. Yet the wealth produced by a constantly increasing number of travellers made Switzerland the first tourist nation, that is, one whose prosperity was based on its visitors. It was numbers more than familiarity that bred contempt, and the Swiss began to dislike those on whom they lived. In the 1890s an American observer found that the Germans 'growl a good deal about the English, and declare that they have spoiled Switzerland. The natives, too, who live off the English, seem to thoroughly hate them.' Swiss landlords developed a reputation for overcharging and dishonesty. 'The abominable money-extracting nature of the Swiss' was another standard comment. Given the increasing number of visitors it was inevitable that there would be a race to find spots not overrun with tourists. A succession of guides and travel books did just this. One such, *A Summer Tour in the Grisons*, written by Jane Freshfield in 1862, lamented, like Wordsworth some forty years earlier, that 'nooks are almost overrun'. The only thing to do was to head for an unspoilt area, the Grison or Graubünden area and when there to go off for walks with a basket filled with an Etna stove, tea, arrowroot and Fortnum & Mason soup. Inevitably her popular book set off a new rush so that her 'secluded Alpine nook' was itself soon overrun with tourists. Earlier travellers would also have been horrified by the illumination of the falls at Giessbach in Switzerland's Oberland. Like the Rhine hoteliers Swiss inn-keepers were keen to add new attractions for their guests. At Giessbach they illuminated the waterfalls every weekday night from June to September. Guests were summoned by a cannon shot to watch the lights change from red to white and then to green.[32]

Another reason for Switzerland's popularity was the quality of the air, which meant that in the summer months it became a place for those with chest problems. Then, in the 1870s, medical fashion, having turned against the Riviera, decided that Switzerland was also good in the winter. As Robert Louis Stevenson wrote, there 'has come a change in medical opinion, and . . . in the lives of sick folk'. The invalid was told to abandon the 'dusty olive-yards' of the Riviera. In the Alps in winter 'a ruder air shall medicine him; the demon of cold is no longer to be fled from, but bearded in his den'. One village in particular, Davos, became the favourite of British consumptives. Located in a valley some 5,000 feet above sea level, it was transformed into a major tourist centre largely because of its appeal to invalids. This change was helped by the writings of John Addington Symonds, who first visited there in 1863, to help his consumption. In July 1878 Symonds wrote an article in the *Fortnightly Review*, a journal appealing to those very people who could afford to spend winters in the Alps. He admitted that it required 'courage to face the severity of winter in an Alpine valley', yet, despite the intense cold and frozen snow, invalids 'can drive in open sledges with impunity, expose themselves without risk . . . or sit upon their bedroom balconies, basking in a hot sun, with the world all white around them'. The secret was the 'pure mountain air and . . . the keen mountain sunlight'. The 'fever, restless nights, cough, blood-spitting, and expectoration' subsided as his strength returned. Although Symonds built a house in Davos, he knew he had not been cured; but he also felt that 'the disease had been arrested'.[33]

When Robert Louis Stevenson arrived, he found 'half English' sanatoriums with *tableaux-vivants*, balls, bazaars, libraries, chess, draughts, billiards, whist, a local English newspaper, *The St. Moritz Post and Davos News*, and tobogganing. (It was actually Symonds who organized the first international toboggan race at Davos in 1883, demonstrating that curious love of sport and organization that mark the British.) Stevenson recommended the village to yet another writer, Conan Doyle, whose wife was consumptive. The Doyles came in 1893, by which time there were more than 1,700 British visitors: there had been a mere seventy in 1869. The writer found it a 'most glorious place . . . The air too so exhilarating!' The ill were advised to give up all medicines, to eat as much as possible, and to exercise. If Symonds popularized tobogganing, Conan Doyle helped to popularize the new sport of 'ski-running' in the winter of 1894. Even if not cured the sick would still feel 'an enthusiasm of the blood unknown in more temperate climates. It may not be health, but it is fun.' Davos's great disadvantage lay in the growing numbers who went there: 'For this publicity there is no cure, and no alleviation.' In 1884, a tourist was told that 'out of a hundred people at least sixty get well again', but he still found the place 'sad and mournful'. By 1907 the village had grown to forty hotels and pensions and about 5,000 people to which an almost equal number of invalids were added in the high season (December and January).[34]

The unending success story that was Swiss tourism shows the dilemma that increasing travel produced, a dilemma which only magnified the dislike of fellow travellers. Tourists came not just to see the scenery but to see it in splendid isolation. When they found the mountains they were covered with the British. In 1870 the Anglophobe Tchaikovsky was thrilled with the beauties of Interlaken but moaned that 'wherever you turn you come face to face with a son of Albion'. What he did not realize is that most of the British shared his dislike of their fellow Britons. By the end of the century writers were complaining that in Interlaken 'you are beset by troops of trippers . . . with the stolid self-suppression of the mountain cattle'. The British seemed to regard Switzerland 'as a kind of private park or preserve'. By 1902 newspapers were noting that 'complaints are constant that Switzerland is overcrowded and dearer every year' and, even worse, the Swiss 'have organized their country so completely upon a tourist basis that one is in a danger of forgetting that it is a real country at all'. Ten years later things had not improved: Switzerland now had 12,640 hotels with 384,744 beds and 168,625 British visitors. The country could not stop being successful, and just as it had benefited from the railways, mountaineering and health resorts (to be discussed below), so it now benefited from the new phenomenon, 'winter sports'. Sir Henry Lunn took up where Symonds and Conan Doyle left off. Lunn was not just a tour operator but a keen organizer of sporting activities which included tobogganing, skiing and bobsleighing. By 1909 his Alpine sports company was booking sixteen hotels for the whole of the winter for sporting holidays in the snow. Three years later some 18,000 British tourists were coming for curling, skiing, skating and tobogganing, and the number was steadily increasing.[35]

Part of the criticism levied against Switzerland was in fact criticism of mass travel. One consequence of offering the same thing over and over again to the same sort of tourist was that the guide heard the same reactions. The end result is boredom or, worse, cynicism. Occasionally a perceptive traveller saw this. When Lord Fortescue went on his walking tour he admitted that his pleasure had been undermined:[36]

> The great drawback to my enjoyment was its being all so completely matter of exhibition, every cascade & glacier . . . as perfectly known as any turnpike road. This hurts one's feelings some times strongly "en contrast avec la position" amidst these wild romantic beauties, & I have felt quite provoked more than once at the novelty of my own admiration when the same things shown by the same guides & accompanied by the same remarks must have produced exactly the same feelings in hundreds of travellers before.

Lord Fortescue wrote this not in 1914, after a century of tourism, but in 1815, only a year after travel to Europe resumed.

The love of the Alps, Lord Fortescue's 'wild romantic beauties', was largely a creation of the Romantic movement in literature and music. Although this vast range is found in France, Italy, Germany, Switzerland and Austria, the Victorians' attention centred on one mountain, Mont Blanc. As Thomas Guthrie wrote in 1872, 'When the rising sun first flashed on the highest summit of Mont Blanc . . . we were dumb with wonder and admiration . . . of the might and majesty of God.' When one climber looked back to his teenage years in the 1870s he remembered seeing 'Jungfrau, Mönch, Eiger and the rest' for the first time. It was 'a new revelation, unimaginable, indescribable . . . and from that moment I also entered life'. Even if Conway found the Alps 'undescribable' he went on, like many Victorians, to use quantities of ink in making the effort. Mountaineering books became one of the most popular of travel books and mountaineers, at least to the middle class, were 'heroes of the heights . . . with flayed face and slightly frost-bitten fingers'.[37]

The interest in Mont Blanc, at just over 15,620 feet the highest mountain in the Alps, became almost an obsession. In 1819 an Oxford don 'before leaving England, set my heart upon ascending Mont Blanc'. In the event he had to turn back after an avalanche killed three of his party's twelve guides. The fact that the highest mountain had been climbed in 1786 by a Frenchman made it all the more necessary that British climbers succeed in climbing every possible mountain. In 1854 Mr Justice Wills, later notorious for presiding over Oscar Wilde's criminal trial, climbed the Wetterhorn from the Grindelwald side. However, the real mountaineering 'hero' was the writer and traveller Albert Smith, after he climbed Mont Blanc in 1851. He then became a lecturer–showman and did more than any man to popularize mountaineering by describing his own daring feats. Ironically, his main impact was on tourism to Switzerland, despite the fact that Mont Blanc is on the Franco-Italian border. He did this first in the 'The Ascent of Mt. Blanc', the extraordinary show he put on between 1852 and 1858. During the performances he used all sorts of illustrations – views of the Rhine or the vast glacier known as the Mer de Glace. As St Bernard dogs wandered down the aisles, Smith played a tin fiddle and sang patter songs poking gentle fun at tourists, many of whom he had inspired to see the Alps.[38] In 1853 Smith enhanced his takings with his book *The Ascent of Mont Blanc.*

The public felt that Mt. Blanc 'belongs . . . to him who has popularized it among us'. Almost a million people saw his show, which he performed in a Piccadilly theatre for over six years, and many, such as Queen Victoria, saw it several times. Smith kept his songs up to date and varied the routes by which he 'took' the audience to Mont Blanc; he even included Mt Vesuvius, Capri and the Bay of Naples! Probably no single person did as much to introduce the idea of continental travel to a popular audience and to show that it could be exciting and, quite frankly, fun. Smith was considered vulgar by many, which he was, but he appealed to the the overwhelming self-confidence of the age: the economy was strong; the empire was growing; the navy guaranteed peace. Mountains were now another challenge to be met and defeated. There was one drawback: Albert Smith and the railways had so increased tourism to Switzerland that hotel prices went up by one-third in the ten years after his show started.[39]

A more serious tone crept into the growing obsession with mountains after the Alpine Club was formed in 1857. Most of its members were professional men – lawyers, doctors, Oxbridge dons, civil servants and judges. Albert Smith was a founding member, and important figures in the scientific and literary worlds were enthusiasts, men such as Leslie Stephen. The son-in-law of Thackeray and father of Virginia Woolf, Stephen admitted that his best known mountaineering book 'is offered chiefly to those fellow-lunatics . . . who love the Alps too well'.[40] A large proportion of these men were liberal or radical in politics and seemed to have found in mountain-climbing a form of spiritual experience to supplement or even to supplant Christianity. Illustrations helped: Edward Whymper, for example, was a talented engraver who like his father was involved with illustrating travel books but his real fame came from being the first to climb the Matterhorn in 1865.

His *Scrambles Amongst the Alps* (1871) was probably the most popular of all mountaineering books.

However much men dominated mountaineering, lady climbers were always part of the scene, both on the mountains themselves and in published accounts of their adventures, as evidenced in Jane Freshfield's book. In the event, books and articles, particularly those in the Alpine Club's journal, spread the lure of the Alps as a place to see and to conquer. Albert Smith, who had made fun of these fashionable but serious enthusiasts, added a new and accurate verse to one of his patter songs, 'The Young English Traveller', in 1856:[41]

> He next proceeds to Chamouni [sic], and up Mont Blanc he
>   climbs,
> And coming back, of course, he writes a letter to The Times.
> In fact, he climbs up anything, without an aim or view
> Because he has a notion it's the sort of thing to do.

Once again, tourism took its toll. Swiss plant life suffered as the British pursued one of their favourite activities, 'botanizing'. The plants they dug up were taken home for the 'rock gardens' which were laid out according to William Robinson's *Alpine Flowers for English Gardens*, first published in the 1850s and in print until 1910. The mountains themselves suffered: by 1912 a railway had been built up the Jungfrau which allowed the peaks and glaciers to be seen by those who preferred to do so from heated railway cars. Mountain climbing by the few had yielded to mountain sight-seeing by the many.

'Italy is the schoolroom of the world' was one guide-book's description, and it fairly well sums up what might be called the British love affair with that country. In architecture, literature and music Italy had long been an inspiration to wealthy British travellers, antiquarians, architects and artists. Likewise the love of, or at least the interest in, the Classics sent travellers to Rome and books on Italy poured forth: between 1818 and 1825 there were 540 books and guides on the country published in Britain. But after 1814 there was also a new and powerful attraction, Italian nationalism. The vision of uniting the peninsula's various kingdoms into one new liberal nation and of ousting the 'reactionary' Habsburgs in Tuscany, Venetia and Lombardy, the Bourbons in the Two Sicilies and the Pope in the Papal States was irresistible to Victorians.[42]

Byron worked himself into one of his passions in *Childe Harold* in 1818 and wrote in the Fourth Canto:

> *Yet, Italy! through every other land*
> *Thy wrongs should ring, and shall, from side to side;*
>
> . . . . .
>
> *Europe, repentant of her parricide,*
> *Shall yet redeem thee, and, all backward driven,*
> *Roll the barbarian tide, and sue to be forgiven.*

Italian radicals such as Mazzini and his disciple, Garibaldi, remembered the French-imposed republics of the 1790s and longed for a republic to include the whole of Italy. In Turin the King of Sardinia saw himself as the unifying force and, starting in 1858, began a campaign in an uneasy alliance with Napoleon III. Within thirteen years Sardinia had absorbed, through plebiscite or military victories, the states of Tuscany, Lombardy, Venetia, Modena, Parma, the Kingdom of the Two Sicilies and the Papal States in order to create the new Kingdom of Italy. For tourists this meant that trips to Italy between the 1840s and 1871 were to a country in the making. The movement, which its supporters christened *il Risorgimento*, or resurgence, was not just to unify but to create a new, 'modern' Italy in which nationalism would be the cement that would bind together the different countries. There was a strong anti-clerical element because of the Church's opposition and the Pope's position as a temporal sovereign. Some supporters liked to quote the eighteenth-century saying 'Let us strangle the last king with the guts of the last priest.'

For the British middle class, which always enjoys sorting out the complex politics of other nations, the Risorgimento had a quasi-religious importance, especially when combined with traditional British anti-Catholicism, while Garibaldi was credited with those mythical qualities frequently associated with foreign revolutionaries. British visitors had no doubt: the development of British-style constitutional government in Sardinia was an 'advance in the *moral* liberty and civilization of the people'. It would soon spread to all Italy. Those with greater knowledge realized that the movement 'was the work of a few great protagonists . . . and . . . comparatively few actors who play to a small actively interested audience'. But for those in that audience, intellectuals such as George Eliot, the 'new' Italy was a 'Resuscitated Italy' and the history of the Risorgimento was the history of a 'widening life'. The Horner family, from Edinburgh's intellectual classes, went on extended trips to Italy in 1848 and in 1861, when they naturally had their carriage stop at the place where Garibaldi had set forth with his 'thousand men' to 'liberate' Sicily the year before. This was perhaps the most theatrical act in the unification melodrama – and the stone on which he had stood had been marked with a star. Joanna Horner was so 'eager to taste the waters of the Mediterranean on this spot' that she climbed onto the rock. According to her sister, Susan, the silly woman 'slipped . . . and came sitting down; but Zileri [the guide] assisted her to rise . . . as we returned we saw our coachman grinning at us from above, as he said, he thought the Signora wanted to take a bath in the Mediterranean'. Susan was wiser and simply dug up a plant to take back to England as a relic, along with some of Garibaldi's hair.[43] As middle class visitors the Horners naturally enjoyed supporting a middle class movement; the peasants were content to sit back and enjoy the show.

For most visitors, whatever their politics, the four places they most wished to see were Florence, Rome, Venice and Naples. As the capital of the Grand Duchy of Tuscany, Florence had been a favourite with the British in the days of the Grand Tour. For centuries it had been the 'focus of intellectual life' in Italy and had 'an amazing profusion of treasures of art, such as no other locality possesses within so narrow limits'. People started arriving soon after 1814 and by 1828 a flourishing British 'colony' had been established. It was large enough that the Commune provided land for a Protestant cemetery that would eventually hold the graves of Elizabeth Barrett Browning, Walter Savage Landor, Arthur Hugh Clough and Frances Trollope. The British were described by the American poet William Cullen Bryant in 1834: 'As the day advances, the English, in white hats and white pantaloons, come out of their lodgings, accompanied sometimes by their hale and square-built spouses, and saunter stiffly along the Arno, to take their way to the public galleries and museums. Their massive, clean, and brightly-polished carriages also begin to rattle through the streets.'[44]

Travellers who were staying for any length of time could join the Gabinetto Scientifico-Litterario, better known as the Gabinetto Vieusseux from its founder's name. In addition to books in English, French and German, it received journals and in time provided a tea-room. Members could join for a day, a week, a month or a year and the fees were remarkably small: a lira a day in 1860. The library's membership books show a steady increase in British names from 1820 to 1914: in 1842, for example, of some 660 entries over half are British. Throughout many decades there were prominent writers including Ruskin, Thackeray, Kipling, Robert Browning and D. H. Lawrence. The library also had a reputation for progressive views and its privacy allowed Italian nationalists to meet liberal intellectuals from abroad and, before the end of the Grand Duchy, to exchange enlightened views.[45]

However, Florence's real appeal was always its works of art and its architecture, although we should remember that the Duomo did not get its west front until 1889 nor its bronze doors until 1903. When Elizabeth Barrett Browning came in 1847 she called it 'the most beautiful of the cities devised by man', a view shared by almost all British arrivals. In the next year, when Susan Horner arrived, her excitement was so great that she left out the subject of her sentence in her diary: 'Here [we] are in Florence!' She also recalled what happened as their carriage drove along the Lungarno. A flower-girl was standing before her shop door and 'as the carriage drove by, she threw two camellias tied up with geranium leaves to us. Charles told us . . . of this custom of the Florentine flower-girls to welcome strangers to their city.' 'Florence,' she noted the next day, 'does indeed exceed all my expectations.' When she returned in 1861 her enthusiasm had not abated: 'Florence is of itself so attaching – so soothing in its loveliness, and yet not the dead feeling of a country town in England – life everywhere, in the sun, in the river, in the hills with their thousand villas – in the living present – in the living past . . . There is much republican equality and brotherhood of feeling.' The British were also pleased that begging was outlawed.[46]

Florence's fame meant that Sardinia's Victor Emmanuel had set his eyes on the city as a new capital once he acquired the Grand Duchy in 1860. Three years later he and his bureaucrats arrived from Turin. Property prices soared, rents rose and the future, at least for those who had not been thrown out of their homes, seemed bright. His campaign against the Church meant that monasteries and convents were closed, including Santa Croce in 1866. Ironically, its west front had only been finished three years earlier thanks to the generosity of a British resident and supporter of the Grand Duke. The ancient city walls were pulled down and urban expansion took off, much to the disgust of those who loved the old, quiet Florence. Along with the rents, taxes rose sixfold, a rise described at the time as 'unfavourable'. Then in 1871 Victor Emmanuel moved to Rome. This exodus began a long depression which ended in the city's bankruptcy in 1884. After that the situation improved and tourism increased. The population, which had been about 60,000 in 1861, soared to 200,000 by 1910. So too did the number of British visitors and tourism, as is its wont, took its toll. Writers bemoaned the 'barbarian, exclamatory souls who in . . . cockney English snort . . . at the beauties industriously pointed out by a loud-voiced cicerone'. Florence 'has lost her soul for the sake of the stranger'. Yet, this same writer continued, 'for all her modern ways, her German beer-houses, her English tea-shops, her noisy trams on Lung' Arno, her air as of a museum, her eagerness to show her contempt for the stranger while she sells him her very soul for money, Florence remains one of the most delightful cities of Italy'.[47]

One of the most stirring experiences travellers to Italy could enjoy before the arrival of railways occurred when the driver of their carriage stopped on a hill near Rome from which one could make out the dome of St Peter's. He would then turn round, swing out one arm, point his whip and cry '*Ecco Roma!*' Most travellers were thrilled by the little drama: 'Roma. After a weary drive over the Campagna in a dull day, the cupola [dome] of St. Peters [*sic*] appeared in the far distance, which we hailed with great joy, and a couple of hours brought us to the gates of *Rome*.' Most, but not all. When the Duke of Buckingham's guide went through the 'Ecco!' performance in 1827 he obviously expected his passenger 'to be sentimental and cry, or to be extatic [*sic*] and dance'. The Duke did neither. To explain His Grace's lack of enthusiasm we must remember that in the early decades after Waterloo the joy of seeing St Peter's was somewhat diminished by the threat of robbery and, sometimes worse, from *banditti*. To combat this, the Pope's government cleared the roadside of trees, which had acted as cover, but this left blackened stumps to create a rather dismal scene. The desolation was enhanced by the proliferation of tall posts: having tried and executed the criminals on their portable guillotine, the government then hung the severed arms and legs from posts every two to three miles. While one early visitor admitted the practice 'does not tend to inspire pleasing ideas', it clearly worked and robberies began to decline. In the Duke's case he was aware that shots had been fired at carriages the night before. When the would-be robbers were arrested they turned out not to be 'real' *banditti* but merely amateurs from Apulia who had come not to rob Italians but only *'le Signore Inglese ... senza fare male'* – the English gentlemen . . . without harming anyone. The fate of these men's arms and legs is not recorded. Eventually this feature of travel gave way to kidnapping for ransom. As late as the 1880s it was reported that the Italians never asked for more than £1,000 for British tourists because of the 'plentiful supply . . . who annually visited south Italy'.[48]

Rome itself was filled with 'lions', the most popular of which were seeing the Vatican's museum by torchlight and wandering round the Coliseum with its heady recollections of debauchery and martyrdom. Many travellers took a serious approach to understanding Rome's history. For such people there were books such as Augustus Hare's two-volume *Walks in Rome*, which went into twenty-two editions. Rome's greatest appeal was her imperial past. Young James Estcourt wrote to his grandfather in 1831 that *'you would visit me within a month*, if my description could afford any adequate view of the delight of wandering among the . . . remains of antient [*sic*] Rome, of their grandeur and beauty, and of their great number. These only duly depicted would bring you here.' Such sights would make anyone forget that 'all officials in this country are corrupt, shabby, plundering rascals up to the very Cardinals'. Until 1870 Rome was ruled by the Pope and his government administered mainly by clerics. It was 'a city by itself . . . a strange blending of pomp and misery, of wealth and squalor' in which the grand coaches of cardinals, complete with footmen and umbrellas laid over the roofs, passed beggars and dogs which roamed the streets unchecked. (At night it was the cats' turn.) Stendhal, who arrived in February 1817, remembered that in the streets there was 'the smell of rotten cabbage; and through the beautiful windows of the palaces on the Corso, one sees the wretchedness inside'. When the actress Fanny Kemble arrived in the 1840s she was delighted: 'I was in Rome, and it was the very Rome of my imagination.' However 'the filth and stench of the streets give one an imaginary fever as one drives through them'. Despite its reputation for dirt and *mal aria** it attracted invalids, the most famous of which was, of course, John Keats. Indeed, from the outset of renewed travel the British flocked to Rome. In February 1818, two years before Keats arrived, one visitor wrote there were 2,000 British visitors there. By 1863 this number was said to be 10,000. Rome also remained a relatively small city – by 1871 the population was only 212,000 and it was an inexpensive place to visit.[49]

Although the papal government was always anxious to please British tourists, on whose spending it depended, it was almost universally denounced by British writers and guide-books: 'The government is ecclesiastic and despotic' said *Bradshaw's Hand-book to Italy*, and after 1850 the forces of Italian unification were only kept at bay by 12,000 French troops. Sometimes censors kept British papers out of the city and in the 1860s banned *The Times* for its support of Italian unification. For years grass grew in the streets, which were badly lit if lit at all. Rome lacked pavements and roofs, had no gutters or drainpipes, which meant that when it rained, pedestrians got soaked. When visitors came out of St Peter's 'the beggars literally swarm, a dozen hands were stuck through the door [of the carriage] for bajocchi [halfpennies]; the dirt and poverty is [*sic*] striking after Tuscany'. Along the city walls, every one to two hundred yards were 'small wooden pens painted red for foot people to escape into from the buffaloes', presumably the buffalo cows that grazed in the Campagna and were brought in for milking to make mozzarella cheese. The city also had its own currency and time because the day began with the Angelus at sunset. Although many of the famous ruins we know were still undiscovered there had been improvements. In 1829 one English visitor was impressed with the work undertaken since her visit in 1818; but hers was not a view widely held.[50]

---

* *Mal aria*, literally bad air, was produced in the Pontine Marshes south-east of Rome. By the 1820s the British were combining the two words to describe the disease spread by the mosquitoes that thrived in this atmosphere.

However, the 1860s also saw the beginning of civic improvements and Rome learned to accommodate herself to the English. From the 1830s hunters had been able to join *La Societá Romana della Caccia alla Volpe*, which was established after the banker, Torlonia, got Pope Gregory XVI to rescind his Bull against fox-hunting, issued after a rider had broken his neck. The city had an English church, English banks, a reading room, club, physicians and by the 1890s its famous Babington's Tea Rooms. When Caroline Edgcumbe arrived in 1864 she was delighted that 'there are most interesting excavations going on' inside the city and in the district round about. Pius IX 'is very busy, doing a great deal in the way of restoring & embellishing Churches', and during these improvements workmen frequently uncovered the original churches underneath. A defence of papal government was published in 1860 by an Irish MP which showed that much material progress had been made in education, hospitals, roads and railways. That token of progress, gas lighting, had been introduced in 1854 by British engineers. By 1860 both the Quirinal (the Pope's palace) and the Vatican were lit with gas, as were many streets. But the image of backwardness had been created, and it was one the British did not want to give up.[51]

Under papal rule one of the city's greatest attractions was the grand ceremonies of Holy Week and Easter, around which many people planned their entire continental journey. So popular were they that papal officials reserved special areas for British tourists, and as early as 1839 an English Catholic priest in Rome published a special guide, *The Ceremonies of the Holy-Week at Rome*. In 1858, when Thomas Best and his wife arrived at the Sistine Chapel to hear Allegri's *Miserere* they found a queue of some 2,000 but luckily their courier had booked their seats. The next day, Maundy Thursday, they could not get in for the Washing of the Feet or the Mass of the Last Supper but were able to join the crowd watching the Pope eat with the men whose feet he had just washed. 'The rush & the crush was [*sic*] awful & we had quite to *fight* our way in, many of the ladies lost their veils, pins for the hair, & had their dresses torn ... one [man had] the front of his shirt all torn open, collar & all.'

On Good Friday the Bests went to the English Church and then on Easter Sunday they left their hotel at 6.45 a.m. for the High Mass at St Peter's. At the elevation of the Host 'silver trumpets which are placed in the lower gallery of the dome sound forth, the effect of which can never be forgotten'. When, afterwards, the pope gave his blessing to the kneeling, bare-headed crowd below, 'the guns of the Castle of St Angelo thunder forth, the military bands strike up, all the bells of St Peters [*sic*] are set ringing ... a sight one never can forget'. After a comparatively tame Eucharist in the English Church the couple returned to St Peter's at 7 p.m. to sit in special stands to watch the illuminations. Seeing the dome illuminated by hundreds of candles lit by 400 men swinging on ropes was stupendous. Altogether there were 6,000 candles placed on 'every column, cornice & frieze ... all the details of the building even to the cross are lighted up & the gigantic mass of building stands out against the dark sky in a complete blaze of light ... It is worth coming all the way from England to see this sight alone.' The next evening there were the famous fireworks or *Girandola* on the Pincian Hill, 'the finest display of fireworks in the world' during which two military bands played and the display ended with 5,000 rockets set off 'in one discharge'. The Bests were a devout couple who came to worship as much as to watch, but this was often not the case and many 'foreigners of influence came as to a show'.[52] If it was a show it was one that was set to close.

The old Rome disappeared on 20 September 1870 when Victor Emmanuel's men finally took the city after Napoleon III withdrew his army. Troops seized Pius IX's palace for the king's new home, and the Papacy retreated into what we now call 'the Vatican'. A new spirit was abroad. Monasteries were closed and Eucharistic processions with bells tinkling and priests walking under white umbrellas as 'every body, right & left, held alighted candles' were consigned to history. On Easter Sunday in 1872 visitors to St Peter's found that 'the service was disappointing as the Pope would not allow anything special'. We have some insight into this new world through the letters of Anne and Matilde Lucas, two Quaker sisters who lived in Rome from 1871 to 1900 and delighted in entertaining *monsignori*. The city they described was a divided one, as seen when Pius IX and Victor Emmanuel died within weeks of one another in 1878. Two of their friends who were fanatical Roman Catholic converts were in deepest mourning, relieved only by the papal colours. 'Their bonnets were tied under their chins, with a yellow key in each bow and a tiara in the middle.' They met another English woman, Mrs Bowen, who supported the 'new Italy'. 'They shouted after Mrs. Bowen that there could be no compromise between the Pope and King, and that theirs was the way to Heaven. Mrs. Bowen shouted back that she was for the King and hoped to meet them there [in heaven].'[53]

The changes that began in 1871 transformed Rome into the city we know today. The city of 'sentimental reminiscences' was swept away in a massive building campaign. The ancient city walls were pulled down. Drains were improved so that tourists no longer feared staying in the city during hot weather. The bureaucrats now flocked to Rome from Florence and extensive gardens were broken up for new houses. Streets were cleaned and widened. The trees, flowers and shrubs growing in the walls of the Coliseum were cleared away and the earth round its sides was removed. 'The building that is going on everywhere is quite dreadful. Ever since I left, all sorts of high edifices have sprung up – Rome is getting quite spoilt, as far as the picturesque goes . . . and there is quite a new town on the other side of the Tiber where Cinsinatus [*sic*] ploughed his fields.' Whole areas of Renaissance structures were pulled down on the Capitoline Hill to make room for a most spectacular new structure designed to embody the new Italy. This was the monument to Victor Emmanuel II, the Risorgimento and the new kingdom and it would only be finished in 1911. At 440 feet across and 230 feet high the glaring marble structure was wider than St Peter's and almost as tall. *Il Vittoriano* was, and is, loved and hated in equal measure – Henry James, Augustus Hare and the

art critic Julia Cartwright 'sighed over the ruin wrought there and
. . . the horrid Victor Emmanuel monument' – but it asserted that
there was now a new Rome in a new country.[54]

With its unrivalled architectural and artistic heritage, Venice should
have been more popular than it was. Ruskin's greatest work was,
arguably, devoted to the city and the opening lines of *The Stones of
Venice* pointed to the city's particular relevance to the British: 'Since
first the dominion of men was asserted over the ocean, three
thrones, of mark beyond all others, have been set upon its sands:
the thrones of Tyre, Venice, and England. Of the First of these
great powers only the memory remains; of the Second, the ruin;
the Third, which inherits their greatness, if it forget their example,
may be led through prouder eminence to less pitied destruction.'
To Ruskin, Venice was 'in the final period of her decline: a ghost
upon the sands of the sea'. Some joked that the British preference
for Florence was because Ruskin's *Mornings in Florence* was a one-
volume work whilst his *Stones of Venice* was in three. More likely it
was because the pattern of travel, created before railways, was to
cross the Alps and proceed on to Milan, Genoa, Pisa and then
Rome. To visit Venice meant a diversion to the East.[55]

From 1815 Venice was part of the Austrian Empire and the
presence of a garrison was increasingly disliked by many Venetians.
It was a city of 'stagnant waters and stifling back slums' in which
'Austrians and Italians kept jealously apart'. In 1848 rebels tried
to re-establish the Republic but were defeated by the Austrians after
a fifteen-month siege and bombardment. In the aftermath of this,
the relatively few visitors often agreed with Ruskin's view and
commented on the 'death-like stillness of all around'. After 1849,
however, Austria did embark on various public works and trade
increased so that by 1879 Venice was declared 'one of the greatest
seaports on the Adriatic'. Even before the rebellion the Austrians
had built a railway bridge from Venice to Marghera, the first link
to the mainland in the city's history. Needless to say many hated it
and were glad to arrive at night because 'the darkness hid a few of

the horrors of arriving at this most beautiful city at a nasty dirty railway station'. It was a 'great and terrible sacrifice of beauty to speed'. If railways were bad, the sewers were worse. While complaints about smells in Italian cities were universal they reached a crescendo when it came to Venice. One visitor wrote that there was 'no small advantage from carrying with me, as I usually do, a good supply of eau de Cologne; but at Venice I should recommend otto [attar] of roses, – eau de Cologne not being strong enough'.[56]

Venice's absorption into the expanding Italian kingdom in 1866 did not lead to a vast upsurge in British visitors: the attractions of Florence were too strong, but those who did come were mainly pleased. Chaloner Chute was delighted with his five-day visit in 1873. On Sunday, he heard the band play in the Piazza and saw the moon over the Laguna. He toured the Doge's Palace and 'then went up the Campanile & enjoyed the sunny view of Venice surrounded by water, the Cathedral St Mark's under our feet, the Laguna on the other side, churches & towers all about, & high tide looking cheerful & bright'. He hired a gondola, bought some bread and wine and saw the sights. He complained that 'Ruskin had given me no idea of the beauty of Murano & Torcello & the "drive" there in gondolas was lovely.' He tried to 'bargain for some old lace, & not succeeding, went on to the Ducal palace to look at some old friends [paintings]'.[57]

The new political regime made some improvements and tried to encourage the major industry, tourism. The Lido, which the Austrians started developing in 1833, became the home of grand hotels for the wealthy. 'Little steamers, overcrowded as penny boats on the Thames, were plying at short intervals from the Riva dei Schiavoni; tables were at a premium in the verandahs of the cafes and *osterias*, minstrels, puppet shows . . . the scene was a Venetian version of Ramsgate sands in the season.' Venice couldn't win: if she did nothing she was said to be 'stagnating'. If she encouraged tourism she was accused of converting Ruskin's 'ghost upon the sands of the sea' into Ramsgate. The new hotels helped the economy and earned a place in German literature when one of the guests in the Grand Hotel de Bains, Thomas Mann, used the location for his 1912 book, *Death in Venice*. Likewise there were improvements to St Mark's – there was a new floor and repairs to the front and, when the famous Campanile collapsed on 14 July 1902, it was carefully rebuilt and re-opened in March 1912. Yet a quarter of the declining population was still listed as paupers in 1889. Whatever improvements the Austrians and then a united Italy could make, the future of Venice lay with tourism, as Henry James saw in 1881: Venice was 'a vast museum'. 'You are reminded . . . that Venice scarcely exists any more as a city . . . it exists only as a battered peep-show and bazaar.'[58] Tourism was its life-support system.

Naples had been the goal of the Grand Tour, and amid its warmth and splendid scenery, the *milordi* had lingered through the winter months exploring antiquities and sampling fleshier pleasures. In the first half of the nineteenth century this tradition carried on, albeit with diminishing fervour. Most people accepted that Naples, facing its much lauded bay, had an exquisite setting, perhaps 'the most beautiful site in Europe'. In the 1830s Lady Blessington and her husband were so pleased that they spent almost three years there. To her it was a picture of Romantic beauty:[59] 'Here, all are gay and animated; from . . . the coroneted carriage down to the lazzaroni, who in the enjoyment of the actual present, are reckless of the future . . . iced water-melons were sold in slices . . . the sounds of guitars were heard mingling with the joyous laughs of the lazzaroni . . . above this scene of life and gaiety . . . was spread a sky of deep azure studded with stars.'

There was something exotic and almost overwhelming about Naples. While most British visitors heartily disliked the conservative Bourbon government, they were fascinated with the hoards of *lazzaroni*, the virtually homeless people who lived in or sometimes under the streets. Visitors found them 'very amusing. This morning four of them stripped stark naked under my window, put off in a boat and fished . . . by diving like ducks, throwing their feet up in the air ... they don't care who sees them, and their forms are perfect.' In addition there were the *facchini* or ne'er-do-wells who were 'infested with vermin'. They either sprawled in the streets while they picked lice out of each other's hair or swarmed over carriages and besieged tourists.[60]

In 1859 Thomas Best and his new wife arrived in the city:

Here we are in beautiful Naples bright sun, blue sky, & still blue sea with old Vesuvius smoking & spitting in the back ground. All Naples seems to live out of doors, rattling about here & there in every sort of vehicle, horses decked out with smart trappings, & a quantity of brass & silver ornaments. 12 or 15 in a gig sometimes, some 3 or 4 being stowed away in a sort of net under the axle, half-suffocated with mud & dust ... bagpipes, punchin-ollo, buffo singer with guitars, ragged lazzaroni lying asleep in every direction. Flower girls, & ... innumerable swarms of beggars, all help to contribute to the gay & busy scene.

Yet again, when an Aylesbury solicitor visited with his sketch pad in 1885 he found Naples a wonderful city to draw, 'a smokeless city' and 'hardly any chimneys ... Beggars, idlers and scamps generally all equally cheerful ... Being spotted as an Englishman [I] have [the] *London Standard* thrust at me constantly.' While the cheapest wine cost only a penny for a half-pint, 'drunkenness [was] apparently unknown'. Although the hotels could be quite expensive (even more so if Vesuvius were acting up), many other prices were quite cheap, especially if a traveller rented a villa or rooms and was prepared to haggle. A favourite sight was the reputed tomb of Virgil, which produced some odd behaviour by visitors. In the 1820s 'some foolish Englishwoman' left her own tribute to the author of the *Aeneid* by burying her beloved dog near the tomb. Others were content with just stripping the leaves from a bay tree growing nearby.[61]

There was no other city in Europe that was such a complete contrast to Victorian Britain and no other that aroused so much affection or hatred. To a Scottish visitor who was there at about the same time as the Blessingtons, 'Naples was a piece of paradise fallen upon earth and inhabited by devils'. Edward Lear's description was: 'all noise, horror – dirt, heat – & abomination & I hate it'. Equal with the climate were, again, the lazzaroni and facchini, which gave the city its reputation for noise, begging and pickpockets. 'Naples is one of the noisiest cities in Europe . . . [with] the ceaseless importunities of drivers, guides, street-vendors, beggars etc', and ladies were warned, 'the constant use of cabs [is] the only sure method of escaping annoyance'. Visitors were appalled when surrounded by gangs of 'deformed beggars waiting outside' tourist sights, and it was hard work trying to get about the large city while constantly being solicited for small coins. Guide-books warned that Neapolitan pickpockets were 'the most expert in Europe' and men's silk handkerchiefs were favourite targets. Visitors had to be careful even in church. Bishop Hynes wrote that in 1843 a friend 'returned yesterday from Naples. Lost his gold watch . . . taken . . . by some clever thief whilst witnessing the liquefaction of the blood of S. Januarius. His companions, each, lost something – handkerchiefs, hats, umbrellas, coats etc., etc.' There were also frequent references to immorality, that is prostitution, but Bishop Hynes, on a second visit, wrote that 'in all my rambles I have not encountered a single case of that flaunting, unblushing exhibition of female indecency which shocks the sight in every city . . . of England'.[62]

Until 1860 Naples had the attraction of a court with a Bourbon king who ruled over southern Italy and Sicily. British visitors were always anxious to be presented but could not do so in Lent when the king was in the countryside 'hunting boars rather than receiving them'. In 1860 things changed when Garibaldi seized Naples and the Bourbons fled the city. He delighted some British travellers by giving land for an English church while other visitors praised him for making Pompeii's pornographic artefacts in the museum more available, at least to men. But once Naples was no longer a capital, the city was less attractive for lengthy stays. Travellers still came but visits were shorter, especially with growing concern about sanitation; but in 1897 the British Consul reported that it was the healthiest large city in Italy thanks to the improved drains. Because 'educated Italians are fully alive to the evils which beset the traveller in and around Naples', a prominent nobleman started the *Società Pro Napoli* in 1891. Its badge-wearing officials were stationed about the city to help tourists and it tried to curb the tricks played on travellers by hoteliers, cab drivers, shop keepers and guides. By 1913 Naples was advertising itself in British newspapers as a modern commercial city that was also the 'Home of the Picturesque'. The inflated prose urged people to arrive by ship so that they 'might fairly believe themselves to be at the gate of Paradise'.[63]

In Murray's *Handbook*, what gave Naples 'an interest beyond any other city in Europe' was the proximity of Pompeii and, to a lesser degree, Herculaneum. Popular fascination with Pompeii greatly increased after 1834 when Edward Bulwer-Lytton published *The Last Days of Pompeii*. This novel had a phenomenal success and was the bestselling book in the 1830s after Sir Walter Scott's *Waverley*. By 1838 the number of people visiting annually had increased to 7,000, even though that same year saw the last excavation until the 1870s. The interest in Pompeii was kept alive by plays and paintings by Poynter, Leighton and Alma-Tadema as well as by the sermons of the famous Baptist preacher C. H. Spurgeon, who saw the city's destruction as a powerful example to the decadent. Visitor numbers were helped by the fact that Italy's first railway ran from Naples to Portici, near Herculaneum.[64] Although only a third of Pompeii had been discovered, visitors like Dickens's Mr Meagles in *Little Dorrit* still arrived and left with 'morsels of tessellated pavement from Herculaneum and Pompeii, like petrified minced veal' (Book I. xvi). It is surprising that anything was left.

Years before *The Last Days of Pompeii* appeared, classicists such as Henry Matthews visited the ruins and went on to the Museo Borbonico (later the National Museum) to see the 'Secret Cabinet'.

Matthews tells his readers that these rooms had items 'which will scarcely bear a detailed description', after which he provides a long footnote describing the various phallic items on display. In Pompeii itself, offensive murals were encased within shuttered boxes which could be opened on request, and it was said that some murals had been plastered over after excavation. When Robert Louis Stevenson's family went in 1863 their servant left a moving account of her visit. She had read of Pompeii but had never thought she would be there herself: 'I shall never forget my visit to the ruins . . . and shall look upon it as one of the most interesting days of my life.' Like many of us, when she left she 'turned again to take a last look of it. What a melancholy ruin it appeared . . . lying before the eye like a map, studded with broken marble pillars and statues.' When the Aylesbury solicitor Walter Hazell visited Pompeii in 1885 he was fascinated by the graffiti left 'by vulgar Pompeiian boys' and by evidence that the bread eaten in AD 79 was of the 'same size and appearance of loaves' in 1885.[65] Seeing Herculaneum was more difficult because for much of the century large sections were still under lava; tourists were given candles with which to follow the guides down the tunnel-like streets.

To visit Vesuvius was a far more challenging matter and the risks visitors took before 1880 were remarkable: there were, after all, nine eruptions between 1814 and 1914. When the 'invalid' Henry Matthews came in 1819 he was too weak to make the climb and was carried up in an armchair by eight 'stout fellows'; it was 'not the pleasantest ride in the world'. The porters enjoyed it, though, because they were well paid and because he was much lighter than the Princess of Wales, who had required forty porters. To Matthews the volcano was 'more like hell, than anything that human imagination could suggest'. When the Bests arrived there in 1859 they followed the usual procedure. They hired guides who led them up the volcano's side to have a picnic a few feet away from the new lava poured out the year before. The men made trails for them by putting sand over the lava, some of it red hot. One had to keep moving because of the ground's heat and sometimes guides would fry eggs on the lava. 'The guides had quite to drag one across, as fast as ever they could. I was very thankful, when we got safe across again.' They ended their tour at night when the scene was lit up by the light of cascading red lava. 'The spectators all standing about. The guides calling to one another & rushing about with their torches – altogether it was one of those scenes, which could never be described, & if seen, never forgotten.' Much of the adventure of these visits ended in 1880 when a funicular railway took people a distance up the side and they could now take tea with sweet pastries in a tea-room. To mark the event, the Italian journalist Peppino Turco wrote the song, '*Funiculì, Funiculà*', with music by Luigi Denza. Seven years later Thomas Cook & Son purchased the railway and established something of a monopoly over British travel to the volcano. Whether at Vesuvius or in Rome, Naples or Florence Italians had learned to take tourism in their stride. There had, after all, been many invaders before the British, but few had done as much good. In 1912 a leading Italian banker said that his country was making about £18 million a year from tourism, and this did not include money spent by the British 'colonies' in Florence, Pisa and Rome. Italy, he claimed, only survived economically due to tourism and the money sent back by emigrants.[66]

The Austrian Empire was the farthest east of any country that attracted significant numbers of British travellers. Austria was often praised by conservative writers such as Mrs Trollope, who spent some time there; but the 'politically correct' view of the time denounced it as a 'tyranny'. This view was not helped by the fact that Vienna governed large sections of Italy until 1866 or by the empire's Catholicism. A good indication of popular attitudes is seen in an article on Vienna published in an Anglican religious magazine intended for the working classes. The Gothic St Stephen's Cathedral was praised but the Baroque Karlskirke (St Charles's Church) was dismissed: 'our countrymen speak rather contemptuously of its gilded frippery as offensive to pure taste'. Vienna was also said to have the reputation for being an extremely dissolute city, which was rather ironic given the level of vice in London. In addition, Austria's bureaucratic passport rules were particularly resented and hostile stories about them appeared regularly. In one celebrated case in 1853 a merchant from Manchester (to Austrian officials a hotbed of radicalism) was stopped, struck and stripped by an Austrian officer.[67] After 1866, when Austria no longer had Italian possessions and passport restrictions eased, tourism increased and hostile comments diminished.

The principal attractions were the capital, Vienna, along with music, spas and mountains. The main problem for Vienna was that it was so far from Britain: even with friendlier feelings, it was still seventy-one hours from London in the 1850s. Those who did make the journey, however, were often delighted with what they found. In 1858 George Eliot was particularly enthusiastic about St Stephen's soaring spire, which she felt was worth going to Vienna to see. Once the city walls were taken down and the spectacular Ringstrasse was built, the city became monumental as well as spacious. As to music, an 1842 visitor was amazed how much it dominated conversation: 'The people of Vienna are not allowed to meddle with politics . . . so they talk and differ about music and the merits of the two great Waltz composers Strauss and Lanner.'[68] Throughout the century Vienna was associated with the greatest names in music: Beethoven, Brahms, Schubert, Bruckner, Mahler and, of course, the Strauss family. Seats at the Opera were cheap while for five shillings a visitor could watch Johann Strauss conduct his haunting waltzes in the Volksgarten.

The famous spas were an even greater attraction and by the early twentieth century one writer claimed that twice as many Britons went to the spas 'for their liver's sake' as to Vienna 'to be amused'. The spas in Bohemia (currently the Czech Republic), especially Marienbad, became popular with British travellers once railways made getting there so much easier. 'So many corpulent ladies' was the first sight that struck visitors, but it was comforting to be assured that an overweight English woman 'is stout symmetrically' whereas Germans were 'strangely disproportioned'. It was the stout

Edward VII's annual summer visit which made visiting Marienbad the height of fashion during his reign. When in Marienbad the King could consult his equally stout Prime Minister, Sir Henry Campbell-Bannerman, who had been visiting for thirty years, or he could talk with his most important admiral, 'Jacky' Fisher, or, less likely, the radical Welsh MP, David Lloyd George not to mention several celebrities of the London stage. Fisher enjoyed three weeks at 'beloved Marienbad' for £25 including his travel expenses.[69] The 'cure' helped people of 'luxurious habit' shed a few pounds through some mild dieting, mud baths and gentle walks through pine forests. There was also, of course, the water to be drunk while the band played.

This charming spa town had the two essential signs of a strong British presence – an English church and a golf course – and people felt relaxed. It was in Marienbad that an Austrian journalist studied the British on the eve of the First World War. He described them in the same terms in which they had seen themselves since Waterloo: 'As ever, the English . . . were distinguished by their restraint. Some splendid specimens of both sexes were to be seen . . . It was easy . . . to single out the Britons . . . they had more assurance, more self-reliance, a freer bearing.' Campbell-Bannerman saw another side because 'in this small Society of English people, quite half of the ladies either have already been, or are qualifying themselves for being divorced: and a considerable number of the men are helping'.[70]

The empire's most famous mountain range lay in the Tyrol. When Frances Trollope visited the region in 1836 she lavished praise on its beauty but deplored 'the total absence of . . . comfort' in its primitive inns. Conditions had greatly improved when, thirty years later, her son, Anthony, set one of his short stories – *Why Frau Frohman Raised Her Prices* – in a Tyrolean inn. This, he wrote, was quite comfortable and cheap: for four shillings a day guests enjoyed snug rooms and huge meals. Thirty years after that, his widow spent much of her time at a hotel in Kitzbühel for 'wonderfully little money', that is, six shillings a day including meals. Murray's 1879 *Handbook* praised the 'highland peasantry' of the Tyrol for the 'kindness and simplicity of manners' tourists found. The Austrian government made considerable efforts to increase tourism by expanding the railway network through some of the splendid mountain scenery. In 1873 Vienna also launched an International Exhibition to increase tourism and commerce, and to show the Empire's achievements to the world. A visiting squire's wife was 'charmed (as who could help being) with Austrian bands' and was 'more and more charmed with Vienna'. Murray agreed that the coffee in Vienna's famous cafes was wonderful and cheap at about fourpence (2p) but the smoke was 'perfectly overpowering', which was intolerable, especially for ladies. It was best to go when the Viennese were at home having lunch. In addition, there was always the *trinkgeld* or tip to the head waiter. Indeed, tipping reigned throughout the city and was 'a considerable item in the week's expenses'.[71]

By 1888 Vienna had made great strides in becoming an important tourist destination. In that year *The Times* devoted two large articles to the city and concluded that the *Kasierstadt* had met many of the desires of modern tourists but its expensive hotels still lacked many amenities. This made the 'Imperial City' less attractive to visitors than its beauties merited. At the start of the twentieth century, guide-books warned Vienna's hoteliers that they could only attract more Anglo-Saxons by 'providing the bedrooms with *large* basins, foot-baths, plenty of water . . . the sanitary arrangements [must be] . . . in proper order, including a strong flush of water and proper toilette-paper'. In 1904 Austria became one of the first countries to set up a travel bureau in London where people could ask for brochures, 'engage rooms and do anything to facilitate travel'. By 1908 the bureau was using a highly professional approach to tourism. It advertised winter sports in an attempt to cash in on the new passion for skiing, but also pointed out that in the summer, tourists would find 'Superb Mountain Scenery, Famous Watering Places, [and] Quaint National Costumes'.[72]

The Continent from Paris to Vienna, from Boulogne to Naples, and from the Rhine to the Alps offered a staggering number of 'lions' for the ever-rising number of British travellers. Yet these enthusiastic Britons always had to cope with a formidable number of practical problems to reach their goals.

Chapter 4

The Englishman's Bible

*I*n 1853 a censorious Englishwoman glared at British tourists striding across Florence's Ponte Vechio. With the practised sneer of the resident of a foreign city bewailing the 'vulgarity' of visiting compatriots she noted they were 'all distinguished by their red-bound Murray's guide-book . . . the national badge . . . "the Englishman's Bible"'. The very word 'guide-book' appears to have been first used in 1814, the year that travel resumed, and its development kept pace with the growth in travel.[1] This new type of publishing venture would become something resembling an all-wise friend. It was both a result of the new tourism and a factor that shaped it. As these books expanded in size, travellers used them not just as guides but as aids to plan their trips. To a large extent they not only determined where people went and what they saw but often what they thought.

Once large-scale continental travel began, Paris resumed her place as the first major destination for most travellers. Publishers were not slow to spot a market and almost immediately new guides to the city appeared. The best known was Edward Planta's *A New Picture of Paris; or the Stranger's Guide to the French Metropolis*, prepared at the end of 1814. Planta was much franker than later guide-book writers about certain attractions. True, the Palais Royal was celebrated for its gourmet restaurants, but it was also the centre of 'gambling and ruin' and the haunt of the 'fashionable impure'. The Palais Royal 'has not its parallel in any city of Europe', by which he meant brothels and prostitutes. Yet in spite of, or sometimes because of, that distinction another guide-book published only a few years later noted that most Britons preferred to lodge within a quarter of a mile of the Palais Royal. It was, so it was said, the best place to observe French manners.[2]

Dominating the publication of guides to the French capital was a family firm whose name would become synonymous with travel, Galignani. The Galignanis were an Italian family who had been in publishing since the early sixteenth century. By the start of the nineteenth century they were involved in numerous activities promoting the English language on the Continent. By the time of Napoleon's first abdication in 1814 they were publishing English books and in that same year began an English-language newspaper for travelling Britons and a series of guides in English, which the firm carried on, under a variety of titles, until 1900. *Galignani's Paris Guide* was annually 'revised and verified by Personal Inspection' and by the early 1850s had grown to over 600 pages. It provided practical information about French history, government, society, business and religious institutions. It listed hotels, restaurants (including seven English ones), dancing-masters and even English pastry-cooks, not to mention a variety of shops for the latest fashions. Those seeking more discreet but essential items such as corsets were directed to the Mesdames de Vertus. The *Guide* even provided the address of the official responsible for private showings of the guillotine at £4.[3] Galignani soon began widening its range to cover Switzerland, Italy and the whole of France, but then decided to limit itself to the French capital.

While visitors to Paris were well served with guide-books, those who embarked on more extensive travels had less choice. The earliest travellers to the post-Napoleonic Continent often consulted two books published shortly before the fall of Napoleon and still read in the 1850s. Joseph Forsyth, a Scottish schoolmaster, wrote *Remarks on Antiquities, Arts and Letters during an Excursion in Italy in the Years 1802 and 1803*. His book became 'a standard authority' on Italian life, and John Murray wrote that 'we know no work . . . to which the traveller will recur with so much pleasure'. Yet with travel changing so rapidly this became dated by the 1860s, when a young girl visiting Italy wrote to her father that she had found an old copy of Forsyth: 'It is so quaint, and amusing to compare with the present day.' Forsyth paid virtually no attention to practical details, preferring to speculate on Classical windows. Regarding present conditions, he usually restricted himself to the dreadful roads and to sneers at Catholic priests who were 'guarded in their debauchery', which therefore allowed him to make allegations without providing any proof.[4]

Another book firmly in the Grand Tour tradition was *A Tour through Italy* by John Chetwoode Eustace, a Catholic priest. This was published in 1813 and on its republication in 1814 the title was changed to *A Classical Tour through Italy*. The author's own bias was clear: 'Virgil, and Horace, Cicero and Livy . . . should occupy a corner in every carriage'. Eustace, even more than Forsyth, reflected the bitterness at the end of the long war against the French. He was 'a thorough . . . prejudiced Englishman . . . [who] hated France'. Indeed, his strictures on the French would provide a battleground for those with pro-French views: Lady Morgan insisted there was no foundation to his story that the French had used Christ's head in Leonardo's *Last Supper* for target practice, but others disagreed. Eustace, like Forsyth, continued to be used until at least 1857 when Dickens referred in *Little Dorrit* to 'the celebrated Mr Eustace, the classical tourist'. Dickens, precisely the type of tourist that Eustace would not have relished, described a scene in which 'everybody was walking about St Peter's. . . . Nobody said what anything was, but everybody said what . . . Mr Eustace, or somebody else said it was. The whole body of travellers seemed to be a collection of voluntary human sacrifices . . . to Mr Eustace and his attendants, to have the entrails of their intellects arranged according to the taste of that sacred priesthood.' (Book II. v, vii) But such criticism really applied not so much to guide-books but to how some people used them.[5]

In addition to Forsyth and Eustace, there was a growing range of books for the increasingly diverse British market. Some, such as *The Pocket Courier or Traveller's Directory* published in Brussels in 1830 by 'A British Traveller', were strictly practical. It was almost modern in the way it apportioned time for seeing the basic sights: one hour was suppose to suffice for Vicenza although it boasted fifty-seven churches and Palladian architecture that had had a considerable influence in Britain. Travellers worried about where to leave their carriages before taking a gondola to Venice were told of a post house where they could leave their vehicles under guard for one franc a night. However, they were warned, one must never allow the men to wash one's carriage because they used sea water which would damage it.[6]

According to that most vigorous of Victorian travellers, Anthony Trollope, 'in travelling these are the things which really occupy the mind. Where shall I sleep? Is there anything to eat? Can I have my clothes washed?'[7] The answers to these questions came in one of the most influential guide-books, one written by a remarkable woman who changed the nature of these books and of travel itself. Mariana Starke spent her youth in India and, once back in England, she became a controversial playwright. Stung by attacks on her works, she withdrew from the stage. She re-emerged in the 1790s when, having accompanied an invalid relative to Italy, she became fascinated with travel. Her two-volume book *Letters from Italy between the Years 1792 and 1798* not only dealt with the upsets caused by the French invaders but acted as a guide to works of art and to economical travel. Its success gave her an established reputation even before Napoleon's fall.

In the euphoria after Waterloo, Mariana Starke appealed to the new rage for travel with the clumsily titled *The Traveller's Guide To Italy, Chamouni, and all the most Frequented Passes of the Alps, Germany, Portugal, Spain, France, Holland, Denmark, Norway, Sweden, Russia, and Poland*, a book which provided a résumé of recent history and described the principal art treasures of Italy's cities. She 'borrowed' from other works but she also drew on her own experiences. The book's lengthy subtitle told readers that it contained information about 'the Expense of Residing in Various Parts of Italy, France, &c. so that Persons who Visit the Continent from Economical Motives, may Select the Most Eligible Places for Permanent Residence: with Instructions for Invalids, and for the Use of Families, who May Wish to Avoid the Expense Attendant upon Travelling with a Courier'. This covered not just the traveller for pleasure but those going for health and those who needed to be relatively careful with money. Women were especially relieved to have the advice of an experienced woman about the practical and domestic concerns of travel.

After her mother's death in 1816 Mariana Starke was free to return to Italy and to devote the rest of her life to continual revisions of her guide into a more popular vein. Her real fame began when a new version, *Travels on the Continent: Written for the Use and Particular Information of Travellers*, was published by John Murray in 1820, a year in which thirteen travel books were published just on Italy. Four years later the title was improved to *Information and Directions for Travellers on the Continent* and for two decades this remained the principal travel guide. She concentrated on Italy and France, but covered other places including Scandinavia and Russia, for which she drew on the work of others. The fact that the most famous early guide was by a woman showed that travel in the new century would be something in which women would play a major role.

Although Mariana Starke was in her sixties when *Information and Directions* first appeared she still had formidable energy. Her book was a tremendous achievement for someone working on her own. In one way it harks back to the Grand Tour because its focus is on lengthy trips through France and Italy. Yet there is one crucial difference. She assumed her travellers would not be young aristocratic men but families. She also assumed they were concerned about money and wanted information about taking long-term lodgings. Finally, she understood that many families would include an invalid. A considerable proportion of this large book of more than

600 pages is devoted to the actual mechanics of travel, with instructions about getting passports and coping with foreign money. Her seemingly endless list of what to take included locks for hotel doors, carving knives and the all-important teapot and kettle as well as an array of medicines. She offered space-saving tips such as the suggestion to put sheets and blankets in leather cases, which could serve as cushions in carriages. Her own carriage was so loaded with practical items that she could scarcely fit into it herself.

Like Eustace, Mariana Starke assumed most readers would be in private carriages and therefore anxious to know about roads, the costs of post horses, and any extra fees. She advised that if the road surface were too rough they should shout to the postillion, '*Allez sur la terre!*' She offered short and often pithy comments about hotels. Thus a traveller approaching Genoa could stop at one small town nearby which had three inns. The first was 'very tolerable'; the second 'remarkably dirty with a bad larder'; the third 'very clean and comfortable'. Travellers to Pisa were reassured that 'the nobility of Pisa and all the gentlemen belonging to the University, are remarkably civil and kind to foreigners; the lower classes . . . [are] respectful and humane, but exacting'. She was herself 'exacting' on prices: it would cost four French francs to hire a gondola for a day in Venice and under two francs to enter La Scala in Milan. The great drawback to her book was its division in two sections: the first part was an account of places and sights while the second provides details of routes. This division made it difficult to locate information quickly.

One of Mariana Starke's most important innovations was to indicate the best works of art by putting exclamation marks – !, !! or occasionally !!! – next to entries. Knowing that many readers would settle in one city for long periods she was precise about the cost of food. In the section on Sorrento, where she lived, there is advice on where to get English cheese, beer, medicine, mustard and sauces. Yet those who only wanted a day-trip to that exquisite spot from nearby Naples were told it required four hours for rowers to get to Sorrento plus three hours to rest before the long row back.[8]

One critic sneered that her book so extolled Sorrento that the city should put up her statue.

The revisions of *Information and Directions* give good indications of the evolving interests and concerns of travellers. The fifth edition, published in 1826, opened with a notice trying to calm travellers' fears about the much discussed Italian banditti. 'English travellers . . . have rarely been robbed, unless owing to imprudence on their own part, or on that of their attendants.' There was also more information about the climate of southern Europe and about the ruins of Pompeii. She noted improvements to roads and inns and the introduction of street lamps in Italy. This made large towns 'tolerably well lighted' and led to a decline in 'the dreadful practice of assassination'. She boasted that 'the great influx of British Travellers' had led to much improvement in the 'comfort of travelling'. Taking account of increasing worries about safety and political unrest, especially in Italy, she proclaimed in her ninth edition of 1836 that she had 'lately visited almost every part of Italy' and everywhere found 'the peasantry, mechanics, and tradesmen well disposed toward their rulers, civil . . . and honest'. She concluded that 'travellers may with safety, frequent the high roads and the most secluded parts of the Alps and Apennines, without the slightest probability of being annoyed by popular tumults, or plundered by banditti'. While concerned for economy, she still felt that 'persons blessed with health and affluence should always travel in their own carriage'.[9]

Mariana Starke's books made her a minor celebrity, especially to those who visited Naples, where she often entertained fellow countrymen with picnics of English food on the slopes of Mt Vesuvius. Such jaunts also allowed her to hear the latest news and to pick up information about the parts of Europe that she had not visited. One writer claimed that she was 'profanely called by the multitude "Jack Stark" from her predilection in favour of a man's hat and riding habit, which formed her usual attire'. It was also said she liked to wear men's boots and carry a huge umbrella. (Her title of 'Mrs' reflected her venerable years, not any married status.) Men who remembered their schoolboy Latin delighted in pointing out minor mistakes, yet one aged traveller remembered that because of her book, he was 'never at a loss what hotel to go to, what to look for, or what to do'. She was 'the friend and companion of all travellers in France and Italy, and the dread of all innkeepers ... "I will complain to Madame Starkey, and you'll see what she says of you in her next edition"' became the penultimate threat of the outraged travelling Briton; the ultimate was a letter to *The Times*. On the other hand 'greasy rogues' who ran dreadful Italian hotels pretended that they had been praised by the *illustrissima Signora Starke*.[10] She even found a place in French literature: in *The Charterhouse of Parma*, Stendhal refers to a travelling British historian who 'never paid for the smallest trifle without first looking up its price in the Travels of a certain Mrs. Starke, a book which ... indicates to the prudent Englishman the price of a turkey, an apple, a glass of milk, and so forth' (Chapter 13).

Mariana Starke died in 1838 while on one of her research trips. By the 1850s travel writers were denigrating her books, although one was honest enough to admit 'It is the fashion now to deprecate her work but I know not what the English could have done ... without the benefit of her experience.' An American magazine claimed she went into excessive detail about what to take in order to cater for the British obsession for 'comfort'. Her books were 'an exhortation to take up your house and travel, if you wished to be comfortable ... but John Bull soon found it easier to make the continent supply him with clean sheets ... He has warmed the bed for the rest of the world.' In her pioneering work to make travel easier, she became the mother of the modern guide-book and in many ways the grandmother of modern tourism. Two decades after her death some doggerel was found in a copy of her once famous work. It could serve as her epitaph ('Vet' is short for *vettura*, an Italian public coach):[11]

Mrs Starke, that most learned old matron

. . .

Will chatter of flannel and thread, like Minerva
Weird woman, indeed! Human things and divine,
She crams in one page, nay, and oft in a line

. . .

From the price of a house to the pace of a Vet
From the relics stupendous of Rome . . .
The old woman's always at home.

'Much delight and instruction have I had . . . from my guide,
philosopher, and friend, the author of "Murray's Handbook" . . .
Every English party I saw had this infallible red book in their
hands.' When Thackeray wrote this in 1845, Murray's *Handbooks*
were still a relatively new venture for a publishing house that had
been founded in 1768. John Murray II (1778–1843) had enhanced
its reputation by publishing not only Byron, Scott and the presti-
gious *Quarterly Review*, but Forsyth and Mariana Starke. His son,
John Murray III (1808–92) was very much a man of his time,
having had 'from my early years . . . an ardent desire to travel'.
Throughout his long life 'travelling was his chief pleasure' and his
work would make it a pleasure to thousands more. His 'very
indulgent father' agreed his travel plans provided he learned
German. As soon as young Murray, fresh from the University of
Edinburgh, had brushed up his German he arrived in Rotterdam,
'notebook in hand'.[12] His aim was to gather facts as he wandered
through the Low Countries, much of Germany and the sprawling
Austrian Empire, including Hungary and even parts of the Balkans.

When John Murray III returned home he began compiling a
guide to the countries he had visited. For a title his father borrowed
the German term *Handbuch*, and in 1836 the first *Hand-Book for
Travellers on the Continent* appeared. (The hyphen was eventually
dropped.) Devoted to Holland, Belgium and northern Germany, it
was followed a year later by one on southern Germany and Austria.

Both were written by the young Murray and both did very well: by 1840 the first title was in its third edition with 9,000 copies sold, and this third edition itself enjoyed seven printings. The success launched a series of *Handbooks* that continued through the century. One of the most popular, *A Hand-Book for Travellers in Switzerland*, appeared in 1838 to cash in on the craze for Swiss holidays. It was written by Murray and the Alpine artist and traveller William Brockedon. Because Murray could not possibly compile all the volumes he recruited distinguished writers, though he remained in overall control. He even kept surplus copies unbound so he could make changes. Within a short time every region and country of Europe had a Murray guide devoted to it. The series was so profitable that he was able to buy several acres on a hill in Wimbledon for a country house from which he could gaze out over the still rural prospect.

New editions, all bound in red, came forth every few years, incorporating changes sent in by travellers or writers trusted by Murray. The *Handbooks* normally had large folding maps in pockets fixed to the inside of the back cover and smaller maps in the text. He increased his profits with the 'Advertiser', a substantial section filled with advertisements from hotels and other businesses. This section was brought up to date even more frequently than the text. Sometimes the *Handbooks* would be thoroughly revised. The seventeenth edition of the *Handbook for Travellers in France: Part One* was revised by Murray's son, Hallam, for £80. A clergyman who contributed some sections received £20 while three other authors had smaller payments of about £5 each. Murray recruited several women to write individual sections such as those on art or architecture. When the radical travel writer Matilda Betham-Edwards sent Murray some comments about Dijon, he commissioned her to revise both volumes of a later edition of the *Handbook* on France. Julia Cartwright Ady was delighted when Hallam Murray asked her to write the art section of the *Handbook* on Rome in 1898, but at three guineas she felt he was trying to get her on the cheap: 'I could not work at such low terms.' This pioneering art historian was delighted when Hallam then offered ten guineas for her fifteen pages. Her work led to a profitable career writing biographies of her beloved Italian artists, no bad thing for the wife of a badly paid clergyman.[13]

By mid-century Murray's *Handbooks* had become an accepted part of travel. In 1857 a contributor to the *Quarterly Review* wrote that he could not recommend a better 'grammar' for a walking tour of Switzerland than Murray's *Handbook* and observed that each new edition both reflected and encouraged the growing fashion for climbing Swiss mountains. This was certainly the case, although anyone with a tincture of cynicism (or realism) might have remembered that the Mr Murray who published the *Handbooks* was also the Mr Murray who published the *Quarterly Review*. William Wetmore Story, a fashionable American sculptor in Rome who entertained scores of visiting Britons, said 'Every Englishman abroad carries a Murray for information, and a Byron for sentiment, and finds out by them what he is to know and feel.' The increasing number of travellers wanted precisely the sort of information that could:[14]

> *Be found by those who hurry*
> *From place to place, from dawn till dark,*
> *Whose only guide is Mrs Starke*
> *Till they can get a 'Murray'.*

The reference to those who travel 'from place to place' reminds us that Murray drew on the format laid down by Mariana Starke. He listed in considerable detail a sometimes bewildering selection of numbered 'routes' which travellers could follow. The first Swiss *Handbook*, for example, had 136 routes to, within and even beyond the country. There was basic information regarding distances, hotels and transport as well as local sights. Thus Route Fourteen covers the eighty-two miles between Zurich and Coire, which could be done in twenty-three hours in a very slow coach. The book included accounts of 'picturesque' old towns as well as news about an 'ingenious' way in which flooding was recently prevented. Murray's routes basically set the itineraries of his readers and much of modern tourism is still influenced by them. Curiously, it was only in 1864 that a *Handbook* for Paris appeared but, as Murray observed in his French *Handbook*, to have included it would have doubled the size of the volume. Secondly, there was no real need since *Galignani's Paris Guide* was 'a very good one'. Behind this praise lay the fact that Galignani's bookshop in Paris was a major seller of Murray's *Handbooks*. Even more, Murray was anxious to keep the Galignanis from pirating copies of his profitable series.

When it came to price, the *Handbooks* always varied: in the 1840s the guide to northern Italy sold for twelve shillings, which Elizabeth Barrett Browning found 'rather dear' on arrival in Pisa, but she still bought it.[15] By the 1880s the volume on the Rhine and northern Germany was ten shillings, while less popular destinations such as Portugal and Russia sold for twelve and a hefty eighteen shillings respectively. To put this in context, ten shillings would have provided a reasonable hotel and dinner in Paris for one night. Whereas Mariana Starke had always assumed the bulk of her readers were well-off and led leisurely lives, even if she did include some information for those with small budgets, Murray never assumed extended, leisurely tours. However, he did assume that his readers were comfortably off.

The tone adopted was that of one gentleman advising another, and many of the writers reflected Murray's strong Tory sympathies. In spite of this, the volumes, especially the earliest ones, were filled with references to Murray's most celebrated author, Lord Byron – too many for some users. Murray and his writers also urged British tourists to avoid arrogant behaviour and to behave themselves, especially when visiting Catholic churches. The volumes were also full of *facts*. Hyppolyte Taine, the greatest contemporary French authority on English literature and himself the author of a travel book, saw Murray's *Handbooks* as resembling 'the interior of an English head . . . which contains many facts and few ideas, a quantity of useful and precise information, short statistical

abridgments, numerous figures, correct and detailed maps, brief
and dry historical notes, moral and profitable counsels'. He
believed that an educated Englishman's stock of facts was three or
four times greater than a Frenchman's but, *naturellement*, the British lacked the grace of the French and their love of ideas 'for
themselves'.[16] In short *les Anglais* lacked *sensibilité* (sensitivity).
This brings to mind Palmerston's famous retort when told that the
British lacked a term for this glittering Gallic attribute. The forth-
right Foreign Secretary replied there was a term that covered it
exactly: 'Humbug'.

Taine may have been somewhat too sweeping in his characteri-
zation, but he was correct in feeling that the *Handbooks* appealed
to the educated upper- and middle-class traveller who had a desire
to know something of the countries he was visiting. Therefore some
of the interesting facts about foreign life they included could have
had no practical use. The first handbook on Switzerland, for
example, carried a section discussing the prevalence of the goitre
and cretinism in 'some of the grandest and most beautiful valleys of
the Alps'. Naturally, travellers' letters and diaries comment on both.
Later editions described the new research into these conditions and
by the 1860s tourists were much less likely to be disturbed by
cretins begging for alms. A mid-century *Handbook for Travellers in
Central Italy* had a section on Tuscan manufacturing. This drew
attention to one London company in Prato that employed over
3,000 girls to prepare the straw for the 'Leghorn' hats then so
popular. It puts travellers' own expenses into context to learn that
the girls earned between one and two shillings a day, which they
saved for their dowries. Travellers reading this would be spending
at least double that for a modest hotel for one night.[17]

We should never underestimate the importance of Murray's
Handbooks. They were, an American observer wrote in the 1850s,
'one of the great powers of Europe since Napoleon; no man's
empire has been so wide . . . There is not an inn-keeper who does
not turn pale at the name of Murray.' In an early volume the
Faucon Inn in Berne had been called 'one of the best inns in

Switzerland'. When a later edition noted that it had 'fallen off' the innkeeper 'looked as if he had received an arrow in his breast'. Much later in the century, *Punch* offered some comical advice to Britons going aboard: 'to ensure civility and respect, see that all your portmanteaus, bags, and hat-boxes be labelled MURRAY in the largest capitals'. This was meant as a joke but a similar event had already occurred. Travelling in Switzerland in the 1850s, Robert Ferguson met a man named Murray who had found 'that his fare was generally remarkably good, and his bills remarkably small'. One hotelier 'bowed low' and asked, 'In that case, may I hope to be favoured with a recommendation in the next edition of the hand-book?'[18] The false Murray appears not to have disabused him of his error.

The most helpful information in the *Handbooks* concerned hotels, and no words were used more frequently than 'clean' when it came to good rooms and 'civil' when it came to helpful staff. Murray's comments also give us insights into readers' attitudes. Perugia, where there were three choices, offers a particularly interesting example: the Hôtel de la Grand Bretagne was 'the best but might be improved as regards cleanliness, attendance [service in one's room], and charges'. The Locanda del Trasimeno had 'civil people, clean beds – deserves encouragement'. La Corona was merely 'second-rate, frequented chiefly by Italian families'. Of the inns in Prague the author wrote, 'none very good' while even the promisingly named *Englischer Hof* was 'not over clean'. (An earlier edition published twenty years before said it was the 'best but bad'.) In the late 1850s the hotels in southern Germany were chastised for 'extreme disregard to cleanliness and sweetness [lack of odours], which is most annoying and disgusting to Englishmen'. From the entrances, often used by both people and animals, came the 'oppressive odour of the stable'. 'Let it be hoped,' he added, that the hoteliers' 'increased intercourse with the English will introduce a taste for cleanliness.' As the decades advanced Murray paid even more attention to hotels, so this section of the *Handbooks* grew, partly in response to the increasing number of hotels. The 1899

Handbook for Rome gives information about noise, the nationality of each hotel's clients and the building's proximity to the 'English quarter'.[19]

Murray also warned his readers about various tricks perpetrated by innkeepers. Mont St Michel, for example, became increasingly popular towards the end of the nineteenth century, largely due to the opening of the causeway in 1880. Murray cautioned visitors that 'the drivers of omnibuses etc are in league with proprietor of the Hôtel Lion d'Or to try to prevent travellers from going to the much better Hôtel Poulard', later famous for its omelettes. Murray was always anxious to avoid any imputation that, like the omnibus drivers, he was 'in league' with hoteliers, especially those who paid for advertisements. Normally, therefore, the first pages of *Handbooks* carried a warning against anyone who extorted 'money from inn-keepers, tradespeople, artists, and others on the Continent, under pretext of procuring recommendations and favourable notices . . . in the Handbooks'.[20]

Murray sometimes carried short statements by travellers who had stayed at a hotel. Those from titled people carried additional weight, much as comments made by the transient celebrities from the worlds of pop music or sport do today. Thus anyone looking for Florence's best hotels in Murray's *Central Italy* would have seen that 'Sir J. L'. found 'most attentive people' at the Hôtel de Florence, whereas 'Earl R.' wrote of the Hôtel de la Paix's 'clean, and good cuisine'. As the number of travellers increased so did the facilities offered. In the first *Handbook* for Switzerland, Murray spoke disparagingly of Zurich's hotels as 'notoriously dirty, high priced and ill attended'. However, he did see some hope because two new inns were being built, which would provide an 'induce-ment to improve'. Six decades later things were much improved and praise was lavished on one hotel in Zurich that has 'all English comforts' as well as a landlord who is 'most polite and attentive' and who makes sure that *The Times* is available.[21]

To get some idea of what a Murray *Handbook* was like one can look at the fourteenth edition of *A Handbook for Travellers in South*

Germany and Austria, published in 1879. It has 660 pages of text plus sixty-eight pages of advertisements for hotels, watch shops in Geneva, cigar shops in Frankfort or shops which sell portable Turkish baths 'as used by Royalty'. The *Handbook* opens with general information on passports and money, with advice about the nature of hotels, and a description of the many spas. A large amount of space was devoted to major cities. Munich, famed as a centre of art, had almost forty pages. In addition to information about museums, there were the inevitable facts about the current condition of the Great Prison and various cemeteries. Vienna and its environs get about forty pages. Travellers were told where they could see Johann Strauss conduct or, for the more vigorous, where they could waltz 'far into the morning'. Yet when Murray felt it necessary to criticize a city he would level a barrage just as fierce as those directed at hotels. Few places suffered more than Nuremburg, in many ways the most 'romantic' city on the Continent. 'The pleasure of the visit will be greatly marred by the intolerable smells, which . . . arise from the defective state of the sewage and water supply.' Those who braved the smells were also warned that in the town hall various instruments of torture were on display: '*English ladies are warned not to enter this chamber of horrors.*'[22]

The *Handbooks* were not just used for touring. Many travellers ransacked Murray for facts with which to impress friends and relations in their lengthy letters home. Some, who wrote shorter letters, simply advised their family to read a description in Murray. John Ruskin's wife, Effie, went even further. She wrote from Venice to her parents, offering a gift of the *Handbook* on northern Italy: 'We use it constantly and when I want you to get a more detailed description of any particular Church than I have time to give I will refer you to the particular page in Murray . . . [which] is invaluable.' She added with the pride of a new wife that some descriptions of the churches had been written by her husband. Sometimes Murray's criticisms annoyed travellers. When E. W. Benson and his wife first saw Rouen Cathedral Mary Benson wrote in her diary, 'The Cathedral astonished us both much by its great beauty, for we had only read Murray's description of it in which the style is called "viciously florid".' Such arguments were not uncommon, but for every one who argued there were probably hundreds who accepted Murray's judgements as definitive. An American travel writer describing a party of British tourists travelling up the Rhine described their devotion to Murray: 'With Murray's Handbook open in their hands, they sat and read about the very towns and towers they were passing, scarcely lifting their eyes to the real scenes, except now and then, to observe that it was "*very nice*".'[23]

In July 1869 a young Gloucestershire squire wrote to his mother from Italy. 'I find my Murray very useful indeed; but now everybody has, instead, a book called "Baedeker", by a German of that name, it is supposed to be more correct.'[24] This was the beginning of the end for Murray.

Karl Bädeker (Baedeker in English) was born in Prussia. He opened a bookshop in Koblenz in 1827 and, like everyone else along the Rhine, was aware of the increasing number of tourists travelling up the river. He later bought a bankrupt printing firm and with it a scholarly guide to the river and its sights. When supplies of the guide ran out, about 1835, he reissued it in a more popular format with practical information. Three years later he started his own series of German-language guide-books which he called *Handbüchlein für Reisende*, 'Little Hand Books for Travellers', an obvious reference to Murray (eventually the 'little' was dropped). Throughout this period Baedeker maintained happy relations with Murray, whose first handbook he called 'the most distinguished guide ever published'. He had imitated Murray by listing routes for people to follow and by combining practical advice with information about sights. The Baedeker guides were actually known in Britain as early as 1858 when one writer praised them as being almost as good as Murray's. Baedeker's, he sniffed, were only good for reference whereas Murray's could be read as books. Similarly, the German guide listed all grades of hotels and did not, like Murray, concentrate on the best; but then British travellers came from the 'higher ranks'. Baedeker's were also too detailed: 'the German with his encyclopaedic turn of mind, requires the greatest amount of detail, and cares little for the adventitious charm of style; while with the Englishman just the contrary is thought desirable'. (This is the exact opposite of what Taine concluded.) Even worse, the German gave information regarding beer rooms and cigar shops: beer rooms were patronized by the working class while smoking in public was considered a vice especially popular with German men. While this article concluded that Murray's was the better series, it added what amounted to a warning if Baedeker ever published an English edition. Murray's superiority 'is referable to the different requirements of the German and English public', not to any inherent superiority. By implication, English versions of Baedeker's guides could change all that.[25]

Karl Baedeker died in 1859. Two years later his son, Ernst, made his first challenge to Murray's near monopoly by bringing out English translations of his guides as *Handbooks for Travellers*, the very title used by Murray. (They were also, like Murray's, bound in red.) Baedeker also used symbols to tell travellers which were the most important buildings, paintings or sights; though where Mariana Starke had used exclamation marks he chose asterisks or stars, a format still used today. Baedeker was often regarded as more informed about art than Murray but, unlike Murray, he did not make judgements. Having said that, his guides were not so 'arty' that they dispensed with practical information. In the guide to Paris of 1855 he replaced the poetry that normally graced his opening pages with some straightforward and timeless advice: 'The first, second, and third most important thing in travel is money. With money, most other deficiencies may be remedied.'

True to their original title, Baedeker's guides were smaller than Murray's and lighter to carry by almost half a pound. This appealed to those with little baggage, especially walkers such as Chaloner Chute during his 1873 visit to Switzerland. *The Times* praised their 'terseness and straightforwardness', while their maps were often better. They were also cheaper by several shillings. Murray's 'noble handbooks are principally intended for a class of tourist to whom expenses are of little or no moment', whereas Baedeker's were popular with the growing number of cash-conscious travellers, especially women on their own. In addition, Baedeker's books were better organized than Murray's and listed all the practical details at the start of each entry. Thus a traveller arriving in Brussels in the 1880s would have found almost six pages giving details about the railway stations, hotels and restaurants – with their prices and comments such as 'the viands and wine are excellent but expensive'. There was also information about cheaper taverns, cafes and the once criticized 'beer houses'. Nor was shopping neglected, especially information on buying lace. Also in this section were the addresses of British and American embassies, English banks, physicians, chemist shops, solicitors and even cricket and lawn tennis clubs. This section always gave details of English church services and in the volume on Brussels it also included the synagogue. Unlike Murray, Baedeker carried no advertising section, although this would be tried for a short time in the 1920s.[26]

Baedekers also developed a reputation for painstaking accuracy: stories were told about one of the Baedekers leaving a coin on every twentieth step on the stairs to the roof of Milan Cathedral so that the exhausted man could confirm his calculation of the total number as he came down. (Readers will be delighted to know that the cathedral now boasts a lift.) Yet, even Baedeker's Prussian efficiency could not avoid mistakes, and one outraged traveller was furious to see out-of-date names for the British and American Ambassadors in Vienna as well as for the Church of England chaplain there.[27] Perhaps the most important reason for the success of the German company, which moved to Leipzig after Karl Baedeker's death, was that, unlike Murray, which published a wide range of books, it concentrated on its guide-books.

The two companies' rivalry came to a head in 1889 when John Murray III accused Franz Baedeker, another of Karl's sons, of plagiarism. Franz accepted that John Murray had been 'the first publisher of guide books on a large scale', but for one simple reason: after the devastating Napoleonic wars, only Britain was rich enough to have 'any large section of the public indulging freely in foreign travel'. He admitted that Baedekers sometimes used material from Murray's books but insisted that Murrays had done the same with their German rival. ('Borrowing' was a common practice.) When three years later John Murray III died, his *Handbooks* did not long survive him. The family firm sold the rights to a much smaller publisher in 1901. Murray's *Handbooks* were truly Victorian: they started the year before the Queen Victoria's accession and ended a few weeks after her death. Yet for Murray's the battle had been lost years before. When Mary Eyre visited France in 1863 to see if she could live more economically, she naturally packed 'the "inevitable Murray"'. Forty-seven years later a correspondent in *The Times* advised women travelling to the Continent to be sure to pack 'the inevitable Baedeker'.[28]

In addition to the two giants – Murray and Baedeker – there were a host of smaller publishing houses which brought out guides. *Bradshaw's Illustrated Travellers' Hand Books* were published by George Bradshaw, a Manchester printer and publisher who had started his famous railway timetables in 1839. Soon, like the railways, his timetables were growing in size but, being Victorian, they were also dropping in price. With his name already so associated with railways and timetables, he started *Bradshaw's Continental Railway Guides* in 1847 and opened an office in Paris. By 1894 these *Guides* had grown to over 1,000 pages each and special editions featured hand-coloured maps. Travellers who needed the most up-to-date timetables could buy monthly supplements. In the 1850s he decided to capitalize on his reputation and launched his *Hand Books* to the principal tourist spots. Bradshaw, a devout Quaker, believed that continental travel would promote peace and a 'cheap and portable' guide whose information would be neither 'tedious' nor 'meagre' would increase profits. His 1857 guide to France was, he readily admitted, based on two French guides and were, like Murray's, arranged by 'routes'. Also like

Murray or Starke, his guides were full of practical advice, suggesting, for example, that if your shoes rub, you should grease a piece of writing paper and wrap that round the sore foot. He also suggested that British men try to be courteous to French officials: 'touch your hat (this goes a great way indeed with every native you speak to) ... Above all things do not trouble your head about French politics.'[29] Bradshaw also published an *Invalid's Companion to the Continent* by the most prolific writer about travel and health, Dr Edwin Lee. This provided advice on which places and climates were considered beneficial for particular diseases, especially consumption. Bradshaw's appeal was lower down the social scale than Murray's. He translated French terms and gave far less historical background.[30] With the enthusiasm characteristic of the Victorian entrepreneur, he was always anxious to improve his volumes. In 1853, while visiting Norway, he contracted cholera and died, but his continental guides carried on until 1914 when publication was suspended as railways and their timetables assumed sinister functions.

In addition to Bradshaw there were Bogue's *Guides for Travellers*. Like Murray, David Bogue was Scottish and a London publisher. He launched his series in 1852 with a guide to Switzerland and three years later published *Paris and Its Environs*, which was particularly useful for restaurants. Like Bradshaw, Bogue hoped to break into the travel market by appealing, with cheaper books, to those from lower down the social scale. Prices ranged from 3s 6d to 6s, thereby undercutting Murray. The first guide was praised by Albert Smith, which is not surprising, since Bogue had published Smith's *The Story of Mont Blanc*. John Murray III's relations with this company were even more fraught than with Baedeker, and soon after Bogue began publishing, Murray sued him unsuccessfully for plagiarizing. Another publishing house that aimed its work at the new wave of first-time travellers was Robert and William Chambers, another Scottish operation. *Chambers's Handy Guide to Paris* was, like Bogue's, clearly intended for those with less knowledge, less experience of travel and less money. The Chambers brought it out in 1863 to coincide with Paris's 'Permanent Exposition', which opened that year. Their aim was to provide a 'cheap, concise and comprehensive' guide with 'ample but compressed accounts' of the attractions. At 181 pages they had little choice and devoted far fewer pages to cultural matters. Like other publications they gave practical advice including the location of *'cabinets inodores'* or public conveniences. They warned tourists, 'Be wary of intimacy with people you meet in cafés, restaurants, or public places.'

More successful attempts to break into a market dominated by Baedeker were made by enterprising new publishers such as Macmillan, yet another Scottish firm, which was anxious to repeat Murray's success with its own series. As we saw earlier, the larger travel firms such as Thomas Cook and Henry Gaze brought out their own booklets priced at under a shilling. Appealing mainly to their own customers, these short guides were never intended to compete with Murray or Baedeker; in fact Gaze told his clients to buy Murray's *Handbooks*. As one reviewer put it, 'publishers seem to exercise as much ingenuity as hotelkeepers in laying snares for their lawful prey'.[31] Guide-book publishing would never have existed without the increase in tourism; but that same tourism would never have increased as it did without a variety of 'indispensable' sources to lead people on their great adventures.

'Next to the pleasure of travelling, the greatest pleasure for an Englishman is to read a volume of travel; in this way he augments his store of facts.' As Taine also observed, the publication of travel books was a vital part of Victorian publishing. Britain came to boast the most accomplished travel writers, as one American admitted: 'The Englishman is at once the most national and the most cosmopolitan of men. Wherever he goes, he takes his prejudices and his tea-pot . . . but he sees more, and tells his story of sightseeing better than the traveller of other nations.' There was an ever-increasing tendency for novelists to dash off profitable travel books as a sideline. It was regarded as easy money: 'When a writer has

got a name, the first rational use to make of the charming profession
is to get astride of it, as a witch upon her broomstick, and whisk
and scamper over half the kingdoms of the earth.' Dickens, having
become the most celebrated novelist of the time, also wrote his
colourful *Pictures from Italy*. Frances Trollope would often write a
travel book and then set a novel in the various countries she visited,
while both her sons made careers as travel writers as well as
novelists. Travel writing could occasionally be financially rewarding.
One of the first new travel writers was a young doctor, Richard
Bright, later famous for his research into renal disease. He visited
Hungary, a place so little known that he could only rely on maps
in a 1673 book written by an earlier English doctor. The publisher
gave Bright the handsome sum of £500 – about £28,000 today –
for the first edition of his book. This was twice the average annual
income for surgeons.[32]

Inevitably some people grew tired of the continual outpouring
which has 'inflicted our generation with one desperate evil', writers
'all determined not to let a hen roost remain undescribed, all
portfolioed, all handbooked'. Particular venom was reserved for
women writers, and one critic longed 'for the return of the happy
period when the chief occupations of the fair sex were cookery and
samplers'. Yet many of the best and most popular travel writers
were women: Frances Trollope, Matilda Betham-Edwards, Margaret
Oliphant and Anna Jameson to name but four. Women, even more
than men, often found travel writing a way to supplement their
incomes and to finance further travels. Women writers also had a
practised eye for the details of daily life that fascinated contemporary readers as much as they do people today, who can easily weary
of the sermonizing and political analyses of many Victorian male
writers. Resenting this female invasion, many men looked back to
more virile times:[33]

> *When English dames kept house at home,*
> *And never thought of seeing Rome*
> *Nor dreamt of reading Dante.*

Magazines quickly realized the public's love of vicarious travel, and travel articles were a constant feature of publications at every level. In the 1830s, for example the Anglican educational body, the Society for Promoting Christian Knowledge (SPCK), was publishing the *Saturday Magazine* with regular supplements on foreign sights or cities. At a penny this was obviously aimed at the lower echelons of the reading public who had very little chance of ever travelling. The supplement for March 1834, for example, had eight pages and three good engravings devoted to Vienna. The supplement is an impressive production that relied on readers' imaginations. As was said in one issue: 'Our readers . . . must carry themselves in fancy to the lofty Alps that separate France from Italy', for in no other way could they expect to see them.[34]

Given the difficulties of getting about in the early years after 1814, writers often emphasized the hardships of travel. With the arrival of steamships and railways, authors began celebrating the pleasures of travel and their accounts were often enlivened by the use of illustrations. Travel books, especially in the early decades, also had their political messages. Tories such as the hymn-writer J. M. Neale visited the Austrian Empire and lauded the 'gentle sway of the House of Habsburg'. Radicals such as Matilda Betham-Edwards applauded republican France where 'class distinction can hardly be said to exist; there are . . . masters and servants, of course, but the line of demarcation is lightly drawn'. In her case it is rather hard to square all this not just with fact but with an author whose hosts prepared for her visits as if she were 'a Royal Personage'. Matilda would send ahead detailed commands about the curtains, sheets and blankets she required in her bedroom – 'the scent of new blankets being very trying to me'. All servants were commanded to be quiet until she arose from her 'unlavendered sheets'.[35]

The single most influential travel writer was John Ruskin, although he would have been horrified to read this description. He was a 'travel writer' by default, his great passions being art and architecture. From the 1840s, when he defended modern art, and Turner in particular, he was a major influence in British intellectual life. But two of his works, based both on years of study and on numerous trips to Europe, had a direct influence on tourism: *The Seven Lamps of Architecture*, published in 1849, and *The Stones of Venice*, published in three volumes between 1851 and 1853. Ruskin hated railways and the growth of travel his works encouraged. He became a major advocate of the 'good old days' syndrome, but if he did glorify the past he also fought to preserve Europe's cultural heritage from the hands of developers. His views were expressed in diktat form, which appealed to his followers as much as it amused his detractors. It is not patronizing to say that his greatest influence was on people who needed, or felt they needed, guidance *before* they set out, the sort of people who flocked to Toynbee Hall and joined the Art Workers' Guild. They were, in George Bernard Shaw's condescending words, 'chock full of Ruskin' – and this was written in the 1890s when Ruskin's influence was supposed to have waned.[36]

On a less serious note, the young Lina Duff Gordon, who lived outside Florence, was visited in 1892 by a Mrs Foster and her daughters. The mother, she wrote, was 'a type of the good english [*sic*] matron. Fat, kind & beaming. Her whole face lights up whenever her eye falls on her two daughters whom, of course, she thinks prodigies of learning. Here goes a list of their virtues.

1° They are very rich.
2° They are fairly good looking.
3° They know Ruskin by heart.
4° They know French[,] German [and] Italian & every picture in Florence by heart, though they are only here since the last 3 days.'

The point is that Ruskin would not have appealed to Lina Duff Gordon, living as she did in Florence, but he would have appealed to the Fosters of this world who wanted to make sense of what they saw. Ruskin's time had really passed when tourists went to enjoy themselves, not to study. Arnold Bennett's tongue was firmly in his cheek when he wrote in 1910 that he was 'in another small provincial town in Central France, where I was improving my mind and fitting myself for cultured society in London by the contemplation of cathedrals'.[37] He did not mention Ruskin by name, but it was Ruskin he had in mind.

Next to Ruskin one of the most influential writers was the exotic Augustus Hare, a popular and prolific author. He produced almost twenty erudite books about virtually all the main European countries from Spain to Russia, each illustrated with his own exquisite line-drawings. His most famous book, still of considerable value, is *Walks in Rome*. Interested only in those of his own cultivated milieu, he stubbornly refused to translate many passages from the Latin or French. With true Victorian earnestness, he preached that people could only really 'enjoy Rome most who have studied it thoroughly before leaving their own homes'. Once there, 'few are able to do more than "read up their Murray"'.[38]

Books by Augustus Hare, Richard Bright or Frances Trollope were part of a literary tradition that reached back centuries. But the new type of travel which began in 1814 also produced new and different types of travel writing. There were books with numerous and lavish engravings, and later photographs, books to show the funny side of travel, books devoted to mountaineering, books for children and, by the late nineteenth century, books that harked back to a golden age of travel. There was also a fashion in the early decades for expensive annuals, with stories and poetry usually alongside engravings of continental scenery. The thrill of 'seeing' famous sights was a new factor in continental travel and these luxurious books did much to encourage the growing fashion for travel. As so often happened, technical advance aided changing tastes: developments in lithography and other improvements to printing played important roles in directing travellers to the Rhine, the Alps and the better-known Italian cities and lakes. Turner, the greatest illustrator of all, had done much work on the Rhine and in Switzerland and it was he who provided illustrations for a new printing of Samuel Rogers's poem *Italy*. It was this edition that caused the Ruskins to set out for the Continent, and they were only one family among hundreds.[39]

Perhaps of equal importance to the works of Ruskin and Hare were the poetry, novels and stories that depicted European travel. Much of the Brownings' poetry reflected their life in Florence, especially Elizabeth Barrett Browning's epic *Aurora Leigh* which drew heavily on her own experience of life and travel. Anthony Trollope set several short stories and novels in Europe while Charlotte Brontë used Brussels in her novels *The Professor* and *Villette*. Possibly more common was the way in which writers made use of their travels for episodes in their works. In *Vanity Fair*, published in 1848, Thackeray had the disgraced Becky Sharpe end her days wandering round Europe. Dickens used his own experiences in France, the Alps and Italy in *Little Dorrit* and George Eliot set part of *Daniel Deronda* in Italy. In addition to these great names there were a host of minor novelists such as Mary Hawker, Lady Georgiana Fullerton, the Gerard sisters and the delightfully named Egerton Castle who used European settings.

Europe continued to feature in the works of the most popular writers up to 1914: George Meredith's *Emilia in England* (1864, republished as *Sandra Belloni* in 1887) and *Vittoria* (1867), Robert Louis Stevenson's *An Inland Voyage* (1878) and *Travels with a Donkey in the Cévennes* (1879), Marie Corelli's *Wormwood: A Drama of Paris* (1890), George du Maurier's *Peter Ibbetson* (1891) and his more famous, *Trilby* (1894), Jerome K. Jerome's *Diary of a Pilgrimage* (1891) and *Three Men on the Bummel* (1900), Beatrice Harraden's *Ships That Pass in the Night* (1893), Elizabeth von Arnim's *Elizabeth and Her German Garden* (1893), John Galsworthy's *Villa Rubein* (1900), Arnold Bennett's *The Old Wives' Tale* (1908) and Katherine Mansfield's *In a German Pension* (1911). The two writers whose use of European settings have had the most lasting influence were Henry James and E. M. Forster. Novels by Henry James that make use of European scenes include *Roderick Hudson* (1875), *The American* (1877), *The Europeans* (1878), *Confidence* (1879), *The Portrait of a Lady* (1881), *The Princess Casamas-*

sima (1886), *The Reverberator* (1888), *The Tragic Muse* (1890), *What Massie Knew* (1897), *The Wings of the Dove* (1902) and *The Ambassadors* (1903). The two most famous novels by Forster which featured Europe were *Where Angels Fear to Tread* (1905) and *A Room with a View* (1908). In spite of their literary distinction these two novelists have distorted the image of continental travel: Forster, by his well-practised sneers at his compatriots and James by his concentration on the idle rich. The world of Victorian travel contained all sorts of people, many quite admirable, who never enter the pages of these celebrated novelists.

A growing number of authors realized the humorous situations that were inevitable once travel began to expand. These writers had great sport with the antics of British travellers, in particular the 'Cockney' or tradesmen classes. The principal theme in most of these works was pretentiousness. Social insecurity was a concomitant of the expansion of the middle class and there was no more popular subject for humour than those people who were getting uncomfortably close to oneself on the shaky ladder of respectability. One of the earliest works to use this theme was Thomas Moore's poem *The Fudge Family in Paris*, published in 1818. The main butt of its humour was Mr Fudge's son, Bob, 'An improving young man, fond of learning, ambitious' who 'just knows the names of French dishes and cooks/As dear Pa knows the titles of authors and books.'[40]

The 1840s saw a host of writers who made fun of the British in Europe. Thomas Hood is now remembered for his moving poem 'Song of the Shirt', which describes the miseries of a poor seamstress. But in 1840 he published *Up the Rhine*, which was devoted to the difficulties of an elderly hypochondriac in search of health. That same year Frederick Marryat, still known for his *Mr. Midshipman Easy*, published *Olla Podrida*, which traces an English family's adventures in Europe. Sadly, its humour has not survived the passage of the years. In 1844 Charles Lever published *Arthur O'Leary* and two years later Lever's whist-partner, Frances

Trollope, brought out *The Robertses on Their Travels*, which portrays yet another English family who live abroad for a year. Thackeray, who had lived in Paris and Germany, relished portraying Britons abroad in numerous works, perhaps best of all in *The Kickleburys on the Rhine*, published in 1849. While Lady Kicklebury of Pocklington Square and her family party gave readers much amusement, Thackeray was concerned to make a serious point about how quickly tourists became blasé about travel. He described 'people asleep in the cabins at the most picturesque parts [of the Rhine] . . . It is as familiar . . . as Greenwich'. He saw this as part of the growing propensity to 'push on again – anything to keep moving' and wondered, 'How much farther shall we extend our holiday ground, and where shall we camp next? . . . Perhaps ere long we shall be going to Saratoga Springs, and the Americans coming to Margate for the summer.'[41]

In 1854 Charles Lever returned to the travel theme with *The Dodd Family Abroad*. At the beginning of this three-volume novel, Mrs Dodd explains the reasons for their jaunt: 'Isn't it worth something to see life – to get one's children the polish and refinement of the Continent – to teach them foreign tongues . . . to mix in the very highest circles.' If Thackeray attacked indifference, Lever attacked pretentiousness in a 'certain class of travellers, the "Dodds" . . . [who] ramble . . . about . . . John Murray in hand, speaking unintelligible French, and poking their noses everywhere . . . [becoming] the prey of innkeepers.' The Dodds are cheated mercilessly but 'You . . . richly deserve it, I say. Had you come on the Continent to be abroad what you were . . . at home . . . You would have seen much to delight and interest, and much to improve you' (Chapters 2, 42). By the time Jerome K. Jerome was turning his attention to Europe the fashion for sermons had passed. In *The Diary of a Pilgrimage* (1891) and in *Three Men on the Bummel* (1900) Jerome was concerned only with humour, a humour that is not derived from looking down on social inferiors but on looking at thoroughly respectable but incompetent middle class travellers, exactly the sort of person who might indeed have read the books.

In popular journalism European trips presented wonderful opportunities for poking fun at tourists. After its founding in 1841, *Punch* found the British on the Continent a perpetual source of amusement, and one of its editors, F. C. Burnand, wrote several volumes of humorous sketches. Most of the magazine's travellers were people presumed to be slightly below the social level of its readers; often they were Londoners – 'Cockneys' again – and often clerks called 'arry. It was only fitting that the magazine published Douglas Jerrold's *Mrs. Caudle's Curtain Lectures* in the early 1850s and equally fitting that Jerrold sent the Caudles on one of the 'excursions' to Boulogne. Also in mid-century there were the works of Arthur Sketchley whose 'Mrs Brown' series was so popular. Sketchley had great fun when he sent Mrs Brown to visit the 1878 Paris Exhibition on one of 'Cook's escursions'. Mr Brown praises the enterprise: 'you can go and see this 'ere Exhibition . . . and stop a week, for about five pounds, as is cheap'. When Martha Brown is convinced that all will be 'fust rate' she agrees to go but remains dubious. Paris, she rejoins, 'is a bold place; and you do ought for to be werry careful 'ow you goes on, for them foreigners is a lot as makes uncommon free'.[42]

Finally we should mention humorous drawings that played an increasing role in what we may call the 'literature of travel'. Indeed, the most impressive production, the 1854 *Foreign Tour of Messrs. Brown, Jones and Robinson* by 'Dicky' Doyle, had nothing but drawings with captions. In this the *Punch* artist portrays the adventures of three young men from London (naturally) who get into various scrapes about their passports, luggage, dress and, as will be seen in Chapter 8, accommodation. This delightfully mild and gentle humour proved very popular and, appropriately, was advertised in Murray's *Handbooks*. Drawings also figured prominently in Jerome K. Jerome's travel books, which were lavishly illustrated in the same style.

By the end of the century, the British passion for travel itself had become a butt of humour. In one serial published in the society journal *Vanity Fair*, 'Cecil the Far-Travelled' worries about 'choosing the foreign country to be favoured by his visit', that is, one without too many other British tourists. Cecil's view is that 'it is the mission of every Englishman to spend a few weeks every year abroad. His presence in their midst enlightens and civilises foreign nations. It is a duty he owes to generations yet unborn.'[43]

Chapter 5

The Curses of the Traveller

When Lord Porchester visited Portugal in 1828 some 'informality' in his passport led to a 'temporary embarrassment', that is to say, his lordship was thrown into prison. Passports were 'the curses of the traveller on the Continent . . . No one can imagine the constant inconvenience and worry caused by . . . having these . . . cumbersome certificates of respectability signed and counter-signed by pompous and often none too civil officials.' Six years later Charles Feilding and his family entered Champlitte, a small town near Dijon. The local *gendarme* examined their passports and decided 'they were not *en règle*' because Feilding had not signed his name. He was arrested and taken to the local *Maire* who pronounced the offence '*très grave*' and ordered him marched off to nearby Gray. He had to walk the ten miles because the *gendarmes* did not want to 'tire their Horses'. Having arrived he was told he could either go to gaol for the night or pay to be guarded in the hotel: 'I resisted stoutly & said I *would* have the business settled at once.' Shortly thereafter the *Commissaire de Police* arrived. As he was 'the greatest scoundrel I ever saw & – the most *intraitable*' Feilding's heart sank. Then, as in a French farce, the *Procureur du Roi* rushed in, anxious to be part of this great drama. He 'soon settled the business' and ordered Feilding released.[1]

From the moment travellers stepped ashore they had to cope with continental rules. European countries demanded that their own subjects obtain passports even if they wished to travel within the country.

'No Frenchman,' Dawson Turner wrote in 1820, 'can quit his arron-dissement unprovided with a passport.' He had heard that 'a week or two ago the Prefect of the police [in Caen] himself was escorted back to Caen, between a couple of gen-d'armes, because he had inadvertently paid a visit to a neighbouring bathing-place without his passport'.[2] Accordingly, foreign governments required those entering their territories to produce similar documents. The difficulty was that in Britain such procedures were unknown. No one needed a passport to move about the country, to leave the country or, indeed, to enter it.

It could be extremely difficult for any Briton actually to prove who he was. The artist Edward Lear once entered a railway compartment where he saw children reading his *Book of Nonsense*. The father explained that there was actually no such person as 'Lear' and that the book was really written by the Earl of Derby. Lear intervened to say that the book was written by a Mr Lear and that he was Lear. The only way he could convince the doubters was to show them his calling card, his monogrammed handkerchief and the name on his hatband. The absence of passports confirmed the view that the British lived in a free country whereas on the Continent the state presumed the right to know and control who travelled where and when. Yet, as one Englishwoman who lived abroad for many years noted, 'I do not remember, by the way, to have met with any recognition of this bit of English freedom, in any book of travels written by foreigners.'[3]

The first thing, therefore, that a would-be traveller needed was to procure a passport. Until the First World War, a British pass-port was a large sheet of paper bearing the royal arms and, if it was obtained in the United Kingdom, those of the current Foreign Secretary. Passports obtained abroad had the arms of the British Ambassador who issued them. The paper, which was then folded some four or five times, gave the name and a very few basic details about the bearer or bearers, in French until 1858 and thereafter in English. It was then signed by the holder(s). When, for example, the Reverend Henry Budd and G. B. Whittaker went to

Europe in 1838 they got a joint passport which described themselves as '*M. Henry Budd, et M. G.B. Whittaker, Gentilshommes Anglais, voyageant sur le continent*'. If the holder did a lot of travelling, extra paper was glued to the bottom of the original sheet: a passport issued to G. P. Jervoise in 1826 ended up being some two feet long. Once obtained, these documents were not given the almost sacrosanct status they have since acquired. Travellers sometimes drew sketches on the back or scribbled notes or poetry. One descendant of Wordsworth even wrote a double acrostic on his as a somewhat doubtful way to aid German innkeepers to pronounce his name.[4]

In Benjamin Haydon's account of his trip to Paris, he stated simply that 'I got passports'. That makes the procedure seem far easier than it was. For those with access to the Foreign Secretary, such as Charles Greville, Clerk to the Privy Council, getting passports was easy. Greville actually had three passports, which could be a great help: when once in a hurry to get to Italy he chose the passport which implied that he was carrying government despatches so that the captain of the cross-Channel steamer left three hours ahead of time. However, for most people during the early decades of the century getting a British passport could be time-consuming and was always expensive. The applicant had to know the Foreign Secretary or 'be known' to someone he 'trusted'. By 1852 the procedures had caught up with the increase in demands: the 'persons known to the Foreign Secretary' had become bank officials. One applied in writing and the day after the letter was received the applicant or his agent collected the passport in London.[5]

People could also ask companies in the capital or, in time, travel agencies, to apply for passports and any necessary *visas*. This service was obviously useful for those who lived outside London. For a few extra shillings, firms would also mount a passport on stout calico, fold it and bind it in a leather pocket book with extra leaves and room to insert yet more sheets if required. As such it resembled a modern passport. Customers could also have the bearer's name inscribed in gilt on the cover while a peer could have a coronet or his own coat of arms added. However travellers got their passports, the cost, £2 7s 6d, was high. Finally in 1852 the fee was reduced to 7s 6d and, not surprisingly, the number of applications jumped sevenfold within a year.[6] In certain cases, as with Henry Budd, the fee was waived: the Foreign Secretary wrote and underscored the word 'gratis' across the bottom.

Another way to save money and time was to include others on a passport. As we saw with Henry Budd, passports could include friends as well as wives, children, relations and servants. Because passports had no expiry dates they were good for life, which could lead to bizarre consequences. When the seventy-year-old Lady Aldborough arrived in Paris in the 1840s for one of her frequent visits, her passport, issued before the French Revolution, stated that she was twenty-five. The official eyed her suspiciously and said he doubted that was her age. To this Lady Aldborough, as notorious for her brazenness as for her long list of lovers, replied *'Monsieur, vous êtes le premier Français qui ait jamais douté de ce qu'une dame lui a dit au sujet de son âge.'* The crushed official bowed low, *'Pardon, Madame, mille fois. Je me suis trompé tout-à-fait.'*[7]

While the great majority of passports were issued in the Foreign Secretary's name, there were other ways to obtain the document. One was through the Lord Provost of Edinburgh who had the right to issue some passports. Far more frequently people applied at a foreign embassy or consulate, a procedure which also cut costs. This would have made sense if one were going there anyway to get a visa. A British subject needed to produce a passport on arrival in Europe but he did not need a *British* passport. Mr Jervoise's 1826 passport was issued by the Netherlands Embassy in London. French passports were free, although small tips were usually given. Obtaining foreign passports was usually quicker in the early decades, which made them attractive to many travellers, especially those in a hurry. The process was also easier, but not always. In 1840 a young Cambridge undergraduate, the future scientist Francis

Galton, had a frustrating visit to the French Consul. He wanted a passport before the family set off for the Continent, but he complained to his father: 'They will not give it me until I get from you a certificate stating that I go abroad with your approbation, I being a minor; so please send me one . . . Only think of the man's insolence in requiring one; it was almost saying: "Does your mother know you're out."' Young Francis also explained that 'to get your passport you must attend once yourself and can represent the family . . . Just come crammed full of information about Names, Height, Eyes, Hair, Complexion, Ages, and all that sort of thing.'[8] It was all very un-British.

Young Galton's frustration about eyes and complexions arose because foreign passports gave a basic description of the bearer. (Presumably Lady Aldborough was travelling on a foreign passport, which is how the French official knew her age.) Like Galton, Anthony Trollope was annoyed when he applied for a Spanish passport and found the official looking into his eyes and then writing that his beard, of which the balding novelist was inordinately proud, was '*poblada*'. He felt better when he discovered that this meant 'thick'.[9] To cope with British passports, which gave no such details, some foreign governments would occasionally insist on adding a printed form with spaces for personal descriptions. This difference between British and European use caused constant friction. In the 1840s a German revolutionary was found carrying a British passport issued by the embassy in Brussels. The new Kingdom of Belgium requested that Britain add some physical description to passports. The truculent Foreign Secretary, Lord Palmerston, then made a great show of demanding an explanation from the Brussels Embassy. It replied that the man seemed 'evidently an Englishman and apparently a gentleman' so no proof of identity had been required. British diplomats were told to be more careful but, at the same time, Palmerston proclaimed that 'the whole System of Passports is so repugnant to English usages that [he] . . . could not propose to British Subjects to submit additionally to the degrading and offensive practice' of having physical descriptions included.[10] When the Belgians refused to allow British travellers, including one prominent peer, to enter without such information, Palmerston told them it was up to them if they wished to injure their lucrative tourist trade. Brussels surrendered.

When, two years later, the Prussians were kicking up a similar storm, *The Times* fought back: 'To a German the pass [*sic*] is the proof of his existence ... An Englishman believes ... that his presence in the shape of five feet nine of respectability on any spot of the earth's surface is proof enough ... that he must once have been born, and had a name. He therefore cares little for his passport ... a fuss is made about nothing.' Foreign governments continued to press for changes, especially Austria when in 1853 someone with a British passport tried to kill the young Emperor Franz Joseph. British diplomats regarded this as 'a most insolent demand' because 'we are not to be dictated to by foreign powers as to the form of our passports or anything else'. Nothing was done until 1858. After that date only Britons could obtain British passports and British subjects could no longer travel on foreign passports. By 1911 a passport cost two shillings with a stamp duty of sixpence if purchased at home. A sign that the world of travel had changed came in 1915 when photographs became a requirement.[11]

If getting passports was troublesome, far worse was the first confrontation with passport inspectors. Dickens described the infamous queues to reach the officials and the treatment people received on a trip to Boulogne in the 1850s:

The road to this dungeon is fenced off with ropes breast-high, and outside those ropes all the English in the place who have lately been sea-sick and are now well, assemble ... to enjoy the degradation of their dilapidated fellow-creatures ... 'Oh! Ain't he green in the face, this next one!' ... The captives, being shut up in the gloomy dungeon, are strained, two or three at a time, into an inner cell, to be examined as to passports; and across the doorway ... stands a military creature making a bar of his arm.

These interviews were usually only tiresome, although occasionally they could be embarrassing. When Caroline Meysey-Wigley, a wealthy young lady, arrived in Le Havre in 1838 the French official wanted her height and then wrote down descriptions of her face on the printed form, beginning with her hair and then moving to her forehead, eyebrows, eyes, nose, mouth, beard – left blank – chin, face or *visage* and complexion. From there he passed to her *signes particuliers*, which in Caroline's case meant a limp due to child-hood polio. When asked if *'vous souffrez du pied droit?'* she replied, *'Des deux pieds'*. As the kindly official handed her the document he said to himself, *'C'est malheureux'*.[12]

These inspections were only the first of many trials, and passport officials were consequently usually loathed: when one traveller's horse was being stroked by an inspector in Calais the animal turned round and bit him. This led to wild cheering, at least among the British. As most travellers landed in France, and as 80 per cent of them went first to Paris, we shall now follow them, although the difficulties they faced applied in other countries. Officials, having interviewed arriving passengers, then took their passports to send to the police in Paris. The traveller was given a police pass or *Passé-port à l'Interieur*. This allowed the visitor to travel to a specific place within a specified time. (When Thomas Trollope arrived in Boulogne on one trip he was only going to Marseilles to take ship for Italy. His *passe*, therefore, only allowed him to travel between the two ports.) On arrival in the capital, the traveller or his agent collected his passport and then took it to the British Embassy to be signed. After that he took it back to the police who would give him permission either to *'rester à Paris'* for a period or to travel on. If the police had given him permission to travel, his destination was clearly stated. Often, when a tourist stopped, some form of the whole procedure of surrender, inspection, signature and retrieval was gone through again. If travellers wanted to carry on to another country they had to get their passports signed by someone in the French foreign ministry (to allow them to leave France).

Then they had to go to the embassies of all those countries they wished to visit to get their passport *viséd* (that is, seen and approved) if those countries demanded this: Sardinia, for example, did not.[13]

All this bureaucratic toing and froing made deep impressions on British visitors, who were blessedly free of officialdom at home. As one writer put it, 'neither spirits nor health mend under the passport ordeal: the being bandied from hand to hand like a bad shilling, – from Ambassador to "Bureau of Passports," thence to Prefecture of Police; from the clerk "at the top" of the "Prefecture," to Clerk "at the bottom;" – to the Ambassador's again, and again to the Police . . . what a fuss a poor traveller has to go through in this country.' There were constant complaints about this 'absurd, clumsy, and cumbrous machinery', and returning travellers were 'forcibly impressed with the freedom and security we enjoy in this country' without the 'humiliating scrutiny and suspicion' found in Europe. Of course if one left France and then returned, one had to start all over again. There was, however, one bonus to having a passport – holders could get into galleries and palaces on days when they were closed to the general public.[14]

Having left Paris, the traveller's troubles did not cease. Henry Budd's passport, for example, had signatures and stamps from officials in Cologne, Koblenz, Stuttgart, Vienna, Leghorn [Livorno], Florence, Rome, Milan, Bologna, Venice, Strasbourg, Perugia and Brussels. At Rome before Italian unification, anyone going on to Naples had to endure further rigmarole involving signatures by the British Consul General, the police and the Neapolitan Ambassador. Every country had different rules: in Naples Bishop Hynes had 'to go to the *Intendenza* to sign my name in the passport book' and, to add insult to injury, he had to pay '1 dollar to the *Intendente*, a tax on every traveller leaving'. Surviving passports show that all these signatures and stamps often made the documents unreadable and meant that people got muddled. In 1823 Dr Henry Percy was stopped by officials as he crossed back into France from Switzerland. The French had 'plagued him amazingly' because his passport had not been *viséd* in Geneva by a French official. When the French tried to pull it out of his hands (to send to Paris) he held on and was ordered to pay four francs. He was still given his *passé-port à l'Interieur*, which allowed him to '*quitter le Royaume dans dix jours par Antibes*'.[15] He was probably happy to get out. All this visiting foreign consulates and embassies to get passports *viséd*, along with surrendering and reclaiming passports, was one of the greatest nuisances of travel up to the 1850s when the rules were relaxed.

There were occasionally moments of light relief and even humour. In 1816 one aristocratic traveller reported that passport inspectors

> ask perpetually for one's passport & last night I was very minutely examined upon my motions [movements] by a *gens d'arme* who came to the inn & took down every particular not omitting the exact hours of my arrival & intended departure. The maid [said] . . . that he not put down my name. . . . '*Bah!*' replied he '*qu'est ce que cela signifie? J'ai bien tout le reste*' – so his information was '*Seigneur Anglais arrivant du Mans allant à Tours.*'

It is slightly ironic that the name the French official did not want was none other than that of the young Lord Palmerston who, as Foreign Secretary, never ceased attacking the very use of passports. However, even the signature of the mighty Palmerston when it was known did not always save travellers from trouble. Earlier we saw that Edward Lear had difficulty proving who he was when in Britain. When sketching in Calabria he had more difficulty in proving who he was not when accosted by a drunken Italian policeman to whom he showed his British passport. When the policeman saw the name 'Palmerston' he promptly arrested him. Lear was then 'trotted ignominiously all down the High-street, the *carabiniere* shouting . . . "*Ho preso Palmerstoni!*" [I've got Palmerston!]'.[16]

Passports were ridiculed in popular fiction and attacked in the press. In *The Times*' leader quoted earlier, the paper referred to 'the pestilent frivolity of passports' and predicted that they would soon fall victim to the march of progress. The march of progress, in the shape of larger ships, railways, and cheap excursion tickets, meant that instead of small numbers of arrivals, officials had to cope with large groups. The constant examination of passports was becoming impossible: 'It is not easy,' rejoiced one radical encyclo-pedia in 1849, 'to enforce the regulations . . . where railroads have become almost the only mode of travelling.' France accepted the inevitable and in the early 1850s introduced a reform: Britons who wished to visit Paris could get a 'pass' from the French Consul in London for five francs. This let them proceed directly to the capital and was good for one month. Gone was the toing and froing to the police for a *passé-port* and 'the visitor will not be annoyed,' wrote one guide-book, 'if its date is expired by a few days'.[17]

The delay in rationalizing the system was largely due to Britain. To most continental governments, Britain was not the home of liberty but a refuge for terrorists and a country that encouraged its people to interfere in other nation's politics. Frances Trollope arranged in the 1820s for radical English papers to be smuggled into France for Lafayette to read; and others did the same. Austrian, Neapolitan and papal governments resented Britain's unquestioning enthusiasm for Italian unification. Hostile articles and poems by Britons resident in Italy and tourists who forced their way through military parades were the least of the problems local officials had to face. Terrorism and assassination were real threats and, as we saw earlier, Austria protested when a man holding a British passport tried to murder the Emperor. Five years later, in 1858, there was another outrage in Paris when the Italian nationalist Count Felice Orsini threw a bomb at a carriage in which Napoleon III and Empress Eugénie were sitting. Orsini had gone to France on a British passport that he had acquired under a false name. French public opinion was inflamed by *Le Moniteur*: Britain was 'that lair, that den, the nest of homicide'.[18] It seemed this would lead to a return to stricter controls, and, as we saw above, Britain did made it illegal for British subjects to travel on foreign passports and for foreigners to travel on British passports.

Ironically, the real decline in the use of passports came almost immediately after the Orsini attack. Napoleon III had the sensible view that 'passports . . . are an embarrassment and an obstacle to the peaceable citizen but . . . utterly powerless' against trouble-makers. (Napoleon well knew how passports could be falsified. In 1831, the future Emperor, then himself a revolutionary, escaped from Florence with a false British passport given him by the British Consul.) Among the 1858 changes was a loosening of the rules governing passports: now mayors and magistrates could support applications and, as noted earlier, the cost fell dramatically. Within two years, one estimate puts the annual number of tourists passing through Calais and Boulogne alone at not much under 180,000. In 1859 Norway abolished the need for passports and Sweden followed the next year. Then, on 16 December 1860, France abolished the need for passports for British subjects. If one so desired one could take a passport or simply write one's name on a piece of paper or a card. This would then be stamped by an official after one had 'declared' that one was British. The new Kingdom of Italy followed France's lead in 1862 and in 1870 this was extended to all Italy. At last, passports were 'falling into disuse in other countries'.[19]

Broadly speaking, from the 1860s tourists did not need passports to travel to the most frequently visited areas, although those venturing off the beaten track could meet policemen who knew nothing of the changes. Two London architects discovered this in 1864 when they were arrested for not having passports while walking in the south of France. A mounted gendarme would not believe that the British did not require them: 'How can that be? No Frenchman can go from one village to another without a passport.' The architects further enraged the slightly drunken official by offering him a five-franc bribe and were lucky to be released by a higher official after they, like others before them, had been marched to a nearby town. Travellers making short trips to countries such as Belgium and the Netherlands increasingly did not bother to get the documents, as they were only occasionally useful, but those penetrating into the remoter reaches of the Russian or Turkish Empires were advised to have them. When, in 1882, Belgium announced it was once again going to demand passports in an attempt to fight terrorists, *The Times* exploded: 'Never was a more senseless custom instituted than that of passports ... Not a conspirator in Europe has been stopped by want of a passport from eluding detection.' Even where there were supposed to be passport inspections, passport officials often just waved people through. Even so, almost every guide-book still urged travellers to get passports (or have cards with their names stamped by an official) simply because it still provided virtually the only authoritative form of identification. Tourists used them to pick up letters at a *post restante*, to claim the service of a British Consul or to verify their signature on a cheque. Certain sights, such as the Arsenal in Venice or private art collections owned by various noblemen still insisted on passports.[20]

As noted earlier, in February 1915 Britain finally gave in to the demands that bearers be identified. All existing passports were declared invalid. The new passports, for the first time in British history, were issued for specific periods, in this case, two years and included photographs.[21] However, in 1915, people travelling to Europe were usually carrying rifles, not passports.

In the early decades of the nineteenth century, crossing the Channel was the most difficult, unpleasant and sometimes danger-ous part of a European trip. In the years immediately after Waterloo, travellers going by the shortest route (Dover–Calais) faced a number of hurdles. The trip from London to Dover by coach could take anything from twelve to twenty-four hours. On arrival they would have to find a ship to take them and would then have to negotiate getting out to the ship, after which they would wait for the outgoing tide. If lucky the passage might take only six hours.[22] Having arrived, travellers, such as the artists Haydon and

Wilkie, then had to get ashore. After this they had to cope with Customs and passport officials and then they faced a forty-eight-hour trip to Paris. Travel was not for the faint-hearted.

The four most popular points of departure were Brighton, Dover, Folkestone and London's Tower Stairs, although travellers could also use any place on the coast where they could find a ship. Folkestone had a harbour as did Dover, where the pier was a 'great use in protecting the packet'. Brighton had a good coach service from London but no harbour, and its fares were not the cheapest. Southampton (usually used for Le Havre) was harder to get to from London but had a harbour, which meant that, like Dover and Folkestone, carriages could be taken. If passengers were wealthy enough to take their own carriages (and sometimes horses) the vehicles and horses would be sent ahead. The carriages could be dismantled and placed on board or, weather permitting, hoisted intact on to the packet and secured to the deck. The horses would be transferred in slings and the owners could retire to their carriages for privacy if not comfort. Few could afford this luxury: 950 packets arrived in Calais in 1835 with 15,019 passengers, but there were only 485 carriages and 605 horses. Of the 924 packets that left Calais for England there were only 368 carriages and 66 horses. If we assume that most people returned home that same year we can also assume the 117 carriages that did not return were either sold or owned by people staying longer. What happened to the 539 horses is anyone's guess. Given French appetites, one fears the worst.[23]

In the early years travellers made their own arrangements from wherever they departed. One army officer on his way to Paris in 1821 found that at Dover 'the English packets would not sail as they had not passengers enough so we took our passage in . . . a small french [*sic*] vessel'. He was furious when forced to pay sixpence 'for the ladder to go down into the vessel'. However they travelled, people could never be sure where they would land because of the prevailing winds. As one lady wrote from Dover, 'We embark tomorrow morning, but whether we land at Calais, or Boulogne depends on Signor Vent.'[24]

At London's Tower Stairs, Dover, Folkestone and Southampton, packets could make use of the quaysides or harbour at high tide and could do the same at Calais, Boulogne and Le Havre. Where there was no quay or harbour (as at Brighton) or when the tide was out and the ships could not get close to the shore, they stayed anchored some way off. In 1814 a traveller described how people coped at Calais:

> The tide being out . . . we could not get into the harbour, and . . . we were glad to accept the offers of some boats which hastened . . . to offer their services in landing us; this, however, they did not exactly perform, being too large to get very near the shore, to which we were each of us carried by three Frenchmen, one to each leg, and a third behind. This service I had often had performed by one of my fellow-subjects, and it seemed to verify the old saying, that *'one Englishman is equal to three Frenchmen.'*

To add insult to injury this 1814 traveller had to pay each porter a shilling and the boatman five shillings, a total of eight shillings in his case. Young Edward Hawtrey was amazed when he landed in Calais the next year to find 'hundreds of ragamuffins dirty and half naked leaping and dancing about in the water'. Whether the boys were begging or offering to carry luggage, they were a standard sight in the early years of travel. As this 1814 visitor noted, the use of men's, and occasionally strong women's backs to carry passengers to the rowing boats, which in turn took them to the packets, was not confined to France. Nor were the exorbitant fees which amounted 'in many cases to the whole cost of the passage'. When the poet and banker Samuel Rogers left for France he noted in his diary that he had 'Set sail at dusk from the beach at Brighton in a crouded [rowing] boat. A luminous sea . . . Met with the packet, & after many attempts, got on board. A long calm & short rolling sea . . . a voyage of 30 hours.'[25]

Rogers's was undoubtedly a long crossing, but he was lucky in having a calm sea. Most passengers, crowded onto small packets, were less fortunate and accidents were not unusual: Lady Stanhope, for example, twice broke her arm while getting into rowing boats at Calais, while Fanny Burney, who went over late in November 1814, endured 'such violent and unremitting sufferings, that when arrived, I was unable to walk on shore'. The poor woman had nearly drowned while her husband and another man received almost fatal injuries while rescuing her. Despite his injuries her husband 'hired me an escort . . . to carry me, by relays, on an armchair to Calais's famous Dessein's Hotel'.[26]

A minority of travellers made their own eccentric arrangements. When Colonel Thomas Thornton, a wealthy Yorkshire sportsman, left Southampton for Rouen in September 1814 he was determined not just to take his three carriages but his coachman, dog-feeders, chief butler, falconer, keeper, two grooms, three hawks, ten horses, thirty guns, 120 hounds and six travelling companions. Predictably he had difficulty finding a vessel and ended up paying the enormous sum of £150. It is not surprising that there were 'thousands of spectators' to watch this extraordinary embarkation. After a thirty-hour crossing the party reached the mouth of the Seine at Le Havre, where Thornton became frustrated: the ship was too heavy to sail to Rouen but he got a £30 rebate. Seven years later the radical journalist Leigh Hunt set off in November 1821 to join Shelley and Byron in Italy to 'set up a liberal periodical'. Hunt, never the most practical of men, admitted that 'it was not very discreet to go many hundred miles by sea in winter-time with a large family; but a voyage was thought cheaper than a journey by land'. On 16 November the party sailed from Tower Stairs to go round the coast to Plymouth. Hunt's small brig was loaded (unbeknown to him) with fifty barrels of gunpowder destined for Greek rebels fighting Turkish rule. Whilst Hunt comforted himself by reading Condorcet's *View of the Progress of Society* his wife and family devoted themselves to seasickness. They eventually arrived at Plymouth, where they waited until 13 May 1822 for ship to Italy. They finally reached Leghorn (Livorno) early in July, exhausted, emaciated and ill.[27]

If Hunt had paid more attention to the news he could have saved his family and himself a lot of trouble because on 10 June 1821 the *Rob Roy*, the French Post Office's first paddle-steamer, entered Dover Harbour. Five days later the ship returned to Calais and, although she only had a few passengers, a new age had begun. By August there were daily crossings and increasing numbers. Within a year the Royal Mail was using two paddle-steamers to carry post and passengers from Dover to Calais and by 1826, it was using only steam ships, admittedly with sails in case of emergencies. From 1823 there was publicity for the new vessels in Regent's Park's famous Diorama, a form of panorama. Spectators could 'travel' without the usual discomforts on a steamer from Dover to Calais, thanks to the use of painted scenes and special lighting.[28]

The new vessels were only about fifteen feet wide and eighty feet long. Driven by a thirty-horsepower engine, each had a displacement of about 100 tons. (A modern cross-Channel ferry can be over 100 feet wide and over 600 feet long and have a gross tonnage of over 40,000.) However, unlike sailing ships they were no longer at the mercy of the wind. Passengers could be sure of their destinations and departures and could now consult printed timetables. Sadly, these improvements did not necessarily make for more comfortable trips. When Lady Blessington crossed the Channel in 1822 she watched the ship 'tossing and heaving near the pier' and noted the misery that 'makes us acquainted with strange companions . . . I have never entered one without beholding a most heterogeneous medley of people, the greater part with countenances indicative of sufferings actual or prospective.' Three years later the poet Thomas Campbell found that the ship was 'more noisy and turbulent in her motions than a sailing packet; very sick, and slept but little'. However, with increasing numbers of travellers the ships got larger and by the late 1830s, at the height of the travelling season – the summer and early autumn – they were carrying about 300 passengers each even if half 'had to walk about or sleep on tables'.[29]

There were also widespread improvements in getting people on to the ships. After the Royal Suspension Chain Pier was opened in

Brighton in 1823 passengers could board packets when the tide was in. As so often in the history of travel, improvements bred further improvements. Starting in 1824 a nine-hour crossing, operating twice a week, was organized between Brighton and Dieppe where the incoming British paddle-steamer was announced by the town crier marching up and down the Grande Rue ringing his bell. When Mariana Starke published the fifth edition of her guide-book in 1828 she could refer to 'persons who prefer crossing the Channel in a Sailing-Boat, to going in the *usual* way [authors' emphasis], in a Steam-Packet'. Steam-packets, she insisted, 'are less liable than other vessels to produce sea-sickness'. With greater accuracy she reassured wealthy travellers that 'carriages, without being dismounted are safely conveyed'.[30] By 1827, only six years after the *Rob Roy* arrived, steam ships dominated the scene with daily sailings during the summer and early autumn.

The cost of getting to the Continent was considerable: ships travelling between Dover and Calais charged the same as those travelling between Holyhead and Dublin, although the cross-Channel route was only one-third as long. In part this was due to the high taxes levied by French ports. In 1814, when travel resumed, these stood at £14 to £15 a ship regardless of size. What travellers paid depended on not just on the number in their party but on whether or not they took their servants, carriage, and horses. A couple with two children over twelve, a four-wheel carriage, two horses and two female servants leaving from London in 1828 would have paid the enormous sum of £21 for the best cabin. Members of our travelling family would each have been allowed 112 pounds of luggage free of charge but dogs would have cost five shillings each. The family had to send its luggage to the London Custom House no later than 1 p.m. on the day before sailing. The keys to their trunks went to the packet agent. If this family had opted for the cheapest fare it would still have cost them £12 12*s* and in neither case did the figure include the various harbour and Customs' fees. These were not inconsiderable: when George Jervoise left Dover in 1826 he had to pay 10*s* 6*d* for his carriage, five shillings for his servant, four shillings for sundries, a shilling for town dues and another shilling for harbour dues. All this was in addition to the £8 he had already spent for his passage An individual travelling without carriage or servant from Dover could cross for as little as ten shillings and sixpence but this did not include the fares to Dover and the various fees. A final but daunting choice was to book an all-in trip on a public coach from London to Paris, Switzerland or Italy. Costs ranged from £2 14s to £5 return per person.[31]

Having finally made it on to their ships, travellers now faced getting across the Channel. When Edward Hawtrey crossed in August 1815 he told his mother that 'for three or four hours, which seemed ten, I was in a state which is indescribable. It finished when, I firmly believe, no particle of gastric juice remained in my body.' The lucky ones could actually fall asleep. Mary Shelley was one of these but her suffering came when she woke up from time to time to ask where the boat was, only to receive the 'dismal answer each time, "Not quite half way"'. Most retired to the cabin below, which resembled a 'field of battle littered by the slain' as people collapsed on to tables, bunks, chairs and the floor to vomit their way across the Channel. Stewards handed round basins and some heartless wretches even demanded tips. Rumour had it that Lord Henry Seymour had been so sick on one crossing to France that he vowed never to return home. He made do with a life in Paris, devoted to racing (he established the Jockey Club) and 'eccentricities'. When he died he left bequests to maintain his four favourite horses and an annual income of £36,000 (some £2,635,200 today) to Paris's hospitals.[32]

The greatest complaint was the new ships' noise and vibrations from the engines. Emma Roberts, who crossed in 1839, agreed that the ship was handsomely fitted up and with state-cabins, one for men and one for women, with sofas and beds. Meals were served for those who could keep them down. The only drawback was 'the tremulous motion and the stamping of the engine'. Still, she consoled herself that these were preferable 'to the violent rolling and pitching of a sailing vessel'. Charles Greville, with his collection of passports, cynically noted later that on his ship from London to the open sea 'all the people were very merry and very hungry . . . It was ludicrous to see the disappearance of their hilarity and to contrast it with their woebegone faces when they were heaved about in the Channel.' Greville was one of the lucky few who 'slept very comfortably'.[33]

Whatever Mariana Starke had written, sea-sickness – 'preaching to the fishes' to use the Victorian phrase – remained a curse to many if not most travellers, and there was no end of suggested remedies. Marianne Thornton's party tried religion in 1817: one member read one of Dr Watts's sermons but 'before he could finish it everyone began to feel sick'. Marianne went to her bed but still had 'no relief but in silent prayer'. In one crossing during the early 1820s Sir Richard Phillips, a publisher, amused fellow passengers by arranging for an armchair to be placed on the deck. Sir Richard then sat down and began to 'raise himself up and down, as on horseback' as they crossed the Channel. While others called for basins Sir Richard bounced his way to France. This idea may have inspired the invention of another device, a 'sea couch', advertised in 1827 as a 'swinging seat, couch, or bed' based on springs and suspended from the ceiling. William Ewart, the radical MP who was responsible for creating our system of free libraries, crossed in the 1850s. He preferred an 'old-fashioned precaution' and had himself 'mesmerized' or hypnotized. (His biographer does not say if this worked.)[34]

When Joanna Horner crossed in the next decade she walked round the ship distributing homeopathic 'pillules to ward off seasickness' with what results we are again not told. Henry Gaze advised his clients to get berths in the centre of the ship where they should lie down and sleep. If they could not sleep they should stay in their berths and concentrate on pleasant (non-nautical) thoughts. If *this* did not work they should try the new drug from France, 'anti-Nausea'. Above all they must not take creosote as some recommended because it did not work. Lady Augusta Stanley was more realistic twenty years later when she 'took some drops of chloroform, to the great contempt of the steward' who told her that 'nothing keeps off sickness except staying on shore'. Lord Salisbury, Queen Victoria's last Prime Minister, remained firmly convinced that eating dry biscuits prevented seasickness. Real relief came when ships grew large enough to minimize the effects of the Channel. Chaloner Chute noted in 1873 that on his trip from Calais to Dover there was 'a good wind blowing, but the boat being a large one we did not suffer'. Such was not always the case and occasionally when sea-sickness did occur, in others that is, it brought satisfaction: a Miss Fife was delighted in 1897 when she saw 'the girl who had jilted Charlie Branch extremely sick and waited on by a poor specimen of a husband till he fled out of sight to be ill too – I did enjoy that'. Finally, some felt seasickness was related to one's social class. On one 1913 crossing the usually acerbic Lytton Strachey, when not himself being sick, noticed that 'the English Upper Classes remained life-size to the end'.[35] That must have been very reassuring.

Novelists had great sport with Channel crossings because of their inherent excitement and because they brought together groups of disparate people. In 1839 Thackeray wrote about 'Wives, elderly stout husbands, nursemaids, and children . . . a *danseuse* from the opera . . . a group of young ladies . . . going to Paris to learn how to be governesses . . . two splendidly dressed . . . milliners from the Rue Richelieu, who have just . . . disposed of their . . . Summer fashions . . . [and] the Rev. Mr. Snodgrass, with his pupils.' There are also a 'few Frenchmen' and 'many Jews'. The food served was as exotic as the mixture of passengers. For the main meal travellers could select from boiled beef, pickles and a 'great red raw Cheshire cheese' consumed with bottles of stout. Afterwards came tea and then brandy-and-water, consumed because it was said to be yet another way to prevent seasickness. Just in case the beef, the brandy, the pickles, the cheese, the stout and the brandy did not quite agree with sea travel, the steward reappeared with 'a heap of round tin vases, like those which are called, I believe, in America, *expectoratoons*, only these are larger'.[36] After all that food they would need to be.

The same year in which Thackeray described his crossing, Charles Lever, like Thackeray a frequent traveller, included a Dover–Calais crossing in his novel *Harry Lorrequer* (Chapter 23). As the ship approached Calais, Lever described behaviour which survives today in aeroplane journeys: 'Friendships, that promised a life-long endurance only half an hour ago, find here a speedy dissolution . . . All the various disguises which have been assumed . . . are here immediately abandoned, and, stripped of the travelling costume of urbanity and courtesy, which they put on for the voyage, they stand forth in all the unblushing front of selfishness and self-interest.'

Dickens described another aspect of a crossing when the steamer was approaching France, an aspect that also survives in air travel: 'And now I find that all the French people on board begin to grow, and all the English people to shrink. The French are nearing home, and shaking off a disadvantage, whereas we are shaking it on.'[37]

The next great advance in cross-Channel traffic, and one that would lay the foundation for modern tourism, occurred not at sea but on land: the railway. Britain led the world in the creation and spread of railways and the first connection to a port came in 1840 when Southampton was linked by railway to London. That same year the lawyer John Torr noted, 'Yesterday in London I could scarcely get credited when I said that twenty-four hours previously I was in Brussels. Having steam the whole way, it is a very quick journey.'[38] In 1841 Brighton got its link followed by Folkestone and Dover three years later. Newhaven got its railway in 1847 and began regular sailings to Dieppe. The year before, the Belgian government had begun its own steamboat services between Ostend and Dover. For the majority of travelling Britons, journeys to the Continent and holidays abroad would now be based on railways, on the rivalry between Folkestone and Dover and on that between the two major railway companies: the London, Chatham & Dover (LCD) and the South Eastern Railway (SER).

The South Eastern bought the harbour at Folkestone in 1842 and in the next year the town celebrated the beginning of a regular steam-packet service to Boulogne with a public breakfast and other festivities at the South-Eastern Pavilion Tavern. The directors laid on a special trip to Boulogne where the British were fêted by local dignitaries. The return trip took thirteen hours and forty-five minutes. The company announced that with a planned new steamer the trip would be reduced to four and a half hours. If people left at 6 a.m. they could have a day trip to Boulogne. Five years later the SER announced an 'express steamer', which allowed travellers to go from London Bridge Station to Paris's Gare du Nord via Boulogne in ten hours and thirty minutes. This was surpassed in 1850, when a group left London at 4 a.m. and reached Paris in ten hours and 20 minutes. After five hours and forty minutes in the French capital the visitors departed at 8 p.m. and arrived in London after nine hours and fifty-five minutes. True, the travellers had a 'contrary wind' and also had to use rowing boats to get to the packets, but as compensation they were on an 'express train'. The 500 mile return trip was covered in twenty hours and fifteen minutes and showed what could be done. For the first time in history, Londoners could have a day out in Paris, even if it did leave them shattered. The next advance came in the early 1850s when Parliament authorized the London, Brighton & South Coast Railway to operate its own ships. We can get an idea of the effect of all these changes by looking at the number of passengers who passed through the ports of Calais and Boulogne: in 1840 the total stood at just over 73,000; twenty years later it had soared to 180,000.[39]

For travellers the most important things were time and bother. By 1852 the normal journey from London to Paris via Folkestone and Boulogne was twelve hours and, via Dover and Calais, fourteen and a half. The fierce competition between the two companies was the stimulus for continued improvements, and in 1853 *Galignani's New Paris Guide* told readers that things were changing so fast that they must go to the railway offices in London for information.[40] In 1861 Victoria Station was opened as the SER's principal London terminus and the LCD's Charing Cross followed three years later. The difficulties of Dover Harbour were overcome with the opening of Admiralty Pier in 1862. (Calais would not catch up for almost thirty years.) Dover was a deep-water port, which meant that, regardless of the tide, ships could steam up to the quayside to meet the 'down trains' from London. In 1865 the South Eastern arranged for the luggage of returning passengers to be examined by Customs at Victoria and not at Dover, thereby ending one of the most irksome aspects of landing. By the end of the century, if passengers registered their bags at the station they would not be examined until arrival in Paris. Two years later the average time from London to Paris via Folkestone had fallen to ten and a half hours.[41]

There were also constant improvements in the vessels, especially those on the Dover–Calais route, which remained the shortest if sometimes the roughest. In the 1870s there was a spate of new designs because inventors were keen not just to improve the safety of ships but to increase their size and speed, and also to eliminate sea-sickness. One of the best known was Henry Bessemer, famous for his work in steel. Bessemer had suffered so badly from sea-sickness himself that in 1869 he began work on a radical new design. He wanted to mount the passenger cabins on axles which were controlled by hydraulic power through a gyroscope. While the hull of the ship would roll and pitch, the cabins would stay horizontal. He set up a company and poured the enormous sum of £34,000 into the project. On 8 May 1875 journalists were invited to Dover for the maiden trip. Sadly, the ship proved difficult to steer and on arrival in Calais it smashed into the pier. The Bessemer Saloon Ship and the company behind it disappeared from the scene.

More successful was the London, Chatham & Dover's *Castalia*. This had two 'half-ship' hulls with a four-foot gap between them which was bridged by a strong platform. In the gap were two paddle wheels, one behind the other, and four engine rooms. Soon there were 'enthusiastic accounts of the new channel steamer'. It was said she would be 'an effectual preventive of sea-sickness' and an early passenger, the Swiss historian Jacob Burckhardt, wrote in 1879 that 'we hardly felt anything, though we saw little ships quite near us pitching quite a lot'. However, what the *Castalia* gained in stability she lost in speed and could not make ten knots in an age where speed was becoming essential. There were also continuous efforts to increase the comfort of passengers. The *Invicta* was launched by the LCD in 1882, and combined speed with luxury. She had large promenade decks, electric lighting and a 'neatly-arranged refreshment bar', admittedly only in the first-class saloon. In addition, the designer had reduced the level of noise by use of 'Messenger's silent blow-off, which wholly obviates the roar of escaping steam, so trying to the nerves of susceptible passengers.' The unpleasant aspect of continuing improvements had been revealed by Henry Mayhew in the 1850s. Sailors suffered because 'every usable part of the vessel is sacrificed for passengers and for cargo'. The walls were wet and cold. When combined with the heat of the engines, they produced a steam-bath. Mayhew was told that 'a man . . . should have the constitution of a negro by day and an Esquimaux by night'.[42]

The *Invicta* was also the first steel ship to cross the Channel. At twenty-two knots she travelled from Dover to Calais in one hour and thirteen minutes. In the following year the company, using the same ship, was the first to begin a daily cross-Channel service year round and one that ignored the tides: the boat train left Victoria at 10 a.m. and passengers reached Paris at 6.50 p.m. – and this was seven years before Calais got a new deep-water harbour. The South Eastern Railway caught up in 1885, when Boulogne got its new harbour. The port's numerous grand hotels now offered weekend breaks with bed and board for as little as six francs or 4s 9d a day. In 1894, the first screw ship appeared, though widespread use had to wait for deep harbours. Two years later passengers were leaving Dover and arriving in Calais in just over an hour. Ships were becoming bigger as well as faster: that same year the

LCD launched three ships and each was 320 feet long, carried 791 people and had a horsepower of 6,450. (Seventy five years earlier, the original steam packets were 80 feet long, had thirty horse-power engines and carried about 60 passengers.) In 1903 the two major railway companies, now united, launched the *Queen*, the first turbine-driven ship to cross the Channel. She carried 1,200 passengers and was much faster though using the same amount of coal. The last paddle-steamer was withdrawn in 1909, the same year in which ships were being equipped with 'wireless tele-graphy'.[43]

Given the Victorians' success in railway tunnelling, proposals for a cross-Channel tunnel were inevitable and came from engineers in France and in Britain. The most promising appeared in 1867 when Monsieur Thome de Gammond published his plan for a Dover–Calais tunnel. The Franco-Prussian War delayed any action until 1873, when there was renewed talk. Supporters were anxious about the government's position whilst ministers were in their turn anxious about national security. The Conservative government's view was one of benign neutrality, but Queen Victoria was in no doubt: 'If England is to be connected with the continent, we shall have to keep up double Army, which we so *unwillingly* afford now!' There was some experimental boring both in France and in England, and by the early 1880s workmen had excavated a mile-long tunnel at Dover. In 1882, however, Parliament rejected the proposal to the great relief of many: the *Illustrated London News* had no doubt it was 'pleasanter and healthier to be ferried across the Channel ... than ... to undergo the gloomy penance of a submarine railway tunnel ... with a stifling atmosphere'. This did not stop further digging, although tunnel bills were again rejected in 1887 and 1890. The idea was revived in 1906 and again in 1913. In France there was a desire to draw closer to Britain as imperial Germany grew stronger; but in London people were less keen. The outbreak of war meant the end of discussions. In addition to tunnels there had also been proposals for a railway bridge to span the Channel in the 1890s, but these got little support.[44]

By 1914 fares in general had fallen, so that low costs were added
to efficiency, regularity and speed as natural attributes of travel.
Likewise, people increasingly came to regard crossing the Channel
as a means of entertainment. As the *Illustrated London News* put it,
'the short sea-passage either from Dover or Folkestone is a refreshment to the Londoner; and it is amusing, for a couple of hours, to
observe the figures . . . of those on board'. Such an assertion would
have been incomprehensible to early travellers, such as Edward
Hawtrey, Fanny Burney or Samuel Rogers.[45] Much of the excitement
had, perhaps, gone but so had many of the problems and dangers.
Few people whose letters, diaries, articles or published memoirs
cover these later decades even refer to their crossings. When the
Anglo-Irish writers Somerville and Ross described their trip to
Europe in the 1890s all they had to say about the crossing was 'there
is happily little to record'.[46] They were much more exercised by
learning to operate their new Kodak camera. By July 1914 there were
four daily crossings from London's Victoria Station to Paris via
Dover–Calais, each taking six hours and thirty minutes – a far cry
from the seventy-three hours endured in 1816. Was there any surer
sign of the unending progress of which the British were so proud?

'A Tyranny most repulsive to our British notions' was one travel-
writer's description of French custom officials, who introduced
tourists to European bureaucracy. *Douanniers* would come on
board to organize the disembarking of passengers in small batches,
so that they could then be 'marched to the Customs house'. Once
on shore they were pestered by 'touters' for hotels and petty
shopkeepers as they queued. The 'crush to get to your place for
your turn was dreadful'. After the passport inspection, described
above, they had to face Customs inspectors who were keen to find
contraband items and were known for their 'incivility, rapacity, and
wilful infliction of annoyance'. French officials who became irritated
by the tourists' 'occasional sallies of impatience' would call out
'*Cochons Anglais.*' The replies from the 'English pigs' were not
mentioned, which is probably just as well.[47]

These searches were particularly annoying to ladies. In 1819 Martha Bradford was on her way to Vienna with her husband, the newly appointed Embassy Chaplain. Coming ashore at Calais she was 'searched by a female Dragon' who 'examined us . . . She felt down our backs, up our stays and maul'd us all over.' The wife of a Nonconformist minister was 'taken by a class of men who looked, to her, the meanest set of ruffians she ever saw, and posted away, to a prison looking house, where they put her in the custody of some old French women, to be searched. She scolded, in her language, and resisted all she could, but they continued unpinning, etc, until they had searched her person thoroughly.' Luckily the inspectors found nothing and she was released, but 'she was so frightened, that she looked unnatural', at least to her husband. Even when the search did not take place immediately after landing it was an unpleasant experience, especially for first-time travellers.[48]

There were ways to make the ordeal less unpleasant. Travellers prepared to spend a night in the port could postpone their suffering by leaving the bulk of their luggage with the Customs' officials. They were allowed to keep their overnight bags and could go straight to their hotels. Of course this only delayed the torment, as William Etty – later the pious painter of voluptuous nudes of both sexes – discovered. He stumbled ashore at Dieppe in 1816, after a horrific crossing. His hand luggage was examined by an official in a cocked hat and he was let go. The next day he was summoned to the Customs office for the searching of his trunk and portmanteaus. Etty unlocked his trunk and the porters began to unpack the carefully arranged items. Out came a tea canister followed by a large supply of sugar, then a cache of tea and a kettle. The officials began to get suspicious when they found a second kettle which was confiscated because it looked unused and they assumed he was going to sell it. However, Etty's landlord came to his rescue and got his extra kettle restored. Arriving travellers could also follow one of the '*Commissioniares*' (or 'touts') from local hotels who had been pestering them. These men could sometimes 'persuade' the officials to be lenient. Occasionally officials would examine only the servants, presumably on the ground that ladies and gentlemen did not smuggle.[49]

European countries, Britain included, prohibited the importation of certain items in order to protect native industries, tax revenues or state monopolies. For travellers this was a nightmare: they were obliged to tell officials of any object that was new – and of course many objects would have been bought for a trip. They therefore had to prove that they were not going to sell that object, as we have seen with Etty's difficulties with his second kettle. While some items were absolutely forbidden (clocks, embroidery and gloves were but three) others could be brought in. However, if judged not to be for private use, they would be taxed up to 43 per cent of the value as determined by the officials. The list of items that could be brought in subject to duty was incredibly long and included books, shoes, cards, horses, carpets, cheese, picture frames, jewels, lace, leather, linen, cotton, silk, woollen cloth, musical instruments, paper, jewels, walking sticks, wine, toys, gunpowder and steam-engines, although we can assume the last item was not usually found. Worst of all, tea was on the list. The system was a virtual invitation to bribery.[50]

In Sardinia officials were concerned with smuggled arms and salt, which amused one traveller: 'Only fancy a gentleman . . . being supposed to carry *salt* in his portmanteau!' In the event, some five months earlier custom officials in Venice had confiscated a 'jar of Maldon Salt' which another traveller had packed because he could not 'eat the dirty stuff' used there. However, while some places, such as Venice, had a monopoly on the sale of salt, all officials were obsessed with tobacco. As French import duties on cigars were about thirteen shillings in the pound, we can understand the British willingness to smuggle: thirteen shillings could pay for a day in Paris. The continual search for tobacco caused annoyance to men, since most felt that European tobacco, with the exception of the Spanish, was inferior.[51]

During the early decades of the century in Italy and Austria, officials were also keen to find prohibited books and sometimes

English newspapers, which were regarded as particularly dangerous. The Authorzed (King James) Version of the Bible was prohibited in most Catholic countries. (As most continentals did not read English the ban seems rather pointless.) The Nonconformist minister Thomas Sheardown was lucky that his Bible, hidden inside his coat, had not been confiscated. In the Papal States inspectors also looked out for banned books, which in 1850 included works by Schiller, Shakespeare, Molière, Lamartine, Ovid, Lucian and Sophocles.[52] Even in France, where there was less concern about books, there still was, up to the end of the 1850s, a duty of ten francs on every 100 kilograms of books but 100 francs or £4 if the books were in French. This was a special burden for the many travellers in the early days who carried numerous books, especially if they were going on a long tour in their own carriages. The concern about books and newspapers had disappeared by the late nineteenth century.

As with tobacco, so with tea: high duties encouraged smuggling. On one crossing, an observant American noticed two good-looking young English women wrapped in an extraordinary number of woollen garments and shawls. Being particularly observant of female legs, or at least of the little he could see, the student also noticed that their stockings were bulging in a rather peculiar way. Eventually the young tea-smugglers asked other female passengers to wear some of their shawls in which tea was hidden. The next day the two triumphant women called round the various Calais hotels collecting their illicit goods.[53] It was commonly believed, at least by men, that women were the greater smugglers, usually because of their love of lace. Writers such as Douglas Jerrold were quick to seize on this and in 1845 his *Punch* serial, *Mrs. Caudle's Curtain Lectures*, featured a Customs house scene. Mrs Caudle, who had persuaded her henpecked husband to join the ranks of Boulogne 'excursionists', was beside herself when he does nothing to prevent her hand luggage from being examined for smuggled lace. 'And you could stand by, and see that fellow with mustachios rummage my basket and pull out my night-cap and rumple the border . . . it

went to my heart like a stab – crumpled it as if it were any duster
. . . I don't speak their nasty gibberish . . . to be searched, indeed!'[54]

In England, once people left the ports they were finished with
Customs, but on the Continent this was never the case. In the first
decades after Waterloo people faced numerous encounters with
Customs officials, particularly if travelling through the mosaic of
states that made up Germany and Italy. Not only did travellers find
them on entering a country but often on coming into a province
within that country and then on entering a city within that province.
The annoyances persisted on the return journey as well. One way
round this was to have one's trunks 'plumbed', that is, sealed with
lead to show they had not been opened since the last inspection.
But this was only good within the country where the plumb was
fixed. On entering another country the plumb would be broken
open. In Italy there were always fees to be paid and a little
something extra. If the bribe was sufficient, the official replied, '*Va
bene.*' If he did not, the wise traveller gave more.[55]

As well as passport checks and Customs' inspections, travellers
also had to cope with the local import duties that were levied by
most continental cities. These were usually known as *octroi* and
were particularly heavy on food and drink: anyone taking cheese
into Paris, for example, would have to pay ten centimes per kilo.
Few people would have been travelling with agricultural products
that were subject to duty, but searching for these was yet another
nuisance. Etty complained about being stopped 'by the paltry
rascals . . . to pay for a few pounds of sugar . . . it is difficult for an
Englishman to restrain his indignation at the wretches who annoy
him everywhere, like mosquitoes'. The outraged Yorkshire painter
saw his poor tea things gone over yet again when he arrived in
Paris. The most popular guide-book to the city warned that 'no
individual, whatever be his dignity or functions is exempt' since his
carriage, possessions and person would all be searched.[56]

Customs officials throughout Europe were disliked, but in Italy
they were often loathed because of the continuous demands for a
buono mano – a 'good hand' or tip. In 1831, when young James

Estcourt landed at Civitavecchia, Rome's port, 'it was not [until] the evening before I could get away even though I bribed the Custom House officer with about *a shilling* to let my baggage pass un-searched. Two other officers of the Pope's I afterwards treated in the same manner and with the same good results. They take the money willingly and openly.' Twenty years later, little had improved. Bishop Hynes, himself a Catholic, fumed in Naples: 'The abuses connected with the Dogana [Customs] are flagrant enough in the Roman [Papal] States, but through the Neapolitan Dominions they are a great deal worse. At every step you are asked for money or threatened with a visitation of your luggage. After passing the first and real custom house today, we had to bribe the soldiers at two gates besides before we got to the Hotel.' Guide-books and experi-enced travellers advised tourists that in Italy, excluding the areas governed by Austria, bribes were a recognized part of salaries. Even in English ports one travel writer saw half-a-crown (two shillings and sixpence) handed over because British officials 'are by no means free from the itching palm of their race [occupation]'.[57]

Travel books and guides were often guilty of double standards concerning Customs. While denouncing continental rigour they less frequently criticized the stringent rules in Britain, as seen in the fate of Mrs Onslow's dress. In 1820 Cranley Onslow and his wife, whilst visiting his cousin in France, crossed into Switzerland. On re-entering France 'some ... French Custom house scoundrels' claimed that Mrs Onslow's dress had been bought in Switzerland and charged him '3 Napoleons and a half' [almost £3] to release it. When the couple arrived back in Dover, still smarting from their treatment at the hands of the French they met another 'Custom House scoundrel', this time English. This man claimed Mrs Ons-low's dress had been made in France, and duly confiscated it. Having already paid French duty, the poor woman now lost her dress to the 'rapacious vigilance' of the hated British Customs official just as her husband had lost his three-and-a-half Napoleons to the equally hated French.[58]

By the 1850s there were demands for reform as part of the

crusade for free trade, and the House of Commons appointed a Select Committee to look into the matter. In December 1851 the committee was supported by a public meeting in London at which merchants expressed their 'great and general dissatisfaction' with the way the Board of Customs worked. The committee's report devoted an entire chapter to 'Passengers' Luggage' and complained of the 'very disagreeable impressions' Customs officials made on arriving passengers. Reform was now in the air, and three treaties greatly reduced the number of dutiable items in France and Britain. Of even greater importance, the sheer number of tourists meant that rigorous standards could not be maintained. The system had to give, and complaints about Customs steadily declined from the 1860s. People arriving at St Malo in 1906, for example, noticed that officials marked the bags with chalk as quickly as they could without opening any of them. The overwhelming number of passengers left them without any alternative. The pressure was greatest on Paris since the city was always '*un pôle exclusif du tourisme britannique*'. By 1874 a minor poet arriving in Paris was relieved to find 'great improvement on old times in the ease with which luggage passed the Customs-house, the officers only opening and scarcely looking at one portmanteau, & only enquiring about *tabac*'. The same was true of Italy, where any examination 'was generally lenient'. When it came to the *octroi*, 'a simple declaration' from the tourist was sufficient. By 1908 tourists were advised to hand over their luggage and keys to hotel porters who would simply tell officials that 'all is well'.[59]

When bags were opened, the thing that most annoyed people was having to repack them. One traveller had his revenge in late nineteenth-century Germany. On his way to Berlin, Henry Labouchere, a radical MP and proprietor of the feared scandal sheet *Truth*, had all his possessions unpacked by a German official. 'Labby,' as he was known to his few friends and many enemies, demanded that the man repack the bag. The man refused and warned that the Berlin train was departing. The fuming MP would not budge and asked to send a telegram. The telegrapher was soon hurrying back to his superiors to read what he had just sent to Prince Bismarck. Labouchere deeply regretted that he could not accept the Reich Chancellor's gracious invitation to dinner because he had been detained by the rudeness of some petty officials. The officials were soon apologizing and bowing to 'His Excellency' and laid on a private train to take His Excellency to Berlin, free of charge, in time for His Excellency's dinner appointment. Labby's anger was assuaged, his bag was repacked – by the officials – and he went luxuriously on his way. An embarrassing international incident was avoided – or would have been had Labby not been lying through his teeth.[60]

Chapter 6

Keep Moving!

*I*n his 1824 poem *The Delinquent Traveller*, Samuel Taylor Coleridge bemoaned the new age of foreign travel:

> *Keep moving! Steam, or Gas, or Stage,*
> *Hold, cabin, steerage, hencoop's cage –*
>
> . . .
>
> *For move you must! 'Tis now the rage,*
> *The law and fashion of the Age*

Travel may have become the fashion of the age but it was a fashion that required a great deal of those involved, especially in these early years. Having survived a crossing, the most important challenge facing travellers in the decades before railways arrived was choosing how to travel. As today, the choice depended on the size of one's purse.

British travelling carriages had long been famous for their quality: 'every thing [was] so compact, so snug, so finished and fitting. The wheels that roll on patent axles without rattling; the body that hangs so well on its springs.' Carriages were expensive and those who bought them knew that their vehicles were signs of status. The one owned by Ruskin's parents had a 'general stateliness of effect' designed 'for the abashing of plebeian beholders'.[1] The abashed

European plebs would have been slightly less impressed if they had known that Ruskin's papa was only a wine merchant.

The fashion for travelling carriages was largely formed by two of the century's great Romantic heroes. Napoleon's 'military carriage' had been captured after his flight from Waterloo and was exhibited in Britain where it 'excited more interest . . . than anything for a number of years'. The second fashion-setter was Lord Byron, who used Napoleon's carriage as the basis for the one he designed for his continental rambles, which he began in 1816. This vast and elegant vehicle required at least four horses and featured a library along with facilities for sleeping and dining. Like Napoleon's, Byron's met a sad fate in Belgium. Although the carriage had been built by the well-known carriage-maker Baxter, it broke down three times in the first few days. Byron was furious since Baxter had charged the huge sum of £500. 'We broke down by a damned wheel (on which Baxter should be broken)', Byron moaned to a friend who was told to demand a reduction. Before we feel too much sympathy for the poet we should remember that when Baxter asked for payment his claim was airily dismissed: 'Baxter must wait – at least a year.'² After seven years, Baxter was still waiting.

Travelling carriages modelled on Byron's provided many comforts: Martha Bradford, the clergyman's wife whom we met earlier, said that her children were 'enchanted with the Coach'. Its size allowed them '*riotous* enjoyment . . . to the great anguish of our shins'. Many of these coaches had a form of commode, and since it was the custom for men to have lengthy walks along the route, ladies could take advantage of their absence to use the *chaise percée*.³ Wealthy people with large families could afford more than one carriage; in October 1840 George Lucy, a Warwickshire squire, brought two for his wife, Mary, their five children, a fourteen month old baby, its nurse, a tutor for the elder children and a footman. The Lucys were embarking on a tour which was planned to last at least two years and they had let their country house, Charlecote, where one of the coaches can still be seen. Underneath they had 'every possible thing . . . we might want', including three beds for the smaller children, three tin baths, a supply of school books, bed linen, tea and arrowroot. However, the baby died as the coaches were ascending the Alps and Mary Lucy recalled, 'for eleven long hours did I travel with his dear lifeless body on my lap ere we reached Turin. Never can I forget that night of anguish.' Once in Turin they arranged for the body to be sent home for burial.[4] Other carriages, such as the Ruskins's, had 'store-cellars under the seats, secret drawers . . . invisible pockets under padded lining' as well as cushions that would not slip and rounded corners 'for more delicate repose'. Some, like Admiral Boyle's, sported a small table and a cupboard for the luncheon basket and tea-making things. Underneath was a hamper containing the Scotch terrier bitch which was allowed out when they stopped. She obviously made good use of her free time for by the time they reached Florence she had her own 'small family'.[5]

When Charles Dickens decided on a long family trip to the Continent he had a look at Lord Vernon's carriage, referred to in Chapter 2, and was suitably impressed: 'You touch a spring and a chair flies out, touch another spring and a bed appears, touch another spring and a closet of pickles opens, touch another spring and disclose a pantry.' There were also storage areas for food, while underneath were nine portable baths, one inside the other. Nothing confirmed British wealth more than the spectacle of such carriages. Complete with gilded coats of arms, they made stately trips along continental roads or through crowded streets. This was all the more impressive because in these years comparatively few private carriages belonging to other nationalities were seen on the roads.[6]

Less well-off travellers could buy used carriages on arrival on the Continent. *Gailgnani's Messenger*, the newspaper for Britons in Europe, frequently advertised bargains ranging from 'a fashionably built Cabriolet with horse' for 4,000 francs to a 'nearly new Travelling Calèche' at 1,000 francs. (Like their descendants in the used-car trade, carriage salesmen preferred 'nearly new' to 'used'.)[7] Likewise, travellers could have bought a used carriage in London.

$\mathcal{B}$ad behaviour by British tourists during Mass in Catholic churches was frequently censured in guide books and by writers and illustrators including Richard Doyle in *The Foreign Tour of Messrs Brown Jones & Robinson*, from which this illustration section is taken. It shows the three eponymous heroes, and others in the background, interrupting the service. The artist, Richard Doyle, was himself Catholic.

$\mathcal{A}$nother place where bad behaviour was condemned was in theatres and opera houses. Then, as now, travellers frequently behaved abroad in ways they never would at home. Jones, like so many travellers, also 'dressed down' as seen in his plaid trousers and 'wide-awake' hat.

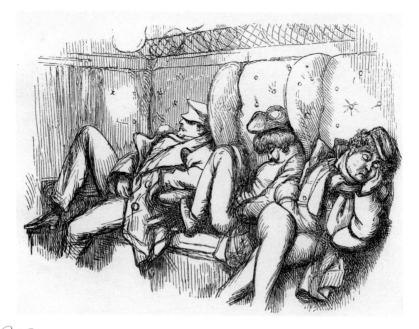

Here, Brown, Jones and Robinson sleep their way across Belgium en route to Germany and the Rhine. The popularity of the Rhine trips, the attractions of Paris and the appeal of French ports meant that for most travellers, Belgium became little more than an extended 'railway platform' as *The Times* put it.

Cologne was not just famous for its perfume but for its sewers. Brown, Jones and Robinson are all wearing the 'wide-awake' hats and in one case, the checked trousers favoured by male tourists.

COMPANY ON BOARD THE RHINE BOAT.

This drawing of passengers on a Rhine boat shows both British tourists and Germans. On the far right is the 'English Grumbler', a British matron (stout), a tutor with his students, and numerous 'hairy, smoky young Germans' with long beards. On the far left were British women with their notorious protective head gear or 'uglies'. Behind them stand a Catholic priest and two nuns, unusual sights for the British.

Here we see Doyle's version of the pompous British traveller, complete with his checked trousers, figuring 'how many thousands a-year' he would need to maintain one of the castles he is observing along the Rhine. Behind him, Brown is making this sketch.

$\mathscr{R}$obinson is searching his German bed for fleas. The presence of fleas in hotels and on trains was a constant complaint and the British were warned by travel-writers to take protective measures.

$\mathscr{S}$ketching was a favourite pastime of many travellers in the era before cheap photography, and even beyond. Here we see Brown, wearing his 'wide-awake' hat and with his courier's bag, sketching two German *fräulein*, one of whom is pleased, the other less so. The British were fascinated by the dress of European peasants which began to disappear toward the end of the century.

ROME—THE BRITISH TOURIST AND THE DYING GLADIATOR

*B*ritish tourists shown in a drawing from *The Graphic* of 13 April 1872. The man is holding the relevant Murray's *Handbook*, which has a diagram of the rooms in Rome's Capitoline Museum, and he appears to be following its advice: 'No one can mediate upon it without the most melancholy feelings.' *The Dying Gaul* (as it is now usually known) was much admired: Napoleon had included it among his loot and Byron celebrated it in *Childe Harold*.

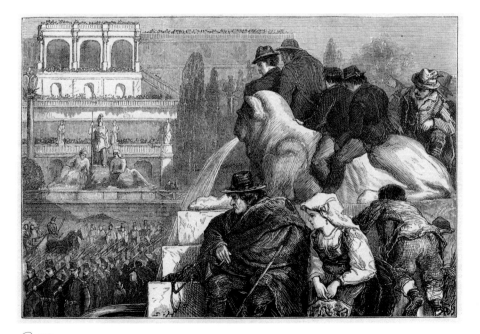

*A*fter Rome became the capital of the new Kingdom of Italy in 1870, the new Italian monarchy put on military shows in an attempt to rival Papal ceremonies but few tourists were impressed.

*B*eggars in front of St. Peter's in Rome from *The Graphic* of 24 February 1872. 'Most of the Roman beggars exhibit mutilated limbs' claimed *Blackwood's Magazine* in 1829 and British tourists constantly moaned about being beset by beggars throughout Italy.

*F*ox hunting in the Campagna with a Roman aqueduct in the background. In the 1830s the Pope allowed English residents to establish a hunt, *La Società Romana della Caccia alla Volpe* which still meets. By 1899, according to Murray's last *Handbook for Rome*, it had about 100 members and hunted twice a week from November to March. The Campagna was a favourite spot for riders as well as hunters.

$\mathcal{T}$wo sketches from *The Graphic* of 24 October 1874 show (above) a group of tourists scrambling across a mountain in the Alps. The celebrated glacier the Mer de Glace (below) was larger in the mid-nineteenth century than today. Murray advised that those who did not intend a long walk to 'gain a just idea of its character should walk, far enough upon it, 50 or 100 yards . . . to enjoy the novel feeling of walking on a glacier and finding the sun intensely hot upon the ice.' Few of these walkers seem equipped with *alpenstocks*, let alone sensible shoes or clothes, although the second man from the left has got a veil to protect him from the sun.

THE TIME-HONOURED BRITISH THREAT

Indignant Anglo-Saxon (to provincial French innkeeper, who is bowing his thanks for the final settlement of his exorbitant and much-disputed account). "Oh, oui, mossoo! pour le matière de ça, je paye! Mais juste vous regardez ici, mon ami! et juste—vous—marquez—mes—mots! Je paye—mais je mette le dans la 'Times!'"

*A*mong periodicals, *Punch* had most fun with British tourists. Here the British paterfamilias utters the ultimate threat of all dissatisfied British travellers. Complaints about foreign hotels were a frequent topic in letters in *The Times*.

*A*s travel expanded so did complaints about one's fellow travellers, especially if they were 'cockney' or lower down the social scale. *Punch's* Mr. 'Arry Belville sports a fashionable white top hat, speaks bad French and drops his 'h's.

This is what Dickens did in 1844: he found one 'about the size of your library; with night-lamps and day-lamps and pockets and . . . the most extraordinary contrivances . . . amply provided in all respects' for £45.[8] Also, well into the twentieth century it was common for people to hire carriages from rural inns or city hotels for short excursions. Amelia Edwards did this to explore the Dolomites.

Carriages were, of course, only as efficient as the horses that pulled them. While travellers could bring their own, this was very expensive and very hard on the animals. It was better to hire horses from a *voiturier* in France or a *veturino* in Italy. The *voiturier* supplied horses and a driver who looked after the carriage and the luggage. He was sometimes helped by a postilion who rode the lead horse.[9] Travellers needed to be precise about what they wanted. In 1836, Robert Hudson wrote out the terms for his *voiturier*: to provide 'a pair or return horses to Bern or Schauffhausen . . . 2 horses & the man to drive – agreement in writing at 10 francs a day each horse – to stop at such places as we may wish – to include all turnpikes, barriers, & additional horses if necessary.' The Liberal MP Edward Horsman was less fortunate in 1846. He hired three horses in Basle at an 'exorbitant price'. The driver was 'the very ugliest wretch in the human form . . . face similar of [to] Punch's. NB. Never again to hire voiturier's horses without making a distinct bargain about the rate.'[10] Whatever arrangements people made, they were always restrained by the fact that horses were valuable animals and could not be overworked. They required frequent 'baiting' or stops for rest and feeding, which naturally slowed down the journey to an average of four to five miles per hour.

The one way to speed things up was to 'post', but this was extremely expensive: Sir Thomas Fremantle moaned about paying eight guineas a day when he was 'posting' to Paris. Under this system people sometimes hired a coachman but they always needed a postilion with his team of horses. The carriage proceeded to the next stop or 'post' where the postilion unhitched the horses and led them back to the previous 'post' whilst a new team with a new postilion took their places. The new horses and postilion would go to the next post and so on. Posts were about five miles apart so the longer the route, the greater the cost. Extra horses, mules and sometimes even oxen, were added when mountains had to be crossed. The costs were strictly set down by government according to the number of 'posts'. Between Calais and Paris, for example, there were 33¾ posts. The advantage of posting lay in the frequency of 'posts', which meant that horses could go faster.[11]

In addition to various port fees on carriages, amounting to about £2, any vehicle brought into France was valued at the custom house and the traveller had to deposit one-third of that value. When leaving France the owner would get back two-thirds of his deposit; if he stayed beyond three years he forfeited the whole. The duties levied were substantial: Martha Bradford was outraged that her husband would have to pay 40 Napoleons [£32.00]. They were lucky, however, in meeting the ambassador to Vienna, where William Bradford was going as his new chaplain. Through ambassadorial 'influence' their fee was waived and '40 Napoleons at least have been saved to us and our heirs for ever'. Of course, such problems were not confined to the Continent, as William Fox Talbot, a Wiltshire landowner, discovered in 1823. On his return home, he wrote that Dover was 'the land of extortion & exaction – I blush that it sh^d be an English town'. Custom officials charged him £11 19s for the carriage he had bought in France. He had been assured by the salesman that there would be no duty.[12]

For those travelling in carriages, getting meals could be a major headache. Many of the 'posts' were at inns where travellers might get some food. However, many inns prided themselves on how quickly they could change teams and food was considered less important. If one's French were weak one could, like Elizabeth Stanton, ask for 'a piece of cake or a cracker' but get 'a piping hot plate of sweetbreads nicely broiled' just as the carriage left. If people had forethought they could, like Lord Vernon, enjoy 'picnics' en route; those less careful, such as the Fremantles, had to exist on tea. Worse was the fate of Isabel Arundell who had to endure 'a twenty-four hours' drive' from Padua to Milan 'without a stoppage, without a crumb of bread or a drop of water'. In years to come, some looked back on carriages with great fondness, especially Ruskin. Writing in the 1880s he recalled 'the complex joys, and ingenious hopes, connected with the choice and arrangement of the travelling carriage in old times'.[13] One suspects Isabel Arundell would not have agreed.

In 1852 one travel writer advised 'all families travelling abroad' to hire couriers whose 'services are almost indispensable on an extended tour'. Until railways connected all the principal cities, couriers took the strain out of travel for those who could afford them. Their cost was 'pretty near that of a third individual added to a couple'. Even after the rail network was established, couriers still saved travellers from 'disappointments and worry, wear and tear' by acting as travel guides, personal servants and translators. They also looked after the luggage, booked tickets, secured hotel rooms and sometimes taught their clients foreign languages. Just as postilions were famous for their huge jack-boots, couriers were known for the leather bags which they wore round their necks. (These set a fashion for male tourists such as the terracotta 'English traveller' described in Chapter 2.) Some couriers were famous for different reasons. In 1820, when George IV tried to divorce his estranged queen, it was alleged that her courier had confined most of his work to a more personal nature. The unconventional Caroline Meysey-Wigley, whose limp was noted by the passport official in the last chapter, shocked the French by asking her courier to accompany her to the Paris Opera.[14]

It was obviously important to find a reliable courier as 'many of them are not altogether to be trusted'. Some people turned to experienced friends for help. In recommending his courier, Thackeray praised a trait inherited by today's tour guides: 'He . . . will often amuse the solitary tourist by appropriate anecdotes.' When Robert Hudson set out in 1840 a friend recommended Constantine Coradi

who had 'served me so faithfully and actively that I can safely recommend him as a confidential & trustworthy Courier'. A traveller
could approach travel agencies in London or one of the couriers'
organizations that placed advertisements in Murray's guides. The
Swiss and United Couriers' Society provided men for those who
'desire to rid themselves of the annoyances and encumbrances
attending a tour in foreign lands and thus "save time, temper, and
money"'. Some people arranged to have couriers start work before
their employers left the country: when the Bests set off on their
wedding tour in 1858, they had already sent Giovanni Borzelli ahead
with their luggage. Other travellers would hire couriers on arrival,
on the recommendation of their inn-keeper. Guide-books warned
people to ask for references and written agreements: Robert Hudson's reads 'Robert Hudson Esq. agrees to engage Constantine Cor-
ati [sic] as his Courier & travelling Servant, during the time of his
absence on his Tour at 2£10s per week . . . But if at the end of the
time, there should be any days over, R.H. will pay C.C. 7s/6d per
day for the additional days.' Both men signed and Conradi wrote 'I
agree to the above' beside his signature.[15]

Couriers stood between the traveller and the unfamiliar, exotic
and sometimes incomprehensible. As well as pointing out the sights,
couriers often entertained clients with anecdotes of earlier travellers they had assisted; a suspiciously large number had worked for
Napoleon or Byron.* Usually couriers were French or Italian, but
there were some English. Whatever the nationality, a quick-thinking
man could be invaluable. In 1815 the Irish banker J. L. Maquay
was furious: he had almost booked rooms in Bagni di Lucca when
the Duchess of Devonshire's courier appeared, offered more and
bagged the accommodation. In 1839 Lady Ravensworth's coach was

---

* Occasionally the claims were true. Disraeli, who was much influenced by Byron's
example, was visiting Lake Geneva in 1826. There he made sure that Byron's handsome
boatman, Maurice, rowed him about the lake at night on the same route that Byron
described in *Childe Harold*. Disraeli went on to bring Byron's favourite Venetian
gondolier, 'Tita' Falcieri, back to England.

en route for Boulogne when her courier learned that the carriage in front was Lord Bingham's. Because the rule of the road forbade overtaking, the courier was worried lest his lordship should grab the rooms at the next inn. Not to be outdone he galloped ahead, arriving just before the Binghams. Lord Bingham was 'furious, abused him in the most unmeasured terms, and was about to collar him' when the courier called out ' "Take care what you do, my lord, for I am an Englishman" whereupon Lord Bingham let go' and, Lady Ravensworth's daughter remembered, 'we got our rooms'. What Lord Bingham would have done in this early example of 'road rage' if the courier had not been English remains uncertain.[16]

Couriers earned good money: in 1817 Matthew Todd acted as courier to his employer's uncle. Todd, a gentleman's manservant, was not keen but was rewarded with the large sum of '10 shillings per day'. By the 1860s couriers were averaging about £11 a month plus second-class railway fares.[17] When couriers were good they were indispensable. When the Lucys were in Nancy the squire's wife gave birth to a son who appeared to be still-born. Their courier, who had been waiting outside her hotel room rushed in with a warm bath that he had been keeping just in case. He plunged the child into the water and the infant quickly let it be known that warm baths were not to his taste. Less dramatic was the crisis faced by the popular poet Martin Tupper, when an expected banker's remittance did not arrive in Switzerland. The family simply had no money and told their courier, Pierre, that they must return to England. Pierre insisted that they must see the Simplon Pass and Italy and loaned them the enormous sum of £100. When Tupper repaid the loan, Pierre refused any interest: '*Non, Monsieur*, pardon; I could not, I always bring money to help my families.' Mark Twain wrote in one of his travel books, which were so popular in Britain, about his Polish courier:[18]

He is always at hand ... You tell him what day you will start, and ... leave all the rest to him ... he has packed your luggage ... he has paid all the bills ... On the journey ... the courier comes to your [train] compartment to see if you want a glass of water . . . at eating-stations he sends luncheon out to you, while the other people scramble . . . He spoke eight languages . . . he was shrewd, prompt, posted, and punctual . . . handy with children and invalids; all his employer need to do was to take life easy.

Often couriers and their employers became actual friends. In Lucca the couriers and 'upper servants' organized a ball in the local theatre and their British employers were invited to sit in the boxes. The servants were 'received at the entrance . . . according to the rank of their masters and mistresses'. Thus the Duchess of Lucca's lady's maid was received 'with royal honours, everybody curtseying and bowing'. The friendship between Dickens and his courier meant that by the 1840s couriers in general were becoming a feature of the rapidly developing field of travel articles and books. In his *Pictures from Italy* he introduced his readers to 'the radiant embodiment of good humour who sat beside me in the person of a French Courier – best of servants and most beaming of men!' The hotelier, Dickens wrote, 'dotes . . . upon the Courier'. This was hardly surprising since much of the hotelier's income depended on couriers, who usually got a back-hander from the owner. The courier 'is everywhere: looking after the beds, having wine poured down his throat by his dear brother the landlord'. Before leaving, the courier disputes the bill with the landlord who lowers it, knowing 'that he will be returning that way . . . with another family'. Dickens employed his courier, Louis Roche, for a second tour, and the man began to spend time in England. When, in 1848, he became seriously ill, Dickens arranged a bed in St George's Hospital. Sadly this 'most faithful, affectionate, and devoted man' died the next year.[19]

Sometimes the courier seems to have been the only European whom tourists got to know. The Birchalls, a Gloucestershire squire and his wife on their wedding tour became devoted to their courier, Perrini, from the time they met him at Charing Cross. He was a source of 'perpetual amusement' with his denunciations of republics and priests (one of his wives had run away with a priest) and his opinions and antics play a large role in Emily Birchall's enthusiastic diary. Even his native Italy was denounced as a 'nation of liars' and he said he 'would rather be dead in England than alive in any other country'. The Birchalls were genuinely distressed when the illness of yet another wife compelled this 'capital fellow' to leave. The next courier, an 'old fogy', was dismissed after two days, and the couple continued on their own.[20]

Of course most travellers never used couriers because they were simply too expensive or were regarded as aristocratic luxuries. The majority put their trust in guide-books or hired local guides. These men showed them the attractions and took them to shops where they would, allegedly, get good buys and where the guide would probably pocket back-handers. They were known by a variety of names: *lacquay de place, valet de place* and even the old term, *cicerone.* Guide-books strongly urged visitors to hire such guides and to pay them about six francs a day: 'active and intelligent as most of them are ... they can save the visitor much time and trouble'. In some cases guides were asked to take their customers to brothels, though some refused.[21]

Those who did use couriers were not always enthusiastic. Some felt that the courier 'becomes, in fact, the master'. Because couriers often had to 'find for themselves' their costs were, it was claimed, often added to hotel bills. The American novelist James Fenimore Cooper discovered in 1830 that his man was eating better than Cooper. The favourite criticism was that the commission paid by hoteliers did not work to the travellers' benefit. Hoteliers, some felt, 'hate the whole system'. Rosamund Talbot told her brother in 1867 that her courier 'foolishly took us (as he had already done at Geneva) to the dearest Hotel in the Place, *le Grand Hotel de Cannes* ... When we found this, of course we would not stay more than one night.' John Ruskin's father never used couriers and neither did Frances Trollope. In part this was because she spoke French and in part because she had to be careful with money. 'I have never yet tried travelling in what is emphatically called good style.' The comfort of 'always finding rooms and refreshment ready on arriving' could only be gained by accepting the courier's schedule, and so her eldest son often acted as courier.[22]

By the 1860s couriers were in decline, although the term survives today, ironically, in packaged tours. They were killed off by the growth of railways, tourist agencies, organized tours, the spread of guide-books, bigger hotels with *concierges*, and the growing use of English as the language of tourism. Where they did survive they became in effect tour guides. Perhaps the last word on couriers should be left with Sir Arthur Sullivan and F. C. Burnard in their 1894 operetta *The Chieftain*. This had begun life in 1867 as *The Contrabandista*; when re-launched in 1894 Burnard added the character of Ferdinand, the Polish courier. The action was set in Spain where couriers might still be thought essential. In Act Two, Ferdinand sings of the honeymooning couple he is escorting. He reminds the audience of the much publicized back-handers and refers to guide-books, organized tours and the travel books of Jerome K. Jerome and Mark Twain:[23]

> *A courier all of you welcome in me,*
> *Whom Boniface grudgingly greets,*
> *I bring him the guests, but insist on my fee*
> *Of twenty per cent on receipts.*
>
> . . .
>
> *They gaze on a lake with a Baedeker book,*
> *'Three men in a boat' over-oar'd,*
> *They travel through France with a trustworthy Cook,*
> *And everyone says from their much Murray'd look,*
> *'Mark! Innocents Twain all aboard!'*

Earlier it was noted that wealthy tourists could bring their own carriages and hire horses from a *voiturier* in France or a *vetturino* in Italy. But these men could also provide a carriage (*voiture* or *vettura*) and a driver which could be cheaper than taking public transport: in 1818 Robert Parker hired his *voiturier* in Paris for the reasonable sum of £16. This was for a two-months' tour of Switzerland. A contract was drawn up detailing the contents of meals and the number of beds which the *voiturier* would find each night. Under this arrangement, travellers avoided the high costs of posting and the bother of acquiring a coach, driver and horses. If the *voiturier* negotiated with inn-keepers this could in theory save money.[24] Of course, those who took on a *voiturier* could be at his mercy when it came to stopping and eating. Also, because the *voiturier*'s own horses were used, travellers could never expect to go more than forty or fifty miles a day, assuming they spent ten hours on the road.

Charges of dishonesty were not unusual. Murray's *Handbooks* urged travellers to examine a driver's testimonials and to show any contract to some 'respectable inhabitant' to confirm that the *voiturier* was reliable and that his *voiture* was clean and sturdy. This was especially the case at ports where *voituriers*, having dropped off a departing party, waited for a new customer. Murray recommended that one pay nine francs per horse per day for a *voiture* from Calais to Switzerland plus another franc per horse as a *pour boire*, or tip. When Leigh Hunt left Italy in 1825 he agreed a fee of 82 guineas with a *vetturino* to take a party of ten for about one month's journey. There were to be several rest or sight-seeing days and the *vetturino* agreed to provide dinner and breakfasts of eggs, coffee, bread, milk and fruit. Hunt decided his driver was an 'honest rogue' but warned others to examine the contract and to watch the *vetturino*. Another British traveller exploded in his diary in 1842: 'A Vetturino [is] a class of persons notorious for their rascality.' The *vetturino* in question had not provided the stipulated milk with coffee and had tried to force this diarist and his companion to share a bed 'not in accordance with English habits!' The Englishmen subsequently got their milk and separate beds, and afterwards the Italian behaved himself. One retired naval officer and his family who went by *vetturino* to Lausanne in 1829 paid £160 but, coming back, he drove his own carriage and paid £115.[25]

Once railways were established, *voituriers* tended to confine themselves to tourist centres where they acted as guides or took people to see sights in the surrounding countryside.

The actress Fanny Kemble did not mince words when she described the diligence, or *diligenza*, which took her from Città Vechia to Rome in the 1840s: a 'crazy, rickety, dusty, dirty, ragged, filthy conveyance'. To add insult to injury, the postilions demanded a *buono mano* at every stop. In the decades before the railways, most travellers without carriages had no choice but to endure 'the jog-trot of the Diligence'. The 'dilly', as the British called it, resembled 'two coaches stuck together' and dominated continental travel until trains arrived. This enormous vehicle was a large version of the 'stage coach' and could hold up to eighteen people. It was 'not infrequently drawn by nine horses. A cavalry charge, therefore, could scarcely make more noise.'[26] At the ports they awaited arriving ships but elsewhere they ran according to schedules. Some French inn-keepers, such as Charles-Augustin Meurice in Calais, ran their own coaches to take passengers to Paris. In 1818 his son built a second coaching inn which later became Paris's Meurice Hotel, known as the 'City of London' because all the staff spoke English. Today, having been recently fully restored, it still welcomes visitors – at prices that would have left earlier travellers reeling.

These extraordinary vehicles usually consisted of four separate parts: the *coupé*, the *intérieur*, the *rotonde* and, finally, the *banquette*. English travellers usually preferred the privacy of the *coupé* (with only three seats) because it was perched on the front of the vehicle and separated from the main body. It was 'the favourite place of the luxurious'. The *coupé* was also the most expensive part: when Ruskin travelled from Rouen to Caen he had to pay 16½ francs plus three francs for luggage. 'Bagging the *coupé*' meant one could keep foreigners at bay and Victorians frequently rejoiced at their cleverness in securing these treasured seats, especially if they were travelling with ladies. Sometimes men sought the seats for different motives, if one can believe the account in *My Secret Life*, the notorious pornographic 'autobiography' published between 1888 and 1894.[27] The author, still known only as 'Walter', recalled: 'I travelled in the *coupé* . . . with a tall, dark-eyed, handsome lady, looking thirty . . . She was well, even expensively dressed, but most quietly . . . Eight hours were we together. It was very cold, and I longed to get near her . . .' and so on and so on until they ended up in a bedroom in Grenoble when Walter got very close indeed.*

The *intérieur*, the main body of the coach, held varying numbers of people in degrees of discomfort. The *rotonde*, normally with six passengers, was at the back and was open to the elements. The *banquette* or *impériale* consisted of three seats on the roof of the *coupé*, which passengers shared with the driver. These seats were the choice of 'the admirer of the sublime and beautiful' and had splendid views, less dust than in the *rotonde* and fewer neighbours, but the only protection from the elements was a hood over the seats and a leather apron over passengers' legs. Access was really confined to the agile, while ladies were advised not to try it lest foreigners get a glimpse of their ankles. Not surprisingly, there was often anxiety for seats, something witnessed by Henry James as he sat on top of a diligence in the Alps. As he nibbled Italian peaches he enjoyed watching his fellow travellers, all British, experiencing 'false alarms about the claim of somebody else to their place for which they produced their ticket, with a declaration in three or four tongues of the inalienable right to it given them by British gold'.[28]

These large vehicles also carried a vast amount of freight and luggage, since each passenger was allowed between 40 and 50 pounds. They were also noisy, frequently slow and crowded. The sixteen-year-old John Blackwood complained of 'the infernal machine containing sixteen greasy ruffians, packed as tight as herrings in a barrel, on a hot, smoking evening'. When Frances Trollope, already in her mid-sixties, travelled 240 miles from

---

* Those interested in learning more of the lady's fate, or in deepening their knowledge of Victorian literature, may consult the text at *www.my-secret-life.com*.

Florence to Turin in 1844, her journey took an exhausting ninety-seven hours. Diligences criss-crossed Europe, trundling from posting inn to posting inn and often travelling through the night. What comfort and speed there were depended largely on the roads. While Charles Greville, travelling overnight from Calais to Paris in 1830, found the roads 'horrid in most parts' he still made the journey in five hours. For some, such as the fanatical Nonconformist minister Thomas Sheardown, a trip in an Italian diligence was also a trial for religious reasons. 'It was,' he complained, 'almost a daily occurrence to have to take off my hat to the images of their saints, posted at the corners of the roads; and on one great festival day, I had to bow my knees in the street until the *Grand Costodia* [the bust] of St. Peter, and other relics, which were carried upon the shoulders of twelve priests had passed by!' Perhaps the best summary of most journeys comes from the much-travelled Bishop Hynes: 'tedious'.[29]

Diaries and letters abound with stories of unpleasant experiences in diligences. One of the earliest was in 1814 when Matthew Todd found himself on roads so rough that the journey 'began to affect my bowels, as well as it did also a French or Swiss gentleman . . . whose breath was extremely offensive, as also from the jolting of the carriage he was continually emitting voluntary posterior declamations, which made the carriage so offensive one could hardly keep one's head in for 5 minutes together.' Fourteen years later a young clergyman, the Reverend George Brett, had a journey only slightly less horrific. His diligence was 'more than half full of very vulgar English' and, even worse, they had got the best seats. Alexander Shand remembered that in Italy fellow passengers 'fed promiscuously, at all hours . . . and the interior – the windows were hermetically sealed – was reeking of rancid oil and garlic! A child or two were crawling about your legs, and babies in arms were satisfying insatiable thirst.' Getting food, especially hot meals, was a problem because of the short breaks. In the early 1840s Emma Roberts was surprised at 7 a.m. to see 'a party of persons running, gesticulating, and talking . . . who brought hot coffee, milk, bread, and fruit to the carriage-door'. The British passengers were naturally 'disinclined to avail ourselves' until they learned that if they did not they would have no breakfast. They gave in and found the food 'very good of its kind'. Praise indeed. More experienced travellers would take potted beef and bread to keep them going. When the carriage did make a prolonged stop, travellers would rush into the inn or hotel for food.[30] Many men liked to get out and walk. This gave them some fresh air and a chance to relieve themselves.

The attacks on diligences, especially those written after the advent of the railways, were almost universal: 'The summer dust ... ramshackle post-yards, with all the beggars (who used to turn out at night with bits of lighted candle, to look in ... the mouldy cafes ... the grass-grown little towns ... the pains in my bones ... the Frenchman with the nightcap who never *would* have the little coupe-window down, and who ... slept all night snoring [and reeking of] onions.' On top of all that, long journeys produced 'swelled feet and ancles' much as long-haul flights do today. Occasionally, very occasionally, someone popped up with a good word and remembered, for example, the pleasures of a trip across the Alps: 'A seat up above, on the banquette of a diligence ... with room for the feet, and support for the back, with plenty of rugs and ... tobacco, used to be ... a very comfortable mode of seeing a mountain route.' But even this writer had to admit that when wedged inside 'with two priests, a dirty man who looks like a brigand, a sick maid-servant, and three agricultural labourers' things were not quite so nice. An even worse problem was when a 'foreigner' got one's seat: when two little Frenchmen grabbed the seats reserved by Anthony Trollope and his older brother, they took matters into their own hands. The older brother entered the coach and shouted 'Stand below, Anthony, and I will hand them down!'[31] Hand them down is exactly what Tom Trollope did and Anthony placed the two men on the ground and resumed his seat beside Tom.

The greatest challenge facing travellers, as well as the greatest thrill, confronted those wanting to visit Italy. Before the first trans-alpine railway tunnel was opened in 1871, travellers had three ways of getting to Italy. The first was to travel by ship, usually from Marseilles to Leghorn or Città Vecchia. The second, after 1827, was to travel to Nice and then to take the Corniche Road, which hugged the Mediterranean. However, the majority preferred the romantic journey across the Alps, using the same passes that people had used for millennia. The fascination with the Alpine routes increased in the late 1820s when the artist William Brockedon published *Illustrations of the Passes of the Alps*, based on his more than sixty crossings. While there were some hundred routes across the mountains, six – the Simplon, Splügen, St Bernard (two routes), St Gotthard and Mont Cenis – were the most popular and all except the Splügen had historic religious hospices to care for travellers. Getting over the Alps was a major task – to cross the thirty-seven miles that made up the Simplon pass, for example, could take seventeen hours, even in the height of the summer.[32] The most important of the hospices was the monastery at the top of the St Bernard pass, made famous in Landseer's painting of its dogs. This painting, first shown in 1820 and followed by numerous prints, appealed to contemporary tastes and was not an insignificant stimulus to travel, even if the dogs' caskets of brandy never existed. The monastery's fame was increased further in the 1850s when Dickens painted a lyrical picture of the famous hospice in *Little Dorrit* (Book II. i).

Dickens also mentioned the monastery's notorious morgue. Visitors could look through a grated window to see the still-frozen bodies, 'some leaning against the wall, staring at you, just as they died . . . some crouching, as if vainly trying to hide against the storm . . . 'Tis a hard fate, to be within a few hours of the sunny plains of Italy, and – all on a day of May – to meet a winter's death.' In fairness we must remember that at one time the monks had simply flung the bodies into a deep crevice, so the morgue was actually an improvement. Also there was so little ground available that it was impossible to effect burials. The lack of trees meant that all wood had to be brought up the mountain: no wonder the twenty-one-year-old Edward Horsman, who visited in August 1828, said the temperature was below freezing. The buildings were 8,000 feet above sea level. When almost forty years later one of the Torr family stayed in the monastery he did not remember the morgue as much as the 'thirteen great dogs, which were inclined to be almost too friendly'. He was 'much pleased with the hospitality we received'.[33]

Yet it was the route over Mont Cenis that was most often described by travellers and writers. 'Few scenes can be more astonishing or more truly sublime,' wrote Mariana Starke, in an enthusiasm shared by Byron and Wordsworth. Generally British travellers suspended their traditional view of Catholic monks and Napoleon and praised both for making Alpine travel easier and safer. The Cenis route, like the Simplon, had been made into roadways by Napoleon's troops and for many years tourists could still see the frozen remains of French grenadiers who had fallen to their deaths. Mariana Starke's view, that the road over Mont Cenis was 'safe and good at every season', was not shared by everyone: Lady Fremantle noted that the 'strong railing or wall' by the side was 'broken down in some parts & . . . the precipices are really frightful'.[34] In the winter months, diligences often had a terrible time with ice and snow up to twenty feet deep. In those frozen months travellers desperate to get across had to be carried in baskets. For the journey back into France, they could, if brave enough, be put on sledges, which made the descent in about seven minutes, a choice not for the timid.

It seems that most people travelling over the Alps felt compelled to record their experiences. In 1816 William Etty, the Yorkshire artist, described his night-time trip in a letter. The road was 'bad, narrow [and] encumbered with stones'. Every five minutes the postilion stopped 'to chain and unchain the wheels' to prevent slipping. 'All,' he wrote, 'is darkness, silence and solitude, save the rushing of the waters deep in the valley below us . . . we were often within a yard, – two feet, – sometimes one of the edge . . . hoping every mountain was our last.' When Caroline Edgcumbe crossed in December 1834, her carriage had to wait until the passes were clear as 'a Diligence that had crossed was only prevented from blowing over the precipice by being fastened with ropes to the railing'. The next day she got up at 5 a.m. and, like so many other travellers, walked virtually the whole way revelling in scenery 'peculiarly grand . . . with thin, transparent vapours flitting over the different crags . . . lit by the sunbeams'. Some twenty-five years later Isabella Arundell went up the same mountain one winter's night in a diligence pulled by fourteen mules and two horses, but the vehicle 'went at a foot's pace, and . . . could hardly stand . . . Everything tumbled about . . . in a snowy, dreamy state of confusion.' In 1860 George Eliot had an even worse night as she was among passengers from three diligences transferred to sledges pulled by donkeys. Warmed by a cup of coffee in an inn she contrasted 'the human bustle and confusion' with the 'sublime stillness of the starlit heavens spread over the snowy tableland and surrounding heights'. She felt herself on 'a visit to Nature in her private home'. But her feelings were not enough to keep her from falling asleep only to awake as dawn rose over the Alps.[35]

The advent of railways did not spell the end for carriages, *voitures* and diligences even if 'the railway spoils you for the old fashioned diligence'. Diligences remained the only form of public transport in many areas. In 1864, for example, the young architect Thomas Jackson got as far as Clermont Ferrand by train. He then switched to a diligence for Le Puy – a seven-hour journey over only twenty-five miles. From there he and his companion set out to walk into Italy but their plans were disarranged when they were arrested for not having passports. For a while, carriages and diligences, with the passengers still aboard, were put on to trains to be ready when the railway line came to an end. But by the 1880s, for travellers visiting the main tourist destinations, the diligence was 'rapidly dying out, since mountains are being tunnelled and the iron road laid everywhere'. An American writer warned those who would romanticize the good old days that 'the diligence for a mountain day trip is very delightful travelling; for a night journey it is a horror'. One final comment on these extraordinary vehicles should come from William Etty travelling from Geneva to Paris in 1823: 'A conveyance I never wish to enter again . . . To be three whole nights and four days, without a bed: – one meal in the twenty-four hours; – exposed to wet, cold, and night-air; – or, if inside, stewed up with a host of all sorts.' For Etty and thousands more, deliverance was not that long in coming.[36]

'*The Railway!* What a sense of bustle, what a confusion of tongues.' It includes 'the field-marshal and the man-milliner in France . . . And thus we fly along . . . It gives me more the idea of the passing of objects in dreams.' The coming of the railway revolutionized travel. Instead of travelling at five miles an hour in a carriage, people were travelling ten times as fast. As noted in Chapter 3, the first continental railway to affect travel, from Ostend to Brussels, was opened in 1838 and was in part a response to the increasing tourist traffic from Britain. In French ports the effect of the railway expansion was marked. After Rouen got a trunk line to Paris in 1843 traffic increased through Dieppe, even though passengers still had to take a carriage to Rouen for the train. In 1847 George Bradshaw began publishing *Bradshaw's Continental Railway Guide*, although travellers had to wait two years for Calais, Dieppe, Boulogne and Le Havre to be linked to the French capital. The effect on tourism was phenomenal: two years after the ports were connected to the capital the annual number of travellers had risen by 300 per cent over the annual totals for the late 1830s.[37]

In 1852 a guide to Paris proclaimed: 'Steam . . . has placed nearly all Europe within reach of the summer holiday-maker by economizing time and money.' Gone were 'a score of . . . nuisances that in old times made travelling costly and troublesome'. Paris and the Riviera were linked by 1864 and in the following year travellers could go by rail all the way from Calais or Boulogne to Brindisi in the heel of Italy although, before 1868, they still needed diligences to cross the Alps. (Brindisi was important for crossing the Mediterranean en route to India and Australia.) The railways not only made travel by land easier but, from the 1870s, led to major improvements in the harbours at Calais and Boulogne: from 1876 passengers could leave their steam packets and find a Paris train waiting on the jetty. Arriving passengers could leave for Paris within five minutes after clearing Customs: 'Twelve hours from London drop them in Paris, twenty-four carry them to the Alps, and . . . before them . . . Rome or Constantinople or . . . the world's end.' Another enthusiast declared, 'Speed and safety are wisely judged to be valuable compensations for state and seclusion.'[38]

People began to feel that 'a carriage has now become almost a useless encumbrance'. In 1856 the American literary historian George Ticknor, who had not been in Europe since 1816, revisited Germany and the Austrian Empire. He found that the improved railways and hotels meant that 'wholly contrary to my expectation, I enjoy travelling. Changes I find on all sides; enormous, and sometimes startling'. He was especially pleased with the improvements in Austria since his train went over the newly built Semmering line, one of the major engineering achievements of the nineteenth century. It was, and remains, 'one of the grandest things that can be seen anywhere'. If Ticknor had travelled between Lyons and Paris he would have been equally surprised. In 1815 the diligence took four days. By 1850 trains took eight hours. Ticknor's enthusiasm was shared by John Delane, editor of *The Times*, when in 1859 he had 'a very pleasant run across France, doing the whole distance from Calais to Chambéry, which has twice cost me seven days, in rather less than twenty-four hours'.[39]

The British were impressed by the comfort they found on continental trains as early as 1847: the Boulogne train had 'a most luxurious carriage . . . which exceeded those in our rail-roads in elegance . . . the men . . . well-mannered, above all they were very punctual'. By the 1850s guide-books were pointing out that in France, first- and second-class seats were not only 'stuffed' but, in the winter, were covered in sheep skins and heated with hot water cases underneath each seat. If the trains did not run quite 'so often or so fast' they were cheaper than in Britain: first-class fare was, on average, 1½*d* per mile while at home it was double that figure. Writers were already moaning that 'in this dear old England of ours, where with highest fares we have the shabbiest accommodation'. Within twenty years other writers stated simply that 'French railway carriages are better than the majority of English ones.' The French second class was now 'nearly equal to our first', while French first class 'are like little parlours, with tables, footstools, and curtains, and plenty of windows to let in fresh air'.[40]

However comfortable the trains might be, waiting to board them infuriated travellers because of the French custom of 'penning-up railway passengers like sheep'. Only when the train came into the station were passengers released, causing 'serious inconvenience and injustice, particularly to female travellers'. The only way round this was to arrive early, buy the tickets and then go to the buffet. One could then board at leisure. As always, luggage was a problem. An 1862 guide warned that, on French railways, passengers must check in all bags and collect them at the end of the journey but only after examination. This was 'tedious and annoying' and if possible one 'should leave the matter in the hands of his servant'. If a traveller had pre-booked a hotel he could arrange for it to send someone to cope. Accordingly, guide-books warned travellers to reduce the amount of luggage 'to the lightest possible weight, and the smallest practicable bulk'.[41]

The same 1862 guide also told readers that in Germany carriages were 'notably fitted up in a superior manner, and the second class so nearly approaches . . . the first, that few persons travel by the later'. There was a saying in Germany that only 'princes, Americans, and fools ride first-class'; a tourist writer added English tradesmen to the list. Because smoking was allowed in second-class carriages, ladies were warned that only first class was free of tobacco. Austrian trains were 'not so comfortable' while those in

the Netherlands were 'generally well managed ... and comfortably appointed'. However, the third class consisted of wagons
'open at the sides, and fitted up with wooden benches'. In Belgium
there was a 'moderate rate of travelling, and a low scale of fares',
while the first-class accommodation was 'luxurious' and the second
class 'comfortable for males but not for females'. As to Italian
trains, a 1909 Baedeker guide said they were 'unpunctual, and
booking is a provokingly slow process. Tickets must be taken
before admission to the waiting-rooms. The first class is more used
than in most other countries, especially when ladies are of the
party. The second is fairly good; the third is used by the lower
orders only.' At least in Italian stations, passengers were not herded
into pens. The Swiss railway network was late in coming but when
it did appear it was praised: 'Swiss railway-carriages are as superior
to English, as broughams are to prison vans.' The trains also had
seats with 'low slanting backs, which can be turned over, so that
the passengers can sit with their faces or their backs towards the
engine, just as they please' to allow them to see the scenery more
easily.[42]

One problem for passengers trying to save money was the fleas
left behind from the clothes of the poor. The young architect
Thomas Jackson, travelling through the Auvergne in 1864, discovered that 'as we went southwards the garlic and the fleas became
more aggressive, and after retiring from one railway journey with
sixty-seven wounds I protested against the economy of travelling
third class'. After fleas came food, and here opinion was less hostile,
at least towards French railways. Until the 1880s passengers were
expected to bring their food with them or to get their meals in
stations, and many European refreshment rooms received full
marks: a writer in *Punch* remembered that 'our *déjeuner* at Calais is
as good as it usually is at that haven of Restauration. After the
buffeting of the waves, how sweet is the *buffet* of the shore.' In
Dickens's *Mugby Junction* (Chapter 3), 'Our Missis,' in charge of
an English refreshment room, goes off to France to see how the
'frog-eaters' operate. On her return she tells her staff:

Shall I be believed when I tell you, that no sooner had I landed
... on that treacherous shore, than I was ushered into a
Refreshment Room where there were – I do not exaggerate –
actually eatable things to eat?' 'I should not enter, ladies,' says
Our Missis, 'on the revolting disclosures I am about to make, if
it was not in the hope that they will cause you to be yet more
implacable in the exercise of the power you wield in a constitutional country, and yet more devoted to the constitutional motto
which I see before me,' – it was behind her, but the words
sounded better so, – 'May Albion never learn!'

It remains debatable if Albion ever has.

The next great innovation came in 1868 with the creation of the
*Compagnie International des Wagons-Lits et des Grands Express
Européen*, founded by the Belgian Georges Nagelmackers, who had
had ridden in a Pullman Sleeping Car in America. This had made
it possible for passengers to sleep comfortably on a moving train.
Nagelmackers, support by the Belgian king, set up the new company. It built its own trains, and in 1872 introduced the first
sleeping car from Paris to Vienna. Five years later the company
put the new cars on trains between the French capital and the
Riviera. It was also Nagelmackers who introduced restaurant cars
in 1881. Two years later the company added a new dimension to
travel when its Orient Express left Paris's Gare de l'Est for Constantinople. It departed at 7.30 p.m. on a Tuesday and arrived in
the Ottoman capital on the following Saturday at 7 a.m. That same
year sleeping cars were introduced on the Calais to Paris line. At
the other end of the scale, it was claimed in 1914 that those in third-
class carriages throughout Europe had 'no more discomfort' than in
their British equivalents.[43]

The single greatest advance in Europe's rail network came when
engineers conquered the Alps. The proposal for a tunnel through
Mont Cenis was first made in 1832. It was adopted by Sardinia in
1846 and work began eleven years later. The tunnel was a feat of

Italian engineering, although it eventually became a joint operation with France, the cost shared by both countries. The French authorities also wanted a railway that could cross the mountains while everyone waited for the tunnel to be finished. Officials investigated a new railway built by John Barraclough Fell in Derbyshire, which allowed trains to climb and descend steep gradients: that at Mont Cenis was one in twelve. Fell was asked to design the 'Mont Cenis Pass Railway', which was forty-eight miles long and opened in 1868, the first rail link between France and Italy. The line, which followed the route of Napoleon's road, was 7,000 feet high at its peak. There were two trains a day and the journey took five and a quarter hours. 'Fell's Railway' was dismantled and sold when the Cenis tunnel was opened in September 1871. Then one could 'cross' the Alps in thirty minutes or less and in comfort. Reactions to the new era in European travel were, as always, mixed. Some felt that the new tunnel 'smells of the time to come' and 'is certainly not a poetic object'. Yet it enabled people to travel from Paris to Turin in twenty-four hours. This meant that travellers with only a week or fortnight's holiday could visit Italy and indulge in what a Sullivan operetta called 'the love of arts in foreign parts'.[44] In addition, a trip to Italy in the winter months, when Britain was freezing and smog covered, was now not much more difficult than going to Paris. The snows of the Alps could be glimpsed from the warmth of a train.

In 1871 most people thought the Cenis tunnel would be the only one, but the year after it opened work began on the St Gotthard tunnel, which was opened to traffic in June 1882. As one traveller boasted, he could 'leave London, we will say, on a Monday morning and be at Faido [on the Swiss-Italian border] by six or seven o'clock the next evening.' 'True,' he added, people missed the majesty of the Alps but 'mountain scenery, when one is staying right in the middle of it, or when one is on foot, is one thing, and mountain scenery as seen from the top of a diligence . . . smothered in dust is another'.[45] Then, in June 1913, came the third tunnel, the Simplon, between Switzerland and Italy. At just under twelve and a half miles, it was until 1984 the world's longest. While the three great tunnels were built as much for political or commercial purposes as for tourism, their benefit to travellers was tremendous. Only four decades after Dickens had depicted his leisurely tour round Italy in his carriage, a late Victorian biographer of the novelist could exult: 'Ah, those eventful, picturesque, uncomfortable old travelling days, when railways were unborn . . . those interminable old dusty drives, in diligence or private carriage . . . What an old-world memory it seems, and yet, as the years go, not so very long since after all.' In 1900 the poet A. E. Housman, in a train bound for Milan, noted prosaically that the journey through the St Gotthard tunnel took seventeen minutes. Other than that he had no comment.[46]

However much travel between cities had improved, once tourists got off the train and wanted to travel outside a city the only choices were to go by diligence or to hire a carriage. The Horner family twice visited Italy and during their 1847–8 trip they took the train as far as they could in France and then hired a carriage. Their plans came unstuck in Arles on Christmas Eve when they discovered they had a coach and horses but no driver. The young man who came to their rescue matched the glamorous portrait of postilions in their 'immense jack boots'. 'He was the smartest looking postilion we have yet had; his jacket was trimmed with fur, his glazed hat had ribands on one side, and his cloak lined with scarlet tied before him. He was a good looking youth besides, and was not unconscious of his personal advantages.' With him came a 'nice little shaved French poodle', which ran beside the coach. The Horners realized that the young man's good looks were not matched by his driving skills when they found themselves in a ditch in the middle of the night. The postilion, crying *'Oh! Mon Dieu, ah, quel malheur!'*, set off for help while nearby cottagers righted the coach. 'A pretty Christmas eve' was Susan Horner's comment.[47] For those without the Horners' money there were always the diligences, which operated right up to 1914.

Of course trains were never without their critics. Railways were a symbol of the march of progress, which was led by Britain. Italy's slowness in building railways, even bad railways, was seen as indicative of her place in the world. As one traveller wrote to her sisters, 'Nobody knows, that comes from a . . . rising country, how sad is the impression given by a declining ill-directed "state" like this.' Even worse, this criticism was levied at Sardinia, the most 'progressive' kingdom in Italy before unification. In central Italy, much of which was still governed by the Church, authorities originally fought against railways, an attitude which of course confirmed traditional British anti-popery. (By the 1850s the Pope was promoting railways: the problem was lack of finance.) Going further south, in the Kingdom of the Two Sicilies Ferdinand II decided in March 1856 to attend a military review rather than the opening of the new railway to Brindisi. One letter-writer to the radical *Daily News* concluded: 'The King, dull though he be, is gifted with sufficient instinct to feel that tyranny cannot cope with "the rail."' Many had also seen railways as agents for the unstoppable march of an egalitarian society: 'of all levellers' railways 'are the greatest . . . Cabinets, and even queens, now abandon their easy, but lazy equipages for the bird-like flight of iron and fire'.[48]

There were also those who did not object to the new technology but wondered about its effects on travellers. The Edinburgh academic John Stuart Blackie, travelling in the 1850s, asked, 'What earthly good is got by the modern fashion of being literally shot through a country without having time to look, or even to breathe.' When the young Oscar Wilde, still a disciple of the railway-hating Ruskin, was lecturing in America in 1882, he complained about 'the train that whirls an ordinary Englishman through Italy at the rate of forty miles an hour'. Such a journey 'finally sends him home without any memory of that lovely country but . . . that he got a bad dinner at Verona, [and] does not do him or civilisation much good'. Yet within two decades Wilde would be enjoying the next stage in technological progress – a rapid motor tour through Switzerland. George Ticknor, quoted earlier, noticed the expanding numbers of tourists and wondered if they were people 'who only care to be able to say they have been there, having little comprehension of what they see, and none of all what they hear'. The most trenchant comment came, not surprisingly, from Ruskin, when he described tourists as 'the poor modern slaves and simpletons who let themselves be dragged like cattle . . . through the countries they imagine themselves visiting'.[49]

Ruskin here touched on those perennial hallmarks of British travellers. The first was a dislike, bordering on contempt, of one's fellow countrymen encountered on holiday. The second was the view that at some previous stage in history all travellers were of a 'better quality'. Likewise we can never totally rule out snobbishness as part of Ruskin's or Ticknor's observations. However, if we are honest, do we not feel a similar distaste when pushed aside for tourist groups 'doing' Notre Dame in the twenty minutes allotted by their guide, while we take three hours?

Although 'bone shakers' and other primitive bicycles had been available earlier in the nineteenth century, cycling only really became popular in the 1870s. Improvements, including the 'safety' bicycle and pneumatic tyres, came in the 1880s, and by 1899 the Cyclists' Touring Club had over 60,000 members. What is more, the club was publishing guides to the Continent. In addition, the price of bicycles fell, and by 1905 they could be bought for about £5. All these factors opened up continental holidays to thousands of new travellers with limited funds and strong legs, the successors of those hearty youths who had 'pedestrianized' their way round Europe in earlier decades. Cyclists shared and spread the late nineteenth-century view that there was a 'real France' and a 'real Italy' beyond the tourist routes. How better to find them than by cycling? Even Switzerland was a possibility because 'Swiss roads are all that could be desired'. This 1904 *Macmillan Guide* did note the somewhat obvious point about the roads: 'they are very hilly'.[50] Cyclists naturally tended to prefer flatter countryside, including Holland and especially France. Tourist agencies recognized this new market and by the late 1890s were offering all-in cycling tours either to Holland and the Rhine or to Normandy and Brittany, both for just over £6, which included second-class Channel crossing and fifteen nights in hotels.

One of the most useful cycling books appeared in 1904 when the Reverend Percy Dearmer wrote that 'One can stay almost anywhere for a month's holiday,' in Normandy 'without exhausting the number of excursions possible to a moderate cyclist.' Striking a note that still applies he praised the hotels where 'one is treated twice as well and charged half as much as in England'. The Vicar of Hornsey bought Dearmer's book and recorded in his copy his own tour in May 1905. It lasted twelve days after he crossed by steamer to Caen and he managed to visit most of the main Norman towns. The next year an Oxford schoolboy set out for Brittany. T. E. Lawrence embarked on the first of several summer expeditions round France, often covering up to 114 miles per day. His first trip was to Brittany in 1906 when there were 120 bicycles on his boat to St Malo. Two years later, he realized a long held dream when he spent a night at Mont St Michel. His 1908 trip was daunting: starting in Normandy he visited medieval glories such as Chartres, Vézélay and Carcassonne before pedalling to the Mediterranean to bathe in the sea. This tour covered 2,400 miles and it is little wonder that he now began to contemplate buying a motorcycle. His hotels were cheap at two francs a night but punctured tyres could be expensive: in Provence a new one cost him almost a pound, because the garage had to telephone to Dunlop in Paris.[51]

Cycling was never confined to men or to the young, since adventuresome middle-aged women also embraced this liberating means of transport. Among them was Margaret Fountaine, a Norfolk clergyman's daughter. In February 1898 she and her sister, both in their mid-thirties, sent their bicycles by train to Cannes and soon they were cycling through Provence: 'Such a road and such scenery and such weather ... Oh, surely life was worth living.' How enchanting to hop off and take a picture of grinning peasants with her Kodak. She knew cycling was 'in the fashion' when she saw that one hotel's billiard room had been converted into a 'bicycle stable.' After the Riviera, the two sisters cycled across Italy, passing through Genoa, Piacenza, Mantua, Verona and on to Venice sometimes doing forty miles a day in searing heat. They were amused to meet a cycling German woman armed 'with a revolver to protect her virginity'. Margaret cycled into the Austrian Empire towards Trieste and then went off to Hungary on her perpetual quest for rare butterflies.[52] Even Lawrence would have been impressed.

The most important effect of cycling was the development of organizations such as the Cyclists' Touring Club, which negotiated lower import duties for members' cycles and better road signs. The French government eventually removed virtually all fees for members of the club and by 1898 it had made reciprocal arrangements with twelve similar European groups. The International League of Touring Associations, which met in London in 1899 for the first time, was the first 'pressure group' for tourists. There was a missionary zeal in cyclist organizations but their crusades, such as that for better road markings, benefited everyone. Cycling clubs and 'automobilists' then formed the International Alliance of Tourism. This became the first non-governmental body to promote both tourism and the interests of travellers. Tourism was now being organized and promoted as never before. Ten years later, largely motivated by cycling clubs, the French government set up a *Conseil Supérieure de Tourisme* to coordinate local efforts to attract even more British travellers. Two years after that there was talk of a 'Franco-British Travel Union' to encourage travel between the two countries.[53]

The Touring Club de France had copied the English clubs as the French embraced 'the British sport of "*tourisme*" with enthusiasm' and soon the 150,000 strong club began campaigning for better roads and hotels especially in rural France, largely ignored by earlier travellers. The French club inspected inns and arranged for badge-wearing cyclists to get reduced rates. They also promoted *chambres hygiéniques* by urging hoteliers to clean premises and paint dreary bedrooms white. Ironically hotels now began removing

the heavy carpets that they had bought to meet the British demand
for 'comfort'.[54] 'Comfort' to one generation of travellers had become
'dust-traps' to another.

It is somewhat ironic that the last development in travel before 1914
was actually reactionary. If bicycles were 'democratising' travel,
motor cars were reverting to the world of private travel for the
wealthy few, even if one MP assured motorists that they were
'aiding the cause of peace and international understanding'. The
favourite country for motoring was France where 'automobiling has
"caught on" to an extent . . . that those who have not run over
there recently will find difficult to realise.' The very phrase, 'run
over there', shows how the whole attitude to travel had changed.
As soon as one left Paris there were no speed limits and so
'automobilists have a high time' even if from the beginning there
were problems. In 1907 'a moderate motorist' complained that noisy
motor-cars were creating 'a veritable *petit enfer*' in fashionable
French resorts such as Cabourg.[55]

The 'automobilists' going to the Continent faced many of the
same problems that their great-grandparents had faced. The cars
had to be slung onto boats and on arrival owners had to pay large
deposits that, unlike the deposits on carriages, were fully refunded
when the cars left France. By 1914 arranging these deposits as well
as coping with French driving licences was made easier because
people could get an International Pass from a British motoring association that was good for all of Europe. Every car brought into
France also had to have a white and a green lamp, some form of
horn 'or other sounding apparatus' and a number plate. In France,
Baedeker told automobilists, 'motoring enjoys immense popularity'
and there were garages and 'depots of petrol and workshops' in 'the
smallest towns'. This was good news, given the frequent break-
downs, problems with tyres, accidents and untoward incidents:
when Arthur Balfour, the former Prime Minister, was motoring from
Cannes to Nice to play in an international tennis tournament he was

hit on the cheek by stones thrown by outraged villagers who hated the new vehicles. He carried on, played and lost.[56]

As we have seen already, France was regarded as the 'one land for motoring . . . for the devotee of speed . . . where he can peg down the accelerator pedal and go out all day'. Motorists also had the benefit of the hotels they could find in small towns. *The Times*, with a large readership among the motoring classes, continued, in an article published in 1912 but one that could have been written yesterday: 'Perhaps it is because the smell of coffee is the smell of France . . . at all events, when it arrives in company with delicious *croissants* and snowy napkins . . . it is very good . . . France is happy in its hotels.' In addition, these hotels would cost 40 per cent less than in Britain. Readers were urged to take their cars via Boulogne, the same route the paper had recommended to carriage owners six decades earlier. It cost £4 for a car to cross the Channel and by 1912 the steamers were carrying enough cars to make booking ahead advisable. Motorists were warned that 'Paris itself is to be avoided.' Once in France and assuming one started by 9.30 a.m., motorists going at 25 mph could achieve seventy-five miles before stopping for lunch. 'A comfortable day's run' on the Continent was said to be 125 miles: one could get from Boulogne to Monte Carlo in five days. As to costs, one had to allow £1 a day for petrol and, when hotels and meals were added, a party of three with a 'motor man' (engineer) would cost about £5 a day. (This amount could provide others with a week's holiday.) Those travelling to the south often preferred to have their car and chauffeur shipped from London Bridge to Bordeaux. This was a favourite route for travellers such as Lord Sandwich who would go to Bordeaux by train and then be driven to Pau where he could watch 'several aeroplanes' at work.[57] The idea that Pau was a quiet retreat for invalids had obviously had its day.

Another *Times* article, this time containing 'simple hints for Women', reminded them that the worst feminine fault was not to be ready when their husbands wanted to drive forth because waiting was 'sorely trying to the masculine temper'. (Men, of course, are never late.) However, motoring offered women 'freedom and independence from all the regular duties' and made them blessedly free of the need for maids. As to those worries entertained by travellers a century earlier, ladies were reassured that French hotel bedding was now better than the English and 'baths and sanitary arrangements, even in small towns, are astonishingly good'. On this 'the demands of the English . . . have been generously met'. Yet there was one new worry in 1910: 'motor fever'. Those afflicted 'never want to get anywhere; you only want to go on'. (Washington Irving had said the same thing about the British in 1824.) But with cars, travelling was so easy that one might end up doing nothing but driving. In short, 'the car must remain our slave and not become our master'.[58]

The car's importance in changing fashions in travel is seen in Rudyard Kipling's admission that he had known 'little of France' beyond Paris but 'the coming of the automobile . . . revealed . . . the immense and amazing beauty' of the country. He became an enthusiastic advocate of motoring holidays in spite of the shouts of 'Assassin' from peasants on the road. Those who did not have their own cars could go as a party on a 'Private Motor Car Tour' of Switzerland and northern Italy (the modern 'lakes and mountains'), offered by Continental Travel for 50 guineas. In Nice, visitors could have a tour of the city for 15 francs for three people. People could also hire cars and drivers abroad, which is what A. E. Housman, did. The effect of the car on France's rural inns and hotels was even greater than that of cyclists because their owners had more money and clout. In 1911 a writer pointed out how 'the small French country hotel is coming into its own, largely through the *Touring Club de France*, which has done great work in improving the French hotel of all grades. Especially . . . the small hotel of the countryside'. The club published its own guide and described what facilities an inn offered: 'those cabalistic letters "W.C.", opposite the name of a hotel . . . indicate improved sanitary arrangements of a kind that scarcely existed a few years ago'.[59] What the British had done a hundred years before in their carriages, motorists, both British and French, were doing now to the ultimate benefit of all tourists.

Motoring further afield presented additional problems, and the benefits were slower in coming. Lieutenant Francis Grenfell was in Germany in 1912 when Germans were worried about a possible war with France. He hired a car, in part because so many trains were cancelled because of 'repeated alarms'. He drove with a companion from The Hague to Berlin, some 256 miles, but found the roads difficult and was 'much delayed by asking the way'. There was even more trouble when he left for Dresden – 'splendid road but difficult to find & so wasted much time'. On top of everything else he had trouble with the car, a situation that one suspects was probably fairly typical: problems with tyres and with pieces falling off even affected Edward VII's cars when taken to Marienbad or Biarritz. Whatever problems Lieutenant Grenfell had in Germany, in Italy the roads were 'so discouraging' that many early motorists avoided the country.[60] There was also a fascination for Alpine motoring. Just as William Brockedon had produced his book about Alpine passes for those in carriages in the 1820s, so Charles Freeston published *The High-Roads of the Alps. A Motoring Guide to One Hundred Mountain Passes* in 1911.

By 1914 there were 196,783 cars in Britain or roughly one for every 200,000 people, and many of the owners had enjoyed or were looking forward to enjoying continental holidays. That enthusiastic motorist Rudyard Kipling gave a lecture on travel to the Royal Geographical Society that year and spoke of the 'fascinating subject of smells in their relation to the traveller'. He noticed how often travellers lovingly recalled the characteristic odour of a place but warned that soon all we shall speak about is the smell of petrol.[61]

Chapter 7

Is the Luggage Safe?

'*T*he married Briton on a tour is but a luggage overseer: his luggage is his morning thought, and his nightly terror.' If he is on a train 'he is always thinking, or ordered by his wife to think, "Is the luggage safe?" . . . It never leaves him (except when it DOES leave him . . . and make him doubly miserable).' Despite the contemporary ring, Thackeray's depiction of a man's worries about luggage dates from the 1840s, from his *The Kickleburys on the Rhine*. The first consideration for the 'luggage overseer' was the limit imposed by carriers, and frequent were the laments that 'the amount allowed to each person is ridiculously small'. In the 1820s a traveller going directly by the public coach from London to Paris was allowed only fourteen pounds while in France even those using private carriages were restricted to 140 pounds if they were posting with three horses. The second consideration was the fees charged by luggage handlers. At Ramsgate in 1836 porters charged one shilling for a portmanteau and 1*s* 6*d* for a trunk or box weighing more than half a hundredweight or 56 pounds, sums that would have easily paid for an entire meal in France or Italy. Few travellers, it seems, were inhibited by such charges, as Percy Fitzgerald saw when he watched the steamer being loaded at Dover: 'One gazes in wonder at the vast brass-bound chests . . . caught so deftly by the nimble mariners . . . Every instant the pile is growing . . . Hatboxes and light leather cases are sent bounding down like footballs . . . forming the mountain.'[1]

Henry Gaze had advised a traveller to take only a knapsack and a portmanteau, but he assumed travellers were going for only a week or ten days and wanted to avoid porters' fees. Experienced travellers agreed: a 'carpet-bag, with a coat-case at bottom, is enough for any man and a small tin case to hold a uniform, which is an absolute necessity'. Some went even further: the architect Augustus Pugin, on a hurried tour to study continental buildings, stuffed all he required in his pockets; but his moderation was rarely followed. Lady William Russell had no fewer than seventy-six boxes, labelled with her name, as she wandered about the Continent. In the 1850s an American observed that 'English travellers generally . . . were laden with luggage' and two decades later Augustus Hare was in a train compartment and noted that his seven fellow passengers had between them twenty-eight hand bags. One can only wonder how many items were in the luggage van.[2]

Ladies were not, of course, expected to carry heavy luggage; that was the man's duty. As the feminist writer Emily Lowe quipped, the 'only use of a gentleman in travelling is to look after the luggage, and we take care to have no luggage', except one carpet bag. Any man would have needed to be strong to cope with Victorian luggage. When the Birchalls arrived in Vienna on their honeymoon they told the waiting porter their bags weighed 300 pounds. The porter's cry of *'Jesu Maria!!!'* was 'in accents of such genuine horror that we could not help laughing'. However, this couple was exceeded by one Hampshire vicar who looked after some 1,300 pounds of luggage for himself, his wife and two nieces. When the Swiss officials said there was not enough time to weigh all this before the train left, the clergyman unleashed some 'most fearsome objurgations'. He still had to wait for the next train.[3]

What other people pack in their luggage is always mystifying, whatever the century. William Fox Talbot moaned to his mother from Calais in 1824, 'I am nearly overwhelmed with luggage. I bring you . . . a shawl from Aunt Louisa . . . I have myriads of English Novels which I shall never get into the Sardinian States, & a monstrous telescope, which I am to try in Italian skies.' One guide-book even had to warn against taking pianos, since they could be hired abroad, as the Masons did when in Montpellier, as we have seen. Most continental railways were as strict as coaches had been and insisted on weighing and registering luggage. These procedures could cause problems, as one young man discovered in the 1840s. Not only did his luggage contain several horseshoes as a gift, a 'large canister of tea', and numerous books 'which I had brought out for my own amusement . . . and for rainy days . . . the books were distributed amidst the contents of two densely-filled portmanteaus and a large waterproof carpet bag – novels, romances, and French and German grammars, dictionaries, and dialogue-books – some five-and-thirty volumes'. The 'wretches' insisted on emptying out all this to weigh it, leaving him but a few minutes to race for his train:[4]

> I am naturally very alert in all cases of emergency; but my present discomfiture was . . . so extreme, that I remained . . . in a sort of stupor, staring at my pile of things . . . I had to be told three times to 'pack' before I came sufficiently to my senses. However, by dint of desperation and recklessness of consequences to many articles inside, I did manage to cram everything in, and was in time for the train.

Unlike travellers today, Victorians always assumed there would be people to help. Those planning extended 'pedestrianizing' in Switzerland for example could arrange for their heavier baggage to be forwarded to post offices along the way at only seven pence for twenty-two pounds. At ports, coaching inns and later railway stations there were always swarms of porters and hotel *commissionaires* to assist. A man arriving in Calais in 1817 was besieged by six porters: one grabbed his portmanteau, another, his *sac de nuit*, the third, his greatcoat while the fourth carried his umbrella, and yet others followed, beseeching him for something to carry. In France it was quite common for porters to be women. One traveller admitted: 'I felt ashamed to let her do it, but it was her vocation, and she strode away, though but a girl of eighteen, bearing a large portmanteau and a carpet-bag.' As early as the 1820s there were firms such as the Commercial Shipping Agents who insured baggage while later the Gaze agency provided 'Gaze's International Baggage Service'. This was only one of many such services that insured luggage and arranged for it to be sent ahead.[5]

As today, there were basically two types of baggage: hand luggage or *sacs de nuit* and larger items, mainly portmanteaus and trunks, which were placed in the storage areas of boats, carriages and trains. Despite their French name, *sacs de nuit* were carpet bags and 'intensely English, so plain, straightforward, sensible'.[6] They were like today's 'over-night' cases and held essential items. Fortunately, French Customs officers allowed passengers to take them straight to their hotel if the bulky luggage was being left for inspection. A traveller in a hurry could move quickly if carrying only this one bag since these passengers were usually allowed ashore first. A carpet bag was also useful if travellers wished to leave the bulk of their luggage in one place when they travelled about. Some economical travellers made their own bags. Turner converted the binding of a battered book into a case for painting supplies while Mary Eyre, a thrifty Yorkshire woman, made her own bag from some old plaid material. A portmanteau was literally a 'portmanteau word', although most were quite large and increasingly divided into several compartments, which made it easier to find items. The compartments might also encourage prying Customs officials not to disarrange everything, or at least that was the hope.

Somewhat perversely, guide-books both told people to take as little as possible and advertised an ever-expanding range of cleverly contrived items for comfort and safety. Indeed, there are few better examples of the Victorian ability to meet the needs of an increasing market. Murray's 1857 guide to central Italy contained advertisements for travelling desks, railway rugs, travelling and pocket inkstands, travelling soap, door and window fasteners, cash belts and straps, and, for a shilling, polyglot washing books 'to save

Travellers the trouble of translating their Washing Bills'. There were also portable baths and even portable chamber-pots. The London firm Allen's widely advertised their catalogue of 500 articles for travellers, which included 'Allen's patent quadruple portmanteau' and the 'Lady's Wardrobe Portmanteau'. Although sold in a wide variety of prices, luggage remained, in proportion to other travel costs, far more expensive than today. An American visitor was impressed by all these bags and saw them as symbols of a Briton's pre-eminence: 'You may know him by the quantity and variety of his luggage, by every ingenious contrivance for comfort . . . There is no . . . adaptation to circumstances and . . . He must stand forth, wherever he goes, the impersonation of his island-home.'[7]

Packing was in itself quite an art. Mrs Beeton offered the consoling thought that 'the improved trunks and portmanteaus . . . in which there is a place for nearly everything, render this more simple than formerly'. She provided instructions for maids because packing required 'not only knowledge but some practice'. One must first line the case with paper before wrapping the best clothes in calico. Unpacking was less of an art and, in the case of ladies, was something often undertaken by a maid. In 1854 an exhausted Lady Shelley arrived at Lord Brougham's villa in Cannes without a maid. She thought it worth noting in her diary that 'for the first time in my life, I unpacked my carpet bag'. Her Ladyship was sixty-seven.[8]

In addition to portmanteaus, carpet bags and trunks, most travellers had dressing cases, which were regarded as badges of maturity for both men and women. These elegantly worked boxes remain highly desirable objects to anyone interested in antiques. At its simplest a man's case held little more than shaving equipment and a few basic items such as combs. At its most elegant it boasted silver-topped crystal bottles of colognes, powders and, perhaps, some discreet hair dye as well as, in some instances, tea-making equipment. Ladies' cases were more intricate, with bottles of perfumes and other essentials carefully fitted into secure compartments. At the 1851 Great Exhibition a Parisian jeweller exhibited a dressing case of ebony inlaid with marquetry. Inside were eighty items in silver and gilt. Locked dressing cases were also a favourite place to carry money, documents, cherished photographs and letters. The leading manufacturer, Mechi, advertised cases from £1 to £100 so 'the man of fortune or he of moderate means,' could each afford a case.[9]

In the decades before beards became fashionable, many men took the opportunity to stop shaving even if they still carried razors in their cases. Bishop Hynes commented in 1853 that 'some of our English travellers are so bedizened with beard and moustache that one can hardly distinguish them from foreigners'. This novelty naturally provoked humorous comment: 'A razor would be super-fluous as you will aim at being horribly *hirsute* on your travels.' After 1856 fashions were changed by soldiers returning from the Crimean War. Before then, while moustaches might be sported by officers, beards were emblems of continental students and, even worse, radicals. After 1856 it was a different story. Henry Gaze advised his male clients in the 1860s to avoid this 'needless daily infliction', and one architect concerned with sanitary reform went even further: 'shaving brush, razor and strop, are of course superflu-ities, being not merely cumbrous, but injurious to the health'.[10] This shift in fashion had one advantage: it lightened men's luggage.

In addition to looking after dressing cases, portmanteaus, carpet bags and trunks many men had a small, leather 'Courier's Bag' slung across their chests, as in the 1840s German figurine of the 'English Traveller'. This had been the virtual badge of couriers, but others found them useful too, for keeping money and documents. If all this were not enough, a 'considerable number' of passengers on Channel boats also carried 'a comfortable picnick [*sic*] box or basket'. On the feminine front, many ladies never travelled without their 'work', the sewing or knitting that helped to pass the time. Some 'work' was of immediate use: domestic manuals contained instructions for all sorts of cloth bags, including one to enclose costly dressing cases. As always there were dissenting views. Among the innumerable manuals of advice for women an 1857 book pronounced that a lady needed only three objects on the train: a book, sandwiches and smelling salts.[11] Presumably her husband carried the rest.

Finally there were those awkward but necessary objects that came to mark the British tourist. Almost every illustration featuring travellers showed them with several walking sticks, umbrellas and sometimes alpenstocks wrapped in travelling rugs. With all this impedimenta it is easy to see why one Italian novelist described the British on a train as 'hedged in on either side by a fabulous outwork of carpet-bags, work-bags, dressing-case bags, leather hand-bags, books, baskets, cushions, shawls, cloaks, wrappers etc.'. The search for comfort was never-ending.[12] Having said that, as continental hotels improved, at least the need to lug baths and chamber-pots decreased.

What did travellers stuff into this staggering array of bags and trunks? There were, as already noted, a variety of books. Next came boots, blue-tinted spectacles (sunglasses) and veils to protect the eyes and back of the neck. Then there were numerous medicines of which Mariana Starke provided a long list: liquid laudanum (tincture of opium), James's Powder (for fevers and inflammation), oil of lavender (antiseptic and good for flea bites), spirit of lavender (lavender water), sweet spirit of nitre (diuretic), antimonial wine (renal problems), supercarbonated kali (a form of sodium bicarbonate), vitriolic acid (to purify water), ipecacuanha (laxative), emetic tartar (skin ointment), bark (quinine), sal volatile ('smelling salts'), that popular but dangerous remedy for bowel problems, Calomel, and if the tincture of laudanum were not enough, some 'pure opium'. Then there was sulphuric acid, used as a tonic, an astringent, a 'refrigerant', a gargle, and a remedy for skin infections (and pain relief) if mixed with lard. Travellers should not forget lint and plasters and most important of all, a good 'dispensary' or guide so that they would not end up killing themselves. Matches were needed to light candles (and later oil lamps), while soap was essential because continental hotels did not provide any. One comic account sneeringly advised: 'If you are an Englishman, you will take soap; if a German, you will dispense with it.'[13]

In the early decades a surprisingly large number of men also carried weapons because people had a well-founded fear of banditti in Italy, Greece and Spain. One of the most experienced early travellers, William Brockedon, said that travelling Britons were 'usually armed' with pistols, and guide-books advised keeping pistols in every carriage. Lord Byron travelled with a veritable arsenal while in 1829 Lord Malmesbury, a future Foreign Secretary, was arrested for having a swordstick in his carriage at Mt Vesuvius. By mid-century, governments, especially in Italy, were taking action against the outlaws and by the last decades of the century these were no longer such a problem, at least outside Spain and Greece. With the virtual disappearance of the banditti, weapons disappeared as well, so much so that Baedeker's 1909 guide to Italy warned that Customs officials would seize all weapons including *armi insidiose* or concealed weapons such as sword sticks.[14]

As in any era, clothes made up the bulk of what people packed. As to what ladies took most writers, male and female, were rather coy. This notwithstanding, in the 1850s the 'Roving Englishman' offered some advice. A lady's dresses 'should be as close fitting as possible, yet perfectly easy' as 'tight lacing has spoiled many a pleasant tour'. She should avoid lace, flowers and hanging sleeves because they will get torn. The dresses, shawl, bonnet and gloves should be grey, brown or black (so as not to show dirt). Brown and grey were preferable because they could not be mistaken for mourning. In Augustus Egg's well-known 1862 painting *The Travelling Companions* we see two ladies in a railway carriage with a Mediterranean landscape visible through the window. This also shows how beautiful grey dresses could be, and how much room they took up in the compartment. Ladies were also urged to take Eau de Cologne to revive themselves in crowded trains in an era before deodorants. A drop or two could also purify water for washing and 'teeth-cleaning'. A woman should wear dark boots, not shoes, and take a brown or black parasol. Finally there was a warning: second-class carriages are 'not fit for ladies' because men might smoke or eat sausages.

Because all clothes, and women's in particular, were far heavier than today's, ladies were urged to wear thinner dresses in the summer. As most people seem to have travelled between June and October, the reminder was sensible. However, even in summer ladies' garments were still heavy, and from the 1840s expanded in bulk. At their bulkiest stage in the 1850s and 1860s a woman's dress could use up to forty yards of fabric. In addition, ladies wore three or four petticoats in 'layers varying from flannel through muslin to white, starched cotton', and underneath, a muslin shift and under this, underwear. Over the shifts were corsets and, between the 1860s and the early twentieth century, bustles. Ladies also had capes or coats (in the cooler months), muffs, bonnets or hats, gloves, bags and parasols. By the 1880s the size of dresses began to decrease. Straighter skirts replaced the billowing effect of the crinoline era and the number of petticoats was reduced; but much of the paraphernalia remained the same. Yet despite male stereotypes, some women did travel lightly. When Mary Eyre went to France she packed 'a spare dress, a thin shawl, two changes of every type of underwear', two pairs of shoes, and writing material, as well as her Prayer Book and 'the inevitable "Murray"'.[15]

For men the main problem was the jacket. Henry Gaze, concerned with lower-middle-class travellers, recommended a lightweight 'tourist's suit', a light felt hat with a wide brim or a stitched cloth hat, linen or paper collars, a waterproof coat or silk umbrella, a tourist's or courier's bag, a pocket knife, nail scissors, wax matches, pocket comb, paper and envelopes, pens and portable inkstand, nail and tooth brushes, an extra pair of wool socks and handkerchiefs, shirts, night shirt and stout purse. There is no reference to underwear. In addition, travellers should pack soap, slippers, and shaving apparatus if required.[16] 'The Roving Englishman', a diplomat and reputedly the illegitimate son of a duke, assumed his traveller would be, like himself, higher up the social scale. This man should wear 'a plain black morning coat' with dark trousers and waistcoat. In his suitcase he should pack a black coat, light dress waistcoat, one pair of dress trousers (these three were in effect evening dress), six shirts, six pairs of socks, two neck and six pocket-handkerchiefs, 'a rolling Russian-leather dressing case', a second pair of boots ('elastic kid dress-boots' were best), one pair of slippers, some Mordan's pencils (propelling pencils first invented by Sampson Mordan in 1822), a sketch book, sponge, soap, his India rubber bath, his Murray and a 'strong' purse (sturdy rather than well filled).[17]

When the Roving Englishman gave advice about suitcases he stated that a man must have 'a small tin case to hold a uniform which is an absolute necessity'. (In a middle class journal such as *Household Words* this must have been written with tongue in cheek.) A uniform could be 'an absolute necessity' for two reasons. First, it provided the proper attire for presentation to royalty. Second, in Europe a uniform showed the wearer was a man of importance. In 1820 young Joseph Strutt was told by Lord Lauderdale to be sure to take a uniform to receive better treatment in places open to the public, including churches, and Lord Lauderdale was right. When Granville Lloyd Baker was in Rome in 1864 he was late for the singing of Allegri's exquisite *Miserere* in the Sistine Chapel, a favourite event for tourists. However, to be sure of a seat he had worn a uniform and was given an excellent place.[18] Privy Councillors had Court dress, which Gladstone took to be presented to the Pope, but most men, such as Lloyd Baker, opted for the militia uniform. Thackeray often made fun of this practice, but when he was studying in Grand Ducal Weimar he asked his parents to send him the Devonshire militia uniform, which he had no right to wear. Ladies who hoped to be presented or to grace royal or aristocratic receptions had an even harder time of it. They needed elaborate Court dresses with trains as well as plumes for their hair – and all this meant yet more trunks.

The majority of travellers had little hope of being presented to Popes or Grand Dukes and ignored the advice about uniforms.

However, men should not have ignored the Roving Englishman's advice about taking a 'plain black morning coat'. Gentlemen might relax their dress codes during the day but not at night and many expected to wear formal evening attire at the theatre, at receptions and parties, at concerts and, in more expensive hotels, at the evening meal. It was not very pleasant to be caught out: in 1860 an Eton master was 'in despair' because he had no dress clothes when invited to dine by the British Minister in Turin. He managed to cobble together an almost presentable outfit by borrowing a white tie only to discover the other British guests were 'a motley crew, dressed in lounge suits of every conceivable colour'. Undeterred he swore that if 'I were travelling with nothing but a knapsack I would carry a dress suit in it'. Early twentieth-century guide-books reminded travellers that in the newer, grand hotels 'It is the custom to dress for dinner and in the best hotels in Switzerland it is essential to wear evening dress.' Ladies were also reminded that 'low dresses are not worn in the hotels'.[19]

Where British men ignored the Roving Englishman's advice most was in their choice of daily dress. When one of Jerome K. Jerome's characters set off in the 1890s he never considered a black coat but followed Gaze's advice about a 'light tourist's suit' and bought 'a check-suit, and a blue veil, and a white umbrella, and suchlike necessities of the English tourist'. Because British men were often taller than Europeans, they presented, in whatever they wore, impressive, or at least arresting, sights. One woman boasted that 'wherever an English gentleman is seen, he looks and feels one of the lords of the earth'. Perhaps, but these 'lords of the earth' often looked quite bizarre. These 'tourist's suits' consisted of a checked shooting or short jacket frequently worn with matching knicker-bockers and were the standard 'leisure wear' of Victorian gentlemen *in the country*. This craze for checked suits was surprisingly long lasting, equivalent to today's passion for blue jeans. Although few would have worn the outfit in London, most were happy to wear it everywhere on the Continent. French shops featured caricatures, bronze statuettes and even chocolate models of British tourists in this get-up. A character in the novel *The Cockaynes in Paris*, 'in his plaid sporting-suit . . . proceeded to "do" Paris. In London Mr. Cockayne was in the habit of dressing like any other respectable elderly gentleman' but in his informal outfit 'he had a notion . . . that he had done the "correct thing" for foreign parts.' The British treated Paris 'as though it were a back garden, in which a person may lounge in his old clothes' (Chapter 5). Yet in another book the novelist describes his own parents' delight in visiting France and discarding 'the stiff dressing, the conventional laces, of the West End'.[20]

The jackets, trousers and waistcoats of these 'sporting suits' were often in tweed and sometimes in the boldest check patterns. So distinctive did this way of dress become that to one American observer the Briton's 'shooting jacket, checked trowsers [*sic*], and brown gaiters proclaim his nationality before he begins to speak.' In 1873 a young Pole wandering through the Swiss Alps glimpsed an 'unforgettable Englishman . . . with the mien of an ardent and fearless traveller . . . clad in a knickerbocker suit . . . [with] short socks under his laced boot'.[21] This exquisite Englishman became 'the ambassador of my future' for the young Józef Konrad Korzeniowski, later known as Joseph Conrad.

Others were less charitable. 'Dicky' Doyle's popular book of drawings, *The Foreign Tour of Messrs. Brown, Jones, and Robinson*, shows Jones dressed in his check suit slouching at the Court Opera in Vienna. This is contrasted with another drawing showing him at the opera in London where he sits upright, properly attired in evening dress. No wonder that a monk at an isolated monastery in Sicily was as astonished at the sight of the Duke of Buckingham's chaplain in a shooting jacket as he was at the Duke's travelling bed. Murray's *Handbooks* did their best to warn travellers that 'a frock-coat is better than that pet dress of juvenile Englishmen – a shooting jacket . . . [which] will attract notice in the streets of a foreign town'. At the other end of the guide-book market, *Chambers's Handy Guide to Paris* almost pleaded: 'Dress as you would in England: the affectation of a *négligé* style not only shows a vulgar taste, but is anything but complimentary to a nation scrupulous of its attire.' Even those who struck back at the criticism were defensive: 'It is true that numbers of Englishmen . . . are so given up to the study of the countries in which they travel that they have no time left to attend to their get-up. Though they are all round, the best-dressed people in Europe when at home, it is true that they often do not look like themselves while travelling.'[22]

When it came to women's dress it was the French who were most fastidious. By 1814 French fashion had played no part in British designs for ten years and if Frenchmen could not defeat the British at Waterloo they could at least fire fusillades at *les Anglaises*. In 1816 it was reported that the French had decided that 'the well-fitting gowns of the English women at the waist and bosom, [are] indecent'. But it was not only the French who laughed; the commander of the Allied forces who fought against Napoleon was an Austrian prince who was aghast when he saw the Foreign Secretary's wife: 'She is very fat and dresses so *young*, so *tight*, so *naked*.' Another Austrian, the Foreign Minister Clemens von Metternich, who was busy buying clothes for his wife and mistress, agreed. He was appalled at the average British woman's dress: 'You have to see it to believe it.' So bad were things in these early years that in Geneva the authorities asked a group of English ladies to remain indoors because a mob had gathered to stare. The main problem was the shorter skirts. Even the most august were subjected to carping as Queen Victoria discovered on her state visit to Paris in 1855. A bluff *Maréchal de France* thought her skirt too short, or as the kindly Empress Eugénie said diplomatically, the Queen's attire was 'so different from our Paris fashion'.[23]

If women's dresses upset the French, so too did bonnets. Victoria was sufficiently intimidated in 1855 that when she shopped incognito in Paris she changed her normal bonnet for one in the French style, that is, with a different shape. Unlike their sovereign, most British women travellers had no choice but to be seen with their own bonnets in Paris. Not only did the French find the British style ridiculous but the head-gear itself was peculiar. 'Anyone who has crossed the . . . Channel, knows that the bonnet as we understand the word . . . is not an article of national costume in any portion of the world except our own island – America and Australia we place, of course, out of the pale of taste' pronounced one supercilious male critic. Even worse than ordinary bonnets were the huge hoods called, quite accurately, 'uglies', which went over the bonnets in mid-century. The journalist George Augustus Sala wrote that 'you meet everybody on the cliff at Capri' including 'Her Majesty's ministers in plaid shooting-jackets, bishops' wives in green "uglies", gouty old generals in wide-awake hats, [and] archdeacons in waterproof coats'. 'Uglies' were folding hoods supported on wires that were fixed to the front of bonnets to shade the face. These were particularly popular on Rhine steamers, Swiss lakes and southern shores and protected the delicate complexion of English ladies. The appropriate name for these 'convenient though unsightly shades' was, according to one account, given by bemused foreigners.[24] When bonnets finally gave way to hats, 'uglies' disappeared, unmourned.

Judgements on British women's appearance when made by European, that is, by French, that is, by Parisian couturier's standards were very important to many women and to a surprising number of men. Travel books often contained passages contrasting not just the fashions but the beauty of continental women with British women. Fortunately, most authors concluded that Britannia's daughters were undoubtedly the more beautiful, but they frequently admitted that their dress was sometimes inferior. Captain Beadles, who was in Paris in 1821, decided that French women surpassed the British in the elegance of their dresses but this could be 'ascribed to the beauty & cheapness of French silks'.[25] Many English women agreed and took the opportunity to replenish their wardrobes when abroad, especially in Paris where they could acquire the latest fashions.

By the 1860s fashionable Englishwomen's clothes were not as heavily criticized by the French as they had been in the decades after Waterloo, yet differences remained that made British women immediately identifiable. In 1860 two English sisters walking along the Boulevard St Honoré were annoyed when a drunken man, 'dressed like a gentleman', tried to grab *l'Anglaise* in her *belle robe*. Worse was to come when later a little boy of *four* saluted them with '*Ah, des belles Anglaises*'. One Scottish traveller assured the 'fair sex' that by 1863, 'in respect of bonnets, cloaks, and other female attire' the styles were virtually the same 'in London, Paris, or Glasgow, the railroad and the steamboat having made fashion the same everywhere'.[26] The sartorial views of an elderly Glaswegian 'invalid' should be taken with a grain of salt. If there was growing uniformity it was because British women were following Paris. Trying to conform was not always easy, however. One young woman, after examining the clothes in a Parisian shop in the early 1890s, described the latest style as having 'the most impressive bustles and the most impossible bonnets. I, walking innocently in my . . . clothes feel half my size when I meet them.' British women's subservience to Parisian fashions grew with the century, fed through the vogue for women's fashion magazines with coloured illustrations of the latest Parisian styles. One book of *Hints to Lady Travellers* proclaimed at the end of the 1880s that '[t]he days are, happily, now long past' when English women's costumes 'excited the derision of foreign nations and made the British female abroad an object of terror and avoidance to all beholders'.[27]

Such confidence was not well founded. In 1898 a New York journalist with tongue in cheek described British women travellers. He praised their sensible if unstylish dresses: 'a dress of any dull-colored cloth, made very plain and rather snug . . . with a skirt reaching barely to the ankles'. The thick, sturdy shoes should 'look like a man's while the hat should be a turban with a feather'. The woman should wear white gloves and carry an umbrella, a guide-book and a lorgnette. When his readers were pondering how a woman managed all that they came to the punchline: 'Many a pretty, rosy-cheeked English girl disguises her beauty in this ungraceful costume.' Bonnets had given way to hats and turbans, which in the 1890s gave way to straw boaters, which remained fashionable until 1914. Shorter skirts remained. But the British could never win, except at war and commerce. As late as 1912 an English woman living in Paris said that the 'French caricature' of the British tourist was of a 'red-haired, flat-chested, protruding-teethed, short-skirted female, and the red-faced, sandy-haired, be-capped male with a pipe'. She admitted that such specimens 'abound'.[28] One suspects the French could never be satisfied.

Among the people George Augustus Sala saw on the cliff at Capri were 'archdeacons in waterproof coats'. The desire to protect oneself against rain was natural enough, especially for the British, and here again entrepreneurial technology in the 1820s and 1830s provided the answer with the 'mackintosh'. Even Pugin, who travelled with everything in his pockets, took a mackintosh, perhaps to have more pockets. The British love of waterproof capes or coats was another source of amusement to foreigners. The French in particular found these clumsy coverings (originally made of India rubber) yet another rich source of humour. One popular number at a music-hall in the Boulevard Montmartre in the 1850s featured a singer who came on as a red-haired 'milord' wearing checked trousers and carrying a carpet bag. He made repeated references to his 'mackintosh' and ended each couplet of his comic song with 'aow yes, aow yes'. Not surprisingly, there were calls for encores. In his 1884 short story 'Miss Harriet' Maupassant made use of this reputation for India rubber in his eponymous character. She was an elderly English spinster who went about trying to convert the natives and who had '*une certaine odeur de caoutchouc* [India rubber]'. But Maupassant was behind the times. Since mid-century Edminston's Pocket Siphonia or 'Waterproof Overcoat' had been on the market. It weighed only twelve ounces and customers were assured that it lacked the smell and stickiness of earlier mackin-toshes. But its high prices – forty-two shillings and fifty shillings (all silk) – made it a luxury item.[29] However, the rigidity and heaviness of the older version did have one benefit: an Oxford don invented a mackintosh that could be put on a frame to serve as a portable bath; his discovery does not seem to have become terribly popular.

Sala's reference to 'gouty old generals in wide-awake hats' reminds us that Victorian men were as devoted to their head-gear as women. In a large picture in *The Graphic* magazine in 1896, showing excursionists arriving in Boulogne, every person is wearing some type of hat: the sole exception is a young girl suffering from sea-sickness whose hat is held by her grandmother. This little girl reminds us that children were not excluded from the wearing of hats. The illustrations in the 1882 children's book *Abroad*, an account of a family trip to Paris, shows all the English children, with one possible exception, in some form of hat when in public. Only when sleeping on trains were hats (but never bonnets) removed. While glengarry caps and German travelling caps were favoured at certain times, the most popular was the 'wide-awake', a wide-brimmed felt hat. This travelled easily and protected the wearer from the sun. However, in many countries it was regarded as the virtual uniform of a revolutionary and some English travellers got into serious trouble for wearing one. A young Oxford man wandering round Prague in 1853 ignored an order to take his off because Austrian officials regarded it as 'a revolutionary emblem'. When he was stopped a second time and threatened with arrest he put it away. Earlier, an Edinburgh lawyer's wide-awake caused alarm in Florence when debates over Italian unification were raging. As his passport was being inspected he placed his hat upside down on a table. An official noticed that the name inside was Mazzini, one of the leading Italian revolutionaries. The lawyer was bundled off to gaol and only released the next day after a protest by the British Minister. The hat had been bought in Genoa from a Signor Mazzini, a distant relation of the revolutionary.[30]

In mid-century very tall top hats were the fashion, even when travelling. One Devon antiquarian noted that his barrister father wearied of his 'chimney pot' in 1851, and plonked it onto the head of a poor Italian standing nearby, thereby causing a sensation among the onlookers. Even so, the generous barrister still ordered that a servant must be ready with a new hat when he arrived in London lest he appear half naked. By 1867 this man had given up the struggle and had stopped taking the cumbersome thing abroad. His antiquarian son remembered that the last time he spotted a 'chimney pot' was on 28 December 1909 at, of all places, the top of Vesuvius. It was worn by a Hindu who was also dressed in a 'very loud check suit', a rare vignette showing how British customs lingered longer among travellers from the empire.[31] Also, for some curious reason, British men also had a penchant for wearing white 'chimney-pot' hats until the 1870s even though men wearing them were not allowed in the Tuileries Gardens. White hats of course became very dirty, but, once again, entrepreneurs provided a solution: hat covers. By the end of the century tall hats had shrunk into top hats and were confined to rather formal wear on holiday. More common were bowlers, Homburgs and straw boaters.

As with later generations, people lugged about clothes that were never used. One way round this was to buy what was needed abroad where clothes were cheaper, but this could produce exotic results, as one German observed while settling into a diligence about to leave Dresden. Suddenly a strangely apparelled Englishman dashed in front of the horses: 'His collar, I believe had been bought in Italy, his trousers in France, his cap in Germany and his manners picked up everywhere. It did not rain, nevertheless he carried a huge umbrella to shield him against the sun.' Having 'slightly adjusted his cravat and dusted his coat' he held up the carriage till his servant ran up with his luggage including the hat box. Then he took his place and told the startled observer that he was going to visit every province of the Austrian Empire although he spoke no German, no Italian, no Polish, no Czech, no Slovak, no Serbo-Croat and no Magyar.[32]

Since walking tours in Normandy, the Tyrol or, most favoured of all, Switzerland were favourite holidays, they influenced the clothes people brought. Henry Gaze recommended men to take flannel shirts, gauze under-shirts (to absorb sweat), a coloured woollen suit, a waterproof suit, leggings called 'Zouaves' and wool socks, which – no doubt by mere chance – could be bought from J. S. Carter of Oxford Street who – no doubt by another mere chance – advertised in the book. In 1873 Challoner Chute actually described the contents of his rucksack when he and his sisters went on a walking tour in Switzerland, and it is interesting to compare what he took with what he was advised to take. Because he was confined to a small space his possessions must have been what he regarded as essential: a nightshirt, a pair of trousers, light shoes, 'warming medicine', myrrh, eau de Cologne, Euchrisma (a per-fumed hair lotion) – the last three being wrapped in three pairs of socks. In addition he had a second flannel shirt, one pair of drawers, a vest, coat and waistcoat, books, glycerine and a Prayer Book. A side pocket contained a brush, sponge, soap, razor, razor paper (to sharpen the blade), shaving soap and a small bottle of camphor (after-shave). In a second pocket he had more socks, a bottle of ink rolled in blotting paper, paper collars and another bottle of 'camph. chl.' (camphor chloride for his portable stove). Between the knapsack's flaps he had his various papers and in his breast pockets he put his money, brandy flask, Baedeker and a German dictionary. His sisters carried hand bags and 'wrappers' containing shawls and waterproofs. A mule carried his sisters' 'leather box'; what this contained is not mentioned. If the knapsack had been too heavy, Chute could hire 'a little ragamuffin to carry it all day, together with your great-coat, for the merest trifle'.[33]

One thing which Chute forgot was a strong cotton umbrella, which was the usual accompaniment of the stereotyped British traveller – or was it? One authority, writing ten years before the First World War, warned: 'Never carry an umbrella. German ped-estrians always carry one.' Even worse, Germans were renowned for tramping about in trousers (not knickerbockers) 'and sometimes in a frock coat!' One might be mistaken for a German and that would never do.[34] It is interesting to note that walkers, and others, particularly in Switzerland, assumed that hotels would provide slippers if their double-soled boots were caked with mud.

Some travellers were keen not just to be properly dressed but to be seen to be properly dressed. One American novelist, writing in 1873, found it all rather amusing:

> The Englishman . . . who has set out to do Switzerland . . . wears a brandy-flask, a field-glass and a haversack. Whether he has a silk or soft hat, he is certain to wear a veil tied round it . . . it looks adventurous . . . Everybody – almost everybody – has an alpenstock . . . We saw a noble young Briton . . . who was got up in the best Alpine manner. He wore . . . an entire suit of light gray [*sic*] flannel . . . His shoes . . . [had] large spikes in the soles; and on his white hat he wore a large quantity of gauze, which fell in folds down his neck . . . He carried a formidable alpenstock; and . . . leaned on it in . . . the most graceful and daring attitudes that I ever saw the human form assume . . . it turned out that he hadn't been anywhere, and didn't seem likely to do anything but show himself at the frequented valley places.

The novelist later saw the would-be mountaineer at Interlaken, 'enduring all the hardships of that fashionable place. There was also there another of the same country, got up for the most dangerous Alpine climbing, conspicuous in red woollen stockings that came above his knees. I could not learn that he ever went up anything higher than the top of a diligence.'[35]

The men may have overdone their Alpine wardrobes but women often ventured up mountains in costumes more suitable for afternoon tea. Illustrations show them climbing mountains in dresses, normal shoes and hats with blowing veils, and even venturing onto the famous glacier the Mer de Glace with no help but an alpenstock. One mountaineering book admitted that 'a lady's dress is inconvenient for mountain-travelling' and advised women to sew heavy rings at the bottom of their skirts to keep them from blowing up. A cord could be attached, which then could be tugged to raise the skirt when picking one's way over stony paths. There was a disadvantage: the rings could dislodge stones that fell onto those below, causing 'painful blows'. By the early twentieth century, common sense was in the ascendant and ladies planning mountain expeditions were advised to take 'a strong short skirt', whatever the French might say. An experienced climber writing in the same guide-book said that women who really wanted to climb should wear clothes 'very like a man's. In climbing, knickerbockers are essential; a skirt is very much in the way.'[36]

Chapter 8

English Comforts and English Sanitation

On 29 January 1901 *The Times* carried an advertisement for a Riviera hotel that boasted 'English Comforts. English Sanitation. English Management. Italian Orchestra.' Such 'comforts' had not always been the case. In 1816 the waspish Lady Holland warned a friend going abroad of 'the coldness of the inns, the bad and uncertain accommodation, the smoky chimneys ... the hatred against the English ... the total want of all comforts'. Lady Holland's emphasis on 'comforts' pointed to a key ingredient in the British view of progress – the increase of personal comfort. At home this meant more efficient heating, better lighting, improved sanitation, thick carpets and more luxurious furniture. Outside it meant better pavements, roads, lighting, drains and sewers. 'Comfort', or the lack thereof, is a word that continually crops up in letters, diaries, guide-books and memoirs. Lord Palmerston supposedly claimed that only the English language had a word for 'comfort'. Even if he did not say it, the *Dictionnaire Français-Anglais* of 1855 did. The nearest French equivalent to 'comfort' was the verb *conforter*, meaning to console or to help. From the very beginning of our period, even those rare travellers who felt that the French were 'in many ways much our superiors' added, 'in the realities of life and in all its comforts we must hold our pre-eminence'. In 1827 one tourist left for France, a confirmed lover of

all things French. After three weeks he burst out: the French were 'still a dirty race of beings with no idea of real comfort (in fact they have no such word in their language and have adopted the English word "comfortable" without understanding its meaning)'.[1]

About the same time that this man was unhappily wandering round France, three other tourists were staying at Viterbo's Black Eagle inn and scribbled on the dining room wall: 'Wm. Arnold, John Righton, Henry Colbrook: three fools for leaving English comfort for the sake of seeing greater fools than themselves'. Underneath, another traveller added 'And three still greater fools for owning it!' Other tourists were moved to verse:[2]

> *Let France for glory play her part . . .*
> *Let Italy reign first in art,*
>
> . . .
>
> *Give us our English comfort, still.*
> *Comfort! Sweetest household word,*
> *Domestic idol, lov'd the most,*
> *In other lands, unknown, unheard,*
> *Comfort! Still be England's boast.*

The idea that comfort lay at the heart of civilized life was one the British felt they had discovered. As Isaac Taylor put it in his children's travel book, 'there is no country like old England for comfort either in riding, walking or sitting'. The advertisement quoted at the beginning of this chapter came at the literal end of the Victorian era as the same issue was filled with details of the great Queen's death. By then British tourism had done much to improve the way in which Europeans designed and ran facilities in the 'tourist industry'. But this 'comfort' was a long time in coming.[3]

In the years immediately after Waterloo travellers expected pretty much what their fathers had expected in the eighteenth century and put up with what they found, whatever their background. One of the favourite anecdotes of the nineteenth century concerned the Duke of Devonshire and his brother – scions of a family renowned for long silences. They were told that the only room left in a German inn contained three beds, one of which was already occupied. Before retiring to a sound sleep each man had a quick peep behind the curtains of the occupied bed. It was only after the Duke had paid the bill the next morning that he asked his brother, 'George, did you see the dead body?' 'Yes' was his brother's laconic reply as their coach drove away.[4]

More frequently travellers moaned about the 'narrow, uncurtained bed ... bare floor ... [and] three hard cane-bottomed chairs' in French hotels. Some hoteliers responded quickly; one banker touring in France in 1814 shared the national obsession about uncarpeted floors and he was therefore delighted when a 'very attentive' innkeeper brought up a carpet and 'placed [it] on our floor'. Most inn-keepers would need prodding: the widely read French travel writer, Antoine-Claude Pasquin, who wrote under the *nom de plume* Valéry, described what was happening. Just as the inns of Italy had been improved by British complaints, so would Corsica's '*détestables et rares auberges*'. By writing their anathemas in visitors' books and on the walls – like Messrs. Arnold, Righton and Colbrook – and by quarrelling with landlords, the British have become '*le terreur des camerieri*' [waiters]. By the 1840s conditions in general, and not just in Corsica and Italy, were said to have improved. One writer in *Blackwood's* knew why: British travellers 'naturally introduce the improvements and conveniences of English life. When they but pass along, they demand comforts, without which the natives would have plodded on for ever.' Hotels 'are gradually provided with carpets, fire-places, and a multitude of other matters essential to the civilized life of England ... England is wholly superior to the shivering splendours of the Continent. Foreigners are beginning to learn this.'[5]

Lady Blessington pointed in vain to the 'fallacy' of 'comparing '*foreign hotel* comforts with those of our own house'. Visitors in Paris, for example, were 'full of complaints of the extravagance of the charges, badness of the dinners, and total want of comfort'. Being an experienced traveller, she also noted that those 'accustomed to even a lavish expenditure at home, are disposed to be parsimonious abroad, and murmur at charges in Paris, that in London would be . . . very reasonable'. The truth was that 'we English are prone to murmur . . . and the moment we are out of England, and are deprived of our never-failing topic for complaint, our climate, we vent our national discontent on other subjects'. One unending source of complaint was the high charges hoteliers made for candles. As a result, many travelled with used candles in their luggage. However, much of the unending British criticism was simply uninformed. In the 1850s a storm blew up over the costs of foreign holidays. Two facts emerged: London hotels were more expensive than European and 'the accommodation is no better, but often very much inferior'. Outraged British travellers were always threatening 'to write to *The Times*' to complain, and the paper did publish many such letters. But in 1853 it also published a leader that said that 'There is no part of civilised Europe . . . [we] exclude some northern and eastern districts, and the Spanish Peninsula generally . . . in which the accommodation at hotels is not infinitely superior and infinitely more economical than in England.'[6] This was not a view heard very often, at least not then.

Leaving aside the debate over quality there was the problem of arranging for places to stay. There seems to have been little idea of booking rooms before departing, even though travellers could have got names from friends or guide-books. Finding hotels full was a 'misery well known to travellers' and many recalled being driven round Paris looking for rooms. Yet as long as people followed the well-established 'routes' they would usually find accommodation because new hotels were continually being opened. The competition for guests became severe and hoteliers took to advertising in guide-books, distributing cards and, in the earlier years, sending *commisionaires* to grasp befuddled passengers leaving ships or trains. Many hoteliers supplied omnibuses to take passengers to their establishments, where they would be greeted by the owner. Some went even further. Marianne North and her family were on a train near Bordeaux when a 'gentleman got into our carriage in a complete *costume de chasse*, dog and all'. He began talking to the English party and strongly recommend they stay in the Hôtel de l'Empereur at a new seaside town. Luckily he 'actually found its card . . . and gave it as a reminder' before he got out at the next station. What the Norths did not know was that he only got out to enter another carriage to repeat the performance at every stop. When they arrived at the town they took his advice and headed for the hotel's omnibus, which was driven by none other than their 'sporting gentleman'. The bus took them to the 'wooden one-storied shanty he called an hotel'. Once inside he welcomed them as the manager. He then cooked the meals, served the meals and, having changed clothes yct again, mingled with his guests. The next morning he was off again to Bordeaux in his sporting clothes and with his season ticket to start all over again. 'That man deserved to make a fortune.' He certainly charged enough by asking ten francs for a tiny room containing, as another traveller noted, only 'a very narrow bed, bowl, tiny table, and one chair'. There was no need for baths because those 'who choose to exhibit themselves' could don a *costume de bain* and walk down to the sea.[7]

In Bradshaw's 1857 *Hand Book* for France the advertisement for Lyons's Grand Hôtel de L'Univers included this italicized warning: '*Travellers are particularly requested not to attend to Touters, Porters &c, for as they receive no bribe* [from the hotel] *they will be sure to say that the Hotel is shut up, full or too far off.*' When Helen Mason and her husband arrived in Montpelier they eluded 'flymen commissioniers &c, we leave serv[an]ts & baggage at the Station & making our escape by a side Sortie, we get hold of a sharp boy, make him show us the chief Hotels, & after deciding on Mons. Hivet's [?] we seek . . . an interview with him'. This way of doing things was replaced for many travellers by the advent of the hotel coupon and the presence of British companies such as Gaze or

Cook: when Sibella Bonham Carter arrived in Turin in 1894 she went to 'Hotel de Londres recommended by Cook's agent close to the station'.[8]

The best source of information remained guide-books. Mariana Starke told readers in the 1820s, for example, that there were about 300 hotels in Paris, some 'splendidly furnished' while others were only 'ready-furnished lodging-houses' without meals or servants. In the late 1820s, a suite of rooms in the capital's best hotels would cost about £20 a month for a small family while the cheapest was £5. The cost of rooms in modest hotels ranged from one franc 50 centimes to three francs a night. If people 'wish to live with œconomy they should rent an Unfurnished Apartment in the Faubourg S. Jacques' and hire furniture from an upholsterer. Information about particular hotels was very limited – 'small but very comfortable' is typical. However, readers were always informed if a hotel was kept by an Englishman or if the hotelier spoke English (these hotels often had English names such as Paris's Hôtel de Hungerford). By the 1850s many of the difficulties people had faced in getting accommodation had lessened for there was 'no difficulty in procuring lodgings . . . to suit the dimensions of every purse'. The total number of Parisian hotels, lodging houses and apartments had soared to some 5,000.[9]

The next generation of guide-books still gave only cursory information. By the 1870s, though, publishers were somewhat more detailed. Murray's 1879 *Handbook for . . . Southern Germany and Austria*, for example, included a few words about the grander hotels, usually commending their cuisine while other references pointed out if hotels were clean or had 'civil people'. It also used frank terms to describe hotels: those in Bohemia were dirty but those in Galicia were 'filthy hovels, perfectly wretched and generally in the hands of the Jews'. Murray's would point out if hotels were 'frequented by the English' and, later, by the 'English and Americans', 'frequented by the clergy', or 'patronised by ladies travelling alone'. By the turn of the century Baedeker's *Paris* still only told tourists that various hotels were 'much frequented by English travellers', while two near the Madelaine were 'unpretending'. Its *Italy From the Alps to Naples* said only that most of Genoa's hotels were 'in noisy situations; opinions as to their merits vary'. Macmillan's *Guides* gave the most exhaustive listings and noted those places 'most frequented' by British and American tourists. They then grouped entries by price but still gave only basic information such as the number of beds and the costs.[10] In Murray's case, the absence was made up by pages of hotel advertisements, which often gave more details and sometimes illustrations.

Inevitably there were problems in finding exactly what one wanted, especially as people often travelled in groups made up of families, friends and, frequently, servants. These groups would take a number of rooms and were advised to ask for a sitting room on the first floor and bedrooms with dressing rooms elsewhere. Servants had rooms at cheaper rates. Better-quality hotels made great distinctions between groups and those travelling on their own, usually bachelors. Such guests were often consigned, much as they are today, to 'pigeon holes, the biggest about the size of a bathing machine'. In the days before lifts, the higher the floor, the cheaper the room. Hotels often assumed guests would be staying for a number of days and many would not offer rooms for just one night. This would only begin to change with the growth of shorter holidays. Spas could be very difficult places during their 'seasons' as the former Foreign Secretary, Lord Clarendon, observed in Wiesbaden in 1861: 'This place is overflowing & yet . . . every day carriages full of folks are sent away . . . the travellers moaned that they would sleep anywhere in the 93 degree heat.' It is astounding that people would arrive for a lengthy stay without having written ahead for rooms. The postal services of Britain and many western European countries had improved tremendously by mid-century, and after 1851 people could send telegrams.[11]

It is perhaps fitting that it was two high officials of the post office who discovered the value of the telegraph in this same decade. When Anthony Trollope, his wife and brother-in-law left their Milan hotel, they asked that a telegram be sent to a hotel in Verona to reserve rooms and a late supper. Arriving at midnight they heard voices crying '*Signor Trollope*' and beheld 'a glorious personage dressed like a beau for a ball'. This was the landlord of Verona's best hotel, the Due Torri, who had arrived at the railway station with three carriages and six servants to assist Trollope and 'his people'. The landlord had assumed that only a great milord with a numerous suite could have afforded a telegram. Increasingly travellers did see the need to book ahead, and by 1903 Baedeker was warning would-be visitors to the south of Italy to write and to 'prepay the answer, to prevent disappointment'. The next year a Macmillan's *Guide* agreed that people going to popular spots in the high season should not only book but send stamps to pay for a reply telegram and, even better, 'to telephone is also a very easy matter'.[12]

It was common for travellers to inspect rooms and then to demand better ones. Of course the British were not only after more 'comforts' but were, on occasion, trying to assert their status. Thus when John Blackwood, of the Edinburgh publishing family, arrived in Cività Castellana near Rome, he wrote home that the 'savages' showed him to 'all manner of back dens' because he was rather muddy after a cooling dip in the Tiber but 'by dint of bullying I got the best rooms they could boast'. Another traveller was more modest: when the Ruskins made their frequent continental rambles, Ruskin senior always asked for the second-best rooms as he felt that the best should always be left in case any British peer turned up. After all, he rejoiced in having noblemen as customers. Tourists were caught between opposite warnings. On the one hand they were told that hoteliers would overcharge them and that they must haggle about the cost, and put it in writing, especially in Italy. On the other hand, they were warned that bargaining with hotel-keepers made the traveller look 'small, and being thought a quiz [odd]'.[13] With the growth of guide-books that listed prices, of coupons, of pre-booking, let alone the growth of organized tours, the need to agree prices began to decline after mid-century.

Some travellers carried on the eighteenth-century tradition of renting furnished or unfurnished apartments or even houses. When Lady Blessington reached Naples in the early 1820s her husband rented the Palazzo Belvedere, 'the perfection of an Italian palace'. However, even it lacked 'comforts', especially carpets. Lady Blessington later recalled that 'now that curtains, carpets, and other adjuncts to comfort are beginning to be placed, the palazzo is assuming an aspect of English elegance joined to Italian grandeur'. Frances Trollope, arriving in Vienna in 1836, avoided 'the very detestable domicile of a public hotel' and instead took a seven-room apartment or 'lodgings' for seven months for £100. This not only gave greater privacy but cost considerably less.[14]

Hotels could also be very noisy, especially with the arrival and departure of carriages and coaches in cobbled courtyards: 'noises of every description, that assail one's ears, from early morn to midnight, in a Parisian hotel!' However, worse than a noisy hotel was no hotel at all. In the 1830s the young artist Charles Cope was touring Italy with friends and stopped in Orvieto, which had wonderful wine but no hotels. The man at the local wine-shop found rooms in a house and 'when we wanted anything we summoned the bare-footed waiter by blowing a trumpet out of the window' to the delight of the neighbours. In the event Cope and his friends did want a rice pudding. The waiter 'brought it in with a flourish, and, while he was re-moving the meat, he placed the rich-looking brown pudding on the floor, and, unluckily for us, in whisking round, he . . . put his bare foot into the middle of it. Our anger was hot; so was the pudding to his foot'. The poor man 'almost prostrated himself on the floor, knelt, and prayed for our pardon', which the tourists gave, but they also refused to eat the pudding. Nonplussed the waiter 'sat on the ground and made a hearty meal of it himself, begging us *"per 1'amor di Dio"* to say to his mistress, if she asked how we liked her dish, that it was *"eccellentissimo"*'. Inns could also be dangerous, as Lord Malmesbury found when he spent the night in 'a wretched tavern for bargemen' on the Rhône. He kept his pistols under his pillow 'by the advice of my courier, who said it was a notorious den of brigands . . . the people stared at us like savages'. On a somewhat lighter note, in some hotels guests were not addressed by their surnames but by their room numbers so that one had 'Good morning, Mr 109.'[15]

Murray's *Handbook* warned travellers that 'one of the first complaints of an Englishman . . . will be directed against the beds. It is therefore as well to make him aware beforehand of the full extent of misery.' When Susan Horner's family stopped at a 'second-rate inn' in Bourges in the 1840s she noted, 'our sheets very clean, as I do not think they had been slept in above once before.' A pair of Cambridge undergraduates were appalled at a French hotel's sheets in the spring of 1857 and after a 'quarrel . . . prevailed . . . on the landlord to allow us clean sheets . . . instead of the dirty ones he and his wife had been sleeping on since Christmas'. At the inn before that, the young men had to borrow the landlord's knife and fork 'as there were no other cutlery available'.[16]

However bad the sheets might be, there was also the problem of other beings in a room, especially in Italy: in 1815 the Maquays found 'bugs, fleas, a lizard, a mouse and a scorpion'. Even worse was what was inside the mattress. In the same year Lord Fortescue stayed in a Swiss inn and had 'an excellent sleep in spite of fleas'. Not for nothing had Mariana Starke advised travellers to bring leather sheets to confine any fleas and damp within the mattresses. She also urged people to place ten drops of essential oil of lavender about the bed – apparently fleas did not like essential oil of lavender.[17] In 1844 *Blackwoods* published a poem describing an Italian inn:

> *Where, in loose flakes, the white-wash peeling*
> *From the bare joints of rotten ceiling*
> *Give token sure of vermin's bower,*
> *And swarms of bugs that bide their hour!*

Fleas could cause great misery, as one diarist noted regarding her brother: 'John's feet were so swelled & inflamed by bites he could hardly walk across the room, so he sat with his feet up on the sofa all day.' Dicky Doyle's *Foreign Tour of Messrs. Brown, Jones and Robinson* shows a hotel guest in Germany killing fleas in his bed with the caption, 'The Right of Search', and suggested that smokers delve beneath the duvets and puff away to fumigate the bed.

The situation was always at its worst if a traveller left the main routes. When John Addington Symonds was touring Sicily with his wife in 1873, he described a typical inn: 'you enter a dark dungeon-like doorway encumbered with filth of every sort' eventually arriving at 'a large bare room with four big trestles on wh[ich] bedding may be put, & [a servant woman] asks if you have brought your sheets. You say No! Then she produces sheets & gives you for dinner some broth & an omelette & lettuces ... legions of fleas then invade you.' He caught seven in one set of underwear yet concluded that 'one somehow sleeps better ... than one does at home – to bed tired at 8 & up lively at 4'. One might have thought the fleas would have vanished by the end of the century, but one of the problems facing the Toynbee Travellers in Pavia in 1891 was the same as that which faced Lord Fortescue in 1815. The solution was to use Keating's Powder to erect 'defensive ramparts around each of the three beds'. Unfortunately they did not reckon on 'the strategical resources of the enemy who, climbing the ceiling, dropped thence on their victims as they lay'.[18]

The next problem was beds that were not sufficiently aired and rooms that were not sufficiently heated. In 1816, when Byron was in Switzerland, he complained: 'Went to bed at nine – sheets damp – swore and stripped them off & flung them – Heaven knows where – wrapt myself up in the blankets – and slept like a child.' Frances Trollope warned readers in the 1830s that 'the habit of using well-aired linen appears ... little known or valued in German inns'. The answer was to bring one's own dry sheets to prevent 'the disagreeable alternative of sitting up all night, or ... pains and aches without end'.[19] Gerald Codrington reassured his mother that he had put 'leather sheets on last night for I thought perhaps the bed might be damp as the room smelt as if it had not been used lately'.

To disguise the smell he 'smoked a cigarette in the room before going to bed to sweeten it'. One American declared: 'damp sheets are the bogie of the English housekeeper, and the opening up and warming of the bed amounts [sic] almost to a religious ceremony in the humid little isle'.[20] We can only assume this writer never slept in a bed with such sheets.

The next problem was the size of foreign beds, especially as Britons tended to be taller than continentals. Not only were beds too short but they were too narrow and often had wooden sides – 'an open wooden box' was Murray's description. Coleridge took his own blanket and slept on the floor 'like a wild Indian' – as Byron did. Even at the fashionable Hôtel Meurice in Paris an American complained about the 'odd little beds, in which a short man cannot lie straight'. Several travel writers advised men to put the mattress on the floor. Double beds also seem, at least in the earlier decades, to have been few and far between. Amorous couples were advised to 'place two together to make believe 'tis one' and then hope for the best.[21] Then there was the detested duvet, known as 'feather mattresses', 'fedder deckers' or 'that stuffed, pillow-like thing which is to do duty for blanket and coverlet'. When the Hills, father and son, arrived in France they found 'a large down mattress, or bag filled with down. I was not sure whether it was meant for us to lie on it, or it on us.'[22] Duvets were widely denounced as 'those stuffy, fluffy, soft, slippery coverings which always fall off a German bed when an Englishman tries to sleep in it'. In *The Foreign Tour of Messrs Brown, Jones and Robinson*, Doyle showed poor Jones in a bed with the duvet reaching to his knees and his feet overhanging, with a caption reading: 'Jones's Night Thoughts. "Man wants but little here below," but "wants that little long"'. Jerome K. Jerome's duvet had 'the appearance of a man suffering from some monstrous swelling'. In the end Jerome's hero, like Byron, Coleridge and others before him, 'camps on the floor'.[23]

After complaints about fleas, damp sheets, short beds, and duvets the most frequent grievance regarding hotels was the general lack of cleanliness. In 1829 James Cobbett decided the dining room table in his hotel in Lyons had never been washed and one of the mirrors had the remains of an exploding bottle of beer. When John Ruskin's mother complained about the filth on the stone stairs at the Hôtel du Mont Blanc the young Ruskin got a broom and a bucket of water and proceeded to clean them. He later noted that the hotel staff 'hadn't washed their stairs since they first went up them'. If we move forward to 1878, when Mark Twain visited Milan, he found that his hotel 'swarms with mice and fleas, and if the rest of the world were destroyed it could furnish dirt enough to start another one with'. Henry James discovered in a Poitiers hotel advertised as '*une magnifique construction ornée de statues*' that in addition to the ornamental statues it had 'immemorial accumulations of dirt'.[24] Every country came in for criticism, but the primitive Spanish inns were particularly lambasted.

Another problem was smells, which could come from outside (drains, cesspits, piles of manure and worse) and from inside (damp, dirt, unwashed bed linen, urine and excrement). In 1818 Robert Parker wrote in his diary that the 'best rooms' of Dijon's Hôtel de Conde 'smell of the stable and something worse'. Guests needed to be constantly on their guard. Almost thirty years later, when the Horners arrived in Paris they found their rooms 'beautifully furnished, with rather a bad smell! By dint of ringing and scolding we have at last got two good fires and an excellent dinner.' They then made sure they got other rooms that were 'very light, and above all, sweet [without odours]'. Sixty years after Coleridge wrote his ditty about Cologne, the British were still referring to 'uncomfortable stenches. It is amazing how the inhabitants can accustom themselves to so much filth.' As late as 1910, visitors to Florence were surprised to see raw sewage still being 'pumped by steam out of a palace'.[25]

Complaints were always greatest in Italy; a typical comment regarding Rome was 'Pheugh! Ramble about a ruin, but hold your nose.' In the 1880s the British were still referring to Europe's 'uncomfortable stenches' but, to be fair, this writer added, 'In the very dirtiest and lowest localities in London the scents are not more disagreeable.' Since most people travelled in the late summer and early autumn smells would have been at their worst. Travelling at this period also meant that visitors to parts of France and in Italy suffered from the heat, especially in their heavy clothes, which would not have helped their levels of tolerance. One barrister visiting Brittany in 1847 wrote that 'the thermometer stood at 80 at night, and in the evening we were oppressed with heat. We walked in vain in search of cool air, and the only relief . . . was an ice at the café.'[26]

One should remember that it was the fashion to complain: as Robert Louis Stevenson said, 'grumbling is the traveller's pastime'. Fortunately some travellers found much to praise. Henry Matthews wrote in 1820 that 'the inns of Italy are generally better than those of an equal class in England', and this included both food and beds. When Thomas Best was on honeymoon in Italy his most frequent descriptions of hotels were 'very clean' and 'comfortable'. George Poore, when touring in the 1870s, found the Gasthof zum Östereicherhof in Innsbruck 'a wonderfully good hotel where they give you English bedding'. There are numerous stories of kindly, efficient and obliging hoteliers who went out of their way to arrange special treats for their guests. In August 1828 Edward Horsman was in Switzerland. After a twelve-hour walk he returned to his hotel but 'was surprised at hearing there was to be a ball in the evening – all the ladies had been on the Mountains during the day & were fatigued'. Although a 'fiddler was found' he 'could only master one German air – a French march & half a Swiss jig'. All seemed lost but then 'to our astonishment there was an excellent piano in the house, & an English lady played quadrilles for us. The Dancers was [sic] neither numerous nor agile – but nevertheless very pleasant – & on the whole was the greatest curiosity in those mountainous regions we had yet met with.' Sometimes the hoteliers could be too obliging. When the Bests arrived in Sorrento they stayed in yet another 'most clean & comfortable hotel'. Because the owners had been in England they made sure that the orchestra, which played during dinner, 'out of compliment to us round up with what was meant for "God Save the Queen" – oh!!'[27]

Sanitary arrangements or the lack thereof figured largely, if discreetly, as another unwelcome aspect of continental travel. However, in 1814 the British had their own peculiar customs as Matthew Todd's diary shows. His 'Capt. B.' was dining out in Paris. After dinner 'a pot de chamber was ... brought in by the waiter on a tray, with all due solemnity, and he was going to set it on the table for he thought it was wanted to make punch in'. The Englishmen told the waiter to put it into a convenient corner and 'in the course of the evening the pot being full, the waiter was desired to empty it'. He refused. Such a task was beneath him; it was the work of a chambermaid. The landlord was sent for and replied that he 'was not used to the English luxuries ... the French never made use of such articles in an eating room. Whereupon ... one of the party took it up by way of showing him that there was nothing derogatory to the feelings of a waiter to do such a job' and chucked the contents out the window. For his part Todd was 'inclined to think' that the custom was 'an indulgence which the English might abolish'.[28]

Todd was right. The custom for men to relieve themselves in the dining room after the ladies had withdrawn was happily on the way out. Standards were rising. Toilets that were flushed with water and placed in 'water-closets' actually dated back to 1778 and by the 1830s their sale was soaring. Bathrooms were also becoming fashionable and washstands in bedrooms were becoming bigger and grander. Thomas Crapper began selling his plumbed-in, cast-iron bath-shower combinations with shower screens, sprays, pedestal washbasins, and hot and cold water taps in the 1860s, and in the 1870s John Shanks and Thomas Twyford started selling their porcelain valve water-closets. Cleaning up Britain's towns and cities was becoming a national priority. With these changes came a new coyness about toilets even among those who rejoiced in being unconventional. Virginia Woolf once remembered how a male friend blushed when she wanted to leave a French train compartment to go to the toilet 'and I blushed too'.[29]

Europe lagged behind Britain in the development of toilets, in improving the supply of water to houses and in building adequate sewers. In 1820 Henry Matthews wrote that French 'offices' [toilets] were 'too filthy for description', while, thirteen years later, a retired naval officer referred to the 'disgusting want of decency in those necessary appendages to every house'. Guide-books reminded travellers that in inns, especially in France, the landlady sometimes 'has a small private establishment of her own, quite unobjectionable, of which she will lend the key to favoured guests, especially Britons'. In Italian inns ladies could ask the landlady to arrange for only female servants to 'wait' on them, that is, to bring chamber-pots, but many Italian inns had only male servants. By the 1850s new hotels were being built and language books were instructing people how to ask for water-closets: '*Ou est les lieux d'aisance?*' Standards started to improve, or so it seemed. Sir Erasmus Wilson found differently. When travelling in Germany in 1858 he noticed an 'abominable smell' from the room next his own. He discovered that it was Room 00 (sometimes numbered 000) or what the hotel staff called discreetly, 'numero null' – the hotel's inadequately ventilated and dirty toilet. As late as 1899 John Oglander and his daughter were in a Brussels restaurant and 'doubted certain accommodation being nice'. When he asked the waiter for help he was told the only facility was 'a place where men had their "*urinoir*" just outside the door. I did not choose our darling to go to that so walked her off up an unknown stairs on the search.' Luckily the landlady 'kindly ran after us and said she would take the *demoiselle au premies* [*prémisse*]'.[30]

The most damning criticism of European toilets was in a remarkably frank pamphlet of 1863. The author, *Viator Verax* ('The Truthful Traveller'), was the Reverend George Musgrave, a prolific travel writer, especially about France. In his *Cautions for the First Tour ... Addressed to the Husbands, Fathers, Brothers, and All*

Gentlemen going with Female Relations on Continental Excursions
he warned men what to expect. What was particularly alarming was
that he did not confine himself to rural inns but to 'good hotels' –
those with sixty rooms or over – on major tourist routes. He
warned that rooms would not have a 'towel-horse – gown horse –
no pegs for gowns . . . no footbath – no chamber-pail for slops . . .
no wardrobe – no hot water can – no soap'. Even worse, guests
should be aware that there will be 'no biedet [*sic*] . . . no night
commode' in the room – everything had to be requested. Therefore
guests should always ask about *le cabinet* or, in Germany, the
abtritt or *commoditat*. 'Impelled by the continual . . . complaining
of their English visitors' hoteliers had begun to introduce water-
closets. These were usually placed next to one another on the first
floor because, if the hotel had plumbing, the water might reach
only to that floor. If there was no plumbing, the water for the
cisterns had to be carried. In a hotel with, say, sixty rooms it was
not unusual to have only four WCs and in some cases these simply
did not work or were just filthy: 'The abominations in this particular department are unspeakable.' Men should always inspect the
toilets before allowing ladies to enter, to check for graffiti and to
make sure that 'moustachioed' foreigners were not using neighbouring closets without closing the doors.

Accordingly, many people, especially ladies, stayed in their
rooms and used the 'usual alternative', that is the *nacht-stuhl* or
chaise percée (a chair with a chamber-pot in the seat). As these were
not usually part of a room's furnishings, travellers had to ask for
them and then wait. 'The custom of the country is *to manage as
one can.*' What this could mean, especially for ladies, was explained
to Musgrave by another traveller. This man's wife, when leaving
one French hotel, tipped the *fille de chambre* because she had asked
for the night commode so many times. The girl protested: the
English lady had not been a nuisance. The problem was those
Frenchwomen who did *not* ring for the commode but pulled out a
drawer from the bureau, used it as a commode and then shut it for
the chambermaid to find later and clean. One way round all these

horrors was to take oneself to Fyfe's Repository of Scientific Inventions for Sanitary Purposes at 46, Leicester Square. For twenty-five shillings one could buy the Inodorous Standard Pail, a metal bucket with a 'hermetically closing cover' and mahogany rim, which ladies could use without having to ring and wait.[31] The chambermaid could then empty it, clean it and return it to its owner. In addition, the pail fitted into what looked like a lady's hat box so there was no embarrassment unless one forgot and reached in for a hat. Not surprisingly, the sixty-one page pamphlet became quite famous and went into five editions within three years.

Twelve years after Viator Verax's pamphlet appeared, Thomas Chambers, who wrote on health problems, reminded would-be travellers that one of the perils they faced was diarrhoea. In addition to dodgy water supplies and unusual food they should beware of 'the pestiferous state of the provisions for daily retirement in Continental inns'. Unlike Musgrave he preferred the coded terms current at the time: in country places gentlemen will do well to 'worship Cloacina sub Jove'.[32] To 'worship Cloacina' was to venerate the goddess who looked after Rome's sewers. To do so 'sub Jove' was to do so 'under the heavens'. In plain English, men should relieve themselves outside. What women should do he did not say. But by the 1870s Chambers was confining his warnings to country inns, whereas Musgrave had criticized the new, larger and better hotels. If the picture both men painted is anywhere near the truth, the British were right to complain about 'dirt'. The warnings continued: in the 1880s Murray told visitors to France that 'some of the most *important essentials to sanitary comfort, and personal decency* . . . evince a state of degradation not to be expected in a civilised country'.[33]

Sometimes the bad reputation was not fully deserved: when in 1868 Queen Victoria travelled to the Continent she chose Switzerland. With her went her physician, William Jenner, who 'has never seen foreign *L* [lavatories] before [and] runs about to each in a state of high disgust and says they must be entirely altered – Jenner was right of course – but he rather over estimates [exaggerates] the idea of bad smells'.[34] Still, it is not surprising that as standards slowly rose, hotels advertised 'English sanitation' along with Italian orchestras to attract the British. It is perhaps a fitting legacy of British travel that in Europe toilets are often referred to as 'WCs'.

Viator Verax also claimed that 'nothing is more annoying to foreign innkeepers ... than our habits of much washing, and our love of hot water'. In the nineteenth century this love of cleanliness was fast becoming a national trait. Fanny Kemble once burst out, 'I believe England is the only place in the world where people are not disgustingly dirty.' Increasingly, this passion for cleanliness divided the British from their continental neighbours far more than the Channel. Edward Lear wrote in his *Illustrated Excursion in Italy* that he once heard some Italians give four reasons for describing a Briton as insane: 'He often drank water instead of wine; he more than once paid more money for an article than it was worth; he persisted in walking even when he had hired a horse; and he always washed himself, sometimes even twice a day!' When the travel writer G. S. Hillard quoted Lear he went on to add: 'consistent and uniform cleanliness is, indeed, an almost exclusively English grace'.[35]

Henry James agreed with this view when travelling in Italy in 1869: 'In the midst of these false and beautiful Italians they [the British] glow with the light of the great fact, that after all they love a bath-tub and they hate a lie.' To an Anglophile such as James, references to bathing were meant as a compliment. To Anglophobes such as the fierce Prussian historian Heinrich von Treitschke, they were not. He informed one university class in Berlin: 'The English think Soap is Civilization.' If soap was not civilization, it was certainly a great help in achieving it. However, a wiser German, Karl Baedeker, repeatedly advised hoteliers to accept the inevitable and provide '*large* basins'.[36]

Travellers were often just as dissatisfied with the amount of water in their basins as with the basins themselves. Mary Wilson noted in her diary in 1847 that in their Cologne hotel 'we began the day by having our hot water to wash with brought up in a teapot'. She was not exaggerating. Small basins and the lack of water became stock ingredients in Victorian writing. Dicky Doyle's three Londoners stared incomprehensibly at the little basin provided for them, while almost forty years later Jerome K. Jerome faced the same problem. He complained to the chambermaid, again in Cologne, that 'we wanted to wash – to clean ourselves – not to blow bubbles. Could we not have bigger basins and more water and more extensive towels. The chambermaid . . . seemed to think the river was more what we wanted.'[37]

One could always ask for a bath to be brought to one's room, although this could be quite a performance. One Oxford don, who spent several years in the early 1880s walking in France, recalled that 'baths were rare. If one could be hired in the village, it arrived at the inn door, borne in a sort of palanquin, draped in a white sheet, escorted by a procession. Sanitation was primitive.' Even people staying at the best Parisian hotels who wanted a really hot soak often had to go to one of the 3,000 public baths that the city had established in the 1830s 'in every street of importance and in many of no importance'. These had price lists giving the cost of scents, shampoos, and even eggs to wash one's hair. One could compromise, as George Poore did when visiting Bohemia, and ask not for a full bath but for a *sitz bad* (sitting bath). It duly arrived but with only two gallons of water, 'barely enough to moisten your surface . . . and . . . instead of cleansing you, merely makes you sticky'. To solve the problem, many British travellers travelled with what they regarded as an essential item, a portable bath made of India rubber. Young Gerald Codrington told his mamma that 'my bath is so very handy . . . & I can jack [it] up so quickly & it is so convenient to put just the things that I shall want next morning on the top'. These devices did have one drawback, they tended 'to fold up unexpectedly and set the floor awash'.[38]

Even when there was an adequate supply of hot water, there was the perennial problem of soap. 'Fail not to take soap with you, a thing never to be found in foreign bedrooms' warned Murray as late as the 1880s. The need to be careful of your soap tablets is seen in an advert for the City Soap Works. Because 'the refined habits of English travellers, [are] as yet imperfectly . . . provided for by Continental Hotel-Keepers' the company was offering not only their Naples Travelling Tablet (made from olive oil) in a 'compact and portable form' but an 'elastic case' to hold it. Maintaining personal hygiene became less of a problem when running water was installed and by the end of the century complaints were increasingly confined to smaller inns and remote hotels. In small cathedral cities in France 'sanitary science seemed to have stood still since the sixteenth century'. Any traveller who complained was thought 'squeamish or effeminate'. This same visitor also noted that these primitive conditions were in 'the towns that lay outside the ordinary routes of tourist travel',[39] another indication of the impact of tourism.

When it came to drinking-water, travellers were told in the early years after 1815 to add five drops of sulphuric acid or twenty drops of 'diluted vitriolic acid' to any 'large' decanter of water. After two hours this should make any 'noxious particles' sink to the bottom. The top three-quarters of the water could then be poured into another jug and drunk. As the jug's capacity was not specified one hopes that those who took this advice properly counted the number of drops, poured carefully and were just plain lucky. Originally this advice applied to all parts of Europe but by the 1880s warnings about water were usually limited to southern Italy. The water here was 'of very indifferent quality.' But by 1903, the same guide could state that the 'immense *Acqua di Serino* . . . now brings a copious supply of good water'. The danger now was no longer water but watermelons, which 'are better left untouched'.[40]

Another threat was bad drains. Travel books, memoirs and guide-books had always urged readers to complain about smells, so that when improvement came hoteliers were keen to inform tourists. San Remo's Grand Hôtel des Anglais advertised in 1890 that not only did it have electric light and a hydraulic lift but 'English sanitary drainage. No Cesspool'. Perhaps the most effective complaint was made from Buckingham Palace. Edward VII particularly enjoyed his annual jaunt to Biarritz, but he had one grievance. He commanded an official to write to his ambassador in Paris: could the French Prime Minister intervene? 'The King,' the official wrote, 'likes Biarritz so much that he would be very sorry to be obliged to forgo his visit there, but both this year and last year the smells and effects of defective draining was so much in evidence that the question of change had to be thought of.' The royal strategy worked and there was a 'decided improvement'.[41]

The British devotion to Switzerland brought benefits for the whole Continent since it was the Swiss who began a new, and cleaner, era in hotel life. As early as 1833 William Fox Talbot wrote from Lucerne that 'it is surprising how many new houses have been built at Berne, Thun & Interlacken, the latter especially now professes 5 or 6 immense Pensions'. In Zurich, Johannes Baur, the son of an inn-keeper, opened his Hôtel au Lac in 1844 and broke with tradition by having the building face the lake rather than the town: his new structure had an impressive 140 beds. Baur was succeeded by his son who also established the first school for hoteliers in the village of Ouchy, near Lausanne. His choice was understandable: by the 1860s the village, on the shores of Lake Geneva, had become 'a centre of the pleasantest Anglo-Swiss society' and the Hôtel de l'Ancre had become the Hôtel d'Angleterre: the owner obviously knew the travel wind was blowing from the west. By 1914 the area could boast four English churches, a hundred English boarding schools, a cricket pitch, a football field and an English library that served afternoon tea. Some of the new structures were 'noble buildings, almost palaces'.[42] No wonder that it was the Swiss who used the term *die Fremdenindustrie* or 'tourist industry'.

Entrepreneurs such as Baur helped to create a new race of Swiss hoteliers especially skilled at managing the new, large hotels that were spreading throughout Europe's tourist centres. As early as 1843 Swiss hotel managers were moving into Italy and sometimes the same man owned or managed a hotel in Switzerland in the summer and one on the Riviera in the winter. Their hallmarks were cleanliness and porters. John Addington Symonds noticed that in this new *Fremdenindustrie* porters came after hoteliers, drivers, guides and shopkeepers as the people who benefited most from tourism. Porters soon developed their own secret 'guild': the luggage of departing guests would be discreetly marked with a variety of symbols understood only by other porters who would know what sort of person they would be dealing with, what to expect in tips and what to offer in service. For their part, innkeepers and hoteliers throughout tourist Europe realized that the key to financial success was to attract British visitors. At the turn of the century one hotelier in Pougnes-les-Eaux, which was not on any tourist 'route', approached that rather fearsome travel writer Matilda Betham-Edwards. The hotelier 'was so anxious to secure an English *clientèle*, the best *clientèle* in the world, so hotel keepers aver, that she offered me a handsome percentage on any visitors I would send her'.[43] The writer declined the commission but still gave the hotel an honourable mention in her next book about France.

These new developments were noted by Anthony Trollope, the most widely travelled of all Victorian novelists, in the 1860s. Trollope was something of an expert on hotels and compared the new structures with those in Britain and the United States. The Swiss, he wrote, 'are the best'. They provided what people want: 'a clean bedroom with a good and clean bed, and with it also plenty of water. Good food, well dressed and served at convenient hours . . . Wines that shall be drinkable. Quick attendance. Bills that shall not be absolutely extortionate, smiling faces, and an absence of foul smells.' Tyrolean inns, Trollope wrote, were the cheapest but were marked by 'stench and nastiness'. Italian hotels, at least in the north, were 'very good' and 'much better than the name they bear'. German hotels 'are not clean, and water is very scarce'. The dearest hotels were in France 'and certainly not the best'. Their cooking was 'often disgusting' and their wines were 'generally abominable'. True, Paris boasted 'luxuries of every description, – except the luxury of comfort'. Good coffee was, alas, 'a thing of the past'. There was some consolation for any French reader: the inns and hotels in England were not much better. Britain's new 'railway hotels' were 'almost suicidal'.[44]

Trollope was describing the new type of hotel that some disliked: 'immense hotels are immense delusions if you are in search of comfort and pleasure. You get lost in the crowd.'[45] But there was no stopping the new fashion for huge structures, which Victorians called 'caravansaries' because they capitalized on increasing numbers. From the 1870s new buildings with up to 600 rooms were being built, particularly in tourist centres such as Paris, and they were often owned by companies rather than individuals. Advertisements in guide-books now boasted of 'English home comforts', sitting rooms, 'elevators' or 'hydraulic lifts'* (both terms were used), 'carefully warmed' bath rooms with hot (or cold) baths on every floor, separate ladies' drawing rooms, orchestras, golf courses, dark rooms for photographers, reading rooms (the Grand Hôtel du Midi in Toulouse boasted a 'Rich Reading Room'), libraries, smoking rooms, 'lawn tennis grounds', carriages for 'excursions', 'English church service', 'English cleanliness', 'rooms carpeted in the best style', hare and partridge shooting, south-facing public rooms, salons and 'ladies' salons', telegraph and post offices, cafes, billiard rooms, restaurants, balconies, 'English servants' (at the Grand Hôtel d'Angleterre' in Rouen), swimming baths, bureaux de change, shady woods, concerts, 'vapour and shower baths', buildings 'heated all over', verandahs, English and American newspapers, stabling, private dining rooms, terraces and telephones (by the 1880s in Paris's Hôtel Belle Vue).

By the time Macmillan's *Guide to Switzerland* appeared in 1904, a large number of the establishments in the forty-one page list of hotels sported the magical letter, 'E', to indicate the presence of

---

* The Grand Hôtel du Louvre et de la Paix in Marseilles advertised in British guide-books that it had a 'machine wagon saloon (known in England as a lift)'.

that newest of comforts, electricity. The St Moritz, opened in 1892, not only had iron baths, electricity and an 'English grill' but 'PERFECT SANITARY, HEATING AND VENTILIATING APPARATUS, Faultless drainage [and] . . . the PUREST MOUNTAIN SPRING WATER laid on throughout'. If this were not enough, 'English and American tastes will be particularly studied as regards SOLID COMFORT and GOOD COOKING.' By the 1890s hotel advertisements, such as that for the Grand Hotel in Rome, noted three things. The building was on the 'highest and healthiest part of Rome', its 'sanitary arrangements have been entirely carried out by Messrs. JENNINGS, of London' and, finally, the managers, 'C. Ritz and A. Pfyffer', were both Swiss.[46] 'C. Ritz' was, of course, César Ritz who, in 1898, opened the first of his 'chain' of luxury hotels in Paris's Place Vendôme. One hotel in Cannes boasted that it had 'three Lawn Tennis Courts considered the finest and largest in Europe' as well as a billiard room; a rival boasted a gymnasium. In the increasingly popular resort of Dinard in Brittany – '11 hours from Southampton' – a hotel appealed 'to Golf, Tennis and Cricket players'. By the end of the century hoteliers had learned to cater for travellers who now looked on the hotel as the holiday itself, not as a place to sleep while sight-seeing.

These new, grand hotels were confined to principal cities and major tourist spots. They were aimed at *'les gens fortunés'*. As today, visitors could still find smaller hotels and country inns. The ecclesiastical writer T. Francis Bumpus (his name should not belie his considerable abilities) toured French cathedral cities at the turn of the century. He could not praise the Hôtel des Négociants in the small and beautiful city of Autun highly enough. He remembered the proprietress's 'anxiety as to what I would do *"pour passer le temps"*'. The *petit salon* had its piano and china dogs, while the charming garden was the perfect spot for afternoon tea. The owner was, in short, an 'ideal French lady' while he was a guest who did not expect the impossible and accepted that he was in Autun, not Paris. It is pleasant to recall that Bumpus proved himself an English gentleman: when out walking in the countryside he picked a bouquet of wild flowers to give to his landlady in return for his afternoon tea. However, he still expected owners to be at the door to welcome him as he stepped down from their omnibus.[47]

Moving from an ecclesiologist to a sexologist, one has Havelock Ellis, who visited Dijon in 1912 and was pleasantly surprised at his hotel's modern improvements in 'the sanitary and mechanical age we are now entering'. In addition to sanitation and mechanics there was organization. By the time Ellis was in France countries such as Switzerland and Italy had national associations of hotels urging continual improvements as well as promoting their hotels through advertisements. The Swiss Hoteliers Association published a booklet each April giving a list of hotels with photographs of each one as well as the costs of rooms, meals and extra charges, including the prices of rooms for servants. However, in rural areas and occasionally elsewhere up to 1914, travellers could still find unpleasant odours and primitive 'washing arrangements', while a 'demand for hot water meets with but slow response . . . because the kitchen fire has to be made up and a casserole or broc of water heated'. Italian inns remained 'bare and gaunt . . . the sleeping-room . . . usually has a portrait of Garibaldi and chromos of the reigning royal family . . . the washing outfit is precariously hung on an iron stand'. In 1903, the Baedeker guide for southern Italy lamented that 'the inns of S. Italy and Sicily, with the exception of those of Naples, Palermo, and a few other towns, are sadly behind the requirements of the age'.[48]

The growth of *pensions* is a good example of how countries adapted to tourism. *Pensions*, which were more 'respectable' than the older 'lodging-houses', grew in number in the second half of the nineteenth century. They first appealed to those with less to spend: the solicitor's clerk who knew shorthand and earned £3 17s a week; the bank clerk on £3 a week; or the vicar and his family who had no more than £300 a year. By 1909 guests could stay in Dieppe's Pension Buckland for 52 francs or about £2 for bed and full board for a week. As one could get a second-class fare to Dieppe for

11*s* 7*d*, people could contemplate a week abroad for under £4. *Pensions* were less 'public' than hotels and were never 'grand'. They were more suited to timid travellers. They were also 'safe' because they were seen as homes away from homes, as a little bit of Britain in a foreign land. Each country favoured its own *pensions* so that one owned by a German would normally appeal to Germans and so on. Katherine Mansfield's short stories, published as *In a German Pension* in 1911, are a vivid depiction of the discomforts that Britons felt if they stayed in a *pension* 'belonging' to another nation.

It was, and still is, difficult to distinguish between a pension and a small, private hotel. There can also be confusion because some hotels used the term *pension* to indicate that full board was included in the price. Unlike smaller hotels, *pensions* were not always self-contained structures and could be found on just one or two floors of a large building. They were almost always located in cities and famous resorts. Quite frequently they were run by women, often English women, such as Elizabeth Barrett Browning's one-time maid, Elizabeth Wilson. They were frequently named after their owners: in Florence there were, beside the Pension Wilson, the Pension Plucknett, the Pension Chapman and so on. Because *pensions* were both cheaper than hotels and yet respectable they were popular with women travelling in groups and with 'English ladies, unattached'. As Henry James put it in *Pension Beaurepas* (Chapter 3), 'as commonly happens . . . The rustle of petticoats was . . . the most familiar form of the human tread.'

To non-British travellers *pensions* were especially associated with the British. When Tchaikovsky, whose hatred of the British has already been noted, was in Florence finishing *The Queen of Spades* he chose, for reasons beyond comprehension, to stay in a *pension*. He described the Pension Modgio in less than flattering terms: 'it is very difficult to . . . live without hearing some English Misses practising on the piano, or singing scales, and horrid sentimental songs'. E. M. Forster was equally damning when he travelled with his mother in 1901. He found it restricting to 'see everything with this horrible foreground of enthusiastic ladies'.[49] The difficulty for many of these women was that they had little choice because many would have been travelling or living abroad on small incomes. The descriptions of *pensions* as places resorted to by spinsterish women in works by Henry James (*Pension Beaurepas*), E. M. Forster (*A Room with a View*) and Arnold Bennett (*The Old Wives' Tale*) have given them a somewhat unflattering reputation.

Pensions also attracted people who did not feel at home in the new, grand hotels or the smaller hotels used by 'foreigners'. When Isaac and Ann Reckitt, whose family firm made Reckitt's laundry starch and bluing, visited Menton they could have afforded to stay in a hotel but they obviously felt more at home in an English *pension*. They chose one that had just been opened by a Miss Stafford, 'who has suffered from ill health'. The Reckitts were charged nine francs a day and had a bedroom for themselves with three easy chairs, 'a fine view' of the Mediterranean and a small bedroom for their son. There was a public drawing room and the staff consisted of a footman and three maids. Breakfast at nine consisted of eggs, bread and butter, and was followed by a 'hot lunch' at two, dinner at five, and tea at eight. The Reckitts had chosen the sedate Menton and the equally sedate Pension Stafford because Dr James Bennett's *Mentone and the Riviera as a Winter Climate* had just been published and had recommended the town and the pension for recuperation. As Quakers the Reckitts attended the French Protestant *temple* and decided to do a bit of proselytizing in the fleshpots of nearby Nice. They tried to hand out New Testaments and tracts but, alas, 'found some difficulty because many could not read English and others were afraid of accepting them'.[50] One wonders if they had ever thought to bring French translations.

One of the last portraits of a *pension* and of the world that existed within its walls comes from 1910, when a young woman and her mother went to Paris to buy clothes 'for my début [coming out]'. Their pension was near the Invalides and was marked by a 'slightly *passé* elegance', which was, again, not uncommon. The dining room was as 'pale and dingy as the milk soups and *blanquettes de veau* we ate there'. Most memorable were the guests, who included a mother and daughter from Dallas, Texas, a young Swede who never spoke, a 'young Jewish American, as conversational as the Swede was silent' and a 'tall and faded lady from the Eastern States'. They were 'stock characters of the *commedia di pensione*' and the *pension* itself was 'the first act of a rather conventional drama, which stopped after the characters had explained themselves but before anything happened'.[51]

On the eve of the First World War a perceptive American writer outlined the variety of accommodation her fellow Anglo-Saxons could expect on the Continent.[52] Blanche McManus's description shows how much hotels had changed, and the picture she painted is remarkably similar to our world today. When describing hotels, *pensions* and inns she put them into groups. The first was the latest in terms of arrival, the *grand* hotels. They were often part of a 'chain', such as the one Ritz was creating, and were all essentially the same. (The use of the word for a group of hotels owned by the same company itself dates from the 1850s.) She wrote that 'the English demand comfort, but the American . . . demands luxury'. These grand hotels (with up to 600 rooms) were luxurious but what they gained in luxury they lost in 'those elements of a personal character which old travellers loved'. They gave guests a distorted impression of a country 'through foreign out-of-focus lenses, rather than from a national viewpoint'. They served French food, offered English afternoon tea and American cocktails at six whether they were in Rome, Paris, Vienna or Biarritz. They were not totally cut off from the past, however: 'To show the length to which a hotel will go in cadging for business, one Italian hotel advertises that the use of garlic is absolutely banished from its kitchen. The refined olfactory nerves of the cultured foreigner are not likely to be offended beneath that roof.'

If the 'grand' hotels cost on average £2 a day, those in the second group, which included small hotels and pensions, cost between ten shillings and £1 a day. Below them were commercial hotels with little luxury but much 'character' at about eight shillings a day. The final group, made up of the *gasthaus*, the *albergo* or the *alberge*, cost about four shillings a day or roughly a tenth the cost of the grand hotels. In many of these inns the 'washing arrangements are usually microscopic, and the bathroom non-existent'. But the food was good and was that of the countries people were visiting. In Italy, while the welcome was warm, the level of service, especially in the smaller hotels and inns, was often minimal: 'The word cosy', roughly the American equivalent of the English 'comfort', 'cannot be applied to the Italian *albergo*'. She did, however, describe one delightful feature: 'On each window ledge is a flat, red cushion, which is convenient for following the Italian fashion and spending your spare moments hanging out the window, the cushion thus protecting your elbows.'

For almost a hundred years the most important thing for writers of travel guides, railway companies and travel agencies was to bring European inns and hotels up to British middle-class standards of domestic comfort and cleanliness. This pressure, combined with the growth in numbers, had led, perhaps inexorably, to the grand hotels. However, a new generation had arrived – as was seen with cyclists – which was seeking not English comforts or American cosiness but a chance to see the 'real France' or the 'real Italy'. In other words these travellers wanted to revert back to the world of 1814. As Philip Herriton put it in E. M. Forster's 1905 novel *Where Angels Fear to Tread*, 'it is only by going off the track that you get to know the country' (Chapter 1). There were now travellers who set out to do just this. Perfect drains and dry sheets were less important. Travel books, such as those by Edward Barker, now rejoiced in the *auberges* he found in France and the peasant life that surrounded them. Difference was not to be avoided but sought.

However, one must not exaggerate. This new development did not affect the majority of tourists, who continued to prefer established routes above discovery and comfort above authenticity, but it did create a new element in tourism. As one Riviera hotelier told

Blanche McManus about those demanding luxuries: 'Oh, I send these exigent foreigners to the big house over the way – every room with a bath.' He was content to have a French clientele, and added, with a shrug of his shoulders, 'Four bathrooms are enough for my people.'

Chapter 9

Men of Garlic – The Tourist and Food

$\mathcal{O}$ne 'excessively warm' spring morning in the 1880s ten English tourists were crammed into a coach travelling through the French countryside near the Spanish border. Despite the discomfort – 'some of the party were of such rotund proportions, that the thin ones were nearly lost sight of' – they admired the Pyrenees and found the staring peasants 'a good-natured lot'. Yet there was that pervasive horror that assaulted them and all Anglo-Saxons in France, Italy and Spain: 'the painful odour of garlic frequently assailed our nostrils . . . to have to talk to a man who has been eating it, is a positive punishment'. 'Fain [to] bring about a reform among the people,' one traveller spent happy moments composing a parody to *Men of Harlech*:[1]

> *Men of Garlic – large your numbers,*
> *Long indeed your conscience slumbers,*
> *Can't you change and eat cu-cumbers?*
> *Men of Garlic, say!*
> *They are sweet and tender,*
> *Short and thick or slender.*
> *Then, we know well your breath won't smell*
> *And sickness' pangs engender.*
> *Men of Garlic, stop your scorning,*

Change your food and hear our warning,
See the day of Progress dawning,
Give three cheers – Hurray!

Almost all nineteenth-century travellers would have been horrified that the 'day of Progress' has led not to the eradication of garlic but to its widespread use among their descendants. Indeed, there are few greater gulfs between the Victorians and us than our attitudes towards garlic and foreign food in general. Today, any account of a continental holiday, be it in a travel article or at a dinner party, usually features ecstatic descriptions of the local cuisine. For many people, food is one of the main pleasures in travel. Yet nineteenth-century guide-books, letters and diaries paid little attention either to food or to places for eating.

Most travellers probably set out with a distrust of foreign food and many returned with that distrust confirmed. (By 'foreign' people usually meant French and Italian. The Germans, Swiss and Austrians received less attention.) Denunciations were common. One example, from the 1860s, will suffice. A 'typical' French hotel meal consisted of thin lukewarm soup; fish served with a 'yellow slime' (sauce); potatoes (not very good but presumably boiled); beef, baked, not roasted, and with no sauces; vegetables; hot cray-fish 'about the size of your little finger' or radishes and '*raw* beef'; leg of mutton, baked and lukewarm; baked duck; rice pudding; baked chickens with cabbage lettuce – 'green greasy leaves'; salad; sweet; cheese; and desserts (usually hard fruit) and sometimes Barcelona nuts and almonds in their shells. If this were not enough, there were usually long pauses between courses during which, in desperation, guests devoured the bread and drank the wine. Frequent were the desires, especially among men, to devote their first day back home to 'a round of beef and a leg of mutton'. If it wasn't garlic it was European food's 'monotonous variety. There is always an embarrassing amount of dishes,' as seen above, but 'with a want of hearty material . . . For genuine soups and solids, commend me to an English cook.'[2]

One writer overheard a conversation about a French meal between two travellers: 'You don't know what their messes are made of . . . I like to know what I eat and you don't mean surely, sir, to say that such as they gave us was anything to compare to a good English dinner?' The happier companion replied: 'I was very much pleased with the *vin ordinaire*, as they call it, and found it a pleasant light wine.' '*Light* enough at any rate,' replied the malcontent 'and well named *vin ordinaire*, for ordinary it is . . . pretty much like themselves for that; but if you like to have any when we are in England, I'll make you some; take a little port wine, put some vinegar and a good deal of water with it and there you have it at once.' Even one of the best-travelled women of her time was perturbed by the foreign refusal to accept 'our outlandish ways,— our preference to one dish prepared in our own fashion, over half a dozen stewed in grease, and the like'. One sometimes comes across someone praising French cooking – 'if happiness consisted in good-eating, I should recommend a man to live in France' – but this was rare.[3]

Given the much discussed dislike of 'foreign' food it is ironic that the British had a reputation among some for gluttony, seen especially in their love of meat: 'Too often the grand business . . . is eating; there is no doubt they carry a mighty stomach with them.' One medical journal lamented this overindulgence, especially for those who went abroad after complaining about their digestions: 'Recovered from his seasickness, he reaches Paris, where the novelties of French cookery are tried . . . tasting a new French wine daily on his way through the Rhône district, he embarks for Italy.' There the traveller has 'doughy bread . . . two daily heavy meals of soup, boiled, roast, fried, and sweet courses without end; the intervals filled in with the "*fungi*" for which Genoa is celebrated' not to mention sardines from the Mediterranean and cheeses from Parma, grapes and melons from the south and 'café noir'.[4]

For most travellers the difficulties were threefold. They demanded British dishes from non-British cooks. When this did not work they had to adjust to unfamiliar food. They also had to cope with strange mealtimes. The problems began at breakfast. As the century wore on Britons liked a large, cooked breakfast with eggs and a variety of meats. One reference work thought that an egg and bacon 'may be advantageously added' to breakfast for sedentary people but the active would want a rump steak, mutton chops or cold meat. As late as 1914, the general view remained that a solid breakfast was necessary for 'holiday comfort' and therefore the French habit of eating little until noon had 'few attractions for the Englishman'. Continentals were satisfied with coffee and a small bit of bread or a 'French roll' with a dab of butter. Readers may be surprised that 'roll' never included croissants: in the hundreds of travel accounts and diaries used in writing this book, there was no mention of croissants for the simple reason that they appeared on French tables only at the very end of the nineteenth century. One of the first references to them in English occurred in *The Times* on 23 September 1899. It was not until the eve of the First World War that one spots references to the smell of France being coffee and 'delicious *croissants*' and not to something altogether less pleasant. Breakfast was even sparser in Italy, at least in the first years of travel in our period: 'people in this country have no idea that a man wants more for breakfast than a little thimbleful of coffee or chocolate and a morsel of bread'.[5]

Because Cook and Gaze knew what was customary in Europe, when they advertised their hotel coupons they boasted that breakfasts would be 'meat breakfasts'. On their own, most travellers were lucky to have their meagre breakfasts supplemented with an egg, at a price of course. Some obliging hoteliers, like Mr Hill's in Mâcon, would even provide a mutton chop along with his 'hard roll' and *café au lait*. Those who went off the main tourist routes could fare even worse, as one man found at a small inn in south-eastern France where he was given 'a bowl of black coffee and a piece of bread'. 'This is the only breakfast that one can expect in a rural auberge . . . If milk is wanted . . . it must be asked for over-night, and . . . it is very doubtful if the cow will be found in time. To ask for butter . . . would be looked upon as a sign of eccentric gluttony,

but to . . . demand . . . bacon and eggs at seven in the morning . . .
would be to openly confess one's self capable of any crime.' This
writer reminded his countrymen that 'people who travel should
never be slaves to any notions on eating and drinking, for such
obstinacy brings its own punishment'. This commendable philoso-
phy deserted him – as such philosophies are apt to do – when the
plump cook announced that having just slaughtered a goose, she
could warm some of its blood for his lunch. This he refused. 'An
Englishman,' he wrote, 'may possibly become reconciled to snails
and frogs . . . but never . . . to goose's blood.'[6]

Of course some people liked the continental breakfast. In the
midst of portraying 'the blond daughters of Albion' breakfasting in
Paris, one Francophile novelist burst forth: 'why is it impossible to
get such coffee in England . . . [as well as] the delicious bread, and
the exquisite butter?' Having returned to his first English breakfast
with 'thick, muddy tepid coffee' one outraged letter writer to *The
Times* likewise recalled breakfasts in Normandy with 'delicious
crisp rolls, sweet butter and hot and well-made coffee'. Throughout
the period visitors complimented the French on their coffee, 'that
Continental beverage which John Bull can no more imitate than he
can the wines of the Rhône', and asked why was it so much better.
Some concluded that it was because the beans were freshly roasted.
Of course the reverse of good coffee was bad tea. If Mr Hill was
pleased with his mutton chop for breakfast in Mâcon he was not
pleased with his tea. The teapot held about a cup and he and his
son survived by constantly appealing for more hot water. As one
saw when talking about Customs inspectors, many people, such as
William Etty and Fanny Kemble, took their own tea with them to
avoid that 'detestable decoction with which travellers are poisoned
in France'.[7]

Breakfasts involved yet another problem – language. What did
people mean by '*déjeuner*' and by 'breakfast'? Diarists and writers
used *déjeuner* to mean a cup of coffee and a piece of bread early in
the morning as well as a substantial meal with meat and vegetables
normally eaten shortly before noon: both were acceptable defini-

tions in French. To confuse matters even further, people sometimes called this meal *déjeuner à la fourchette*. Equally confusing is the use of 'breakfast'. One of the Torr family was in Belgium and 'breakfasted on Beef Steak and coffee'. We only know this was what we would call breakfast because he tells us he had to be at the station by 6.40 a.m.[8] Yet other people had 'breakfast' much later in the day. The term 'luncheon', when used, could mean either a midday meal *or* a light meal at any time. The final meal of the day was similar to the *déjeuner* in content except that it included soup (usually condemned). This raises the problem of mealtimes. In Britain the time of the main meal had been moving steadily towards the evening whereas in Europe people were still taking it earlier. (With small breakfasts they had no choice.) This presented real problems for hoteliers.

Most British travellers preferred to stick to what they knew, both with regard to time and to content. In 1860 that very embodiment of Victorian cookery, Mrs Beeton, visited Paris with her husband. Their breakfast consisted of meat, eggs and coffee, and unlike the French they then had a very light midday meal of just bouillon and then a large dinner at 5.30. One day a business associate arranged a dinner at a restaurant in the Palais Royal: soup, sweetbreads, *Poulet aux Cressons*, Sole *à la Normandie*, and *Charlotte aux Pommes* but Isabella Beeton noted that this was only 'tolerably nice'. In many cases hotels simply learned to prepare British dishes for British diners. The difficulty was that this way of cooking, being strange to them, could produce bad dishes.[9]

Meat was yet another problem. At home, the British, at least those of the travelling classes, normally consumed meat as chops, steaks or roasted joints; indeed, one of the politer French terms for their visitors was *les rosbifs*. On the Continent meat was often baked in an oven (as we do today) rather than roasted before a fire, hence the denunciations of 'baked' meat. Equally condemned was the continental habit of serving meat as a 'made dish' where sauces masked what the British considered cheap cuts. One traveller complained that in France all the *bifsticks* he had were 'tough' and the *cotelets* (both are his spellings), 'bony'. But he discovered a great truth after a good French meal in Dijon: 'the cookery of the country is best suited to the country's meat'. Such insights were not common. One clergyman who had lived abroad as a boy recalled 'how difficult it is to get good, well-fed beef on the Continent'. When a schoolboy in Cheltenham he was ordered to take some sirloin to his family in Belgium. He expected a parcel but was given instead '*half an ox*' sewn up in sacking. Not only was continental meat regarded as inferior but the sauces sparkled with the two dreaded horrors: grease and garlic. A visitor to Amiens noted as early as 1814, 'Our dinner, wholly French, was (with the exception of a small bit of roast veal) all swimming in oil [but] I set out with a resolution to eat without mercy all kinds of sauces, fricacies [*sic*], oils.' Four decades later a honeymooning squire staying at 'horrid dirty smelling' Arles moaned about 'every thing tasting more or less of garlic'. Then there always lurked the menace of unfamiliar food and the fear of eating horse-meat. In 1815, young Clarissa Trant was relieved to get to the top of the Simplon Pass with her father, a retired general. She was also relieved to have eaten the 'remains of some venerable cow' and not horse. But her relief was premature. When she said how much she had enjoyed some tender chicken the general suddenly burst forth, 'Clara, you have been eating frogs.'[10]

Coping with French cooking and mealtimes was nothing when compared with the bewildering and exotic world of Italian cooking and its use of 'macaroni' and 'pizza', which writers struggled to define. In 1843 the latter was 'a sort of cake, composed of flour, lard, eggs and garlick' while '*muzzarella* [was] a vile compound'. As late as 1903, the first modern English gourmet restaurant guide defined pizza as 'a kind of Yorkshire pudding eaten either with cheese or anchovies and tomatoes flavoured with thyme'. By mid-century 'macaroni' was 'coming much more into use' in Britain, especially among the wealthy. The term could mean macaroni as we know it or any form of pasta. One of the 'ludicrous' sights in Naples was watching the *lazzaroni* swallow as much of the long strands of 'macaroni' as possible without stopping. The tourist had his amusement and the poor man at least got a meal. Baedeker warned tourists that 'maccaroni' in Naples was 'generally hard and therefore they should say they wanted it *ben cotti*.[11]

Another feature of a Neapolitan visit was watching 'macaroni' being made, although tourists were not pleased to see the dough being mixed by men's naked feet while other visitors were horrified to see flies crawling over the drying 'strings'. If the prevalence of pasta and the methods of pasta-making were exotic, so too was the widespread use of tomatoes. An 1846 book on popular customs in southern Italy began with macaroni and actually praised the Neapolitan cuisine and explained how Neapolitans ate pasta with 'tomata [*sic*] or love-apple sauce' – 'excellent' meal. Because this was not like the 'pappy, greasy' version made in England, it was 'easy of digestion'.[12]

A modern visitor to Naples has no problem finding a place to enjoy pasta, but for Victorians who were prepared to make the effort it was not so easy. Murray's *Handbook* for southern Italy is emphatic about Neapolitan restaurants and *trattoria*: 'all very inferior and uncomfortable'. There was but one hope: Mrs Brynne, an Englishwoman, ran 'one of the best . . . however it may appear otherwise from the outside'. Forty years later, at the start of the twentieth century, things had somewhat improved. Baedeker announced starkly that 'restaurants of the first class do not exist in Southern Italy', but 'in the smaller towns the traveller will have little difficulty in finding a tolerable, though not often scrupulously clean' *trattoria*. But there was one Neapolitan treat which everyone praised, including one young man who wrote home enthusiastically that 'the macaroni here is good [but] the ices here are certainly delicious'.[13]

In 1821 Captain Beadles described a novel experience when visiting Paris. He went to a 'restaurant' where 'the scene was quite new to me'. The chandeliers made the large room look like a ballroom. There was a woman, dressed in the height of fashion and sitting on a raised platform who took customers' money while the menus featured between 200 and 300 dishes. He was surprised to see ladies sitting at the tables and to discover that on the menu each dish had its cost listed beside it. The captain was right to be surprised. At no time between 1814 and 1914 were such 'restaurants' – large and elegant public places where people chose a selection of dishes from menus – common in Europe. For many decades, they remained virtually unique to Paris. One of the few wholly beneficial results of the French Revolution was the growing popularity of these Parisian restaurants although the term had been used before 1789. The name came from the fact that the earliest establishments advertised broths as restoratives or *restaurants*. It was well into the middle of the nineteenth century before the term was fully accepted into English and no longer italicized in print. Mariana Starke, writing in the 1830s, paid hardly any attention to them and what she does say makes one wonder if she had ever been in one. In 1815 an official register showed only a handful outside Paris: Bordeaux, for example, had only four and even by the 1850s the majority of French *départments* still had none. The 1914 Baedeker guide to southern France announced bluntly: 'except in larger towns there are few restaurants in France suitable for tourists'.[14]

The aristocratic travellers who flocked to Paris after Napoleon's two abdications often joined Wellington's victorious officers in savouring the delights of famous restaurants in the Palais Royal. Here, said a duke's son, they delighted in *'les pieds de mouton* and *gras double sur le gril* . . . sheeps trotters and tripe. Many a squeamish lady and gentleman who would be horrified at the mere mention of the above dishes in England, would be delighted to partake of them under a foreign name.' Fortunately, one early traveller pasted a restaurant menu in his notebook and the large sheet, about one foot square, shows a staggering choice including seven soups, meats ranging from a *bifteck aux pommes de terre* for one franc to half a chicken or turkey. There was even a rare English item, Cheshire cheese at ten *sous* (about one English penny), but far cheaper was Brie at six *sous*. Vegetables were comparatively expensive and fruits, especially exotic ones, were even higher since elaborate desserts were a restaurant speciality. Many wines were listed but with little information: a costly bottle of St Emilion was four francs. Ordering from such a large menu was considered an elegant accomplishment for gentlemen and real connoisseurs would arrange a meal hours or days beforehand.[15] Since portions tended to be huge, gourmets always advised visitors that one portion would feed two people.

Travellers, frightened of the complexities of fashionable restaurants, could always resort to *cafés* for a quick meal; but these, warned one author, might be 'receptacles for sulky husbands, swell shop-boys, and dirty and idle politicians – to say nothing of the delight of sitting in a concentrated essence of bad smells, animal and vegetable, and in the midst of a shower of refreshing expectorations'. Murray's *Handbook* hoped that if one did frequent *cafés* one would choose 'the superior class'. While it was respectable for ladies to go to such places in the afternoon, in the evening even the better ones could be full of 'tradesmen, soldiers and men in blouses [workmen]'.[16]

Eventually cheaper, less elegant restaurants began to spread throughout Paris, and by the 1860s there were said to be a grand total of 500 such establishments. Even in the centre there were places serving meals consisting of soup, two other courses, desserts, bread and 'a modicum of wine' for twenty-two *sous* or about 2*d*. There was a particularly notable chain called Duvals where women felt comfortable dining on their own. Arnold Bennett, a devoted gourmet who lived in Paris, often frequented them, and it was there, while observing two women, that he got the idea for his greatest novel, *The Old Wives' Tale*. When young Rudyard Kipling was taken to Paris for the 1878 Exhibition, his busy father told the boy there were 'lots of restaurants all called Duval' where he could eat for one franc. Of course, restaurants, whether grand or part of the Duval chain, could take too much time from a hard-pressed tourist's schedule. Many followed the advice given to one teenage boy: 'order something simple'. He ordered *bifsteak* and potatoes but it still took three-quarters of an hour.[17]

Throughout the century every gourmet always had his favourite restaurant – and it was almost always *his* – be it *Le Café Anglais*, *Les Trois Frères Provenceaux*, known for its cod in garlic sauce, or *Véry*. In virtually every gourmet's account one theme was constant: 'culinary art has sadly fallen off in Paris'. This quotation comes from 1852, but similar statements were made in every decade. A second theme was that the cost of restaurants was always increasing. For the novice gourmet, however, almost all guide-books were virtually useless concerning restaurants or, indeed, any other place to eat outside hotels. It was not until 1903, with the appearance of *The Gourmet's Guide to Europe* by Lieutenant Colonel Newnham-Davies and Algernon Bastard, that people had a real guide to European restaurants. This book was a turning-point because it showed a new attitude towards dining out in Europe, especially in France, when it declared, 'Paris is the culinary centre of the world.' Newnham-Davies was the first serious restaurant critic for a newspaper and his book gave sound advice about where to eat in different cities while his descriptions of lengthy dinners still whet appetites today. His book also shows how far the restaurant had developed from its Parisian beginnings and how travellers, both men and women, could now eat well throughout Europe. The colonel, however, warned that some Parisian restaurants had attractions other than food: 'At *Maxim's*, any gentleman may conduct the band . . . and a little impromptu dance [is] organised. At the *Café Américain*, the profession of the ladies who frequent it . . . is a little too obvious . . . You should not take [your wife] to *Maxim's* and you cannot take her to the *Américain*.'[18] From the earliest days rumours of immorality had clung to Paris's fashionable restaurants.

Because there were so few acceptable restaurants when travellers did eat outside their hotels, they usually chose the *traiteur* in France or the *trattoria* in Italy, which offered good food but in far less fashionable surroundings. As so often happened, British tourists caused problems for themselves. One man, landing in Naples after years in India, assumed that once in Europe he could get English food. He demanded the perplexed owner give him a chump chop, something unknown in Italy. After a long wait, the chop finally arrived, followed by a staggering bill: to get the chop a sheep had to be found, slaughtered and butchered especially. Long did the Briton's London club resound with his rants against dining in 'foreign parts'. If visitors would only order local dishes they stood a much better chance. Bishop Hynes called into one *trattoria* in Naples and had some 'bouillie [*bouilli* or boiled beef]', bread and wine all for fourpence. 'The things were good, altho' not served in the best style.' *Traiteurs* would also send meals to travellers who had rented rooms. One could order specific items or sufficient food for a set number of people at an agreed fee per day. Henry Matthews and two friends had excellent meals sent to their lodgings in Rome in 1817 for about three shillings a head. They also had a bottle of wine for about sixpence – the bottle held four pints. Three decades later, the newly married Elizabeth Barrett Browning was enchanted with the way in which large meals were brought in a heated box to her rooms in Florence. It cost less than three shillings to feed herself, her husband and her maid with soup, meat, fish, vegetables and pudding with enough left for an evening meal. A guide-book explained how the system worked in Paris: 'a garçon . . . appears with a clean white apron . . . lays the cloth . . . sets the dinner on table . . . [and] waits upon you while you dine'.[19] It was an ideal solution for weary travellers and especially for invalids such as Elizabeth Barrett Browning or Henry Matthews.

As well as having *traiteurs* send food to their rooms, many travellers came equipped with an Etna stove like that displayed at the Great Exhibition in 1851. Naming it after the Sicilian volcano reflected both the device's speed – it could boil water in three minutes – and the influence travel was already having on the language. Travellers could buy an impressive version in gleaming copper for thirty-five shillings or in tin for less than two. Travellers were advised to take the necessary methylated spirits as these could not always be found abroad. The Etna made that perennial problem of obtaining a decent cup of tea less difficult, although it had other uses: soon after it came on the market one retired naval captain was using it to heat up Fortnum and Mason's 'portable soup', which he had packed along with boxes of hard biscuits.[20]

The British passion for tea was already changing hotel life even before the Etna appeared. One German woman who resented the 'barbarians' – 'the innumerable tribe of English people ' – claimed that their annoying devotion to 'comfort' meant that in 'all the hotels throughout Italy the people are prepared for the reception of the *tea-drinking* northerns'. 'Yet 'the barbarians' were served some strange concoctions. One barrister visiting Germany wrote after a meal, 'the tea wretched – mere common herbs of the country and on requiring more hot water the waiter brought a ½ pint cup of warm water and threw it into the teapot'. Far better to pack your own Etna, a pound of tea and potted meat, as Mary Gladstone did when she travelled in the 1890s. But as always things could be carried too far. A general's wife always brought not just her Etna but her own supplies to give tea parties for ten in her rooms in a Nice hotel. The owner, herself English, made up for the lost revenue by simply adding ten francs to the bill. She also ordered the concierge to make sure that ladies did not smuggle food into their rooms. The difficulty was that brandy could be secreted in their muffs – provided they tipped the concierge.[21]

'Great fun', declared Gladstone's teenage daughter about her first continental table d'hôte. Since the majority of British travellers took their meals at their hotel's table d'hôte it is not surprising that restaurants developed so slowly. Guests dined at a set time, paid a set fee, made their meal from those dishes which the proprietor chose and usually sat at one large table. In the early days the host presided at the head of the table and tasted every dish as it was brought in. By the 1830s the Torr family were staying at a hotel in

Brussels that had sixty people at table with at least thirty different dishes and good meat – 'excellent table d'hôte' was the verdict. The custom of eating at a common table (or several tables in large hotels) prevailed in France, Italy, Switzerland and Belgium but was less common in Germany and Austria. Most hotels used the table d'hôte for all meals and often larger hotels had two evening sittings, with the English preferring the later one. For the adventurous, tables d'hôte gave a chance to taste foreign dishes. The practice meant that people did not have to find a place to eat in a strange city and it was especially useful when so many travellers had to be up early every morning. It was also more economical than dining in one's room (usually two-thirds less) or eating out: the two sisters whose clothes had attracted so much unwanted attention in Paris ventured to a Parisian restaurant on their own in 1860. They concluded that they had 'paid more for fewer things than . . . at the table d'hote' and they were right. Finally, some tables d'hôte were open to the public. The writers Mary and William Howitt took 'lodgings' in Heidelberg in the 1840s to 'retrench'. At a nearby hotel's table d'hôte, they fed themselves, their five children, one English maid and the delightfully named governess Miss Freelove for thirty shillings a week.[22]

British attitudes towards tables d'hôte were sharply divided. 'Nothing, in general, can be more adverse to the quiet, the ease, or the good-sense of English manners,' fumed one writer in the 1840s. 'The *table d'hôte* is essentially vulgar; and no excellence of *cuisine* . . . can prevent it from exhibiting proof of its original purpose, namely, to give a cheap dinner to a miscellaneous rabble.' For those who agreed with this view, the difficulty was not so much the food but one's fellow diners. One could be placed beside unsuitable people, fellow countrymen whom one would avoid at home or foreigners, often of confusing social rank. One Murray *Handbook* from 1879 tried to reassure people: 'The table-d'hôte is frequented by both ladies and gentlemen, and, . . . by persons of the highest rank, from Grand Dukes and Princes downwards . . . the topics and news of the day are discussed without restraint; and . . . the traveller [can] . . . gain general or local information.' More practically, 'The best dinner is always to be had at the table-d'hôte.'[23]

The criticisms of the table d'hôte system were based on the normal dislike, perhaps more prevalent in the middle class, of close proximity to strangers while eating. People, numbering from a handful in a country inn to hundreds in a city hotel, were thrown together. Experienced travellers knew 'how essential it is to one's comfort to get near to pleasant neighbours . . . it certainly does seem . . . that the musty fusty people, and the nicy spicy people, and the witty pretty people do severally assemble and get together as they ought'. Occasionally this natural segregation did not work, and things could also get quite nasty between the British and foreigners. When Lord Malmesbury was in Holland in 1828 he was at a table that included several Napoleonic officers and 'our gallant Colonel Brotherton', a veteran of Waterloo. The battle was being discussed 'as usual, with great heat by the French' and when the colonel refused to reply, one offensive Frenchman called him a coward. 'Then the colonel jumped up, and, breaking up his wooden chair like a stick, shook the leg in his face. I shall never forget the rapid retreat of the aggressor. All the table cheered.' It turned out the militant Frenchman was actually a 'hell-keeper [keeper of a gambling house] from Aix'. Far more common was the stiff formality and near silence produced when the British sat next to people to whom they had not been introduced. When Miss Bartlett and Miss Honeychurch were discussing the lack of 'a room with a view' in Forster's novel, they were seated at a Florentine table d'hôte: 'Some of their neighbours interchanged glances, and one of them – one of the ill-bred people whom one does meet abroad – leant forward over the table and actually intruded into their argument.'[24]

The vulgarity of compatriots was always far worse than that of local people. In 1828, the Reverend George Brett visited Paris and was not happy at the fashionable Hôtel Meurice's table d'hôte where there were '14 or 16 English'. The young clergyman 'addressed myself to my neighbour, but got nothing – 8 ladies at table – very stupid business – three broad Scotch, 1 lady, 2 gents, talked of *opening* medicines [laxatives]'. Brett fled to a theatre. Although larger hotels tended to have a separate table d'hôte for travellers' servants, some guests insisted on bringing their servants with them so that they could fend off unacceptable neighbours. The risk of having unpleasant company was worse if travellers were staying outside the main tourist cities. In smaller towns, the table d'hôte was frequently dominated by local people and commercial travellers. When Henry James stayed at 'the wretched little Hôtel de France' in Narbonne he 'sat down with a hundred hungry marketers, fat, brown greasy men, with a good deal of the rich soil of Languedoc adhering to their hands and boots [which] . . . they almost put . . . on the table . . . there were swarms of flies; the viands had the strongest odour . . . a horrible mixture known as *gras-double* [tripe], a light grey, glutinous nauseating mess'. However, if travellers had an interest in the area and made an effort, tables d'hôte could be enjoyable, especially for a lonely tourist. We have already met the Gloucestershire landowner Granville Lloyd Baker, when he was a young man in Rome. When in Normandy two decades later he stopped in Isigny, where he had a 'dull evening' since the three other people at the table d'hôte were 'silent'. But when he got to Coutances there were some 'some intelligent French men' and he had a 'pleasant evening'.[25] The key here was language: Lloyd-Baker spoke French.

As hotels became more luxurious so too did their tables d'hôte, and the best could be quite splendid affairs. This is seen in Eugène Lami's detailed watercolour of the elegant Hôtel des Princes near the Boulevard des Italiens in Paris in the 1840s. At five francs, the meal was more expensive than usual but the wine was said to be particularly good and non-residents needed to book ahead. The watercolour shows an elegant room with chandeliers in which a few women and several dozen well-dressed men, including one with a turban, are sitting at a long table while at least eight formally attired waiters attend to the numerous carafes of wine.[26] Large hotels sometimes provided music during meals, which added to the elegance and relieved the silences.

It was not just a table d'hôte's seating arrangements that were so different from modern dining but the way of eating. The following is a menu from a Cologne hotel in the early 1860s: vegetable soup, roast beef and potatoes, cucumber and French salad, stewed cabbage, asparagus, salmon, omelette, sweetbreads, chicken and salad, veal, geese with cherries, plum pudding, ices, cheese and butter, desserts and coffee. All this cost about three shillings and included wine.[27] This bewildering assortment was not usually served in courses but in one go, that is, the dishes were set on the table and replenished as necessary. The joints would have been carved at table and diners would have what they wanted when they wanted it, although desserts, puddings and coffee came at the end. *Vin ordinaire* was usually included in the cost and its quality was high since many hoteliers had a profitable sideline in arranging for the export of wine to Britain: their tables served as advertisements. Guests could always order special wine for themselves and it is an almost inflexible rule in any contemporary novel with scenes at a table d'hôte that the obliging foreign grandee who offers to share his champagne with a pretentious Briton will turn out to be a cheating rogue. The final part of the table d'hôte experience came after the meal when the guests retired en masse into a salon for their tea or coffee and someone might be prevailed upon to play the piano. At smaller hotels this retreat would often be to a nearby cafe. Those who avoided the after-dinner socializing would also miss out on that ready exchange of information that can be so useful when travelling. However, there were two potential draw-backs: if there were many hungry diners, the choicer items might have run out by the time the platters came round to the end of the table, while late-comers might have a hard time of it.

Towards the end of the century tables d'hôte began to give way to separate tables. Why this took place was discussed by one aristocratic traveller in 1905, as he looked back over almost thirty years. In part it was because 'English life abroad has grown more intolerant and exclusive' with increased tourism: 'the "travelling English" are nowadays recruited from a lower class' so that 'the increased toleration of the most refined class of tourists is more than counteracted by the increased vulgarity of an occasional member of the least refined class'. More importantly, hoteliers had slowly realized that they could actually make more money with *à la carte* dining at separate tables. Yet right up to 1914 the older custom delighted those who are amused by the table talk of others. One intellectual girl wrote to another in 1892 from an Italian spa: 'The table d'hôte talk . . . was not always brilliant or interesting. The company consisted of rheumatic aristocratic old ladies and gentlemen & every day they would lean across the table to ask each other – Did you have a good *bagno*? Was it warm to-day? Mine was cold and the water took a long time to come etc. etc.' What Lina Duff-Gordon did not appreciate is that it could have been much worse: they could have been talking about their bowels.[28]

Chapter 10

Travelling is a Very Troublesome Business

*easoned travellers always accept that 'travelling is a very troublesome business',[1] but in the nineteenth century three aspects caused particular problems: language, money and religion.

Mark Twain once wrote of the French language, 'How beautiful that language is! How expressive it seems to be! . . . I always think I am going to understand it.' When it came to foreign languages the British appear to have been defeated, but in their defeat they scored a tremendous victory. In the early years of travel in our period, a large proportion of travellers would have spoken French. In addition, a surprising number, especially women, had some Italian because of the widespread devotion to Dante and Petrarch among the educated classes. Those who knew French often assumed that it would serve them everywhere as it had done in the days of the Grand Tour, but its days as the pan-European language were numbered. By 1870 Edward Peek wrote from Dresden, 'Whilst here I shall try to acquire a smattering of German. I have found absolute ignorance of the language intolerably inconvenient, French does not go far here and is of no use whatever in Austria.'[2]

Tourists with no foreign languages coped as people do today. In Blanchard Jerrold's novel *The Cockaynes in Paris* the eponymous hero found himself in a jewellery shop. 'He might make up for his ignorance of French by speaking in a voice of thunder.' When this did not work, 'the bright idea struck him that he, Mr Cockayne, late of Lambeth, would make his meaning plainer than a pike-staff by speaking broken English also. The jeweller was puzzled, but he was very patient' (Chapter 5). The jeweller was patient because he had to make a living and this, combined with a large amount of sign language and some good humour, offered one means of salvation for the British. This inability to communicate caused 'both annoyance and amusement'.[3]

If tourists would not speak other languages, inn-keepers and tradesmen had no choice but to learn at least some English. As early as 1817 the fourteen-year-old Harriet Campbell noted in France that 'at every petty shop or ale house they hang out a large sign with the french [*sic*] above and the English translation under[neath] . . . the inn cards too have generally the translation into English'. Inns also had 'some one happy person of the house who speaks English'. Young Harriet also remembered that 'all these marks of civility . . . were not practised when we left the continent last year'. Henry Matthews saw the same developments in Florence four months later. A pattern was being established that would in time be repeated round the world: the 'natives' were adapting to attract customers. By 1849 an American traveller found that 'English alone will carry us through France, Italy, Switzerland, Germany, Holland, and Belgium without difficulty . . . as for places where English is not spoken, *there are very few* . . . almost every tolerable hotel has some person whose business it is to speak English'.[4] This only increased as the wandering British were reinforced by their transatlantic cousins. As we saw earlier, by the 1850s railway companies and tourist agencies began placing bilingual officials at major stations.

Problems remained when travellers left major tourist spots or met Europeans privately. When the Bishop of Langres had John Henry Newman to dinner in 1846 neither spoke the other's language so they compromised on Latin which 'went off very well'. Recourse to Latin was, however, not an option open to many. One could, of course, learn foreign languages, or at least foreign phrases, and there were a host of published guides appealing to the many people who saw travel as a serious part of education and culture. In 1844 John Murray began his *Handbook of Travel-Talk* which was 'free from the puerilities and vulgar nonsense ... in similar works'. Murray's volumes included all three major languages and taught people to ask for the water-closet – *les lieux d'aisance*, *il luogo comodo* and *das Privet*. Ladies, well aware that 'tight lacing has spoilt many a pleasant tour', could tell Italian chambermaids *'Allacciatemi il busto. Non melo allacciate tanto streto'* – 'Lace my stays. Do not lace them so tight.' In German one was taught to complain that *'Dieze Ueberzüge sind ganz gewiss schon im Gebrauch gewesen'* – 'These sheets have certainly been used already.'[5]

While we admire those who made (and still make) the effort we can also enjoy the humour this produces. When the Torrs, a family who made annual continental rambles, visited Florence in 1872 they were shown round the Palazzo Vecchio. Their guide spoke only Italian. 'His efforts to make us understand were most ludicrous – Henry took out his Dictionary to ... get up a little talk with him. He took us into the Hall of the Italian Parliament and there Henry sat down to find words ... to ask him if he believed the confusion of languages was the result of the Tower of Babel. The Guide seemed as amused with us as we were with him.' However, French remained the real bugbear. When Dickens landed at Marseilles in 1844, he went to a bank: 'After delivering with most laborious distinctness a rather long address in French to the clerk ... [he] was disconcerted by that functionary's cool enquiry ... "How would you like to take it, sir?"'[6]

Alfred Tennyson suffered even more when he and his brother, Frederick, visited Paris in 1848. Frederick left the hotel and told the concierge, *'Prenez garde de ne pas laisser sortir le feu.'* But he pronounced *'feu'* as *'fou'* so that instead of asking the staff to keep the fire in his room going, he asked them not to let 'the madman'out of the building. Since the poet's 'eccentric manners' had already convinced the staff that he was mad they were alarmed when Alfred tried to go out. The concierge quickly blocked the door and explained very carefully that Tennyson could not leave. Tennyson 'raged and stormed, but to no purpose'. Others came to the concierge's assistance and detained the poet until Frederick returned. It was many years before Tennyson returned to France. Twain also told a story against himself regarding his German: 'When I was talking (in my native tongue) about some rather private matters in the hearing of some Germans one day, Twichell said, "Speak in German, Mark – some of these people may understand English."'[7]

The more typical dilemma was described by a tourist in 1889. 'If the person . . . was a German I must listen to the past participle rattling past like the brake van at the end of a luggage-train, telling one that . . . the German sentence, is finished.' Then 'I gently clear my throat and this would be understood to be a German remark in concurrence.' If his neighbour was French, 'I was at once to attempt that imbecile smile with which an Englishman listens to a Frenchman.' When the Frenchman came to his 'last flourish I was to say "*oui*," but with reserve, as of one who wishes to take the matter into consideration, and after a little add with emphasis, "*oui, oui*," which would ensure another shower of rhetoric'.[8] This remains sensible advice for travellers.

As the range of travellers expanded, the number able to speak foreign languages declined. In *The Prince and Betty*, P. G. Wodehouse described how he was in Paris's Gare du Nord in 1912 and watched how 'obvious Anglo-Saxons wandered about like lost sheep, miserably conscious of linguistic deficiencies' (Chapter 7). A more typical view was expressed by the warden of Toynbee Hall when quizzed by Thomas Okey on his inability to command enough French to buy a collar-stud. '"No," said he; "it's the business of *these people to learn English.*"' In the event the warden was right. 'The English-speaking man stands amid the strangers and jingles his gold. "Here," he cries, "is payment for all such as can speak English." . . . He is the missionary of the English tongue.'[9] Anglo-Saxon ignorance ultimately gave birth to an international tourist language, which played its part in making English the world's language.

'English gold will go anywhere' was not just a patriotic boast but a statement of fact. British currency included gold coins – the sovereign (one pound) and the half-sovereign (ten shillings) – and because gold had an intrinsic value, such coins were recognized wherever travellers went. In addition, British economic power and the strength of her banking system meant that after 1814 her silver and copper coins were also accepted, especially in the main tourist centres, by hoteliers, shopkeepers and even beggars. At Calais, urchins besieged travellers crying, 'Please, please a little English penny.'[10] Furthermore, British economic involvement in Europe meant that some British bankers became partners in foreign banks in the main cities, as much to finance British merchants and engineers as to serve tourists. British financiers also began setting up their own banks, and here tourists could present cheques in exchange for local currency. However, difficulties remained.

In France from 1814 to 1914, the pound was worth about twenty-five francs. (Even during the Franco-Prussian war and the Parisian Commune [1870–1] this exchange rate only rose to twenty-six francs.) Thus an English shilling was worth one-fifth more than a franc. The franc was divided into 100 centimes although five centimes were often called a *sou*. The *Napoleon* was worth twenty francs. These gold coins were often accepted in other continental countries, especially Italy, and were frequently used by the British who became rather fond of 'Naps'. The rate of conversion might fluctuate when people strayed from the main tourist routes.

Once a traveller left France the problem of foreign currencies became more acute, at least during the first two-thirds of the century. Murray's first *Handbook* for Switzerland warned: 'almost every canton has a Currency of its own and those coins that are current in one canton will not pass in the next'. The numerous Germanic states, with their *thalers, groschen, schillings, pfenniges*, and *zwanzigers*, let alone the patchwork of Italian monarchies with their *lire, florins, soldi, scudi, pauli* and *carlini* were simply a monetary nightmare as each kingdom's currency fluctuated in value. If that was not enough, one country's currency was often commonly used in another. The best thing was to read up before leaving: thus a traveller going to Hanover in the 1820s could consult Thomas Hodgskin's book:[11]

> A pistole, or *George d'or*, which is the gold money in circulation, is worth at par about 16*s*.8*d*. It is also worth five thalers, cassen* money of Hannover; each cassen thaler is therefore worth at par 3*s* 4*d*. Conventions, or reichs money, bears the proportion of 10 to 9 to the money of Hannover; consequently, the conventions or reichs thalers, which are most usually in circulation, are each of them worth only 3*s*. Each thaler contains 24 good grosschen, or 36 marien grosschen; consequently, the cassen good grosschens are each worth somewhat more than 1½*d* a marien grosschen more than 1*d*. A conventions good grosschen is 1½*d*. and a marien grosschen 1*d*. Each good grosschen contains 12 pfennige, each marien grosschen 8. A florin contains 16 good grosschen, and is worth about 2*s*.

Anyone emerging sane from all this knew his best bet was to avoid Hanover.

Not only was continental currency confusing but gold coins were in short supply before the California gold rush of 1848–9. As for silver coins, they were often centuries old: their inscriptions and values were worn away and their likelihood of being 'clipped' was greater. Even when new their silver content varied enormously, but retained some intrinsic value. In general, travellers were warned to avoid non-silver coins and, not surprisingly, travellers recalled that the incessant 'wrangling over small change with a knavish landlord, or being woke up in a night drive . . . to tip the driver'. Many

---

* 'Cassen' means the official value as set by the Exchequer in Hanover.

travellers completely failed to make sense of this monetary confusion. The editor of *The Times* boasted in 1854 that, although his
party included highly educated men, he was the only one who
could 'reckon German money'.[12] It is likely that his experience was
typical.

By mid-century, however, reform was in the air. In 1850 all Swiss
cantons adopted the French franc. In the German lands a monetary
union was set up in 1857, and Prussia's currency was adopted in
much of Germany. This was but a prelude to the simplification in
Italy in 1861 when the Sardinian *lira* became the national currency
everywhere except in the area ruled by the Pope. Ten years later
the new currency covered all Italy. The new German Empire
adopted the *Reichsmark* in 1871 which, along with the *lira*, was a
decimal currency. There was a bonus for the British: the new Mark
was virtually equal to one shilling.

Another help for travellers was the Latin Monetary Union, which
France launched in 1865 with Belgium and Luxembourg. Within
the next decade the union recruited the new Kingdom of Italy as
well as Spain, Greece and eventually other continental states. It was
not so much a 'union' as an agreement to maintain the gold and
silver value of members' coins so that these could be used in all
member countries. The higher value coins of each country started
to resemble one another, with the monarch on one side and the
coat of arms on the reverse. Strictly speaking, only higher-value
currency down to the silver five-franc coin was accepted regardless
of national origin, but most people honoured the smaller copper
and nickel coins. Yet, for many decades, worthless coins were
palmed off on foreigners as Baedeker warned in various Italian
guides as late as 1909. For the British this union, although often
ineffective, meant that an understanding of the value of the French
franc provided some vague notion of the value of most continental
countries. There was talk that Britain and even the United States
might join this monetary union. However, the Latin Monetary
Union – a forerunner of the Euro – would be undermined by the
First World War and would collapse in the 1920s.

It was not just British coins that enjoyed a high reputation in Europe: in time British banknotes and sterling cheques had the same standing. By 1904 travellers were assured that 'in all parts of the Continent . . . regularly frequented by tourists, English credit is so good that . . . an English cheque-book is all that is required'. Still, this guide also recommended that a traveller carry a pound's worth of small French silver coins to cope with minor expenses and tips. An example of the respect paid to British currency occurred when one tourist presented a £50 cheque in a Swiss bank. The clerk did not ask for a passport but immediately handed over 1,256 Swiss francs to the astounded tourist, 'a very extraordinary way of doing business I thought as they did not in the least know me'.[13]

The 'Roving Englishman' who advised travellers to take 'a little bag of sovereigns' also advised them to take letters of credit or circular notes. To get such a 'letter' the traveller deposited a sum in his bank and received a letter authorizing him to draw any amount up to that figure in a list of approved banks, which would compare his signature with a sample sent on ahead. The foreign bank would then note on the letter the amount withdrawn. This method required careful planning because the traveller had to ask his bank to send his signature to specified banks in specified cities. But the system could not keep up with the growing numbers who travelled and with the increasing variety of places they visited. In addition, the use of these letters required close coordination among banks and was open to fraud. In 1841 *The Times* uncovered a plan organized by a French baron and some English bankers in Florence to steal the staggering sum of one million pounds or £69,716,000 today. The plan was to cash forged letters of credit – some forgeries had already been accepted in places as far apart as Brussels, Koblenz and Turin when *The Times* exposed the scheme. The paper's Parisian correspondent acted at considerable risk to himself: the baron was a celebrated duellist. If the scam had been successful it would have tarnished the reputation of British travellers across the world and undermined international finance. Rightly did London's bankers pay for a florid plaque to commemorate the paper's action.[14]

Letters of credit were primarily used by the wealthiest travellers, especially those planning long stays in a few places. For the ever-increasing numbers of travellers on shorter holidays, a second and easier method, circular notes, became popular in mid-century. These were an early form of traveller's cheques. The traveller asked his bank for a series of printed forms for any amount above ten pounds. Essentially these were detachable cheques that had to be signed before leaving and then presented to foreign banks (and even some hoteliers) and signed again. In time travel agents began their own 'notes', but there were occasional breaches. Circular notes were safer than British currency because a lost note could not be cashed unless it had the required second signature. This was an advantage because the notes were lost all over Europe. Two English climbers even found a negotiable one in the Alps, though they made sure that the note and its owner were safely reunited. It was perhaps fortunate for the owner that the two climbers were future bishops.[15]

People with circular notes or letters of credit had to visit banks just as much as those cashing cheques; yet bankers, especially British bankers in Europe, provided other essential services for most travellers. 'The English banker has now become an important feature in all continental circles' and only 'unsophisticated beings . . . imagine his duties simply limited to . . . circular-notes . . . His clients' happiness, interest, comfort, and amusement are his engrossing thought; and if, after experiencing an infinity of trouble . . . his only return should be the half-percentage on a £50 draft, he is expected to smile . . . and with undaunted resolution, pursue the same train of kindness . . . towards the next new-comer.' Bankers also acted as translators. They advised on hotels, *pensions*, other travellers' backgrounds, railway timetables, churches and libraries. They wrote introductions to allow customers to visit private art collections. They received and forwarded post and provided British newspapers. The journals of one Florentine banker, the 'excellent, honourable, and hospitable' Irishman John Leland Maquay, Jnr, for example, show how important bankers were. Maquay, who was married to an Italian, entertained visitors, presented Americans to the Grand Duke, worked to establish a free lending library and was involved in the English church in Florence from the 1830s.[16]

Some European bankers were often just as hospitable. Perhaps the most famous was Rome's Prince Torlonia. Mariana Starke praised him as 'highly respectable ... particularly obliging and useful to the British nation'. Torlonia's bank had been founded in the eighteenth century and by 1814 his was one of the richest families in Rome. His princely titles were given him by Pope Pius VII in appreciation for his handling of papal finances. The banker-prince was remarkably sociable and invited visiting Britons to his lavish entertainments. On one famous occasion in 1834 Sir Robert Peel was present when word arrived that he had just been appointed Prime Minister by William IV. But since, to qualify for an invitation, a guest's balance needed only to be above 500 *scudi* (about £11), invitations went out all over Rome. The unknown young artist Lowes Dickinson, who had merely presented circular notes at the bank, was stunned when he received an invitation. He wrote an enthusiastic description of progressing up the footman-lined grand staircase in the Torlonia *palazzo* to drink champagne with Roman princes while cardinals played whist, servants walked round with ices and sherbet and couples waltzed in another room. At almost every one of Torlonia's elegant receptions there would also be a select gathering of British aristocrats looking with bemused conde-scension at the growing ranks of their fellow countrymen from the middling ranks of society. No wonder Dickinson added, 'I felt so strange and so alone.'[17]

The most glaring difference between Victorian travellers and people today is religion. For the British visiting Europe religion had two aspects. The first was their reaction to Catholicism; the second was the provision of Anglican worship in Europe. Both of these were crucial to many travellers.

To the vast majority of the British setting out for the Continent, their country's Protestantism was the bedrock on which constitutional government and 'progress' had been built. For most, to visit Belgium, France, Italy, Austria and parts of Germany and Switzerland was to come face to face with Catholicism for the first time, to go back in time to a 'pre-enlightened age'. The relatively advanced state of Protestant cantons in Switzerland over Catholic ones, along with the poverty they saw in Italy, naturally fed the view that Catholicism equalled stagnation. The state of Rome, the prevalence of beggars and 'dirt' and the wholesale bribery supported the views that Catholic countries were backward and that the Catholic Church was on its last legs. Progress was equated with Protestantism and the hostility to the Church that was part of the *Risorgimento* only enhanced its value in British eyes. Even Catholics such as Bishop Hynes lamented when in Palermo 'There is certainly a vast deal to reform in these Catholic countries ... What a pity such fine countries and people, no doubt capable of rivalling others in every intellectual and industrial pursuit, should be so very much behind the age we live in.' Catholicism was also equated with persecution, a view that conveniently overlooked much of Britain's own history. In *Pictures from Italy* the anti-Catholic Dickens described the Inquisition's chambers in the papal palace at Avignon. As a result this became a tourist 'must', and when the Horners arrived in 1847 they peered into a dungeon into which 'prisoners were let down by ropes, and never heard of more'. (Within four years after Dickens's book, the palace had become a military barracks and the infamous rooms were closed.) For the Horners, worse was to come. In San Giovanni Valdarno they visited the church: 'The first object shewn us, was the body of an unhappy man who had been built up in the church. It was a horrid sight; the skin had shrunk up to the bones, and the arms were crossed, with the fingers pressed on the shoulders as if in pain.'[18]

While many enjoyed the music at High Masses and some understood what was going on, many more disliked '[p]opish ceremonies, this presumption, folly and idolatry are not to be borne.' The majority were horrified when they came face to face with relics, whether virgins' bones in Cologne or the holy clothes

OUR COUNTRYMEN ABROAD.

SKETCH OF A BENCH ON THE BOULEVARDS, OCCUPIED BY FOUR ENGLISH PEOPLE WHO ONLY KNOW EACH OTHER BY SIGHT.

This *Punch* cartoon of 4 June 1870 shows four travellers in Paris: a High Church clergyman, two ladies and a middle-aged businessman who do not speak. They have not been introduced.

The 'love-hate' relationship between the British and Switzerland is caught in this *Punch* cartoon of 14 October 1865. On the left, the Swiss inn-keeper with his bags of gold, derived through over-charging. On the right, the impoverished tourist back in Britain, complete with his travelling suit, courier's bag, backpack, *alpenstock* and empty pockets.

The annual Advertiser section in every issue of Murray's *Handbooks* always featured hotels. As this section was in every *Handbook*, the list of hotels mixed British and foreign. Paris' Hotel Meurice, still flourishing, was a particular favourite of the British. Thackeray advised 'If you don't speak a word of French, if you like English comfort, clean rooms . . . your fellow country-men around you, your brown beer . . . with your best British accent cry heartily: "Meurice".' The hotel had been opened specifically for the British in 1817 by a Calais inn-keeper who arranged coaches to Paris. It was nicknamed 'The City of London.'

The Hotel Continental was opened in 1878 as a symbol that after war and revolution, Paris was once again the great goal of travellers. As the journalist G. A. Sala said, 'this vast and gorgeous hotel has risen, with magical rapidity, from the red-hot ashes of the Commune.' This drawing was on the cover of an 1887 menu. The hotel was among the three largest hotels in the French capital and is today called The Westin Paris.

Déjuener menu at the Hotel Continental, Paris from 1887. Not surprisingly, the cost was quite high. The hotel's wine cellars were renowned: a guest could have a St Emilion for five francs or champagne from five to eight francs. Guests could also order cases of any of the wines to be sent to Britain at trade prices.

DÉJEUNER A 5 FRANCS

Admission de 11 heures à Midi 1/2

(Café Divan)

HUITRES

Marennes 3 50 — Cancales 3 50 — Ostende 4 »
A choisir dans le Menu
Beurre, Hors-d'Œuvre, deux Plats, un Légume
Demi-bouteille de Médoc, Chablis ou bière de Diekirch
Demi-Tasse de Café

Menu du 10 Mars 1887

Œufs à la coque, sur le plat, brouillés
ou en omelette
Filets de Merlans à la Orly
Hachis de Bœuf à la Polonaise
Jambon aux Petits Pois
Bifteck aux Pommes
Haricots verts sautés
Longe de Veau rôtie au Cresson
Viandes froides à la Gelée

FROMAGE — DESSERT — FRUITS

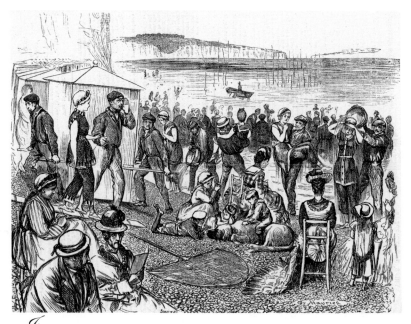

*I*n the second half of the nineteenth century French resorts facing the Channel became popular with the British. In this *Punch* cartoon of 28 August 1875, the British couple (lower left) disagree over the pleasures of the seaside. The wife prefers a book while the husband prefers looking at the young girls and the lucky men who carry them.

A trip to the top of Mt Vesuvius was the goal of most British travellers to Naples. The ascent could be exhausting unless one hired porters to carry one in a chair, as shown in this *Illustrated London News* illustration of 1 June 1872. In 1880 a funicular railway made things much easier and it inspired the Italian song, *Funiculì, Funiculà*. Thomas Cook eventually acquired the railway.

Division of labour

Here's to the milkmaid

a friend of Sir Wilfrid

a Railway Signal woman

The Tourists nuisance

The centre of attraction

Harry Furniss

*S*cenes of a tour in Normandy from *The Illustrated London News* of 10 September 1881 drawn by the well known artist Harry Furniss. The two larger drawings depict early travelling cyclists and the way local people often gathered to stare at any sketching Briton. The vignettes depict women doing manual labour in public, always an amazing sight to the Victorians. They also show a rather prim High Church clergyman in a *café* and an English couple arguing about their luggage with a French official. Sir Wilfrid Lawson, alluded to in the drawing of the water carrier, was a Radical MP and fanatical teetotaller.

This is a print of the Swiss artist Rudolf Koller's most famous painting, *Gotthardpost* (now in Zurich's Kunsthaus), painted in 1873. It captures the excitement of these mammoth coaches as they roared through the St Gotthard pass. This print was in *The Graphic* of 10 November 1888.

Europe's most fashionable spas in the high season represented all that was luxurious. Here we see a montage of various places in Bohemia's Karlsbad (now in the Czech Republic) where people took the waters and promenaded. On the bottom left we see an Austrian army officer and on the right, an Orthodox Jew, both of whom would have been unusual sights to British visitors. (*The Graphic*, 28 July 1900).

The advent of the motor car in the final years of the nineteenth century heralded both a new era and a return to the days of private travel for the wealthy. It also gave rise to motor car races, such as the one from Marseilles to Nice shown here in *The Graphic* of 19 March 1898. The winning car drives along the *Promenade des Anglais* although many cars broke down en route, leaving their drivers to finish their journeys by train.

The expansion of Europe's railway network was in part due to the increasing number of tourists. The Maderan Valley viaduct in Switzerland was part of the St Gotthard series of tunnels and bridges which was opened in 1882. (*The Illustrated London News*, 3 June 1882).

LE MARIN. — J'te dis qu'elle n'a ni gaillard d'avant, ni gaillard d'arrière... Du vent dans les voiles, et c'est tout!

Dessin de ROUBILLE.

Throughout this period Frenchmen laughed at the dress and behaviour of British tourists. This cartoon from *De Rire* magazine, published in the early years of the twentieth century, contains two of the standard French views of British travellers: they were haughty and women always had red hair.

in the cathedral in Aix-la-Chapelle. Here visitors were shown 'the very girdle which Our Saviour always wore – & also that of the Virgin – there was also a gown of the latter upwards of 5 feet long, which would go far to prove that the mother of Our Saviour was a giantess.' These 'beat all I have ever heard of in absurdity'. Yet the corpse of St Charles Borromeo in Milan was even worse: '[a] truly disgusting spectacle' was a typical reaction. Many people tried to be fair-minded without surrendering their own views. A young tourist who stumbled across a Marian devotion in a German church wrote: 'beautiful and solemn, first Roman Catholic service I had been to – much impressed'. When another tourist was walking round an Austrian village he heard 'a murmur of the united voices of families congregated to offer up an evening prayer, and saw, through the windows their uplifted hands and prostrate forms as they bent before the cross . . . if there were error here – there was earnestness.' Of course there was also ignorance and religious intolerance on the Catholic side. Frances Elliot, the wife of an important Anglican clergyman, remembered being approached by a monk asking for alms. In their conversation the monk said there was none of his order in England because there one found ' "so few Christians" – such being the opinion Catholics express when they speak frankly of *us*, who esteem ourselves the lamps of the world, the sun and centre of civilisation! We are not even Christians! *O Miserere!*'[19]

Guide-books repeatedly reminded tourists that while they went to churches to see their art, others went to worship. Murray's guide to northern Italy warned: 'The fact is, that the clergy do not like to have the churches considered as shows, nor are the congregations at all indifferent, as has been asserted, to the conduct of strangers, in walking about and talking during the Divine service. It might perhaps too be suggested to zealous individuals that they are not protesting against Roman Catholic errors by behaving indecorously in Roman Catholic churches.'[20] Where loyalty to one's beliefs ended and bad behaviour began was not always understood by tourists such as Robert Louis Stevenson's servant, Cummy, who tried to convert a French maid, or the Reckitts, who had a go at handing out English Bibles in Nice. This might have been mis-placed fervour, but it was not intentional rudeness.

However, there are many stories of appalling behaviour that had nothing to do with sincere Protestant beliefs. In 1836 Lady Trevel-yan attended a service in the Sistine Chapel. This High Church-woman was horrified at seeing 'English ladies . . . talking, laughing, jumping over the tops of the benches, and striding from one to another in the most hoydenish manner.' In the 1840s the American historian Francis Parkman was disgusted by the behaviour of many of the English in Rome: 'beloved as usual,' he concluded sarcasti-cally. He had been at the Palm Sunday Mass in St Peter's where he overheard one Englishman exclaim, 'How long does this damned Pope expect us to stand here waiting for him?' When rebuked by a priest, the traveller retorted, 'The English *own* Rome.' (At this time there were said to be 4,000 British subjects in Rome and about sixty Americans, many of the latter being rather prim intellectuals.) In Assisi Fr Herbert Vaughan, a future cardinal, had to cope with tourists who were 'poking about everywhere, even round . . . an altar where Mass was going on' – such stories were legion. In his novel *The Bertrams* the ecumenically minded Trollope unleashed an outburst at the tourist in his shooting-jacket:

> standing on the very altar-step while the priest is saying his mass
> . . . while he holds his opera-glass to his eyes . . . All that bell-
> ringing, incense-flinging, and breast-striking is nothing to him:
> he has paid dearly to be brought thither; he has paid the guide
> who is kneeling a little behind him . . . he has come there to see
> that fresco, and see it he will . . . all men of all nations know that
> that ugly gray shooting-coat must contain an Englishman.

Trollope also wondered, what would this Englishman say 'if his place of worship were disturbed by some wandering Italian?' (Chapter 9). Such people were only a small minority, but their behaviour was another proof that the adjective most used to describe the British, 'arrogant', had some substance. Before the 'ugly American' there was the 'ugly Briton'.

One of the worst examples of misplaced conviction occurred in 1875 during a papal audience. When Pius IX came up to a British party one man refused to stand, remaining seated, 'crossed his legs, folded his arms . . . staring rudely at him'. The elderly Pope, who had a temper, 'raised his stick. The Cardinals, fearing an undignified outburst . . . pushed Mr— out of the room.' What is even harder to believe is that Mr— was applying for a diplomatic post at the British Embassy in Rome. Fortunately he did not get it. A few days later at another audience the Pope came across a 'perfectly unoffensive English woman' and her family. When he learned they were *Inglese* he 'made a gesture of disgust and contempt, and passed without even looking at them. The English lady was so much shocked that she nearly fainted.'[21] For several days no British subjects were allowed into the Vatican. This man's behaviour was one of the worst, but not the worst. One Scottish lecturer told his audience how he was visiting a convent when he came across an old man who was praying with his Rosary: 'I could not resist giving him an exhortation above my breath, telling him it was all nonsense; and, pointing him to the simple way of salvation in Christ, finished by a flourish of my hat, which struck his beads, and reversed all his manipulations. The poor man patiently readjusted them, and went on as before. A lady present said something to me in a disapproving tone. Really, I do not wonder at John Knox acting as he did.' Perhaps the most disgusting behaviour was Elizabeth Barrett Browning's in 1847 when she was 'amused' to watch her dog pee on the altar in a Florentine church. Her rightly embarrassed husband 'was in agony'.[22]

While this behaviour was outrageous, it was never universal. Often it was simply the bad manners that 'the holiday spirit' can so easily produce, combined with ignorance. As late as 1902 tourist-guides still reminded tourists to 'walk softly and speak likewise . . . Do not walk the aisles arm-in-arm or point to any object with stick or outstretched arm, or look through opera glasses.' However, in general, anti-Catholic comments and bad behaviour declined by the end of the nineteenth century; tourism had played, in spite of colourful exceptions, a role in this spread of tolerance. Likewise we should remember that it was not only the British who were badly behaved. When one English clergyman went to Parma Cathedral in 1887 he was horrified when the preacher spat into his handkerchief – Italian priests were not allowed to smoke but they could take snuff. Then 'on all sides of me men were spitting on the marble pavements, and even women . . . expectorated as they sat at their prayers'.[23]

'Sunday. May 26th [1895]. Went to Early Service . . . and to 11 o'clock Matins. Auntie and I intended to go to vespers at the Minster . . . but we both fell asleep' is a diary entry that would have been written by thousands between 1814 and 1914, at least with regard to the early Eucharist and Matins. When abroad many tourists made great efforts to worship, and the overwhelming majority were members of the Church of England.[24] Rules governing English churches on the Continent were adopted by Parliament in 1826 and stipulated a cooperative effort between government and church-goers. There were also two societies that helped: the Society for the Propagation of the Gospel (on the 'High' side) and the Colonial and Continental Church Society (on the 'Low'). Most churches were set up in towns or spots where there were British 'colonies', places which were almost always popular tourist destinations. Often the clergyman would be chaplain to the British Consul or Ambassador. Without these 'colonies' the chances for worship would have been far fewer. A mid-century survey showed that there were at least 50,000 British subjects living in Europe in 125 different places but there were only five church buildings. People in Protestant areas often hired a church or, occasionally, as in Belgium, were given one by the government. In Holland the government supported the Church of Scotland as a sign of Calvinist solidarity. In Protestant Berlin the King allowed Anglicans to worship in his private chapel.[25] More often than not, services would be held in the public rooms of hotels and 'the first paper that strikes the eye on entering every Swiss inn is the list of services and chaplains supplied . . . for the season'. The hoteliers' thoughtfulness (or concern to retain British guests) could cause problems: some disliked worshipping in a room used for billiards or smoking the night before while other guests disliked having the British take over.[26] Many continental hoteliers proudly advertised that they had built Anglican chapels in their grounds, although these were open only during the high season.

Guide-books always gave information about Anglican, and sometimes other British, church services at the beginning of an entry. A distinctive feature of the *Macmillan Guide to Switzerland* (1904) was that all the chaplaincies were listed in the Introduction, which made holiday planning much easier. This shows ten permanent chaplaincies, and two closely printed pages listed all temporary chaplains arranged to indicate whether they were High or Low church. Where there were sufficient people either living in a town or visiting for longer periods, the goal was to erect an Anglican church; and many sprang up in the main tourist centres. In Grindelwald in the 1860s, three landlords gave money for an English church, and one of the three was appointed treasurer. In the spa town of Wiesbaden, St Augustine's Church began with services in local Protestant churches and then moved to the Duke of Nassau's private chapel. In the 1860s a new building costing £2,750 was opened on land given by the Duke and the church began a long history. Frequent visitors included Queen Victoria's eldest daughter, who had married the heir to the German throne, and her son, the future Wilhelm II.[27]

Continental churches had two major problems: finding sufficient funds and the endless arguments between High and Low factions. This was made worse because churches in Europe were congregational in government, so majorities ruled. The banker John Maquay attended one meeting in Florence where there was 'a compete scene of disorder and factious opposition. God knows how it can end . . . I could eat no dinner.' In the end Florence ended up with two churches. The Low-church Sibella Bonham Carter went to St Mark's by mistake: "To the English church near the Ponte del Trinità Via Maggio. Service very ritualistic.' In Pau, High church visitors and residents disliked the fact that the English church shared its premises with French Huguenots, and so set out to build another church. Eventually there were not two but three churches as well as a Church of Scotland chapel.[28]

Before 1870 there could be difficulties about building Anglican churches in Italian cities, but often these were overcome through compromise. Buildings had to be inconspicuous lest they offend local people's feelings. In Rome, Anglican worship started in the private rooms of an Oxford fellow in 1816 who then had to find larger premises. Thinking it right to inform the authorities he was told by Cardinal Consalvi that '*Il Papa sa nulla, e concede nulla*' – the Pope knows nothing and concedes nothing: permission was granted as long as the church did not look like a church. In Bagni di Lucca in the 1830s the local ruler allowed a church if it did not appear too ecclesiastical. The *Chiesa Anglicana* was designed to look like a villa with some 'Strawberry Hill Gothic' embellishments. A plaque on the building reads: '1839 Carlo Ludovico, Duke of Lucca, gave permission for a church so long as it was in a building which did not look like a church and which was to be called "The Palace of the English Nation"'. The result was the Palazzo della Natione Inglese – a social centre that included a church. In Florence, St Mark's Church still occupies a floor of a large building which once belonged to Machiavelli's family. Eventually Rome, like Florence, had two churches: one High, one Low. Many would have agreed with the sentiment in one children's book that it was all very well to see the Pope when in Rome, but it was far more comforting to worship at the English church with her prayers of 'matchless beauty'.[29]

The Church of England was remarkably successful in meeting the needs of worshippers, and by 1891 there were 150 permanent chaplaincies in Europe and over 250 seasonal chaplains just in France and Switzerland.[30] These churches not only met the spiritual needs of residents and visitors but acted as valuable social and in-formation centres. Here travellers could meet other travellers and get either the latest news from home or advice about the next place on their routes. The 'wedding tour' diary of Emily Birchall has numerous references showing how she and her husband enjoyed meeting fellow Britons and the 'right sort of Americans' at various Anglican chapels in France and Italy. The Anglican chaplaincies were – and still are – sources of spiritual sustenance and support to weary travellers.

Chapter 11

Hearing from Home

'You cannot think how uneasy one gets abroad at not hearing from home,' wrote a mother to her daughter in 1839.[1] Writing and receiving letters were just two of several ways in which people kept in touch with family and friends, with the news in Britain and finally, on their return, in touch with memories of places they had left behind.

'The bands are very good and I do wish, my darling, that you were here to listen to them with me. You are such a sweet dear wife. I feel as if some time one or other of us would regret every day of the lives God gives us, that we have not spent together.' John Oglander was writing to his wife from his hotel in Vichy in 1894. By the time he wrote, letters were criss-crossing Europe as never before as tourists kept in touch with friends and family. Arriving in Nice just over a week after leaving London, a honeymooning couple were delighted to find seventeen letters awaiting them; they 'virtuously set to work' and replied to all before midnight.[2] The years between 1814 and 1914 were probably the greatest period for writing letters in history, and the people who travelled were the same type of people who wrote constantly. These letters opened up the world of travel to others who in turn could be inspired to cross the Channel themselves.

One of the best insights into the importance of letters is seen in the correspondence of Gerald Codrington, the eighteen-year-old

Gloucestershire squire who spent four months travelling in 1869. Shortly after arriving on the Continent Gerald started writing to his widowed mother. From France, Switzerland, Germany and Italy he wrote regularly but he also expected three letters a week 'because I cannot enjoy what I am doing, unless I *know* that you are all right, Mama-dear'. Some of his letters were sent to his mother while she was in Spa. He told her about Swiss railways and the Jewish quarter of Prague and he described his 'internally deranged' stomach, which he cured with the 'blue pill'. For her part his mother followed young Gerald's wanderings closely and drew up a list of the thirty-three hotels in which he stayed.[3]

Such easy communication was not always the case. In 1814 the post was little better than the Grand Tourists had known: on 7 October a young man visiting Lyons was delighted to get two letters from his father in Suffolk written on 5 July and 5 August. Five years later another traveller complained that it took sixteen or seventeen days for letters to come from England to Florence. The arrival of cross-Channel steam packets and the development of railways helped enormously. By the late 1860s, John Tilley, the head of the post office, boasted to a Parliamentary committee that it took 50 hours and ten minutes for letters to get from London to Florence and 47 hours and 30 minutes, from Florence to London. In August 1850 England and France were linked by underwater telegraph and *The Times* exulted that when Homer had spoken of '"winged" words we doubt if even he imagined they would cleave their way through space at such a rate'. In 1891 a telephone link was established to France but its high cost, eight shillings for three minutes, limited its use. Even so, within a few years many continental hotels were boasting they had a telephone. However, technological improvement did not always make the post quicker. Only a few years after Tilley's boast, his brother-in-law in Florence claimed that the opening of the Mt Cenis tunnel meant it took a day longer for letters to arrive because 'those accursed enemies of the human race, the French' had cut the number of express trains.[4]

So common was letter-writing that guide-books often listed the 'posting times' when letters would be sent to England. Galignani's guide to Paris, for example, said that by the early 1850s there were two posts daily; if a traveller put a letter in the 6 p.m. post, it would be in London the next day. Travellers often described their plans so that correspondents would know where to reply, but if letters arrived after guests had left, most hoteliers and postmasters would forward them. Since so many did not book their hotels ahead, letters would be addressed care of *Poste Restante*, that is kept at a town's post office until tourists could pick them up, provided they produced a passport or, amazingly, just a calling card. Elizabeth Barrett Browning, particularly anxious for family news, instructed her sister to 'direct Poste Restante—*it is safer*'. This may have been true but it was not always efficient. At about the same time, Thackeray was in Rome desperately awaiting money from his publishers. In seven weeks he went to the post office thirty-five times for a letter before discovering that a clerk had filed it under the Js as Jackeray. Thackeray had survived thanks only to money advanced by his Roman banker, which is perhaps why, on his next trip, he had his letters sent care of the bank. Thackeray's problem was not unique: as late as 1899 Murray was advising tourists in Italy to have their letters addressed to their banker as 'officials sometimes regard the Christian name as the surname'.[5]

However efficient the service was, or was not, it was not cheap in the early years. Postage could be particularly expensive when the recipient had to pay, in which case it could be charged double: Mrs Browning never grudged the cost as 'the happiness is more than worth the money'. Mr Browning thought otherwise: he came home from the post office fuming about having to pay almost three shillings for an envelope full of nothing of importance. The cost of postage declined, and by the 1890s a letter to Europe was only 2½*d*. Telegrams, of course, made communication quicker but people seem to have used these only for short messages. Many, like John Oglander, carried a book of codes with single words for basic messages. The post office and travel agents could also arrange for money to be sent quickly by telegram. In 1897 Oscar Wilde implored publishers and friends to send him money in Naples through a Cook's telegram because the Italian post could be so slow.[6]

'The French have a notion,' wrote one British journalist, 'that, go where you may, to the top of a pyramid or to the top of Mont Blanc, you are sure to meet an Englishman reading a newspaper.' For the travelling classes, the newspaper was the prime source of information and to be without it was inconceivable. This was especially true of *The Times*, then the most influential newspaper in the world and one that played a continual role in travel. Because of its pre-eminence, unequalled by any paper today, outraged travellers could always threaten to 'write to *The Times*', and many did. On the other hand, more travellers worried about being without the paper, which meant that many hotels frequently advertised that they took it. Yet many tourists, such as Gerald Codrington, found it difficult to see any London newspaper. How could he keep up to date? The answer, he assured his mother, was that 'I always read "Galignani's Messenger" the only English newspaper out here when I can get hold of it.' Like Codrington, the young Disraeli also depended on *Galignani* and later claimed that it was while studying a file of back copies of 'that excellent publication' that he first became interested in politics. This may have been unusual but he certainly expressed a common sentiment of travellers when he reassured his sister that 'Galignani meets me every morning at my breakfast table, which is very pleasant'.[7]

Galignani's Messenger was established in 1814 by the same Parisian family that published guide-books, and their newspaper quickly became a vital aspect of foreign travel, if it is little remembered today. Although in the beginning they only copied the main items from the London papers, by the 1830s some 4,000 copies were being published in morning and afternoon editions. One traveller, who wandered as far as Hungary, aptly called the newspaper 'the vagabond Englishman's consolation'. While the emphasis was on political and financial news, the paper also appealed to people who had, or thought they had, connections with society. In July 1819, for example, readers learned that several dukes, duchesses and 'a large party of fashionables took an aquatic excursion to Richmond to dinner yesterday'.[8] Like papers in Britain *Galignani's* often noted the arrival of titled people and celebrities. As the paper expanded it began to be more than a 'scissors and paste' production and had its own writers. The cost was always reasonable: in the 1820s it was ten francs a month, delivered to any address in Paris; outside France it cost twelve francs a month.

The issue of 11 December 1828 gives a good example of the contents. There were four pages, each with four closely printed columns. Parliamentary news predominated, but there was French, continental and American news and some financial information, in particular the value of government bonds from which many travellers received income. Travellers would have been interested by French news, including the story about an Englishman who had been walking in the Champs-Élysée when he was approached by a man. This man, an ex-prisoner, 'made proposals for the commission of an abominable [homosexual] offence'. Suddenly two other men appeared, demanding money, but the wily tourist said he had none but would bring 40 francs the next day. He came with a policeman who apprehended the blackmailer who was later sentenced to five years. Brief notices of a somewhat less exciting nature included times of church services and theatrical performances as well as those days on which one could gain admission to the Louvre on showing one's passport. The issue also had advertisements – then unknown in French papers – for Channel packets, diligences, used carriages, servants and travelling hats. In many Victorian novels *Galignani* is mentioned, but few authors felt it necessary to explain what this meant to their readers. Thackeray, in particular, enjoyed alluding to *Galignani's* as he had worked for the newspaper as a young man in Paris.

A final source of news was the local newspapers produced for resident British 'colonies' in popular places such as Florence or Davos. Even in the small town of St Jean de Luz on the Franco-

Spanish border, the British colony had its own weekly newspaper by the early 1900s. The *St-Jean-de-Luz Gazette and Visitors List* had advertisements for English banks, piano hire firms, butchers, ironmongers, upholsterers, car-hire companies, greengrocers and livery stables. This Basque town, nestled between the Pyrenees and the Atlantic, hosted an 'English Club', reading rooms, a Badminton Club, Lawn Tennis Club, Golf Club and an English church with its own library. In February 1903 there was an amateur production in the Casino that raised £20 for charity. Miss W. Porch danced the 'Japanese Umbrella' and the 'Spanish Cachucha'; Miss Kathleen Tandy in flowing white *mousseline de soie* did the Skirt Dance, Serpentine Dance and Irish jig which 'quite brought down the house'.[9]

In 1884 the Galignani family gave up their paper but the renamed *Daily Messenger* carried on until 1904. In that year a new newspaper for Britons abroad, *The Overseas Mail*, began. The next year it became the *Continental Daily Mail* and was part of the 'new journalism' that was aimed at the lower-middle class, the people now travelling in such numbers. Unlike *Galignani's* it was published in simultaneous editions in London, Manchester and Paris with the copy sent by wire. Both in content and composition it signified that a new world was in the making, but its advertisement showed that it also appealed to traditional travellers. These were the people 'who spend a great part of the year away from home "chasing the sun" or simply following the ebb and flow of fashionable distraction'.[10]

In its heyday, *Galignani* had always meant more than just a newspaper. As there was no international copyright, the firm 'pirated' British books, that is, paid nothing to authors or publishers and sold their versions at about a third of the British price. For travellers whose favourite pastime was reading, this was useful since they could acquire cheaper editions of the latest titles. The firm also published each year what was the most popular guide to the French capital and established a reading room and lending library in the 'British quarter' of Paris. This building became a centre for visitors and resembled a club with a garden and, unusually for the time, women members. A conversation room was open until 11 p.m. and messages could be left. The fee was only three francs a month and membership brought access to current British newspapers and journals. It attracted about 300 people a day in the 1830s, and the numbers grew as tourism developed.[11]

'The name of Tauchnitz is as familiar in the mouths of . . . tourists as those other "household words" Murray . . . Bradshaw and Baedeker.'[12] Bernhard Christian Tauchnitz was a publisher in Leipzig who in 1841 started a highly successful 'Collection of British Authors', which by 1884 had reached 2,200 volumes. (By the time the series ended during the Second World War it had exceeded 5,000.) The books, even more than *Galignani's*, appealed to British travellers as well as to Europeans. Each volume cost two francs and was normally issued in paper covers, making it the first large series of paperbacks, yet another way in which British travellers were helping to create the world we know. Unlike the Galignanis, Tauchnitz paid authors – he was no pirate. Eventually he was made a baron by the King of Saxony and was, appropriately, appointed British Consul in Leipzig.

Tauchnitz provided British travellers with 'what they rarely got at home – cheap books, legibly printed, portable'. Britain benefited because the books spread the knowledge and influence of English, and by the 1890s it was said that almost as many continentals could read English as French. Two decades before that, Robert Louis Stevenson and a fellow Scot were on a train to Cologne and became fascinated with a Greek family sitting opposite. They thought the woman was exquisitely beautiful but, they assumed, stupid like Dora in *David Copperfield*. Eventually they began to talk in French to the Greeks until the woman said '*parlez en anglais*', which she well understood as she always carried a Tauchnitz when travelling. She also told the abashed Stevenson that *David Copperfield* was her favourite novel.[13]

There was one disadvantage to Tauchnitz books: copyright

restrictions made it illegal to bring them into Britain, and so the small volumes became favourite items for smuggling. When the four-teen-year-old Charles Brookfield, the son of a prominent clergyman, was on a storm-tossed steamer to Dover, his fellow passengers included the Archbishop of York and the very sick Archbishop of Canterbury 'in all the archiepiscopal panoply of aprons, gaiters, and rosette'. As the boat heaved, young Charles fell and injured himself. He was grateful when the somewhat recovered Archbishop of Can-terbury offered to carry his bag. Fortunately His Grace did not know he was smuggling a hoard of Tauchnitz novels. The British Customs official examined young Charles's hat box but of course did not peep inside a bag carried by the Primate of All England.[14]

'Oh Papa, Caroline has made such a nice sketch. Do come and look.' Observing this scene on a Rhine steamer one writer con-cluded, 'Let us hope that the proud papa felt . . . that the money expended on his daughter's accomplishments was not entirely thrown away.' The unidentified author, himself an artist, was describing a typical scene where, he claimed, three out of every four young British women sat with their sketch books, trying to draw the romantic ruins before them. Even if doing this on a 'throbbing steam-boat' made their ruined castles resemble the Leaning Tower of Pisa, the writer had no doubt that among all tourists 'probably those who sketch possess the greatest qualifica-tions for enjoying a ramble'. They avoided the 'objectless' travel of tourists whose 'aimless rushing about leaves only a mosaic-like impression of the scenes visited'.[15]

Among the features that distinguished Victorian travellers from those before or after was this passion for sketching. What we might call 'visual note-taking' embedded the scenes before them in their minds and later 'kept them in touch' with what they had seen. These sketches, as well as the particularly British art of watercol-ours, also stimulated other people to travel. Lessons in drawing were considered essential for young ladies and often for their brothers. Even if the sketcher had little artistic ability, the time taken to concentrate on an object fixed the impression in the memory. Sketching affected *how* people saw things, much as taking digital photographs does today except that in sketching one did not snap and run. One early traveller made sketches as his carriage lumbered through the countryside near Lucca. He later touched these up to give a 'pretty accurate general idea of any scene' and, he argued, an account more accurate than words written afterwards.[16]

The time and patience taken for sketching testify to the virtual reverence many travellers had for what they were seeing. Yet to Europeans, this sketching, like so many British traits, was yet another example of the islanders' eccentricity. At the very beginning of this book, we saw the incomprehension of an Italian peasant watching Amelia Edwards sketching in the Dolomites. Inquisitive natives frequently infuriated those absorbed in drawing. Peter Orlando Hutchinson, a very talented watercolourist from Devon, discovered this when trying to draw the statue of Jan Van Eyck in Bruges. The people were 'either very simple and ignorant, or very rude . . . peeping and sidling round . . . so as to get a sight of the sketch. This always makes me angry.' Things could be even worse, as another traveller discovered when drawing a church in Brittany. A local lad was so astounded that he ran about urging everyone to see this marvel and some even attempted to examine the Briton's stool whilst he was sitting on it. He escaped to the house of the only resident Englishman who gave him a mixed welcome: 'I settled here forty years ago, because no English had made it their home, and I am still the only Englishman in the place.'[17]

Occasionally sketchers welcomed spectators: while the feminist Emily Lowe was drawing waterfalls in a Norwegian forest, work-men gathered round her and some even stood on a roof to get a better view of this extraordinary sight. When she was finished she passed the drawing round for the men to see as she had no time for the 'sulky way of hiding' her work. For her, sharing her art had a civilising effect so characteristic of her era: to 'link one human being closer to another . . . has accomplished a moral purpose'. It was also common for Britons to set up their easels in continental galleries and copy the Old Masters, while many authors used their sketches to illustrate their books, none more so than Ruskin and Augustus Hare. Hare illustrated his books with charming drawings of buildings and also gave sketching lessons for society ladies in Rome. But by the end of the century he felt that sketching, like so many Victorian delights, was becoming more difficult and less enjoyable. Even in his beloved Rome it 'would be quite like old days if a great tram did not come rushing and roaring by every five minutes'.[18]

When sketching there was always one great risk: people might be taken for spies, especially if they were near military establishments. In 1852, at a time of tension between Britain and Austria, a young British architect was arrested outside an Austrian fortress in Verona. The guard claimed that he was sketching one of the greatest fortifications in Europe. The architect said he was merely studying the plan of the fort in his Murray *Handbook*. He spent a day in gaol and the incident resulted in an outraged letter to *The Times* and a question in the House of Commons. Privately the Foreign Secretary scoffed at this 'absurd young man with a beard and a fancy hat, which are now the symbol of Communists'.[19] In the decades before the First World War there were frequent incidents in which sketching Britons were arrested in Germany and, for that matter, sketching Germans were arrested in Britain.

However, there was one sketching story set in Germany that had nothing to do with spying. One German claimed that while travelling in the Rhineland he saw an English carriage where both the gentleman and lady slept through glorious scenery while on the seat behind was a man frantically sketching. When the German asked what he was doing, the artist replied, 'Oh! my lord wishes to see every night what he has passed during the day, and so I sketch as we go along!'[20]

The Wiltshire landowner William Fox Talbot can be considered the father of photography. Talbot's work made it possible to produce negatives that could be re-used repeatedly. His discoveries also meant that relatively unskilled people could take up this new invention, an invention which helped to sound the death knell for sketching. From the very beginning, Talbot's work was connected with continental travel – he first came up with his idea at Lake Como while on his wedding tour in 1833. One of the first pictures in his pioneering *Pencil of Nature* collection of 1844 was a marvellously detailed photograph of a Parisian boulevard taken from his hotel's bedroom window. Even before that, one of his earliest followers, the Reverend Calvert Jones, informed him that he was off to Italy 'to photographize Venice' and a few years later he took many atmospheric photographs of Pompeii. By 1850 Ruskin was startling the Venetians in St Mark's Square by standing with a black cloth over his head taking photographs. The inhabitants – like posterity – could not decide whether he was 'very mad or very wise'.[21]

Even those who did not 'photographize' were starting to look at places with the camera in mind. 'What a place Ghent would be for photography!' exclaimed Martin Tupper in the late 1850s. 'Every street corner, every canal bridge, every old building is an artistic "thing of beauty and a joy for ever".' By the 1860s photography had become much easier for amateurs and one leading engineer claimed that anyone could learn to do it in a quarter of an hour while the necessary equipment would fit into a gentleman's pocket or a lady's reticule. While portraits required more time and equipment, landscapes were relatively easy since the photographic plates could be prepared ahead. His own travelling camera was about the size of a normal book, weighed two pounds, and could be hung round the neck. Happily, one could buy a walking stick that was convertible into a tripod for a camera and the amateur could develop his pictures in about ten minutes per plate.[22] As mentioned in Chapter 8, some hotels were even providing dark rooms by the end of the century.

As with sketching, however, there could be problems. 'In some of the more unfrequented districts, the boys grow wildly excited and follow you about in droves,' said one Lancashire photographer visiting the Italian Lakes. He soon realized that the best way to make peace with the twenty-one boys who begged to become models was to let them look at his viewfinder. This worked until one dropped it. There were also the usual annoyances from 'fiendish Customs Officers without hearts'. This writer urged photographers going to Italy to have an Italian Consul in England weigh their photographic plates and provide an official form (available in four languages) saying that opening them would ruin them.[23] By the early years of the twentieth century travellers such as Edith Somerville and Violet Ross, Margaret Fountaine and T. E. Lawrence were all packing their Kodaks as casually as their grandparents had packed their sketch-books.

Those who did not wish to take their own photographs could buy views of the principal tourist sights. The continentals led in the development of the picture postcard, which became a popular souvenir. Travellers also found them useful in the last quarter of the century for brief messages home. The sepia photographs of Florence taken by the local firm Fratelli Alinari were amongst the most cherished by British travellers anxious to have views of Florentine buildings, paintings and statues. Art-loving travellers such as Agnes Mason proudly carried her Alinari portfolio back to England and eventually to her convent in Sussex. Especially in places famed as centres of art, travellers spent lavishly on acquiring such souvenirs; young Gerald Codrington was not alone when moaning, 'I have spent my last money, all but a few francs. I have bought such loads of photographs.'[24]

Chapter 12

The Happy Days
Before the War

$\mathcal{B}$y March 1914 Provence's budding mimosas and almond trees showed spring was approaching. Because the ground was still wet from a rainstorm, a middle-aged novelist on a walking tour in the final 'happy days before the war' decided to take the recently completed electric tram that ran from Menton to Sospel. After an hour's journey through orange, lemon and olive groves it reached the mountain resort where a golf course had been opened for visiting Britons. Archibald Marshall was following the Victorian tradition of alternating novels with travel books and was now writing *A Spring Walk in Provence*, a region he knew from several motoring trips. However, during this trip he wanted to 'be done with everything English', especially grand hotels with English-speaking waiters. Exactly eighty years after Lord Brougham had 'discovered' Cannes, Marshall looked down on the 'wealthy and delocalised' Riviera. He was anxious to walk through rural Provence, one of the few areas of Europe 'untouched' by travellers. He had prepared himself by reading a history of Avignon by Thomas Okey, the basket-maker turned Professor of Italian who had been so indispensable to his fellow Toynbee Hall travellers. For Marshall it was, usually, 'fun' to chat to the local peasantry at humble inns costing only two francs a night, to take the occasional snapshot or to watch men playing *boules*. He was not quite so enthusiastic for 'clumsy petrol-driven' omnibuses in which the 'powerful efflux of garlic' could be overwhelming. The real France could sometimes be too real.

After finding that for one penny he could buy a loaf of French bread, Marshall proclaimed in words re-echoed down the years: 'Here is food, food fit for the gods.' Marshall was part of the new generation of travellers who turned their backs on the great tourist industry that had been built up over the past hundred years. He rejected tours, 'routes', and hotels with English sanitation, English management and Italian orchestras. He avoided his countrymen in order to discover the 'real France'. Not far from Nice, Marshall was being 'continually passed by motor-cars speeding along'. Although he had himself made several motoring expeditions, on this trip he admits that when he saw a group 'flushed with food and wine and other liquors' and chatting 'like parrots' before climbing into their cars outside a fashionable country inn, he 'disliked them one and all, and felt vastly superior to them'. It was, he added, 'a feeling which they no doubt experienced towards me'.

At a hotel in the small village of Contes he relished a dinner of soup, omelette, beef, potatoes, carrots, cheese and oranges. After spending the night and having breakfast he was charged less than three shillings. He was amused when the young waiter apologzed because the bill was so high but Monsieur had drunk two litres of wine. Marshall encountered only one other Briton on his wanderings: this man was yet another harbinger of the future, an artist restoring an old Provençal house. When in Aix en Provence he found memorials to British travellers who had died in that once fashionable resort. He also learned that the generosity of one member of the Russell family to the local children almost a century before, when she had her footmen carry baskets of bonbons to children on New Year's Day. Her kindness was still remembered.

From time to time Marshall would hear a distant drummer and then the shouts of drunken French youths coming though the rural byways on their way to serve in the expanding French army. By the time Marshall got down to writing the preface to his travel book, it was August and he was in Switzerland. In that same country, in Lucerne, Walter Ivory, a schoolteacher from Chesham and his fiancée's brother, Fred, were staying in the Polytechnic Touring Association's chalet beside the lake. He wrote to his fiancée, Flos, on 2 August, surrounded by talk of war. Bridges and tunnels were guarded by Swiss troops. Only days before, when passing through the French town of Belfort on the German frontier, he had learned that people's houses had been requisitioned by the French army: 'women & children were in a panic and weeping copiously . . . no time to take anything except the clothes in which they were attired and perhaps a small bundle. If the rumour of war produces such an effect what can war itself be?'

Even the Polytechnic's chalet was surrounded by thirty-seven soldiers and writing-paper had disappeared. What should they do? 'Fred & I are seriously talking about either walking home to Calais, or joining the French Army if they will have us and take our chances, or going to Genoa and coming home by boat. . . . We are in a very strange position.' Unbelievably, British money, which had reigned supreme for a century, was now 'practically of no use'. The tourists' world so carefully built up over exactly a hundred years was in pieces, shattered by the bullets of a Serbian terrorist. The British tourist, that 'grumbling, police-hating, comfort-loving animal, who didn't care much about the politics of the countries he visited, and was fortified in that indifference by an infinite amount of pride in his own nationality', was now imprisoned in a pension, at the mercy of 'the politics of the countries he visited'.[1]

Two days later Walter Ivory wrote again. Things had deteriorated. Martial law had been imposed and he could not get out of Switzerland while the Swiss army was being mobilized. Lucerne 'is nothing but soldiers & baggage varied by baggage & soldiers'. Like thousands of others all over Europe, British and American tourists in Lucerne were 'clamouring for some means of exit & all waiting for their ambassador's decision'. The 'hurry-scurry' of 1815 was being repeated all over again. There was a rumour that by the end of the week the British might be 'conducted out of the country probably under military escort' and 'this morning I heard some artillery firing'. Three days later Walter and Fred finally got their passports from the Ambassador in Berne and a '*sauf-conduit*', which '*autorisà à prendre le train special*'.[2] Once on the special train Walter and Fred could leave. While all this was going on, Archibald Marshall was finishing the preface to his book and recalling those young French recruits. Now he wondered 'what they are doing and how many of them are still alive'. Five years later he added a preface to the second edition in which he wrote: 'The world has changed since this book was written.'[3]

Traces of the Travellers

$\mathcal{F}$our ghastly years followed after those curtailed holidays in 1914, and they took their toll on men such as Captain Francis Grenfell, who had been accused of spying in Dresden, or Walter Ivory and his future brother-in-law, Fred Long, who had been trapped in Switzerland as war broke out. Grenfell earned the VC leading a cavalry charge in Belgium in the first weeks of the war, only to be killed the next year. Ivory, already a middle-aged man in 1914, eventually managed to join up, was gassed but survived to marry his 'Flos', while Fred Long was badly wounded at Gallipoli and invalided out of the army.

Places suffered as well as people. Menton, like all the expanding Riviera towns that Archibald Marshall gazed down upon, at first pretended that the war would change nothing. Its Syndicate of Hoteliers, created to attract British visitors, merrily advertised that 'The Season 1914–15 will be quiet and "Germanless", an old-fashioned Menton Season with Croquet, Tennis and Golf as usual.' Some determined Britons carried on going to the Riviera during the war, having first obtained the new passports with photographs; but the old, seemingly carefree, spirit was gone. Nor did it return immediately when peace finally came because many of Menton's hotels remained closed: so many managers had been Germans or Austrians. In the spa towns throughout defeated Germany and tragically dismembered Austria, it was some time before tourism resumed. In 1914 in Wiesbaden the Rector of St

Augustine's Anglican Church handed the keys to the Oberburger-meister, bidding him 'Auf Wiedersehen'. The church reopened after the war but some two decades later it was vandalized by the Hitler Youth and then bombed by the RAF. This church symbolized so much of what happened to the peaceful and progressive world that the travellers had enjoyed and helped to create between 1814 and 1914.

What remains today of these travellers' impact on European life? Words they popularized such as travel agents, Cooks, WC, toilet, restaurant, café, courier, visa, knapsack, Baedeker, handbook, guide-book, coupon, sleeping car, table d'hôte, à la carte, *pension* and *en pension* survive, albeit with subtle variations in their meanings. If we glance round most major continental cities and many of the smaller ones it is still possible to see relics of the age that created modern tourism. Tourists today often ride on or through some of the greatest remains of the long nineteenth century – the marvellous engineering feats that brought railway lines across Europe and conquered the Alps with tunnels and extraordinary viaducts. The ride south from Vienna on the Semmering railway, completed in 1854, astounded travellers such as Gladstone and Thackeray with its beauty, and still does so in the twenty-first century.

Less fortunate were the great stations used by travellers: few structures suffered more from wars and architectural vandalism. Fortunately, the most important of all survived: Paris's Gare du Nord, Europe's busiest rail terminus, opened in 1864 to replace one built in the 1840s when the French ports were connected with the capital. In spite of expansion, much of the decoration seen by today's Eurostar passengers would have been seen by their predecessors. The carriages and other vehicles that the travellers used can still be seen in museums such as the Château de Compiègne while at Charlcote House in Warwickshire one can see the travelling coach in which Mary Elizabeth Lucy clutched her dead baby on that dreadful Mt Cenis crossing in 1841. Those who wish to experience some of the travelling conditions of the earliest tours, without the worst rigours, can have a short trip in a carriage or even have a fortnight's tour across the Alps from Bavaria to Lake Como.

Many of the hotels, especially the Grand Hotels, established for British travellers remain today. In Paris the Meurice, founded by a man who provided transport from Calais to Paris in the early post-Waterloo years, still welcomes guests. There were of course numerous humbler Parisian hotels such as the Hôtel l'Alsace in the Rue des Beaux Arts, which achieved fame in 1900 because Oscar Wilde died there. Now it is an elegant designer creation called simply L'Hôtel. Verona still boasts the Due Torri, which sent several carriages and servants to greet Anthony Trollope because he had telegraphed for a reservation. Within the walls of Lucca still stands the Universo where Ruskin stayed while sketching and studying some of the city's wonderful churches. Yet another hotel connected with Ruskin and his frustrated young wife is the Danieli in Venice. On the Riviera, many of the grand hotels that Marshall gazed down upon in 1914 still remain, including Nice's then new Negresco. Higher up from Nice, amid the lush greenery of Cimiez, the charming statue of a smiling Queen Victoria still stands before the former Hôtel Excelsior Régina, a lasting testimony to the enjoyment she had when staying there.

On another French coast is Biarritz's Palace Hôtel, much patronized by Victoria's son and successor, Edward VII, and his wealthy subjects. In Switzerland modern tourists will find numbers of hotels reaching back to the nineteenth century. Lausanne still has the Hôtel d'Angleterre where Byron is said to have written the *Prisoner of Chillon*, while Zurich's Baur au Lac, founded in 1844, is still owned by the founding family. In Kitzbühel, Rose Trollope spent many months of her widowhood 'for wonderfully little money' at a hotel run by an Englishwoman. Today the Schloss Lebenberg is one of the most expensive in this Tyrolean resort and, although there have been modern additions, the core of the sixteenth-century castle that Anthony Trollope's widow knew is still there.

While most travellers ate in their hotels, an increasing number favoured the Parisian-inspired restaurant. In Paris itself the Palais Royal, where the British first encountered the very idea of a restaurant, still boasts Le Grand Véfour, founded in 1784. Its rooms continue to sparkle with the gilt decorations and mirrors that delighted and scandalized the travellers from beyond the Channel. Colonel Newnham-Davies, in his *Gourmet's Guide*, praised the restaurants of Vienna, particularly Sacher's, which was 'very well known and . . . the typical Viennese restaurant. It is expensive.' It still is both well known and expensive but it continues to offer the leisurely service of an earlier age. It is not only in capitals where older eating places endure. The *Gourmet's Guide* also pointed to a small inn in Normandy: 'The quaintness of the old inn Guillaume le Conquérant at Dives counts for something, and the 5 franc table-d'hôte dinner there is good of its kind.' Today in the fascinating town of Dives-sur-Mer that same inn continues, though sadly neither the five-franc meal nor the franc itself survives. Finally, some places have retained their old names even though they have both moved locations and changed their characters: Paris still has a Maxim's, but today's raucous entertainment has little to do with the more genteel debaucheries of the past.

Fortunately, most of the museums and a large majority of the churches treasured by the travellers survived the horrors of the twentieth century. Many, including Dresden's Frauenkirche, which were destroyed have been magnificently restored, and in that city an Anglican Eucharist is celebrated once a month to symbolize the two countries' reconciliation. St Stephen's Cathedral (which George Eliot said it was worth going all the way to Vienna just to see) was badly bombed in the last days of the Second World War, but it has been so well recreated, complete even with the Habsburg coat of arms on the new roof, that only an architectural expert could spot the differences. (As we write the magnificent south tower reaching up 445 feet is being cleaned and restored to a beauty the Victorians never knew.) In Pisa the damage done to the Campo Santo by an incendiary bomb has been repaired and visitors can now recapture some of the inspiration Victorians felt when gazing on that medieval building, especially on a moonlit winter night when all the clattering tour parties, successors to Messrs Gaze and Cook, have departed. The Louvre, while no longer bursting with Napoleon's loot, still attracts travellers, and British art-lovers continue to stagger from the Uffizi like Byron, 'drunk with beauty'.

The most extensive memorials – sometimes in the literal sense of the word – throughout the Continent are the many Anglican churches established to meet the spiritual and social needs of travelling Britons. These remain as the greatest living testimony to our travellers and most have some visible link to them. Sometimes it is just a small memorial tablet but at other times it can be a whole building, as in Cannes where a church was built in honour of Prince Leopold, Queen Victoria's son. Some of the churches are in large cities and are very grand, such as Holy Trinity in Nice, which was begun in the 1860s and acquired a splendid gothic sanctuary in 1913. In Cadenabbia on Lake Como, a quiet place favoured by more sedate travellers, the proprietor of the Hotel Bellevue built a chapel in his grounds for his guests in the 1860s and even included a stained-glass window. By 1891 this had given way to a new Anglican church. More than a quarter of a million people have attended services in the hotel's chapel and later in the church. There are today over 300 churches and congregations in the Anglican Diocese of Europe, which is one the fastest growing parts of the Anglican Communion, with growth especially pronounced in France and Italy. In Florence, St Mark's has an enthusiastic chaplain who is restoring the many artistic beauties of the church. Even when a city no longer needed two Anglican churches, the disused buildings sometimes survived. At Biarritz, St Andrew's has been converted into the Musée Historique de Biarritz, where photographs depict some of the visitors and the resort they relished.

After churches, the most prevalent memorials of Victorian travellers are golf courses. The British, or more properly the Scots, set up the first continental golf course at Pau in 1856, and gradually these began to spread across Europe wherever the British spent long periods. In 1889 the British colony in Florence set up the first golf club in Italy, while other tourists were seen playing the sport in German spas such as Wiesbaden. In 1895 Sir Arthur Conan Doyle helped to establish the first Swiss course at Davos. For many years these courses were the exclusive preserve of British visitors and residents: Pau did not admit a French member until 1913. Sports in general were promoted by the peripatetic British: in addition to mountaineering, skiing, tobogganing and cycling, they introduced rugby to France in the 1870s and two decades later, to northern Italy. Britons founded A. C. Milan, and in their honour the club adhered to the English spelling, Milan, not Milano.

When it comes to the 'lions' sought out by the Victorians, some, happily, have ceased to attract: morgues are now off limits throughout Europe, as are private tours to examine Paris's guillotine. Of the many battlefields connected with Napoleon, only Waterloo continues to draw British visitors, though very few would consider a visit their 'first duty'. Those who do go do not have to allow the eight hours (including a three-hour rest for the horses) that Murray advised in the 1850s. Despite the fact that there is now a Wellington Museum in a former coaching inn used by the Victorians, modern Britons are annoyed to find that the vainglorious Emperor is more celebrated than the victorious Duke. Palaces associated with Napoleon such as Fontainebleau remain attractive, but the room where the defeated Emperor abdicated long ago lost the thrill of the immediate past. Napoleon's *dénouement* is just one more event that took place in that exquisite building. Nor do Garibaldi's legend and the whole Risorgimento drama attract many today to Italy. Of those who do go, few follow Joanna Horner's example and drink some of the polluted Mediterranean in his honour.

Fortunately, simple pleasures last the longest and change the least: Lady Burton's favourite pastime at Nice was to sit on the shingle beach and gaze at the Mediterranean as countless thousands of her compatriots still do. In his first Swiss handbook of 1838 Murray mentioned the 'prevailing reverence' for the bears at Berne, and the bears are still there to be admired. One can also get close to an earlier age of travel if one is in Baden bei Wien on a day that the town orchestra is playing in the park. Only the gentle sounds of nearby fountains disturb the strains of Strauss and Lehar, and for a moment one feels as if one were back in one of the elegant spas in search of health, or, perhaps, just a reduction in weight. Tourists still go up Vesuvius, even if there are no longer 'stout fellows' to carry them in chairs, and Cook's famous railway has been replaced by roads. People continue to flock to gaze on the splendours of Alpine scenery even though its spiritual testimony is perhaps not as cherished as it once was. Modern visitors do not often realize that they are treading in the footsteps of those who went before and who made their own visits easier. Those going to see the great glacier the Mer de Glace, where once Victorian ladies sedately picked their way across the ice with their billowing skirts, can stay in the Montenvers Hôtel (established in 1880) and take the Montenvers Railway (started in 1908).

Switzerland, while still a popular destination, is no longer the centre of the British-created 'tourist industry', and gone are the days when the middle classes all knew terms such as the 'Engandine' or the 'Oberland'. Yet tourists still go to the top of the Rigi to behold the dawn and visit the Tellskapelle or William Tell chapel, even if many no longer believe in the invented man with a crossbow who so appealed to Victorian sentimentality and devotion to liberty. Another spot on the borderland between fiction and fact is the Reichenbach Falls where a plaque by the funicular railway records Sherlock Holmes's fatal encounter there. The town of Davos was developed by Britons with lung problems or a passion for winter sports. The once quiet resort, now described on one website as 'a bustling honky-tonk of a place', is today famous for the annual gathering at which plutocrats and vastly important prognosticators (important, at least, in their own eyes) fly in to chat with one another. After dinner they warn others of the sinfulness of aeroplane travel, reminding us of Ruskin's annoyance at others' travelling. Hypocrisy was not exclusively a Victorian vice.

Alpine passes such as the Simplon are still sometimes closed in the winter, although this matters little to the traffic roaring through the tunnel underneath. The revered hospice in the St Bernard's pass is still there providing shelter and refreshment as it has for a millennium. Its famous dogs have, however, been replaced by heat-seeking rescue helicopters. Albert Smith's long-running show in London encouraged hardy Victorians to climb Mont Blanc and many more of the less hardy to gaze upon it. Now the mountain has a traffic-jam as 30,000 people attempt the climb every summer. Local officials, as reported in *The Times* of 28 August 2008, fume that 'The legendary climb to the peak of Mont Blanc is becoming a piece of cut-price, consumer goods.' Perhaps the officials should encourage would-be climbers to visit churches near celebrated mountains, such as that at Zermatt, with their graves of those earlier climbers who went up but did not come back.

Taste in art of course constantly changes, and probably few today would agree that the Raphael Madonna in Dresden is the 'greatest painting in the world'. Likewise, in Rome Guido Reni's baroque fresco of Aurora was much visited by enthusiastic Victorians despite Ruskin's strictures. Today its once-a-month viewing satisfies the demand. With the decline in the teaching of Latin and in our interest in Italian literature, it is unlikely that many seek out Petrarch's house or visit the site of Horace's dwelling, once so popular with the *Inglesi* that local peasants became convinced that the poet must have been an Englishman.

Brussels, which Victorians increasingly ignored, is now a double capital and Lord Palmerston's 'rum English' are now joined by Eurocrats and bureaucrats who may or may not be 'rum'. Paris's Jardin des Plantes is no longer such a 'lion' since Britain has botanical gardens at least as good. Trips up Byron's 'wide and winding Rhine' seem once again to be growing in popularity, but now their appeal, judging by the advertising, is to older, well-travelled people rather than those stepping on to the Continent for the first time. Tours are now advertised not just in German and English but also in Chinese: tourism, once begun, knows no limits. Tourists still visit the Drachenfels and still buy a version of the eau de Cologne so heavily advertised by the Farina family in Murray's handbooks even if German courts have forbidden the use of the family name.

Even in Spain, so little visited by the Victorians, the British are remembered. In the 1990s Córdoba renamed a square La Plaza del Pintor Topham in honour of the painter F. W. Topham who visited Spain in the early 1850s and whose colourful work gave many Victorians their first hint of the splendours of Spanish scenery. He returned to Córdoba to die in 1877. Indeed, it is Spain that provides the most startling change in British travel to Europe. An authoritative letter in *The Times* in October 1860 said that there were about 4,000 British residents in Spain and about twice that number travelling there each year. Foreign Office figures show that in 2006, about fourteen million people visited Spain while about 100,000 reside there permanently.

The rise of budget airlines has restored places such as Pau and Biarritz as familiar names in travel destinations. Inevitably this latest expansion of travel has aroused many critics, and not just those gathered at Davos. They denounce the new travellers with the asperity if not the eloquence of Ruskin, causing the head of one such airline to reply with words similar to those used by the early travel agents Gaze and Cook: 'We are working hard to make travel affordable for everyone, not just those with homes in Tuscany and Chiantishire.' Likewise the collapse of communism has revitalized famous spots such as Dresden and Marienbad, now renamed with much less euphony, Marianske Lazne. Such cities are now happily freed from the drab dictatorships under which they wilted throughout most of the years after 1918. Now in Marienbad, Edwardian hotels are being restored and the Royal Golf Club's course, opened by Edward VII in 1905, is once again filled with British players. Yet one travel goal remains as constant today as it has been since Napoleon's first abdication in March 1814: Paris, even if most of *les Anglo-Saxons* are often American. The rivulet of American travellers in the nineteenth century became a mighty stream in the twentieth. However, in 2007 the number of American tourists fell sufficiently to allow the British to regain their pre-eminence, if only for a period.

Sometimes an alleged 'change' seems more profound than forgotten facts warrant, particularly when describing the behaviour of the British abroad. In recent years there have been numerous articles about the obnoxious cavorting of drunken Britons in Europe, but this is not a change as much as a development. Writing in the 1840s in *The Book of Snobs*, Thackeray attacked the 'boozy' wretches often 'heard yelling, "We won't go home till morning!" and startling the midnight echoes of quiet Continental towns with shrieks of English slang.' It is true that today there are more boozy wretches and 'rum English' but there are also more sober and refined travellers: the change is in numbers, not in behaviour.

On the Riviera the legacy of the British is still strongly felt even if most French guide-books studiously downplay or even ignore it. Dotted about are the splendid villas and great gardens created by Britons, although arguably the greatest garden is just across the Italian border at La Mortola. Here the Quaker Hanbury family, rich from the China trade, created one of the most beautiful gardens in the world. What the French guide-books cannot ignore is Lord Brougham's achievement in creating Cannes nor the statue of him that still stands there as does a plaque at the hotel where he began '*La Colonie Anglaise de Cannes*'. His villa, the Château Eleanor Louise, set the fashion for many other elegant houses built by his compatriots, and many of these can still be seen. Down the coast at Menton, there is a relatively new statue to another Englishman: the Reverend William Webb Ellis. Ellis, the Evangelical Rector of St Clement Danes, followed Dr Bennett's advice and came to the small town in the 1870s because of his weak lungs. He had been the Rugby schoolboy who was credited with picking up a ball and creating a sport. Ellis's grave, which was recently restored by rugby fans, is not far from that of Aubrey Beardsley, the quintessence of decadence. Two men who were light years apart in life are now neighbours in death. A third grave is that of the once well-known historian, whose headstone bears the moving inscription 'John Richard Green, the historian of the English people. He died learning.'

In Nice, in addition to the Promenade des Anglais and Queen Victoria's statue, there are several smaller relics of past travellers that are easily overlooked. One is in the Rue de France: this is a marble cross inside a cupola, which commemorates a meeting in 1538 between a pope, an emperor and a king. To British travellers, this monument had an extra meaning because it marked an important boundary. As Murray's handbook said in 1860, the area round the Croix de Marbre was favoured by the English, some of whom still called this 'Newborough', the term being used a hundred years earlier by the Grand Tourists. If visitors crossed that invisible line they might end up in a neighbourhood where they would see laundry women washing English linen in the dirty river.

Florence, that exquisite Tuscan city that attracted and enthralled so many Britons with a religious-like worship of art, still attracts though she is bereft of many of her old bridges, her walls and her repose. Perhaps the most enduring monument to this devotion is the British Institute, a library founded by a group of Italophiles, which promotes British culture and carefully protects the diaries and letters of many Victorian visitors. The city still boasts numerous other British connections: a plaque on one house records that it was here that a daughter was born to Edward and Frances Nightingale in 1820, a daughter christened with the name of her native city. The Pitti Palace, now a magnificent art gallery, was for early nineteenth-century travellers the place where they hoped to be presented to the Grand Duke of Tuscany and to be invited to a royal reception after which they could pocket all the bonbons. Nearby is Casa Guidi, the eight-room apartment lived in by the Brownings, which shows how well a couple with but a few hundred pounds a year could live, with their two servants. The Strozzi Palace now houses the Vieusseux Library, once the intellectual centre for so many visiting Britons and the meeting ground for Italian liberals. The west fronts of both the Duomo and Santa Croce, the favourite church of so many of the British, were decorated late in the nineteenth century thanks to money given by Francis Sloane. He came as a tutor, made a fortune from copper-mining and used his wealth to restore many buildings. Unfashionable because he was a strong supporter of the Grand Duke, Sloane ultimately did far more good for the city than the chattering devotees of the Risorgimento who snubbed him.

In Florence's Piazza dell' Indipendenza stands a large building now occupied by Italian Railways. It was once the Villa Trollope where lived Frances Trollope and her son Thomas Adolphus, both of whom wrote numerous travel books. This elegant home, with its lush garden, became the centre for visiting writers such as Dickens and George Eliot. A plaque was erected to the memory of Thomas Adolphus's unpleasant first wife, who 'wrote in English with an Italian heart', but who also wished to strangle the last priest with the guts of the last aristocrat. After the Trollopes left, their name was retained and the villa became a well-known *pension* run by a Scottish couple. Frances Trollope, her daughter-in-law and one of their maids now lie in what people call the English Cemetery. Anyone who successfully dashes across the swirling traffic in the Piazzale Donatello into the verdant calm will find a veritable Valhalla of British travellers, including half a dozen Waterloo veterans. Fortunately, the cemetery has been much restored by its well-informed and devoted guardian. Best known of all its inhabitants is Elizabeth Barrett Browning, who eloped to Italy and to life. Her own poem about a small child's burial only a year before her own describes the setting best:

> *And here among the English tombs*
> *In Tuscan ground we lay her,*
> *While the blue Tuscan sky endomes*
> *Our English words of prayer.*

Bagni di Lucca, the Tuscan spa town once an exhausting day's carriage drive away from Florence, was where the Anglo-Florentines went in the summer to escape the heat of the city. It became a centre of English life in Italy. The *Inglesi* tended to live in three distinct sections: the fast set lived close to the casino and ballroom;

the respectable set clustered near the church; the invalids had a third section to themselves. Some of the houses occupied by all three sets still lend an elegant touch to the town. Other traces linger, too: the Royal Arms are still over the local chemist's; the church that the Protestant British were allowed to build is now a library but retains various British heraldic symbols on the outside. Recently a memorial and river walk have been dedicated in honour of the Brownings, who much enjoyed their summers there. Across that same river, the English cemetery with once famous people such as the novelist Ouida, or the fearsome Mrs Stisted, the 'Queen of the Baths', survives; even if it always seems to be locked.

Many continental cities had their 'British Quarter' where the resident 'colony' and the travellers (often relatives and friends of the residents) met; neither could have promoted British 'comfort' without the other. Two cities, Paris and Rome, have the largest number of reminders of this lost world. Britons in Paris congregated on the right bank, in the area round the Tuilleries, where until 1870 any well-connected islander expected to be presented to whichever French monarch was currently on the throne. Close by was the British Embassy, where marriages were often held in the ambassador's drawing room. In the Rue de Rivoli was the Hôtel Meurice and Galignani's, both still there today. Galignani's, which moved there from the nearby Rue Vivienne, no longer publishes a newspaper or provides a club-house but its shop at 224 Rue de Rivoli is one of the most beautiful and civilized book shops in the world. Not far away is the Palais Royal, which provided shopping and pleasures of various sorts to visiting Britons. In the southern suburb at Corbeil, a monument was erected to the two Galignani brothers – one a British subject, the other a French citizen – who did so much to make the life of British travellers more comfortable. Appropriately it shows them holding a copy of *Galignani's Messenger*. The monument also testifies to their numerous charities, including those which helped destitute Britons in France.

Rome's British quarter was in the area round the Spanish Steps where today the Keats-Shelley House is the most famous survivor of the many buildings where travellers rented rooms. Close by is the celebrated Babington Tea Room and near it is the Caffè Greco, where Thackeray met artists from home to drink mezzo-caldo rum (with hot water, lemon and sugar). The famous Torlonia palaces where travellers, be they important figures such as Sir Robert Peel or obscure artists such as Lownes Dickinson, were entertained lavishly by their banker, survive in modern Rome although one, now a museum, was once the official home of Mussolini. Further afield the Società Romana della Caccia alla Volpe still rides out in search of Italian foxes. The Protestant cemetery in Rome is mainly celebrated for the graves of Keats and Shelley but many other travellers lie there as well. Many shared a similar fate with one Yorkshireman:

HERE LIES THE BODY OF WILLIAM HARDING OF SCARBRO GENTLEMAN WHO DIED IN THIS CITY ON THE 22 DAY OF OCTOBER 1821 AGED 31 YEARS WHEN MAKING A TOUR THROUGH ITALY TO SEE ITS CURIOSITIES OF NATURE AND ART ANCIENT AND MODERN

Undoubtedly the most important and lasting legacy of the century of British travellers lies not in Rome or Paris, nor on the Riviera or in the Alps, but in the fervent conviction that every Briton was entitled to an annual 'holiday'. As the distinguished dermatologist Sir Erasmus Wilson wrote in mid-century, 'an autumn holiday is one of the institutions of Great Britain'. He was referring to his own professional class of doctors, lawyers, clergymen, civil servants and university teachers. As travel became easier and in many ways cheaper, thanks to the Victorian entrepreneurial spirit, this 'institution' became prized by people in the lower middle class and even among the better-off skilled artisans. Perhaps no attitude differentiates modern Britons from Americans more than this near universal belief in the 'right' to an annual holiday, preferably one abroad.

Yet going to the Continent, whether across the Channel, above it or beneath it, can still bring those traditional annoyances, many of which have been described in this book. In the *Daily Telegraph* of 16 August 2008 one travel writer, Robert Chesshyre, described his experiences in getting onto the Motorail at Calais. The old pier, on which 175 years earlier Frances Trollope overheard the conversation about 'the smell of the Continent', has gone. However, Robert Chesshyre noted that 'There was the same French drain smell – novel when you first travel, less welcome as the years roll by.' Yet most travellers, in Frances Trollope's day and in our own, would agree with Thackeray when he said that he 'never landed on Calais pier without feeling that a load of sorrows was left on the other side of the water'.

Further Reading

In the years after 1814 thousands of books have been published on continental travel. The following are some that we feel may be of especial interest to those anxious to discover more about travel to Europe during this period. The dates given are those of the books' first publication, although many have been reprinted and also increasingly made available online.

GENERAL HISTORY AND GUIDES

Arengo-Jones, Peter, *Queen Victoria in Switzerland* (1995).

Benjamin, Sarah, *A Castle in Tuscany: The Remarkable Life of Janet Ross* (2006).

Brendon, Piers, *Thomas Cook: 150 Years of Popular Tourism* (1991).

Buzard, James, *The Beaten Track: European Tourism, Literature, and the Ways to 'Culture', 1800–1918* (1993).

Cormack, Bill, *A History of Holidays 1812–1990* (1998).

Feifer, Maxine, *Tourism in History* (1986).

Fitzsimons, Raymond, *The Baron of Piccadilly: The Travels and Entertainments of Albert Smith, 1816–1860* (1967).

Kanigel, Robert, *High Season in Nice* (2002).

Kaplan, Fred (ed.), *Travelling in Italy with Henry James* (1994).

King, Francis, *Florence: A Literary Companion* (1991).

Links, J. G., *The Ruskins in Normandy . . .* (1968).

Morgan, Marjorie, *National Identities and Travel in Victorian Britain* (2001).

Nelson, Michael, *Queen Victoria and the Discovery of the Riviera* (2001).

Newnham-Davis, Nathaniel and Bastard, Algernon, *The Gourmet's Guide to Europe* (1903).

Norwich, John Julius, *Paradise of Cities: Nineteenth-Century Venice . . .* (2003).

Pakenham, Simon, *Sixty Miles from England: The English at Dieppe 1814–1914* (1967).

Pimlott, John, *The Englishman's Holiday* . . . (1947).

Ring, Jim, *How the English Made the Alps* (2000).

Robinson, Jane, *Wayward Women: A Guide to Women Travellers* (1990).

Ruskin, John, *The Stones of Venice* (1851–1853).

Sillitoe, Alan, *Leading the Blind: A Century of Guide Book Travel 1815–1914* (1995).

Varriano, John, *Rome: A Literary Companion* (1991).

Young, George, *Tourism: Blessing or Blight?* (1973).

GUIDE-BOOKS

Between 1814 and 1914 hundreds of guide-books were issued, the most famous of which were those of Mariana Starke, John Murray (the *Traveller's Handbooks* series) and Karl Baedeker, as described in Chapter 4. These may still be found in second-hand bookshops and their contents are increasingly being made available online.

TRAVEL BOOKS

Anon, *Mr. Punch on the Continong with 152 Illustrations* (n.d.). [A collection of cartoons and stories showing the humour of travel, first published in *Punch*.]

Agassiz, Lewis, *A Journey To Switzerland* (1833).

Annesley, Maude, *My Parisian Year* (1912).

Barker, E. H., *Wanderings by Southern Waters. Eastern Aquitaine* (1893).

Blessington, Countess of, *The Idler in France* (1841).

Blessington, Countess of, *The Idler in Italy* (1839).

Bumpus, T. Francis, *Summer Holidays among the Glories of France* . . . (1901).

Butler, Samuel, *Alps and Sanctuaries of Piedmont and the Canton Ticino* (1881).

Cooper, A. N., *The Tramps of "The Walking Parson".* (1902) [This is an entertaining account by a Yorkshire clergyman who made walking tours to Rome, Venice, Monte Carlo and the Pyrenees.]

Crane, Thomas, *Abroad* (1882). [This children's book about a trip to Paris has superb illustrations by Ellen Houghton and gives much excellent information about Victorian travel.]

Dearmer, Percy, *Highways and Byways in Normandy* (1904).

Dickens, Charles, *Pictures from Italy* (1846).

Doyle, Richard, *The Foreign Tour of Messrs. Brown, Jones and Robinson* (1855).

Edwards, Amelia, *Untrodden Peaks and Unfrequented Valleys* . . . (1872).

Eyre, Mary, *A Lady's Walks in the South of France* (1863).

Ford, Richard, *Gatherings from Spain* (1846).

Frye, W. E., *After Waterloo: Reminiscences of European Travel* . . . (1908).

Hare, Augustus, *A Winter at Mentone* (1861).

Jerome, Jerome K., *Diary of a Pilgrimage* (1891).

Jerome, Jerome K., *Three Men on the Bummel* (1900).

Lowe, Emily, *Unprotected Females in Norway . . .* (1857).

Marshall, Archibald, *A Spring Walk in Provence* (1914).

Matthews, Henry, *The Diary of an Invalid . . .* (1822).

Murray, A. H. Hallam, Nevinson, Henry W. and Carmichael, Montgomery, *Sketches on the Old Road Through France to Florence* (1904).

Shelley, Mary and Shelley, Percy, *History of a Six Weeks' Tour through a Part of France, Switzerland, Germany and Holland* (1817).

Somerville, E. Œ. and Ross, Martin, *In the Vine Country* (1893).

Stephen, Leslie, *The Playground of Europe* (1871).

Stevenson, R.L., *Essays of Travel* (1905).

Stevenson, R.L., *Travels with a Donkey in the Cevennes* (1879).

Symonds, J. A. and Symonds, Margaret, *Our Life in the Swiss Highlands* (1892).

Thackeray, W. M., *The Kickleburys on the Rhine* (1850).

Thackeray, W. M., *The Paris Sketch Book* (1840).

Trollope, Anthony, *Travelling Sketches* (1866).

Trollope, Frances, *Belgium and Western Germany* (1834).

Trollope, Frances, *Paris and the Parisians* (1836).

Trollope, Frances, *Vienna and the Austrians* (1838).

Trollope, Thomas Adolphus, *A Lenten Journey in Umbria and the Marches* (1862).

Waterfield, Lina, *Home Life in Italy . . .* (1908).

Wilson, Erasmus, *A Three Weeks' Scamp through the Spas of Germany and Belgium . . .* (1858).

LETTERS, DIARIES AND MEMOIRS

Anglesey, Marquess of (ed.), *The Capel Letters 1814–1817* (1955).

Baring-Gould, Sabine, *Early Reminiscences 1834–1864* (1923).

de Beer, G. R. (ed.), *A Journey to Florence in 1817 by Harriet Charlotte Beaujolois Campbell* (1951) [The impressive diary of an aristocratic fourteen-year-old girl.]

Bennett, Arnold, *Florentine Journal, 1st April–25th May 1910* (1967).

Blakiston, Georgiana, *Lord William Russell and His Wife* (1972).

Cater, W. F. (ed.), *Love among the Butterflies . . .* (1980). [Records the travels of an unconventional late Victorian lady.]

Clive, Mary (ed.), *Caroline Clive . . .* (1949).

Colles, John Mayne (ed.), *The Journal of John Mayne during a Tour on the Continent . . . 1814* (1909).

Dickinson, Lowes, *Letters from Italy 1850–1853* (1914). [Privately published letters of an artist travelling and studying in Italy.]

Emanuel, Angela (ed.), *A Bright Remembrance, The Diaries of Julia Cartwright, 1851–1824* (1989). [These show how travel in Italy affected a woman's whole life.]

Hare, Augustus J. C., *Memorials of a Quiet Life* (1873).

Hare, Augustus J. C., *The Story of My Life* (1896). [The original six volumes were later abridged in two volumes by Malcolm Barnes: *The Years with Mother* and *In My Solitary Life*.]

Jackson, Thomas Graham, *Memories of Travel* (1923).

Londonderry, the Marchioness of & Hyde, H. M. (eds), *More Letters from Martha Wilmot: Impressions from Vienna 1819–1829 . . .* (1935).

Luard, C. G. (ed.), *The Journal of Clarissa Trant 1800–1832* (1925).

Lucas, Matilda, *Two Englishwomen in Rome, 1871–1900* (1938).

Lutyens, Mary (ed.), *Young Mrs. Ruskin in Venice . . .* (1965).

Noakes, Vivien (ed.), *Edward Lear: Selected Letters* (1988).

Okey, Thomas, *A Basketful of Memories . . .* (1930).

Ruskin, John, *Præterita . . .* (1885–9).

Shand, A. I., *Old-Time Travel: Personal Reminiscences of the Continent* (1903).

Simpson, Jennifer (ed.), A *European Journal: Two Sisters Abroad in 1847* (1987). [These diaries also include examples of Victorian watercolours made during a trip through Germany, Italy and Switzerland.]

Skinner, Robert T. (ed.), *Cummy's Diary: A Diary Kept by R.L. Stevenson's Nurse Alison Cunningham while Travelling on the Continent during 1863* (1926).

Torr, Cecil (ed.), *Small Talk at Wreyland* (1918–1924).

Trease, Geoffrey (ed.), *Matthew Todd's Journal . . .* (1968).

Trollope, Thomas Adolphus, *What I Remember* (1887–1889).

Verey, David (ed.), *Wedding Tour . . .* (1985). [The diary of Emily Birchall.]

Vernon, W.W., *Recollections of Seventy-Two Years* (1917).

Walker, Archibald (ed.), *The Letters of John Stuart Blackie to His Wife* (1909).

There are many modern scholarly editions of the correspondence of writers and frequent travellers such as Anthony Trollope, Dickens, Thackeray, Ruskin and, most famous of all, Elizabeth and Robert Browning.

Notes

The place of publication is London unless noted otherwise. If all citations are from one part of a manuscript collection then only the collection's shortened citation will be given. For fuller information, and for the location of collections used, readers should consult the List of Manuscripts below. Given the variety of editions available for novels, references will be to the chapter only. The following abbreviations are used:

A.Y.R.	*All the Year Round*
B.E.M.	*Blackwood's Edinburgh Magazine*
C.J.	*Chambers's Journal of Popular Literature*
d.	Diary entry
D.N.B.	*Dictionary of National Biography (1998): online*
E.C.J.	*Eliza Cook's Journal*
F.M.	*Fraser's Magazine*
H.W.	*Household Words*
I.L.N.	*The Illustrated London News*
M.L.	*The Mirror of Literature*
N.M.M.	*The New Monthly Magazine and Literary Journal)*
O.E.D.	*Oxford English Dictionary (1989): online*

LIST OF MANUSCRIPTS

Austen-Leigh MS: Austen-Leigh Family Papers, Hampshire Record Office, 23M93/87/2/36

Balfour MS: Scottish Record Office, Edinburgh.

Beadles MS: A Fortnight in Paris with Capt. Beadles in February 1821, Bodleian Library, MS Eng. e3438 (rough notes) and 3439 (finished text).

Benson MS: Papers of Archbishop Benson and his Family, Bodleian Library, Oxford.

Bentham MS: Papers of Jeremy Bentham, British Library.

Best MS: Thomas Best Family Papers, Hampshire Record Office.

Bonham-Carter MS: Bonham-Carter Family Papers, Hampshire Record Office.

Bridgeman MS: Records of the Bridgeman Family, Shropshire Record Office.

Budd MS: Papers of Henry Budd, Hampshire Record Office.

Carnarvon MS: Carnarvon of Highclere Papers, Hampshire, Record Office.

Chute MS: Travel Journal of C.W. Chute, 'Voyage to Rome, Hampshire Record Office, 86A06/1.

Codrington MS: Codrington Papers, Gloucestershire Record Office.

Curtis (Journal) MS: Anon. 'Journal of an 13 Months Tour in the Years1842, 1843–Europe', Curtis Museum, Alton Collection Hampshire Record Office, 4M51/396.

Curtis (Woods) MS: Travel Journal of H. H. Woods, 5 June 1827–23 Oct. 1828, Curtis Museum, Alton Collection, Hampshire Record Office, 4M51/395.

Dunne MS: Records of the Dunne Family of Gatley Park, Herefordshire Record Office.

Dyrham MS: Dyrham Park Archives (Blathwayt Family Papers), Gloucestershire Record Office.

Feilding MS: Feilding of Newnham Paddox MS, Warwickshire Record Office, CR 2017/TP431/97–103.

Fortescue MS: Fortescue of Castle Hill Papers, Devon Record Office.

Fox Talbot MS: Papers of W.H. Fox Talbot, Lacock Abbey, Wiltshire.

Freiburg Visit MS: Anon. Diary of a Visit to Freiburg, 17 May–5 Sept. 1895, Authors' Collection.

Fremantle MS: Sir T. F. Fremantle Papers, Letters 1815–1817, Buckinghamshire Record Office, D/FR/83/5.

Gabinetto Scientifico MS: Papers of the Gabinetto Scientifico-Litterario, Archivo Storico, Palazzo Strossi, Florence.

Galton MS: Galton Papers, Birmingham City Archives.

Grenfell MS: Diary of Capt. F.O. Grenfell, V.C., 6 Aug. 1910–1913, Grenfell Family Papers, Buckinghamshire Record Office, D-X835/1.

Hawtrey MS: Elizabeth Hawtrey Papers, Buckinghamshire Record Office, D/65/2/4.

Hazell MS: Walter Hazell, 'Stray notes from Italy. 1885', Hazell, Watson and Viney Ltd. Papers, D/HWV/2. Centre for Buckinghamshire Studies.

Hill MS: Notes of a Tour on the Continent. Bodleian Library, Oxford, MS. Top. Gen. e. 77.

Horner MS: Diaries of Susan Horner, 1847–8 & 1861–2, Susan Horner Collection, Harold Acton Library, British Institute of Florence.

Horsman MS: Horsman Family Papers, Buckinghamshire Record Office.

Hudson MS: Papers of Robert Hudson for his European trip, 8 Sept.–20 Oct. 1836, Bodleian Library, MS Eng. c 7099.

Hutchinson MS: Six Sketch Books of Peter Orlando Hutchinson, Devon Record Office, Z19-2-8C and Z19-2-8E.

Hynes MS: Diaries of Bishop John Thomas Hynes, <www.unisanet.unisa.edu.au>.

Ivory MS: Papers of W.W. Ivory of Chesham, Buckinghamshire Record Office, D/X/712/1-8.

Jervoise MS: Jervoise Family Papers, Hampshire Record Office.

Jones MS: Papers of John Jones, National Library of Scotland.

Lamb MS: Correspondence of Lady Palmerston with Viscount Melbourne, British Library, BL Add. MSS, 45552.

Lawrence MS: Papers of T. E. Lawrence, Bodleian Library, Oxford, MS. Eng. d. 3342, MS Eng. c. 6739.

Lloyd-Baker MS: Gloucestershire Record Office, D3549 26/2/7.

Llysdinam MS: Llysdinam Papers, National Library of Wales.

Malmesbury MS: Malmesbury Papers, Hampshire Record Office.

Maquay MS: Maquay Family Papers, Harold Acton Library, British Institute of Florence.

Marrington MS: Marrington Papers, Shropshire Records and Research Centre.

Oglander MS: Papers of the Oglander Family, Isle of Wight Record Office.

Onslow MS: Papers of Cranley Onslow, Clandon House, Surrey.

Peek MS: Papers of Edward Peek, Devon Record Office.

Poore MS: Poore Family Papers, Hampshire Record Office.

Power MS: Mrs. A.W. Power, 'Notes Upon Italy Written Immediately on my Return to Scotland in 1829', Harold Acton Library, British Institute of Florence.

PTA MS: Papers of the Polytechnic Touring Association, University of Westminster Library.

Rooks MS: Papers of Rooks, Rider and Co., Solicitors (Bingham Papers), Gloucestershire Record Office, D3871/7.

Shelley MS: Robert Parker Travel Journals, Shelley Rolls of Avington Papers, Hampshire Record Office.

Sotheron-Estcourt MS: Sotheron-Estcourt Family Papers, Gloucestershire Record Office, D1571F454.

Thomson MS: Papers of Prof. Allen Thomson in the Library of the Royal College of Surgeons in England, Lincoln's Inn Fields, London.

Torr MS: Diaries of the Torr Family, Devon Record Office.

Trollope Business MS: Bodleian Library, Oxford, MS. Don. c. 10*.

Trollope-UCLA MS: Trollope Family Papers, UCLA Library, Los Angeles, California.

Veale MS: H. M. Veale, Diary of a Journal on the Continent, <www.geocities.com/clayton_veale/journal>.

Villari MS: Letters from F. E. Trollope to Linda Villari, Bodleian Library, Oxford, MS Eng.Lett. d. 493.

Waterfield MS: Papers of Lina Waterfield, Harold Acton Library, British Institute of Florence.
Weld MS: Papers of Edward Weld, Jnr, Dorset Record Office.
Wickham MS: Travel diary and notebook of Helen Mason, 8 Nov. 1859–21 Feb. 1860, Wickham Family Papers, Hampshire Record Office, 38M49K3/13.
Wrest Park MS: Wrest Park (Lucas) Collection, Bedfordshire and Luton Archives and Record Service.

INTRODUCTION

1 Malcolm Elwin (ed.), *The Autobiography and Journals of Benjamin Robert Haydon* (1786–1846) (1950), p. 202.
2 Ibid., pp. 205–6.
3 Quoted in ibid., p. 216; quoted in Adam Zamoyski, *Rites of Peace* (2007), p. 192; Archibald Montgomery Maxwell, *My Adventures . . .*, 2 vols (1845), II, p. 62.
4 Amelia Edwards, *Untrodden Peaks and Unfrequented Valleys* (1872), p. 133.
5 Ibid., p. 313.
6 Philip Gibbs, *The Pageant of the Years* (1946), pp. 135–6.
7 Edward Weld Jnr. to Edward Weld Snr, 2 Mar. and 2 Aug. 1761, Weld MS, D/WLC/C/22.
8 Mrs E. T. Cook, *From a Holiday Journal* (1904), pp. 204–5.

CHAPTER 1 WHY DO YOU TRAVEL?

1 'English in Italy', *Westminster Review*, (Oct. 1826); J. W. Cunningham, *Cautions to Continental Travellers* (1823, 2nd edn), pp. 4–6; Samuel Rogers, 'Foreign Travel', in *Italy: A Poem* (1830), p. 170; Frances Trollope, *Vienna and the Austrians . . .*, 2 vols, (Paris, 1838), I, p. 3.
2 John Ruskin, *Præterita . . .* (1949 edn [1885–9]), pp. 69–70; Rogers, 'Foreign Travel', pp. 172–3.
3 Anon., n.d. [1843], Curtis (Journal) MS; Augustus Hare, *Memorials of a Quiet Life*, 2 vols (1873), I, pp. 9, 19–20, 29.
4 James Paul Cobbett, *Journal of a Tour . . .* (1830), p. 265; 'Back Again', in *C.J.* 10 Jan. 1863.
5 Marianne Thornton to Patty Smith, n.d. [1817], E. M. Forster, *Marianne Thornton: A Domestic Biography 1797–1887* (1956), p. 97; 'Mildred: A Tale,' *B.E.M.* (Dec. 1846); P. H. Fitzgerald, *A Day's . . .* (1887), Part I, <www.bookrags.com/ebooks>.
6 Quoted in E. J. Trelawny, *Recollections of the Last Days of Shelley and Byron* (1859, 2nd edn), pp. 11–12.

7   Lord Byron, *Alpine Journal*, <www.internationalbyronsociety.org>, p. 4; Lady Frederick Cavendish, d. 7 July 1864 in John Bailey (ed.), *The Diary of Lady Frederick Cavendish*, 2 vols (1927), I, p. 228; Bishop Magee to J. G. MacDonnell, 23 Sept. 1869, in J. C. Macdonnell, *The Life and Correspondence of William Connor Magee . . .* 2 vols (1896), I, p. 237; Maude Annesley, *My Parisian Year* (1912), p. 246.

8   J. W. Burgon, *Letters from Rome . . .* (1862), p. 1; Laurence Sterne, *A Sentimental Journey . . .* (1841 edn), p. 16; 'Recent Travellers', *F.M.* (Sept. 1849); John Ruskin, *Præterita*, p. 405; entries for 'tourist' and 'traveller' in *OED*.

9   For a good summary of the debates see James Buzard, *The Beaten Track . . .* (Oxford, 1993); Jerome K. Jerome, *Diary of a Pilgrimage* (1919 edn), pp. 134–5, 131.

10 A. N. Cooper, *The Tramps of 'The Walking Parson' . . .* (1902), p. 253.

11 Blanchard and Douglas William Jerrold, *The Life and Remains of Douglas Jerrold* (1859), p. 168; George Bradshaw, *Bradshaw's Illustrated Travellers' Hand Book in France* (1857), p. xxiv; W. M. Thackeray, *The Works of William Makepeace Thackeray: The Paris Sketch Book*, 13 vols (1902–1905), V, p. 28.

12 W. M. Thackeray, *The Kickleburys on the Rhine, The Works of . . . Thackeray*, vol. 9, p. 211; 'Recent Travellers', *F.M.* (July 1850); Cooper, *The Walking Parson*, pp. 154–5.

13 Anon., *The Enquirer's Oracle . . .* (n.d. [1884?]), p. 18.

14 Thomas William Jex-Blake, *A Long Vacation in Continental Picture-Galleries* (1858), pp. 42–3; Gerald Codrington to his mother, 12 Aug. 1869, Codrington MS.

15 Rogers, 'Foreign Travel', p. 173; [E. C. Grenville Murray], 'The Roving Englishman: His Hints to Travellers', in *H.W.*, 13 Nov. 1852. *Bradshaw's Illustrated Travellers' Hand Book in France*, p. xxiii.

16 Article V, *The Foreign Quarterly Review* (Oct. 1844); Frederick Leveson Gower, quoted in Sir George Leveson Gower, *Years of Content 1858–1886* (1940), pp. 84–6.

17 Charlotte Mackenzie, *Psychiatry for the Rich . . .* (1992), p. 105; Rooks MS.

18 Donald Thomas, *The Victorian Underworld* (1998), pp. 768, 119; see Thomas Hodgskin, *Travels in the North of Germany*, 2 vols (Edinburgh, 1820) and A. K. Gardner, *The French Metropolis* (New York, 1850); J. L. Maquay, d., 16 Nov. 1822, Maquay MS; Hill MS, p. 81; Bishop Hynes, d., 13 Jan. 1860, Hynhes MS; Walter, *My Secret Life*, 11 vols (Amsterdam, 1888–1894), V, ch. 1.

19 Anon., d., n.d. Curtis (Journal) MS; 'The Pleasures and Drawbacks of Travelling', *Temple Bar* (Nov. 1875); quoted in James Pope-Hennessy, *Monckton Milnes: The Flight of Youth . . .* (New York, 1955) p. 79.

20 Anon., *Miss Jemima's Swiss Journal* . . . (1963), p. xiii; J. A. St John, *There and Back Again* . . . (1853), p. 28.

21 Mary Ann Evans, d. 29 Sept. 1854, in Margaret Harris and Judith Johnston (eds), *The Journals of George Eliot* (Cambridge, 1998), p. 25; Sir Wemyss Reid (ed.), *The Life of William Ewart Gladstone* (1899), pp. 347–9; Philip Magnus, *Gladstone: A Biography* (1954), pp. 92–4; S. G. Checkland, *The Gladstones* . . . (Cambridge, 1971), pp. 366–7; Roy Jenkins, *Gladstone* (1995), pp. 93–5, 107, 185, 456–7; Lord Stanley, d. 3 Feb. 1861, in John Vincent (ed.), *Disraeli, Derby and the Conservative Party* . . . (1978), pp. 165–6 and 366 n. 9; F. D. Munsell, *The Unfortunate Duke* . . . (1985), pp. 272–4.

22 Granville Lloyd-Baker, d. [1884?], Lloyd-Baker MS; Pugin to Charles Barry, 1 Aug. 1845 in Margaret Belcher (ed.), *The Collected Letters of A.W.N. Pugin.* Vol. 2: *1843–1845* (Oxford, 2001–), p. 425.

23 R. J. Croft, 'The Nature and Growth of Cross Channel Traffic through Calais and Boulogne, 1870–1900', in *Transport History* (July 1973), p. 131; Paul Gerbod, 'Voyageurs et residents britanniques en France au XIXᵉ siècle', *Acta Geographica* (1988), p. 25.

24 James Bentley, *Oberammergau and the Passion Play* (1984), quoted in Piers Brendon, *Thomas Cook* . . . (1991), p. 116; Sir Charles Oman, *Memories of Victorian Oxford* . . . (1941), p. 185; Mrs Stuert Erskine (ed.), *Memoirs of Edward Earl of Sandwich* . . . (1919), p. 205; *Gaze's Tourist Gazette* (Nov. 1895), n.p.

25 [E. C. Grenville Murray], 'The Roving Englishman: A Ramble to Rehburg', in *H.W.* (14 Aug. 1852). *Boston Daily Globe* (5 Sep. 1897); *Washington Post*, 18 Aug. 1905.

26 A. B. Granville, *The Mineral Springs of Vichy* . . . (1859), pp. 212–15, 227, 228–30, 242; John Oglander to Florence Oglander, n.d. [May or June 1894], Oglander MS, OG/CC/1826.

27 John Oglander to Florence Oglander, 1, 2, 18, 20 Oct. 1897, Oglander MS, OG/CC/1933, OG/CC/1935, OG/CC/1945B, OG/CC/1945D.

28 David Bogue, *Belgium and the Rhine* (1852), p. 173; Charles Feilding to William Henry Fox Talbot, 3 Aug. 1834 in Fox Talbot MS, Doc. No. 02969; the Revd. R.R. Dolling, quoted in Charles E. Osborne, *The Life of Father Dolling* (1903), pp. 300–1.

29 Frances Blathwayt to Charlotte A. Baker, 22 Jan., 28 Mar., 8 Dec. 1865; Frances Blathwayt to Ellen Philips, 22 Jan., 2 Feb., 7 Mar., 27 June & 25 Aug. 1868. Telegram from ? to W. T. Blathwayt, 23 Feb. 1869, Dyrham MS, D1799/C63 and D1799/C103.

30 *The Times*, 26 Sept. 1853; 'Travelling Englishmen', in *E.C.J.*, 22 Oct. 1853, pp. 409–11. *The Times*, 3 Nov. 1855.

CHAPTER 2 EPITOMES OF ENGLAND

1   Geoffrey Crayon [Washington Irving], 'The Adventure of the Popkins Family', *Tales of a Traveller* (1824), pp. 47–8; [Constantine Phipps, Viscount Normanby], *The English in Italy*, 3 vols (1825), vol 1, p. 12, vol. 2, p. 221; Cunningham, *Cautions to Travellers*, pp. 455–7.

2   Lady Fremantle to T. F. Fremantle, 23 Sept. 1815, Emma Fremantle to T. F. Fremantle, 27 Oct. 1815, Lady Fremantle to T. F. Fremantle, 27 May [1817], Fremantle MS.

3   W. W. Vernon, *Recollections of Seventy-Two Years* (1917), pp. 7–9; Charles Dickens to John Forster, n.d., quoted in John Forster, *The Life of Charles Dickens* (n.d. [1879?]), p. 441.

4   G. P. Jervoise, notes in *The Tourist's Pocket Journal* ... (n.d., 'New Edition'), *passim*, Jervoise MS, 44M69/E13/12/159 (2).

5   Robert Parker, d. 4 Sept. 1826, Shelley MS, 18M51/561; Earl of Carnarvon to Lord Porchester, 28 Oct. 1826, Carnarvon MS, 75M91/E4/55.

6   R. N. Talfourd, *Supplement to "Vacation Rambles"* ... (1854), p. 1; 'The Baths of Baden,' *The Lady's Magazine and Museum* ... (July 1837), p. 123; Margaret Price to Daniel Price, 3 Sept. 1841 in Marrington MS, 631/3/1429.

7   *Bradshaw's Illustrated Travellers' Hand Book in France*, p. xxv; R. J. Croft, 'The Nature and Growth of Cross Channel Traffic through Calais and Boulogne, 1840–70', *Transport History* (Nov. 1971), p. 262.

8   Sir Erasmus Wilson, *A Three Weeks' Scamper* ... (1858), p. 5; Account Books of the Revd. R. I. Venable, Llysdinam MS, A 42; Derek Hudson, *Martin Tupper: His Rise and Fall* (1949), p. 143; Charlotte Horsman, d., 8 and 10 Mar. 1847, Horsman MS, D/RA/A/3E/26.

9   Jack Simmons, 'Railways, Hotels, and Tourism in Great Britain, 1839–1914', *Journal of Contemporary History* 19/2 (Apr. 1984), p. 215; Edmund Swinglehurst, *The Romantic Journey* ... (1974), pp. 174–9; *Gaze's Tourist Gazette* (1895–6), *passim*.

10 J. B., *The English Party's Excursion to Paris ... 1849* (1850), pp. 104, 95, 2–10.

11 *The Times*, 25 July and 20 Sept. 1849.

12 Croft, 'Nature and Growth ... 1840–70', pp. 254, 252 *ff*; Simmons, 'Railways, Hotels and Tourism', p. 221 n. 68.

13 [E.C. Grenville Murray], 'The Roving Englishman: A Few More Hints', *H.W.*, 25 Dec. 1852; 'The Roving Englishman ... Hints to Travellers', *H.W.*, Samuel Butler, 'Our Tour', *The Eagle* (Easter Term, 1859), I, p. 5.

14 Swinglehurst, *The Romantic Journey*, pp. 174–9; Henry Gaze, *Outline Plan: Holland and Belgium: How to See Them for Seven Guineas* (n.d. [1864]), p. 1; Henry Gaze, *Switzerland: How To See It for Ten Guineas* (n.d. [1866],

Southampton), pp. 3, v; [Edwin Hodder], *Old Merry's Travels on the Continent* . . . (n.d. [1869]), p. 137.

15 *Gaze's Tourist Gazette* (May 1896), *passim*.

16 H. P. Leland, *Americans in Rome* (New York, 1863), p. 16; John Strang, *Travelling Notes* . . . (1863, Glasgow), pp. 232–3.

17 Gaze, *Holland and Belgium*, pp. 4–5; W. E. Gaze, *Paris and How to See It* . . . (1902 edn), pp. 12, 37; 'The Baths of Baden', *The Lady's Magazine and Museum* . . . (July, 1837); Philip Hone, d., ? Sept. 1836, Allan Nevins (ed.), *The Diary of Philip Hone 1828–1851*, 2 vols (New York, 1970), I, p. 224.

18 Gaze, *Holland and Belgium* . . ., p. 5; *Bradshaw's Illustrated Hand-Book to Italy* . . . (1862), p. xvii; Baedeker, *Italy from the Alps to Naples: Handbook for Travellers* (1909, 2nd edn), p. ix.

19 Leslie Stephen, *The Playground of Europe* (1894 edn), p. 40; quoted in Maude Annelsey, *My Parisian Year* . . . (1912), p. 249.

20 Of the numerous studies of Thomas Cook, the best is Piers Brendon, *Thomas Cook: 150 Years of Popular Tourism* (1991).

21 *The Excursionist*, 6 Aug. 1855; Lucilla Lincolne, d., n.d., quoted in Brendon, *Thomas Cook*, pp. 66 *ff.*

22 [Edmund Yates], 'My Excursion Agent', *A.Y.R.*, 7 May 1864; Thomas Cook, *The Excursionist*, 6 Apr. 1865; Anon., *Miss Jemima's Swiss Journal* (1963), p. 112.

23 Brendon, *Thomas Cook*, pp. 113–5; Charles Dickens, Jnr, *Dickens's Dictionary of London, 1887* . . . (n.d. [1887]), p. 239.

24 Brendon, *Thomas Cook*, pp. 113, 116–19, 168.

25 Dickens [Jnr.], *Dickens's Dictionary* . . . *1887*, p. 239; 'To Engelberg and Back', *Punch*, 18 Oct. 1890; Jerome, *Pilgrimage*, pp. 151–2.

26 'My Excursion Agent.', Anon., d., 8 July 1863, *Miss Jemima's Swiss Journal*, p. 77.

27 Cornelius O'Dowd [Charles Lever], 'Continental Excursionists', *B.E.M.*, (Feb. 1865).

28 Thomas Cook, *The Excursionist*, 3 Apr. 1865 and 6 June 1863; Lionel Stevenson, *Dr. Quicksilver: the Life of Charles Lever* (1939), p. 287.

29 *Vanity Fair*, 6 Sept. 1900.

30 *I.L.N.*, 25 Sept. 1880; T. Adolphus Trollope, 'Recollections of the Tuscan Court', *Lippincott's Magazine*, (Mar. 1875).

31 H[yppolite] Taine [W. F. Rae, trans.], *Notes on England* (1873, 5th edn), pp. 371–2; Henry James, 'The Old Saint-Gothard: Leaves from a Note-Book', Fred Kaplan (ed.), *Travelling in Italy with Henry James* (1994), pp. 314–5; Edwards, *Untrodden Peaks*, p. 1.

32 Lady William Russell to Col Hare Clarges, 19 Aug. 1840, Lord William to Lady Holland, 4 Oct. [1829], Lord William Russell, d., 25 Apr. 1829, q. in

Georgiana Blakiston, *Lord William Russell and his Wife* . . . (1972), pp. 438, 198, 189.

33 Helen Mason, d., 29 Nov. 1859, Wickham MS.

34 C. W. Chute, d., 2 Nov. 1873 Chute MS; Anon., d., 31, 15, 18 July 1895, Freiburg Visit MS.

35 Cunningham, *Cautions*, p. 6; 'Spain As It Is', *B.E.M.*, (Feb. 1845).

36 B. R. Mitchell and Phyllis Deane, *Abstract of British Historical Statistics* (Cambridge, 1971), pp. 6–7. The exact figures were 544,000 in 1821 (the earliest year to include Ireland) and 1,328,000 in 1911.

37 Mrs Dalkeith Holmes, *A Ride on Horseback* . . ., 2 vols (1842), vol. 2, p. 418.

38 Emily Lowe, *Unprotected Females in Norway* . . . (1957), pp. 3–4.

39 Edwards, *Untrodden Peaks*, pp. xxxi–xxxii and *passim*.

40 Alice M. Ivimy, *A Woman's Guide to Paris* (1909), v, vi, 30, vii, 1, 34, vii.

41 *Daily News*, 5 Aug. 1869, quoted in Brandon, *Thomas Cook*, p. 83; Janet M. McNair to Florence Glynn, 8 Nov. 1886, Oglander MS, OG/CC/1579.

42 See correspondence in Villari MS; Vernon Lee [Violet Paget], 'Of Modern Travelling', *Limbo and Other Essays* (1897), p. 91.

43 Arnold Bennett, 'Night and Morning in Florence', *The English Review*, (Apr. 1910).

44 'Travelling Incentives', *M.L.*, 2 Aug. 1828; Anon., *The Enquirer's Oracle* . . . (n.d. [1884]), p. 18.

45 *The Enquirer's Oracle* . . ., p. 18. The Countess of Blessington, d. 27 Aug. 1822, *The Idler in Italy* (1839), p. 3; Lady Monkswell, d. 2 Sept. 1873, E. C. F. Collier (ed.), *A Victorian Diarist* . . . *1873–1895* (1944), p. 4.

46 Quoted in Sabine Baring-Gould, *Early Reminiscences 1834–1864* (1923), pp. 103–4.

47 Thomas Best, d., 10 Jan. 1859, Best MS.

48 Leslie Stephen to O. W. Holmes, 18 Aug. 1867, John W. Bicknell (ed.), *Selected Letters of Leslie Stephen*. Vol. 1: *1864*-1882 (1996), pp. 52–3.

49 Mary Benson, d., 2,5,12,13,14,17,19 July 1859, Benson MS.

50 Mary Benson, d., 17,18,20,21 Mar. 1876, Benson MS.

51 Michael Millgate, *Thomas Hardy* . . . (2004, Oxford), pp. 150–4.

52 Sir William Augustus Fraser, *Hic et Ubique* (1893), pp. 63–4.

53 P.T.A. MS, GB 1753 UWA PTA.

54 Anon [Thomas Wright], *Some Habits and Customs of the Working Classes* . . . (1867), pp. 109-10; *The Times*, 3 May 1859; Susan Barton, *Working-Class Organizations and Popular Tourism, 1840–1970* (2005, Manchester), p. 216.

55 Jehoida Rhodes, 'A Sheffield Workman's Week Excursion to Paris and Back for Seventy Shillings', *Saint Pauls* (Nov. 1867), pp. 195–205; *Saint Pauls*,

Oct. 1867 to Sept. 1868, 'Contributions. Contributions & Payments,' Trollope Business MS, *ff* 19–22.

56   *The Times*, 17 Apr., 22 May and 28 Oct. 1889.

57   Thomas Okey, *A Basketful of Memories . . .* (1930), pp. 63, 66–91; Mrs. S.A. Barnett, *Canon Barnett . . .* (1921 edn), pp. 359–65.

58   Barnett, *Canon Barnett*, p. 361; G. B. Shaw to Sir William Morris, 23 Sept. 1891 quoted in Okey, *A Basketful of Memories*, pp. 119–25.

59   Barnett, *Canon Barnett*, p. 365.

60   Mariana Starke, *Information and Directions for Travellers on the Continent* (1828), p. 43; Helen Mason, d., 8 Nov. 1859, Wickham MS; *A Handbook for Travellers in Southern Italy . . .* (1863), p. 1; *A Hand-Book for Travellers in Central Italy . . .* (1850), p. 288.

61   Mrs Butler [Fanny Kemble Butler], *A Year of Consolation*, 2 vols (1847, New York), I, p. 2; quoted in Lord Albert Denison, *Wanderings in Search of Health* (1849); quoted in Osbert Sitwell, *Left Hand, Right Hand* (1946), p. 71; Lady Burton quoted in W. H. Wilkins (ed.), *The Romance of Isabel, Lady Burton*, 2 vols (1897, 1897), I, p. 99.

62   *Mary Boyle*, p. 76; Matilda Lucas to ?, 10. Nov. 1878; Matilda Lucas, *Two Englishwomen in Rome 1871–1900* (1938), p. 159; Lady Frederick Cavendish, d., 5 July 1864, *Diary*, I, p. 227.

63   Matthew Todd, d., 21 Oct. 1814 & 2 May 1816, Geoffrey Trease (ed.), *Matthew Todd's Journal . . .* (1968), pp. 57, 140.

64   Quoted in J. G. Links, *The Ruskins in Normandy . . .* (1968), p. 48, 46 n; John Ruskin, d., 30 Apr. 1849, quoted in Tim Hilton, *John Ruskin: The Early Years . . .* (1985), p. 132.

65   Alison Cunningham, d., 9 & 11 Jan, 19 Feb., 29 Apr., 9 May, 17 and 30 Apr., 13 and 10 Jan., 4 Feb., 2 Apr., 19 and 11 Jan., and 12 May 1863, Robert T. Skinner (ed.), *Cummy's Diary . . .* (1926), *passim*.

66   Jervoise MS, 44M69/13/12/166; Susan Horner, d., 1 Nov. 1861, Horner MS; Lina Duff-Gordon to Madge Vaughan, 8 Feb. 1894, Waterfield MS; Lina Waterfield, *Home Life in Italy . . .* (1908), p. 43; Matilda Lucas to ?, 2 Jan. & 5 Jan. 1893, Lucas, *Two Englishwomen*, pp. 171–2.

67   W. K. W. Blumenbach, *Austria and the Austrians* 2 vols (1837), I, p. 65. The exact number for 1814 was 8,469. Gerbod, 'Voyageurs et residents . . .', pp. 19–35. The figure for the late 1830s was 'un total de 40,000 voyageurs passes à Calais'. This figure has to be halved and it applies only to Calais. (Michel Chevalier, *Lettres sur L'Amérique du Nord*, 2 vols [Brussels, 1837], I, pp. 352–3.) Figures for the 1860s are based on those for 1865. (Gerbod, 'Voyageurs et residents . . .', p. 28.) The figure for 1862 is 190,213. (R. J. Croft, 'The Nature and Growth of Cross Channel Traffic through Calais and Boulogne, 1840–70', in *Transport History* [Nov. 1971].) Figures for the

final period include 951,078 for 1899 (Croft, 'The Nature and Growth . . . 1870–1900'); 660,000 (Marjorie Morgan, *National Identities and Travel in Victorian Britain* [Basingstoke, 2001], p. 14; and 1 million for the year 1910 (Gerbod, 'Voyageurs et residents . . .', p. 28;'The Cultivation of "Tourisme" . . .,' *The Times*, 16 Nov. 1911). The other sources consulted are: Simmons, 'Railways, Hotels, and Tourism'; *Encyclopaedia Britannica of 1911*, <www.1911encyclopedia.org>; James Chalmers, *The Channel Railway Connecting England and France* (1861), p. 32; John Pimlott, *The Englishman's Holiday* . . . (1947), p. 189; George Young, *Tourism: Blessing or Blight?* (Harmondsworth, 1973), p. 18; Maxine Feifer, *Tourism in History* . . . (New York, 1986), p. 164; Bill Cormack, *A History of Holidays 1812–1990* (1998), pp. 36–7.

68   This section is based on: K. T. Hoppen, *The Mid-Victorian Generation 1846–1886* (Oxford, 1998), pp. 33–4; W. H. Mallock, *Classes and Masses* . . . (1896), pp. 14–16, 10, 28, 31; Lawrence James, *The Middle Class: A History* (2006), pp. 254–5; B. Seebohm Rowntree, *Poverty: A Study of Town Life* (1901), *passim*; P. H. Lindert and J. G. Williamson, 'Reinterpreting Britain's Social Tables, 1688–1913', *Explorations in Economic History* (1983), pp. 94–109; Peter H. Lindert and Jeffrey G. Williamson, 'Revising England's Social Tables 1688–1812', *Explorations in Economic History* (1982), pp. 385–408; G. G. D'Aeth, 'Present Tendencies of Class Differentiation', in *Sociological Review* (1910), p. 3; 'Nominal Annual Earnings for Various Occupations . . .', <www.privatewww.essex.ac.uk>; Baedeker, *Austria-Hungary . . . Handbook for Travellers* (1905), p. xi–xii.

69   Mitchell and Deane, *Historical Statistics*, pp. 343–4; A. L. Bowley, *National Progress in Wealth and Trade* (1904), p. 27. According to the Rousseaux Price Index, the cost of food and principal industrial products can be set at 175 in 1800. By 1900 the figure was 91.

70   C. W. Jones and Edith Ducat to the Editor, *The Times*, 14 Aug. 1879; Boulogne Chamber of Commerce, *Trafic Franco-Anglais* (n.d. [1889]) quoted in Croft, 'The Nature and Growth . . . 1870–1900', pp. 137–9, 128–30.

71   Sibella Bonham Carter, d., 4 & 15 Nov. 1894 & *passim*, Bonham Carter MS, 94M72/F166; Philip Gibbs, *The Pageant of the Years* . . . (1946), pp. 27–8; Cooper, *The Walking Parson*, p. 282.

CHAPTER 3 SEEING THE LIONS

1   Baedeker, *Northern France* . . . (1909, 5th edn), p. xiv; M. J. Torr, d., 10 Aug. 1873, Torr MS 57908 T 009.915.688. Unless noted otherwise, all Torr MS use 'T.009.915.688', therefore only the first five numbers will be given.

When unable to identify the writer of one of the Torr diaries we use Torr Family.

2   *The Times*, 29 July 1879; Bishop Hynes, d., 24 Oct. 1843, Hynes MS; K. Baedeker, *Belgium and Holland: Handbook for Travellers* (1888, 9th edn), pp. 107–21; R. B. Bernard, *A Tour through Some Parts of France* . . . (1815), p. 2 *ff*; Lord Palmerston to Laurence Sulivan, 15 Nov. 1834 in Kenneth Bourne (ed.), *The Letters of . . . Viscount Palmerston to Laurence and Elizabeth Sulivan* . . . (1979), pp. 257–8.

3   Georgiana Capel to the Dowager Countess of Uxbridge, ? Aug. 1815, in the Marquess of Anglesey (ed.), *The Capel Letters* . . . (1955), p. 134. Marianne Thornton to her aunt, n.d. [Sept. 1817], in Forster, *Marianne Thornton*, pp. 103–4; Hudson MS; Marianne Thornton to her aunt, n.d., in Forster, *Marianne Thornton*, pp. 103–4; *A Hand-Book for Travellers to the Continent . . . Holland, Belgium, Prussia* . . . (1838, 2nd edn), p. 151; Torr Family Diaries, 13 Aug. 1868, Torr MS, 57878.

4   A. I. Shand, *Old-Time Travel: Personal Reminiscences of the Continent* (1903), p. 29; 'Brute Life in the Alps,' *B.E.M.*, (Nov. 1853); *The Times*, 29 July 1879; Charlotte Horsman, d. 29 Oct. 1846, Horsman MS, D/RA/A/3E/26.

5   Augustus Hare, *Paris*, 2 vols (1900, 2nd edn), p. 1; Lady Fremantle to T. F. Fremantle, 23 Sept. [1815], Fremantle MS; *Galignani's New Paris Guide* (1853), p. ii; Baedeker, *Paris* (1896, 12th edn), p. 87.

6   Torr Family, d., 15 Aug. 1871, Torr MS, 57907.

7   Thomas Best, d., 4 Nov. 1858, Best MS; Robert Parker, d., 3 Apr. 1819, Shelley MS, 18M51/559. Beadles MS, 3439.

8   [Archibald Alison], 'France in 1833', *B.E.M.*, (Dec 1833); R. P. Graves, *A.E. Housman* (Oxford, 1981), p. 155; F. Hervé, *How to Enjoy Paris in 1842* (1842), p. 33. Richard Mullen and James Munson, *Victoria: Portrait of a Queen* (1987), p. 68; Maude Annesely, *My Parisian Year* (1912), p. 207.

9   David Bogue, *Paris and Its Environs* (1855), pp. 16–17.

10   H. H. Woods, d., 6 June 1827, Curtis (Journal) MS; S. G. Green, *French Pictures* . . . (1878), pp. 1, 182; Lord Fortescue, d., ? Oct. 1815, Fortescue MS; *The Times*, 4 Aug. 1902.

11   E. A. Freeman, *Sketches of Travel* . . . (1897), p. 1; Cyril Scudamore, *Normandy* (1906), p. 3.

12   Gerbod, 'Voyageurs et residents', pp. 27–8; J. P. Cobbett, *A Ride of Eight Hundred Miles in France* . . . (1824), pp. 22–4; Edwin Lee, *Nice and Its Climate* . . . (1865, 2nd edn), p. 32 n.1.

13   Elisabeth Feilding to W.H. Fox Talbot, 2 Jan. 1835, Fox Talbot MS, Doc. 03039; Gerbod, 'Voyageurs et residents,' p. 27.

14 James Bright, A Practical Treatise on Diseases of the Heart ... (1860), pp. 350, 353–4.

15 Edwin Lee, *Nice and Its Climate* ... (1860), 18, 9, 94, 6–13; Croft, 'Nature and Growth ... 1870–1900', p. 131; Tchaikovsky to Anatoli Tchaikovsky, 1–13 Jan. 1872, Piotr Ilyich Tchaikovsky [Galina von Meck, trans.], *Letters to his Family: An Autobiography* (1981, 1981 edn), p. 72; Gerbod, 'Voyageurs et residents', p. 27 ff; *The Times*, 1 Apr. 1911; Susan Horner, d., 31 Dec. 1847, Horner MS.

16 This section is based on ch. 2 of Michael Nelson's excellent book, *Queen Victoria and the Discovery of the Riviera* (2001), pp. 20–36.

17 Bernard, *A Tour*, <www.books.google.co.uk>.

18 Anthony Trollope, *Travelling Sketches* (1866), pp. 101–2.

19 *A Handbook for Travellers on the Continent ... Holland ... and the Rhine* ... (1853), p. 257; *New York Times*, 20 July 1852; see advert in Francis Coghlan, *The Miniature Guide to the Rhine* (1853), p. 395.

20 [Edwin Hodder], *Old Merry's Travels on the Continent* (n.d. [1869]), pp. 144–5; Martin Tupper, *Paterfamilias's Diary of Everybody's Tour (1856)*, p. 40; [W.G.T.] Shedd (ed.), *The Complete Works of Samuel Taylor Coleridge*, 7 vols (1853), VI, pp. 305–6 n. 4.

21 Robert R. Taylor, *The Castles of the Rhine* ... (1998, Waterloo, ON), p. 256; John Barrow, *Tour on the Continent* ... (1853), p. 53; Bishop Hynes, d., 20 Oct. 1843, Hynes MS; Tupper, *Paterfamilias's Diary*, p. 37.

22 For the poem and statue see 'Der Englischer Reisender um 1845', Bonn Stadt Museum, <www.2.bonn.de/stadtmuseum/inhalte/objektbeschereibung_engl_reisender.htm>.

23 Mary Shelley, *History of a Six Weeks Tour* (1817), pp. 68–9; Anon., 'The East and South of Europe', *B.E.M.*, (Jan. 1843); Anon, *What May be Done in Two Months ... Up the Rhine* ... (1834), p. 57.

24 Edward Horsman, d., 25 Sept. 1828, Horsman MS, D/RA/A/3E/20; Anon, *What May be Done*, p. 57.

25 *A Handbook ... the Rhine*, p. 233; S. R. Roget (ed.), *Travel in the Two Last Centuries* ... (1922), pp. 182–6; Sir Erasmus Wilson, *A Three Weeks' Scamper* ... (1858), p. 73; Thomas Dunne to his parents, 8 June 1841, Dunne MS, F76/IV/550–555.

26 W. C. Bridgeman to his wife, 30 Mar. 1899, Bridgeman MS, 4629/1/1899/6; Lord Sandwich, d., n.d.[1908], Mrs. Steuart Erskine (ed.), *Memoirs of Edward Earl of Sandwich* (1919), p. 255; Jerome, *Pilgrimage*, pp. 247–8.

27 Francis Grenfell, d., 10 & 11 Sept., 1 & 25 July 1912, Grenfell MS.

28 *The Washington Post*, 5 Nov. 1860; Emily Foster, d., 12 Mar. [1821]; S. T. Williams and L. B. Beach (eds), *The Journal of Emily Foster* (1938, New

York), p. 5; Jerome K. Jerome, *Three Men on the Bummel* (1962 edn), p. 94; Shand, *Old-Time Travel*, p. 195; Edward Peek to Henry Peek, 12 July 1870, Peek MS, 1405M.add.3/F2; G. E. Biber, *The English Church on the Continent* . . . (1846, 2nd edn), p. 58; Shand, *Old-Time Travel*, p. 125.

29   Mary Wilson, d., 22 Feb. to 1 May 1847, Jennifer Simpson (ed.), *A European Journal* . . . (1987), pp. 36–67.

30   Thomas Guthrie, *Sundays Abroad* (1872), pp. 30, 29; 'Brute Life'; *The Times*, 10 Apr. 1899.

31   Henry Matthews, d., 26 Aug. 1816, *The Diary of an Invalid* . . ., 2 vols (1822, 3rd edn), II, p. 115; Torr Family, d., 11 Sept. 1863, Torr MS, 57888; Chaloner Chute, d., 10 Sept. 1873, Chute MS.

32   Lord Fortescue, d., 27 Sept. and 5 Oct. 1815, Fortescue MS; H. H. Woods, d., 29 Sept., 1827, Curtis (Woods) MS; Sir Edward Harris, d., 6 June 1858, Malmesbury MS, 9M73/598; C. D. Warner, *Saunterings* (1891), p. 57; Mary Benson, d., 14 July 1859, Benson MS; Mrs Henry Freshfield, *A Summer Tour in the Grisons* . . . (1862), pp. 1–5; Baedeker, *Switzerland* . . . (1864, 3rd edn), p. 143.

33   R. L. Stevenson, 'Health and Mountains', in *Essays of Travel* (1916), p. 197; [J.A. Symonds], 'Davos in Winter', *Fortnightly Review*, (July 1878).

34   Croft, 'Nature and Growth . . . 1870–1900', p. 133; Stevenson, 'Health and Mountains', 'Alpine Diversions', 'The Stimulation of the Alps', and 'Davos in Winter', *Essays of Travel*, pp. 193–211; Conan Doyle, quoted in Andrew Lycett, *Conan Doyle* . . . (2007), pp. 190–1, 198, 202–3, 214; Tchaikovsky to Modest Tchaikovsky, 12–24 Nov. 1884, *Letters*, p. 317; J. A. Symonds and Margaret Symonds, *Our Life in the Swiss Highlands* (1907, 2nd edn), pp. xii, viii.

35   Tchaikovsky to Modest Tchaikovsky, 12–24 June 1870, *Letters*, p. 67; Shand, *Old-Time Travel*, pp. 44–5; advert in Continental Travel Ltd., *The Mediterranean, Italy, and Switzerland* . . . (n.d. [1909]), p.iii; University of Basel, Department of English, Literature & Culture Studies: British and American Visitors in Switzerland . . ., <www.pages.unibas.ch>; *The Times*, 1 Oct. 1902.

36   Lord Fortescue, d., 23 Sept. and 5 Oct. 1815, Fortescue MS, 1262 M/FD 20.

37   Guthrie, *Sundays Abroad*, p. 30; Martin Conway, *The Alps* (1904), p. 2; Shand, *Old-Time Travel*, p. 171.

38   J. D., 'Mont Blanc', *N.M.M.* (1821), I, p. 452; Barrow, *Tour on the Continent*, pp. 52–3.

39   *The Times*, 6 Dec. 1853; *The Musical World*, 28 Nov 1857; 'Holiday Walking Tours', *London Society* (1863), IV, pp. 85–94.

40   Stephen, *Playground of Europe*, p. xx.

41   *The Times*, 25 Nov. 1856.

42   G. C. Williamson, *The Cities of Northern Italy* (1908), p. 13.

43   See correspondence in Villari MS, especially *ff* 52–5, 120–1, 165–8, 207–10; Okey, *A Basketful of Memories*, p. 79; George Eliot, 'Recollections of Italy, 1860', *Journal*, p. 337; Susan Horner, d., 29 Sept. and 3 Oct. 1861, Horner MS.

44   Baedeker, *Italy. Handbook for Travellers . . .* (1879), pp. 347, 346; W. C. Bryant, Letter IV (11 Dec. 1834); *Letters of a Traveller . . .* (1851, New York), p. 31.

45   'Il Libro dei Soci, Gabinetto Scientifico MS. n.f. Laura Desideri, Il Vieusseux Storia di un Gabinetto di lettura 1819–2003', in *Chronologia Saggi Testimonianze*, Edizioni Polistampa (Florence, 2004), *passim*.

46   E. B. Browning to H. S. Boyd, 26 May 1847, in F. G. Kenyon (ed.), *The Letters of Elizabeth Barrett Browning*, 2 vols (1897), I, p. 331; Susan Horner, d., 8 Mar. 1848 and 8 Oct. 1861, Horner MS.

47   Susan Horner, d., 16 Oct. 1861, Horner MS; Shand, *Old-Time Travel*, pp. 239–40; Christopher Hibbert, *Florence: The Biography of a City* (1993), pp. 258–9, 288; 'The Peripatetic Politician – in Florence', *B.E.M.*, (Mar. 1863); Edward Hutton, *Florence and Northern Tuscany with Genoa* (1907), pp. 151–2.

48   Susan Horner, d., 30 Mar. 1848. Horner MS; W. E. Frye, *After Waterloo: Reminiscences of European Travel . . .* (1908), p. 170; N. P. Wiseman, *Recollections of the Last Four Popes . . .* 1858), p. 16; [Lord Chandos], *The Private Diary of Richard, Duke of Buckingham and Chandos*, 3 vols (1862), III, pp. 3–4; *The New York Times*, 20 June 1881.

49   James Estcourt to his grandfather, 23 Dec. 1831, Sotheron-Estcourt MS; Shand, *Old-Time Travel*, pp. 266–70; Stendhal, *Rome, Naples et Florence* (Paris, 1865 edn [1817]), p. 235; Fanny Kemble, *A Year of Consolation by Mrs. Butler*, 2 vols (1847, New York), I, pp. 58, 66; Matthews, d., 2 Feb. 1818; *Invalid*, I, p. 187; Strang, *Travelling Notes*, p. 106; Shand, *Old-Time Travel*, p. 294.

50   *Bradshaw's Hand-book to Italy* (1862), p. 160; Susan Horner, d., 1. Apr. 1848, Horner MS; Thomas Best, d., 10 Apr. 1859, Best MS; Harriet Scott to Lady Grantham, 22 Nov. 1829, Wrest Park MS, L30/13/24.

51   Fanny Lewald, *The Italian Sketchbook* (1852), p. 97; *Bradshaw's Illustrated Hand-Book to Italy*, pp. 150–60; Butler, *A Year of Consolation*, I, p. 66; Viscount Hinchinbrooke to Viscountess Sydney, 8 Jan. 1868, *Earl of Sandwich*, p. 87; Caroline Edgcumbe to W. H. Fox Talbot, 20 Feb. 1864, Fox Talbot MS, Doc. 08804; J. F. Maquire, *Rome: Its Ruler and Its Institutions* (1860), pp. 377–80.

52   Thomas Best, d., 10–26 Apr. 1859, Best MS; Shand, *Old-Time Travel*, p. 294.

53   Thomas Best, d., 17 Mar. 1859. Best MS; M. J. Torr, d., 18 Mar. 1872, Torr

MS, 57908; Matilda Lucas to ?, 11 Feb. 1878; Lucas, *Two Englishwomen*, p. 28.

54 Janet McNair to Florence Glynn, 8 Nov. 1886, Oglander MS, OG/CC/1559; Shand, *Old-Time Travel*, pp. 270–5; Julia Cartwright, d., 7 Nov. 1908, Angela Emanuel (ed.), *A Bright Remembrance* . . . (1989), pp. 297–8.

55 John Ruskin, *The Stones of Venice*, 2 vols (1900 edn), I, pp. 1, 2; John Julius Norwich, *Paradise of Cities: Nineteenth-century Venice* . . . (2003), pp. xiv–xv: this is the best account of the British role in Venice's nineteenth-century history.

56 Shand, *Old-Time Travel*, p. 252; Anon., *'Mems' of a Ten Weeks' Continental Trip* (1852) p. 18; Baedeker, *Italy . . . Northern Italy* . . . (1879), p. 220; Charlotte Horsman, d., 29 Oct. 1846, Horsman MS, D/RA/A/3E/26; Barrow, *Tour on the Continent*, p. 77.

57 Chaloner Chute, d., 5–9 Oct. 1873, Chute MS.

58 Shand, *Old-Time Travel*, 259; Baedeker, *Italy . . . Northern Italy* . . . (1889), p. 239; Henry James, *Portraits of Places* (2001 edn [1883]), pp. 13, 15.

59 *A Handbook for Travellers in Southern Italy* . . . (1853), p. 90; Lady Blessington, d., 18 July 1823, *The Idler*, pp. 244–5.

60 Charles Greville, d., 26 April 1830 in Henry Reeve (ed.), *The Greville Memoirs* . . ., 8 vols (1888, new edn), I, p. 353; Shand, *Old-Time Travel*, pp. 301–3; Hill MS, p 139.

61 Thomas Best, d., 7 Feb. 1859, Best MS; Walter Hazell, d., 19 Feb. 1885, Hazell MS; J. L. Maquay, d., 16 Nov. 1822, Maquay MS; Matthews, d., 1 Mar. 1818, *Invalid*, I, p. 229.

62 Power MS; Edward Lear to John Gould, 17 Oct. 1839, Vivien Noakes (ed.), *Edward Lear: Selected Letters* (Oxford, 1988), p. 47; Baedeker, *Italy: Handbook for Travellers . . . Southern Italy* . . . (1903, 14th edn), p. 33; Walter Hazell, d., 19 Feb. 1885, Hazell MS; Blewitt, *Southern Italy* (1853), p. 84; Bishop Hynes, d., 13 May 1843 and 29 Nov. 1859, Hynes MS.

63 Lady Morgan, quoted in Edith Clay (ed.), *Lady Blessington at Naples* (1979), p. 5; *The Times*, 1 Oct. 1897; Baedeker, *Italy . . . Southern Italy* (1903), p. xiii; *The Times*, 20 Mar. 1913.

64 *A Handbook for . . . Southern Italy* . . ., p. lvii; Edward Bulwer-Lytton, *The Last Days of Pompeii* (1850 edn [1834]), Bk I, p. 4; Judith Harris, *Pompeii Awakened* . . . (2007), *passim*.

65 Matthews, d., 19 Feb. 1818, *Invalid*, II, p. 216; Alison Cunningham, d., 13 Apr. 1863, *Cummy's Diary* . . . (1926), pp. 121–2; Walter Hazell, d., 19 Feb. 1885, Hazell MS.

66 Matthews, d., 22 Mar. 1818, *Invalid*, I, pp. 253–4; Thomas Best, d., 12 Feb. 1859, Best MS; R. J. B. Bosworth, *Italy and the Wider World 1860–1960* (1996), p. 163.

67   *Saturday Magazine*, 22 Feb.1834; *The Times*, 23, 30, 31 May 1853.

68   George Eliot, 'Recollections of our Journey from Munich to Dresden', *Journals*, p. 322; Anon., d., 29 Aug, 1842, Curtis (Journal) MS.

69   Nathaniel Newnham-Davis and Algernon Bastard, *The Gourmet's Guide to Europe* (1903), p. 199; John Wilson, *CB: A Life of Sir Henry Campbell-Bannerman* (1973), p. 139; *The Times*, 25 Sept. 1885.

70   Sigmund Münz, *King Edward VII at Marienbad* (1934), pp. 19–20; Camp-bell-Bannerman to Herbert Gladstone, 27 Aug. 1899, quoted in Wilson *CB* . . ., p. 142.

71   Trollope, *Vienna*, I, p. 107; Emily Birchell, d., 7 and 11 May 1873, David Verey (ed.), *Wedding Tour* . . . (1985, Gloucester), pp. 132,137; Richard Mullen, *Anthony Trollope* . . . (1990), p. 658; *A Handbook for Travellers in South Germany and Austria* . . . (1879), pp. 168, 197 *ff.*

72   Baedeker, *Austria-Hungary* . . . *Handbook for Travellers* (1905), p. xvi; *The Times*, 27 June 1904; *The Times*, 20 Nov. 1908, 4 May 1909.

CHAPTER 4 THE ENGLISHMAN'S BIBLE

1   'Gossip from Florence', *N.M.M.*, (Dec. 1853). The first use of 'guide-book' in the *OED* is in J. M. Colles (ed.), *The Journal of John Mayne* . . . (n.d. [1909]), p. 164. It is a diary entry from 25 Oct. 1814: *OED online*.

2   Edward Planta, *A New Picture of Paris* . . . (1814), pp. 55–6; Peter Hervé, *How to Enjoy Paris* . . . (1818), pp. 55, 146.

3   Galignani's *Paris Guide* . . . (1814), *passim*.

4   Robert Chambers, *Cyclopedia of English Literature* (1851), p. 671; *A Handbook for Travellers in Central Italy* . . . (1857), p. xxix; Rosamund Talbot to W. H. Fox Talbot, 31 July 1869, Fox Talbot MS, Doc. 9549; Joseph Forsyth, *Remarks on Antiquities* . . . (1813), p. 221.

5   J. C. Eustace, *A Classical Tour through Italy*, 2 vols (Paris, 1814), I, p. 12; G. S. Hillard, *Six Months in Italy* (Boston, 1854), p. 410; Josiah Conder, *Italy* (1831), pp. 372–3; Louis Simond, *A Tour in Italy and Sicily* (1828), pp. 11–12; Eustace, *A Classical Tour*, I, pp. 7, 2. The last edition appears to have been in 1841.

6   'A British Traveller', *The Pocket Courier or Traveller's Directory* (Brussels, 1830), *passim* authors' collection. There appears to be no copy in the Bodleian Library, the Cambridge University Library or the British Library.

7   Anthony Trollope, *The West Indies* . . . (1861), p. 244.

8   Information for this and the preceding paragraph from Starke, *Information* (1828), *passim*.

9   Mariana Starke, *Information and Directions* . . . (Paris, 1826), pp. iii, vi; Mariana Starke, *Travels in Europe* . . . (Paris, 1836), p. 6.

10 'Are There Those Who Read the Future?', *Bentley's Miscellany* (1848), XXIII, p. 344; W. H. G. Kingston, *My Travels in Many Lands* 1862), p. 50; 'Northern Italy', *F.M.*, (June 1843).

11 British Spinsterhood Abroad', *Dublin University Magazine*, Mar., 1854; 'American Travellers', *Putnam's Magazine*, (June 1855); *Notes & Queries*, 31 Jan. 1857, lines rearranged.

12 Titmarsh [W. M. Thackeray], *Little Travels and Road-Side Sketches*. III: *Waterloo*; *The Works of William Makepeace Thackeray . . .*, VI, p. 296; John Murray, 'The Origin and History of Murray's Handbooks for Travellers', *Murray's Magazine*, (Nov. 1889), quoted in George Paston, *At John Murray's . . .* (1932), p. 304.

13 Matilda Betham-Edwards, *Mid-Victorian Memories* (1919), pp. 156–7; Julia Cartwright, d., 18 May, 15 and 18 July 1898, *A Bright Remembrance*, pp. 226, 229. See W. B. C. Lister, *A Bibliography of Murray's Handbooks . . .* (Dereham, Norfolk, 1993).

14 [J. D. Forbes], 'Pedestrianism in Switzerland', *Quarterly Review*, (Apr. 1857), quoted in 'The Inexhaustible Capital', *B.E.M.*, (Apr. 1863); Charles Hervey, 'La Grotta del Cane: A Neapolitan Legend', *Ainsworth's Magazine* (1843), III, p. 187.

15 Shand, *Old-Time Travel*, p. 136; E. B. Browning to H.S. Boyd, 26 May 1847, *Letters of Elizabeth Barrett Browning*, I, p. 330.

16 Taine, *Notes on England*, pp. 306, 314.

17 *A Hand-Book for Travellers in Switzerland . . .* (1838), pp. lviii-lix; *A Handbook for Travellers in Switzerland . . .* (1867), pp. lxvii-lxviii; *A Handbook for Travellers in Central Italy . . .* (1867), pp. 2–3, 65.

18 Hillard, *Six Months*, pp. 557–8; F. C. Burnand, *Very Much Abroad* (1890), p. 367; Robert Ferguson, *Swiss Men and Swiss Mountains* (1853), pp. 37–8.

19 *A Handbook for Travellers in Central Italy . . .* (1867), p. 380; *A Handbook for Travellers in South Germany and Austria* (1879), p. 492; *A Handbook for Travellers in Southern Germany . . .* (1858), p. 451; *A Handbook for Travellers in Southern Germany* (1858), pp. 1–2; *A Handbook of Rome and the Campagna* (1899), pp. 6–8.

20 *A Handbook for Travellers in France . . .*, Part I (1882), p. 111; *A Handbook for Travellers in Central Italy . . .* (1861,), p. ii.

21 *A Handbook for Travellers in Central Italy . . .* (1867), pp. 77, 80; *A Handbook for Travellers in Switzerland and the Alps of Savoy and Piedmont . . .* (1838), p 24; *A Handbook for Travellers in Switzerland, and the Alps of Savoy and Piedmont* (1867), p. 29.

22 *A Handbook for Travellers in South Germany and Austria . . .* (1879), *passim*.

23 Effie Ruskin to her parents, 19 Nov. 1849, Mary Lutyens (ed.), *Young Mrs.*

Ruskin in Venice . . . (1965), p. 73; Mary Benson, d., 2 July 1859, Benson MS; J. Bayard Taylor, *Views A-Foot* . . . (1847, two parts), I, p. 54.

24 Gerald Codrington to Lady Georgiana Codrington, 8 July 1869, Codrington MS, Dep 1610 C112.

25 'Railway Literature Abroad', *N.M.M.* (1858), CXIII, pp. 109–10.

26 *The Times*, 7 Apr. 1875; Chaloner Chute, d., 10 Sept. 1873, Chute MS; *The Times*, 16 Aug 1879; Baedeker, *Belgium and Holland: Handbook for Travellers* (1888), pp. xi–xx.

27 Letter to the Editor, *The Times*, 21 Oct. 1887.

28 Murray, 'The Origin and History . . .', *Murray's Magazine*; Franz Baedeker to the Editor, *The Times*, 26 Nov. 1889; *The Times*, 28 May 1910. This section has made use of two important websites: <www.bdkr.com>, which incorporates articles from an earlier German website, 'Mitteilungen für Baedeker-Freunde' and other titles, and Edward Mendelson, 'Baedeker's Universe', at <www.ctrarebooks.com>.

29 *Bradshaw's Illustrated Travellers' Hand Book to France* . . . (1857), pp. iii, xxxiii.

30 See Victor Isaacs, 'Bradshaw's Travels on the Continent . . .', *The Journal of the Australian Association of Time Table Collectors*, (Jan. 2002).

31 Albert Smith, *The Story of Mont Blanc* (1853), p. 23; C. S. Drewry (ed.), *Report of Cases . . . in the High Court of Chancery in 1852 to 1859*, 4 vols (1853–60), I, pp. 353 *ff*; *Chambers's Handy Guide to Paris* . . . (1863), pp. i, 177–8; *The Times*, 31 July 1884.

32 Taine, *Notes on England*, p. 101; 'American Travellers', *Putnam's Magazine*, (June 1855); 'Dumas in Italy,' *B.E.M.*, (May 1843). See Richard Bright, *Travels from Vienna* . . . (1818); Pamela Bright, *Dr. Richard Bright 1789–1858* (1983), pp. 93–102.

33 'Modern Tourism', *B.E.M.*, (Aug. 1848); Charles Hervey, 'A Neapolitan Legend', *Ainsworth's Magazine* (1843), III, p. 187. For an excellent guide to women travel writers see Jane Robinson, *Wayward Women: A Guide to Women Traveller* (1990).

34 *Saturday Magazine*, 22 Feb. 1834.

35 J. M. Neale, *Notes, Ecclesiological and Picturesque* . . . (1861), p. vi; Matilda Betham-Edwards, *Holidays in Eastern France* (1879), <www.books.google. co.uk>, p. 5; Mrs Sarah Grand, 'Personal Sketch', in Betham-Edwards, *Mid–Victorian Memories*, pp. xix–xxiv.

36 G. B. Shaw to William Morris, 23 Sept. 1891, Okey, *A Basketful*, p. 123.

37 Lina Duff Gordon to Margaret Vaughan, 9 Jan. 1892, Waterfield MS; Arnold Bennett, 'Holiday Reading', in *Books and Persons* . . . (1917), p. 223.

38 Augustus Hare, *Walks in Rome*, 2 vols (1872), I, p. 24.

39 Ruskin, *Praeterita*, p. 69.

40 *The Poetical Works of Thomas Moore* (1860), p. 446.

41 W.M. Thackeray, *The Kickleburys on the Rhine* in *The Works of ...
    Thackeray*, IX, p. 190.

42 See F. C. Burnand, *Very Much Abroad* (1890); Arthur Sketchley [George
    Rose], *Mrs. Brown's Visit to the Paris Exhibition* (1878), pp. 3–4.

43 *Vanity Fair*, 6 Sept. 1900.

CHAPTER 5 THE CURSES OF THE TRAVELLER

1   ? Lucas to Lord Porchester, 5 May 1828, Carnarvon MS, 75M91/E43/91;
    Lady Dorothy Nevill, *Under Five Reigns* (1912), p. 39; Charles Feilding to
    W.H. Fox Talbot, 3 Aug. 1834, Fox Talbot MS, Doc. 02969.

2   Dawson Turner, *Account of a Tour in Normandy*, 2 vols (1820), II, p. 154.

3   Vivien Noakes, *Edward Lear ...* (2004, Stroud), p. 180; Quoted in F. E.
    Trollope, *Frances Trollope . . .*, 2 vols (1895), II, p. 87.

4   Henry Budd and G. B. Whittaker's passport (15 May 1838), Budd MS, 6/M/
    60/3. Jervoise MS, 44M69/E13/12/159/3; Elizabeth Wordsworth, *Glimpses of
    the Past* (n.d.), p. 76.

5   Haydon, *Autobiography*, p. 201; Charles Greville, d., 6 Mar. 1830, *The
    Greville Memoirs*, I, p. 288; Barrow, *A Tour*, pp. viii–ix.

6   Shand, *Old-Time Travel*, pp. 39–41; Parliamentary Papers, 1852, XXVIII:
    Accounts and Papers (Passports), pp. 545–7. The total for 1850–1 was 1,178
    while that for 1851–2 was 7,304.

7   Quoted in Lionel A. Tollemache, *Old and Odd Memories* (1908), pp. 32–3.

8   An example of a Lord Provost's passport may be found in the papers of the
    prominent Edinburgh surgeon Prof. Allen Thomson, in the Thomson MS.
    Francis Galton to S. T. Galton, 28 Mar. 1840; Karl Pearson, *The Life ... of
    Francis Galton*, 2 vols (Cambridge, 1914–39), I, p. 114.

9   Mullen, *Anthony Trollope*, p. 344.

10 Quoted in Jasper Ridley, *Lord Palmerston* (1970), p. 362.

11 *The Times*, 13 Dec. 1849; G. Harris to Lord Malmesbury, 14 Mar. 1853, the
    Earl of Malmesbury, *Memoirs of an Ex-Minister ...*, 2 vols (1884), I, p. 385.
    See Collection of Passports, 1802–1961, Chief Clerk's Department and
    Passport Office, FO 655, The National Archives.

12 Charles Dickens, 'Our French Watering-Place', *H.W.*, 4 Nov. 1854;
    Caroline Clive, d., 14 May 1838 in Mary Clive (ed.), *Caroline Clive ...*
    (1949), p. 50.

13 Croft, 'The Nature and Growth ... 1840–70', pp. 259–60 and 'The Nature
    and Growth ... 1870–1900', p. 134; Holmes, *A Ride on Horseback*, I, p. 2;
    'General Notes', in travel diary, Fortescue MS, 316.add.3M/F3/4; 'General

Notes. Aug. 1820', Torr MS, 316add3M/F3/4; T.A. Trollope's *Passé-port a l'Interieur*, Trollope-UCLA MS. *n.f.*

14   Alexander Gilchrist, *Life of William Etty, R.A.*, 2 vols (1865), I, p. 63; Leitch Ritchie, *Wanderings by the Loire* (1833), p. 2 n.1; *Notes of a Tour on the Continent*, pp. 178–9, Hill MS; Starke, *Information* (1828), p. 528; Beadles MS, 3438.

15   *A Handbook to Northern Italy Part II* (1856), pp. 447–8, 516; Bishop Hynes, d., 22 Jan. 1853, Hynes MS; W.H. Fox Talbot to Elisabeth Fielding, 2 Nov. 1823, Fox Talbot MS, Doc. 01111.

16   Lord Palmerston to Elizabeth Sulivan, 1 Sept. 1816, *Letters of the Third Viscount Palmerston . . .*, p. 133; Quoted in Noakes, *Edward Lear*, p. 52.

17   *The Times*, 13 Dec. 1849; *The Standard Library Cyclopaedia*, 4 vols (1849), IV, p. 484; *The Times*, 19 May 1851; *Galignani's New Paris Guide for 1853* (1853, Paris), p. 1.

18   Frances Wright to Jeremy Bentham, 12 Aug. 1822, Bentham MS, BL Add. MS 33545 *f* 588; Quoted in Martin Lloyd, *The Passport . . .* (2003, Stroud), p. 15.

19   Quoted in Lloyd, *The Passport*, p. 23; Ridley, *Lord Palmerston*, p. 75; Croft, 'The Nature and Growth . . . 1840–70', p. 262 *ff*; *A Handbook for Travellers in France. Part I. . . .* (1882), p. [18]; Benjamin Vincent, *Haydn's Dictionary . . .* (1892), p. 727.

20   Basil H. Jackson (ed.), *Recollections of Thomas Graham Jackson . . .* (1950), p. 98; See Baedeker, *Belgium and Holland*, (1888), p. xii; *The Times*, 11 Apr. 1882); Cooper, *The Walking Parson*, p. 240; John Jones, d., 2 Apr. 1862, Jones MS, 41674, *f* 14.

21   'The History of Passports', <www.ukpa.gov.uk>.

22   *The Observer*, 18 Aug. 1816; Bernard, *A Tour*, p. 2 *ff*.

23   E. C. Hawtrey to Mrs Elizabeth Hawtrey, 3 Aug. 1815, Hawtrey MS; Michel Chevalier, *Lettres sur L'Amérique du Nord*, 2 vols (1837, Brussels), I, pp. 352–3.

24   Beadles MS, 3438; Elisabeth Feilding to W.H. Fox Talbot, 27 Jul. 1817, Fox Talbot MS, No. 00773.

25   Bernard, *A Tour*, p 4; *Railway Times*, 30 May 1846; E.C. Hawtrey to his mother, 3 Aug. 1815, Hawtrey MS; Samuel Rogers, d., 20 Aug. 1814; J.R. Hale (ed.), *The Italian Journal of Samuel Rogers* (1956), p. 133.

26   Aubrey Newman, *The Stanhopes of Chevening . . .* (1969), p. 314; Fanny Burney to Princess Elizabeth, n.d., Joyce Hemlow (ed.), *Fanny Burney: Selected Letters and Journals* (1987, Oxford), p. 188.

27   Matthew Todd, d., 4 Sept. 1814, *Journal*, pp. 43–5; J. E. Morpurgo (ed.), *The Autobiography of Leigh Hunt* (1949), p. 289 *ff*.

28 Jonathan Law *et al.*, *Brewer's Theatre* . . . (1994), p. 140.

29 Lady Blessington, d., 5 and 27 Aug. 1822, *The Idler*, pp. 1–3; Thomas Campbell to ?, 10 Sept. 1825, *Life and Letters of Thomas Campbell*, II, p. 169; F. M. Hawtrey, The *History of the Hawtrey Family* 2 vols (1903), II, pp. 111–12.

30 Simon Pakenham, *Sixty Miles from England* . . . (1967), pp. 8, 21–2; Starke, *Information* (1828), p. 444.

31 Bernard, *A Tour*, p. 2; Starke, *Information* (1828), pp. 442–5; Jervoise MS, 44M69/E13/12/159/3.

32 E. C. Hawtrey to his mother, 3 Aug. 1815, Hawtrey MS; [Mary Wollestone-craft & Percy Bysshe Shelley], *History of a Six Weeks' Tour* . . . (1817), p. 3; Wilson, *A Three Weeks' Scamper*, p. 6; Henry T. Tuckerman, *A Month in England* (1854), p. 119; *The Times*, 25 Aug. 1859; *Gentleman's Magazine*, (Oct. 1859), II, p. 432; *D.N.B.* (1998), XVII, p. 1261.

33 Emma Roberts, *Notes of an Overland Journey* . . . (1841), p. 27; Charles Greville, d., 19 Jun. 1843, *Greville Memoirs*, V, p. 169.

34 Marianne Thornton to Patty Smith, n.d. [1817], Forster, *Marianne Thornton*, p. 98; *M.L.*, 24 Nov. 1827; W. A. Mumford, *William Ewart* . . . (1960), p. 136.

35 Susan Horner, d., 18 Sept. 1861, Horner MS; Henry Gaze, *Switzerland: How To See It for Ten Guineas* . . ., p. 13; Lady Augusta Stanley to ?, n.d. [1874]; A.V. Baillie and Hector Bolitho [eds.], *Later Letters of Lady Augusta Stanley* . . . (1929), p. 191; Chaloner Chute, d., 2 Nov. 1873, Chute MS; Miss Fife to Florence Oglander, 11 Jan. 1897, Oglander MS, OG/CC/1917B; Lytton Strachey, d., 16 Mar. 1913, Michael Holroyd (ed.), *Lytton Strachey* . . . (1971), p. 133.

36 W. M. Thackeray's *An Invasion of France* first appeared in *The Corsair* in 1839 and was then included in *The Paris Sketch Book* (1840).

37 Charles Dickens, 'A Flight', *H.W.*, 30 Aug. 1851.

38 John Torr, d., 3 May 1840, Cecil Torr (ed.), *Small Talk at Wreyland*, 3 vols (1970, Bath), II, p. 6.

39 *I.L.N.*, 1 July 1843; *The Times*, 2 Aug. 1843; *The Examiner*, May, 1850; Croft, 'The Nature and Growth . . . 1840–70', p. 252. The exact figures, taken from the ports' records, were 73,100 in 1840 and 179,751 in 1860 but these numbers would have included some non-British travellers.

40 Simmons, 'Railways, Hotels, and Tourism', p. 221 *ff*; Croft, 'The Nature and Growth . . . 1840–70', pp. 252–4, 264; Croft, 'The Nature and Growth . . . 1870–1900', pp. 129–31, 133–5; *Galignani's New Paris Guide for 1853*, pp. 1–2.

41 Rixon Bucknall, *Boat Trains and Channel Packets* . . . (1957), pp. 5, 16–17, 82–119; E. W. P. Veale, *Gateway to the Continent* . . . (1955), *passim*.

42 O. W. Hewett, *Strawberry Fair . . .* (1956), p. 247; Veale, *Gateway to the Continent*, pp. 48–9; Jacob Burckhardt to Max Alioth, 1 Aug. 1879, Alexander Dru (ed.), *The Letters of Jacob Burckhardt* (1955), p. 189; Leveson Gower, *Years of Content*, p. 86; Bucknall, *Boat Trains*, p. 108; *I.L.N.*, 30 Sept. 1882; Henry Mayhew, Letter XLVI, *The Morning Chronicle*, 3 Apr. 1850.

43 Boulogne Chamber of Commerce, *Trafic Franco-Anglais* (n.d. [1889]), quoted in Croft, 'The Nature and Growth . . . 1870–1900', pp. 137–9; Veale, *Gateway to the Continent*, pp. 50, 52–3.

44 Lord Derby to Ponsonby, 10 Feb. 1875, Victoria to Ponsonby, [?]11 Feb. 1875, Victoria to Disraeli, 9 Feb. 1875 in G.E. Buckle (ed.), *The Letters of Queen Victoria . . .*, 2 vols (1926), II, 380n and II, pp. 380–1; *I.L.N.*, 23 Aug. 1884; Vincent, *Haydn's Dictionary*, pp. 999, 196.

45 Baedeker, *Paris and Environs . . .* (1896), p. 378–96; Simmons, 'Railways, Hotels, and Tourism', pp. 215–18; Croft, 'The Nature and Growth . . . 1870–1900', pp. 135–40; Gerbod, 'Voyageurs et residents britanniques', pp. 27–34; *I.L.N.*, 23 Aug. 1884.

46 E. Œ. Somerville and Martin Ross, *In the Vine Country* (2001), pp. 16–17, 20.

47 Viator Verax [The Rev. G.M. Musgrave], *Cautions for the First Tour . . .* (1863), pp. 8–9; Hawtrey, *Hawtrey Family*, II, pp. 111–12; 'The English at Home by a Frenchman Abroad', *B.E.M.*, (Jan. 1854); William Liddiard, *A Three Months' Tour . . .* (1832), p. 7.

48 Martha Wilmot, d., 1 Aug. 1819 and Martha Wilmot to Alicia Wilmot, 31 Jul. 1819, The Marchioness of Londonderry & H.M. Hyde [eds.], *More Letters from Martha Wilmot . . .* (1935), pp. 2, 5; Thomas Sheardown, *An Autobiography* (1865), <www.rootsweb.com>, ch. 2. n.p.

49 Gilchrist, *Life of Etty*, I, p. 62.

50 *Galignani's New Paris Guide for 1853*, pp. 28–9.

51 Anon., *'Mems' of a Ten Weeks' Continental Trip*, p. 31; Edward Leeves, d., 3 July 1850, John Sparrow (ed.), *Leaves from a Victorian Diary* (1985), p. 105; Mullen, *Anthony Trollope*, p. 640.

52 Sheardown, *An Autobiography*, ch. 2. n.p.; J. I. Tucker, d., 12 Dec. 1850; C. W. Knauff, *Doctor Tucker, Priest-Musician . . .* (1897, New York), <www.morgue.anglicansonline.org>.

53 Samuel Ward, d., n.d. [Nov. 1832], M. H. Elliott, *Uncle Sam Ward and His Circle* (New York, 1938), p. 46.

54 Douglas Jerrold, *Mrs. Caudle's Curtain Lectures* (1902 edn.), p. 146.

55 Starke, *Information* (1828), p. 528; Cobbett, *Journal*, p. 113.

56 Gilchrist, *Life of Etty*, I, pp. 61–2, 69; *Galignani's New Paris Guide for 1853*, p. 54.

57 James Estcourt to his grandfather, 23 Dec. 1831, Sotheron-Estcourt MS;

Bishop Hynes, d., 6 Jan. 1853, Hynes MS; 'The Roving Englishman', *H.W.*, 13 Nov. 1852.

58 Cranley Onslow to George Onslow, 9 Jan. 1820, Onslow MS.

59 Anon., *A Digest of the Proceedings and Reports of the Committee of London Merchants for Reform of the Board of Customs* (1852), pp. 234, 50; T. E. Lawrence to his mother, 4 Aug. 1906, Lawrence MS, 3342 *ff* 1–3; Gerbod, 'Voyageurs et residents britanniques', p. 27; Alfred Domett, d., 5 Nov. 1874, E.A. Horsman (ed.), *The Diary of Alfred Domett* . . . (1953), p. 135; Baedeker, *Italy* . . . *Northern Italy* (1879), p. xv; George C. Williamson, *The Cities of Northern Italy* (1908), p. 29.

60 G. L.Gower, *Mixed Grill* (1947), pp. 43–4.

CHAPTER 6 KEEP MOVING!

1 Geoffrey Crayon, [Washington Irving], *Tales of a Traveller* (1824, Philadelphia), pp. 47–8, 21; John Ruskin, *Praeterita*, pp. 95–6.

2 'Register: Scottish Chronicle', *B.E.M.* (Mar. 1818); Byron to John Cam Hobhouse, 1 May 1816, Peter Quennell (ed.), *Byron . . . Letters and Diaries 1798 to 1824* (1950, Oxford), p. 336.

3 Martha Bradford to Catherine Wilmot, 3 Sept. 1819, *More Letters* . . ., pp. 10–11.

4 M. E. Lucy, *Mistress of Charlecote* . . . (1983), pp. 62–3.

5 Ruskin, *Praeterita* . . ., pp. 95–6; *Mary Boyle*, pp. 103–4.

6 Warren Vernon, *Recollections* . . . (1917), pp 8–9; Charles Dickens to John Forster, n.d., quoted in Forster, *Charles Dickens*, p. 441; Sir Herbert Taylor, 'Notes on His Journey', Ernest Taylor (ed.), *The Taylor Papers* . . . (1913), p. 415.

7 *Gailgnani's Messenger*, 11 Dec 1828.

8 Charles Dickens, 'Travelling Abroad', *A.Y.R.*, 7 Apr. 1860.

9 Starke, *Information* (1828), p. 3; Cobbett, *A Ride*, pp. 7–8.

10 Hudson MS, *f* 36; Charlotte Horsman, d., 29 Oct. 1846, Horsman MS, D/RA/A/3E/26.4.

11 Lord Fortescue, d., 29 July 1819, Fortescue MS, 316 add.3M/F3/1; Robert Parker, d., 11 Aug. 1818, Shelley MS, 18M51/560.

12 Starke, *Information* (1828), p. 444; Martha Bradford to Alicia Wilmot, 1 Aug. 1819, Londonderry and Hyde (eds), *More Letters* . . ., p. 4; W. H. Fox Talbot to Elizabeth Feilding, 16 Nov. 1823, Fox Talbot MS, Doc. 01117.

13 Lady Fremantle to T. F. Fremantle, 27 May [1817], Fremantle MS, D/FR/83/;. E. C. Stanton, *Eighty Years and More* . . . (1898), p. 94; Isabel Arundell, *My Continental Tour: Switzerland*, quoted in W. H. Wilkins, *The Romance of Lady Isabel Burton* . . ., 2 vols (1897), II, p. 118; Ruskin, *Praeterita*, p. 95.

14 Barrow, *Tour on the Continent*, p. vii; Viator, *Cautions* . . ., pp. 56–7, 43–4; Gerald Codrington, d., n.d., Codrington MS, D 1610 C 112; Caroline Clive, d., 23 May 1838, *Caroline Clive*, p. 54.

15 Barrow, *Tour on the Continent*, p. vii; W. M. Thackeray to Whom It May Concern, 12 Aug. 1843, Gordon N. Ray (ed.), *The Letters and Private Papers of William Makepeace Thackeray*, 4 vols (Cambridge, MA, 1945–46), II, p. 119; ? to Robert Hudson, 26 Aug. 1840, Hudson MS; Advert in *A Handbook for Travellers in Central Italy* . . . (1867), pp. 29, 22; Thomas Best, d., 26 Oct. 1858, Best MS; Hudson MS.

16 Elizabeth Maquay, d., 22 July 1815, Maquay MS; Georgiana, Baroness Bloomfield, *Reminiscences* . . ., 2 vols (1883), I, p. 19.

17 Matthew Todd, d., n.d., *Journal*, p. 149; Mark Twain, *A Tramp Abroad* (1880), ch. 24.

18 Lucy, *Mistress of Charlecote*, pp. 68–9; Martin Tupper, *My Life as an Author* (1880), pp. 181–2; Derek Hudson, *Martin Tupper* . . . (1949), pp. 142–3; Twain, *A Tramp Abroad*, chs. 32–3.

19 *Mary Boyle*, pp. 117–18; Charles Dickens to Angela Burdett Coutts, 1 Nov. 1848, Edgar Johnson (ed.), *The Heart of Charles Dickens* . . . (1952), pp. 131–2.

20 Emily Birchall, d., 25 Jan., 8 Feb., 19 Apr. 1873, *Wedding Tour*, pp. 1, 14–15, 113.

21 *Galignani's New Paris Guide for 1853*, p. 13; Walter, *My Secret Life*, V, ch. I and VI, ch. II.

22 Mrs. [C. M.] Kirkland, *Holidays Abroad* . . . (1949, New York), I, pp. 119–20; James Fennimore Cooper, *Excursions in Italy* (1838), pp. 16–17; Kirkland, *Holidays Abroad*, I, p. 120; Rosamund Talbot to W. H. Fox Talbot, 2 Nov. 1867, Fox Talbot MS, Doc. 09267; Trollope, *Vienna and the Austrians*, I, p. 11.

23 Arthur Sullivan and F.C. Burnard, *The Chieftan*, Act II, The Gilbert and Sullivan Archive, <www.math.boisestate.edu>.

24 Anon., 'The Roving Englishman', *H.W.*, 13 Nov. 1852; Robert Parker, d., 11 Aug. 1818, Shelley MS, 18M51/559.

25 *Murray's Handbook to Switzerland* (1838), pp. xiv–xv; *Autobiography of Leigh Hunt*, p. 400; Curtis (Journal) MS; Lewis Agassiz, *A Journey To Switzerland* (1833), p. 279.

26 Kemble, *A Year of Consolation*, I, p. 65; Martha Bradford to Edward Wilmot, 11 May 1828, *More Letters* . . ., p. 318; *Notes of a Tour*', p. 59, Hill MS; *M.L.*, 10 Nov. 1827.

27 Links, *The Ruskins in Normandy*, pp. 30–1; Walter, *My Secret Life*, V, ch. 1.

28 Henry James, 'The Old Saint Gothard', *Travelling in Italy*, p. 319.

29 *Galignani's New Paris Guide for 1853*, pp. 2–3, quoted in Mrs Gerald

Porter, *Annals of a Publishing House: John Blackwood*, 3 vols (1898), III, p. 7; F. E. Trollope, *Frances Trollope*, II, p. 40; Charles Greville, d., 6 Mar. 1830, *The Greville Memoirs*, I, p. 288; Thomas S. Sheardown, *Half a Century's Labors in the Gospel . . .* (New York, 1865), Tri-Counties Genealogy and History, <www.rootsweb.com>; Bishop Hynes, d., 30 Dec. 1852, Hynes MS.

30 Matthew Todd, d., 24 Oct., 1814, *Journal*, p. 59; The Rev George Brett, d., 7 Aug. 1828; C. H. Dudley Ward, *A Romance . . .* (1923), pp. 52–3; Shand, *Old-Time Travel*, p. 208; Emma Roberts, *Notes of an Overland Journey . . .* (1841), p. 49.

31 Charles Dickens, 'A Flight', *H.W.*, 30 Aug. 1851; Roberts, *Notes of an Overland Journey*, p. 53; Athony Trollope, *He Knew He Was Right*, ch. 37; quoted in Michael Sadleir, *Trollope: A Commentary* (1961), pp. 330–1.

32 Cobbett, *Journal*, p. 9.

33 Robert Ferguson, *Swiss Men and Swiss Mountains* (1853), p. 131; Edward Horsman, d., 28 Aug. 1828, Horsman MS, D/RA/A/3E/20; Cecil [?] Torr, d. 23 Aug. 1871, Torr MS, 009–915 MS 36. Z19/36/22^c.

34 Starke, *Information* (1828), p. 510; Lady Fremantle to T. F. Fremantle, 17 Oct. 1815, Fremantle MS.

35 William Etty to Mrs Bodley, n.d. [Sept. 1816], Gilchrist, *Life of William Etty . . .*, I, p. 66; Caroline Edgcumbe to W. H. Fox Talbot, 19 Dec. 1834, Fox Talbot MS, Doc. 03022; Isabella Arundell, *My Continental Tour*, quoted in Wilkins, *The Romance . . .*, II, pp. 118–19; George Eliot, 'Recollections of Italy, 1860', *Journals*, p. 336.

36 George T. Lowth, *The Wanderer in Western France* (1863), p. 2; Basil H. Jackson (ed.), *Recollections of Thomas Graham Jackson . . .* (1950), pp. 97–9; N. Robinson, 'The Comforts and Discomforts of Travel', *Frank Leslie's Popular Monthly*, (Aug. 1882); William Etty, d., ? Oct. 1823, quoted in Gilchrist, *Life of William Etty . . .*, I, p. 201.

37 'Paris in 1851,' *B.E.M.*, (Aug. 1851); Anon., *Adventures with my Stick and Carpet Bag . . .* (1855), p. 9; Pakenham, *Sixty Miles*, p. 41; Croft, 'The Nature and Growth . . . 1840–70', *passim*.

38 *Bogue's Guides for Travellers: Switzerland and Savoy* (1852), n.p, 'The East and South of Europe'.

39 Anon., 'The Roving Englishman', *H.W.*, 13 Nov. 1852; George Ticknor to W. S. Dexter, 24 Sept. 1856 and George Ticknor to Mrs W.S. Dexter, 26 Sept., 1856, quoted in [G.S. Hillard], *Life, Letters, and Journals of George Ticknor*, 2 vols (Boston, 1877), II, pp. 334–5; Georges d'Avenel, *L'Evolution des moyens de transport . . .* (Paris, 1919), pp. 54, 102; J. T. Delane to G. W. Dasent, 29 Sept. 1859, quoted in Arthur Dasent, *John Thadeus Delane . . .*, 2 vols (1908), I, pp. 319–20.

40 Susan Horner, d., 27 Nov. 1847, Horner MS; *Bradshaw's Illustrated Travellers' Hand Book in France* (1857), p. xxxiv; Walter White, *On foot Through Tyrol* . . . (1856), p. 13; [Hodder], *Old Merry's Travels*, p. 10.

41 Strang, *Travelling Notes* . . ., p. 50; Thomas Best, d., 24 Nov. 1858, Best MS; Anon., *The Railway Traveller's Handy Book of Hints* . . . (1971, Bath edn), pp. 90–2; Baedeker, *Italy from the Alps to Naples: Handbook for Travellers* (1909), p. xii.

42 *The Railway Traveller's*, pp. 90–2; Erasmus Wilson, *A Three Weeks' Scamper* . . . (1858), p. 27, quoted in W. P. Fetridge, *Hand-Books for Travellers in Europe* . . ., 3 vols (New York, 1896), II, p. 549; 'Paris in 1851'; [Hodder], *Old Merry's Travels*, p. 39; Baedeker, *Italy from the Alps to Naples*, p. xii.

43 Jackson (ed.), *Recollections*, pp. 96–7; 'Some Circular Notes: Chapter II', *Punch* (Aug. 1891); Archibald Marshall, *A Spring Walk in Provence* (1914), p. 41.

44 'The Mount Cenis Railway and Tunnel', *Harper's New Monthly Magazine*, (July 1871); *A Handbook for Travellers in Switzerland and the Alps of Savoy and Piedmont* (1867), pp. 445–6; Henry James, 'From Chambéry to Milan', *Travelling in Italy* . . ., pp 305–6; Burnard and Sullivan, *The Chieftan*, Act I.

45 'The St. Gothard Tunnel', *Harper's New Monthly Magazine*, (Oct. 1878); Samuel Butler, *Alps & Sanctuaries* . . . (1986, Gloucester), p. 22.

46 Frank T. Marzials, *Life of Dickens* (1887), p. 93; A. E. Housman to Lucy Housman, 27 Sept. 1900, Archie Burnett (ed.), *The Letters of A.E. Housman*, 2 vols (2007, Oxford), I, pp. 123–4.

47 Susan Horner, d., 25 Dec. 1847, Horner MS.

48 The Hon Mrs Ellen Twistleton to her sisters, 26 Dec. 1852, quoted in [Ellen Twisleton Vaughan, ed], *Letters of the Hon. Mrs. Edward Twisleton* . . . (1928), pp. 64–5; *Daily News*, 28 Mar. 1856; 'The East and South of Europe'.

49 J. S. Blackie to his wife, 24 Apr. 1853, in A. S. Walker (ed.), *The Letters of John Stuart Blackie to his Wife* . . . (1909), p. 129; Oscar Wilde, 'Art and the Handicraftsman', *Essays and Lectures* (1909), p. 295; George Ticknor to W. S. Dexter, 24 Sept. 1856 and George Ticknor to Mrs. W.S. Dexter, 26 Sept., 1856, quoted in Hillard, *Life* . . ., II, p. 335; Ruskin, *Praeterita*, pp. 95–6.

50 Bill Cormack, *A History of Holidays 1812–1990* (1998), p. 58; *Macmillan's Guide to Switzerland* (1904), cviii.

51 Percy Dearmer, *Highways and Byways in Normandy* (1904), pp. 1, 3; Itinerary of the Rev. C. J. Sharp, Vicar of Hornsey, in Dearmer book, authors' collection; note on Lawrence to his mother, 6 Aug. 1906, Lawrence

to his mother, 4 Aug. 1906, 26 Aug. 1907, 2 and 28 Aug. 1908 Lawrence MS 3342 *ff* 1–3, and Jeremy Wilson, *Lawrence of Arabia* (1989), pp. 25–52.

52   W. F. Cater (ed.), *Love Among the Butterflies* . . . (1980), pp. 107–16.

53   *The Times*, 8 June 1899 and 16 Nov 1911.

54   *The Times*, 25 Feb. 1913.

55   William Joynson-Hicks, MP, quoted in *The Times*, 9 July 1909; *The Graphic*, 12 May 1900; *The Times*, 9 Sept. 1907.

56   Baedeker, *Southern France* . . . (1914), p. xvii; *The Times*, 19 Mar. 1914.

57   *The Times*, 2 Apr. and 11 June 1912; Erskine, *Memoirs*, p. 258.

58   'Motor Touring Abroad: Simple Hints for Women', *The Times*, 28 May 1910.

59   Rudyard Kipling, *Souvenirs of France* (1933), *passim*; advert in Continental Travel Ltd., *The Mediterranean* . . ., p. ii; Baedeker, *Southern France* (1914), p. 567; R. P. Graves, *A.E. Housman: The Scholar-Poet* (1981, Oxford), p. 155; Blanche McManus, *The American Woman Abroad* (1911), ch. 12. n.p.; <www.kellscraft.com>.

60   Lt. Francis Grenfell, d., 25 July, 11 Aug., 6 Sept., Grenfell MS; Erskine, *Memoirs*, p. 243; C. W. Stamper, *What I Know* (1913), *passim*.

61   *The Times*, 18 Feb. 1914.

CHAPTER 7 IS THE LUGGAGE SAFE?

1   Starke, *Information* (1826), p. 329; Lillias Davidson, *Hints to Lady Travellers* . . . (1889), p. 238; Hudson MS; Fitzgerald, *A Day's Tour*, Part III, 'The Packet'.

2   'The Roving Englishman', *H.W.*, 13 Nov. 1852; J. F. Clarke, *Eleven Weeks in Europe* (1852), p. 168; Augustus Hare, d., 30 Jan. 1874, Malcolm Barnes (ed.), *In My Solitary Life* . . . (1953), p. 40.

3   Lowe, *Unprotected Females*, p 3; Emily Birchall, d.,1 May 1873, *Wedding Tour*, p. 124; William Hardman, d., [29] July 1863; S. M. Ellis (ed.), *The Letters of Sir William Hardman* . . . *Second Series* . . . (1925), p. 58.

4   H. F. Talbot to his mother, 5 Mar. 1824, Fox Talbot MS, Doc. 1174; *Stanford's Paris Guide* (1858), p. 18; 'Three Weeks in Bonn', *The Illustrated Parlour Miscellany* (1849), pp. 168–9.

5   *Macmillan's Guide to Switzerland* (1904), p. lxxxiv; 'Memorandums of a View-Hunter', *B.E.M.*, (July 1817); 'Zig-Zag to Paris, and Straight Home', *Ainsworth's Magazine* (1850), XVII, p. 212; *Galignani's New Paris Guide for 1827* (1827), p 2; *Gaze's Tourist Gazette*, (June 1899), p. 1.

6   'The Carpet Bag', *C.J.*, (30 Sept. 1854).

7   C. M. Sedgwick, *Letters from Abroad* . . ., 2 vols (New York, 1841), I, p. 182.

8   Isabella Beeton, *The Book of Household Management* (1861), p. 965; Lady

Shelley, d., 5 Nov. 1854, Richard Edgcumbe (ed.), *The Diary of Frances Lady Shelley* . . ., 2 vols (1912–13), II, p. 382.

9   *Notes & Queries*, 25 Jan. 1851; *Official Descriptive and Illustrated Catalogue By Great Britain Commissioners for the Exhibition of 1851* (1851), p. 1229.

10   Bishop Hynes, d., 1 Jan. 1853, Hynes MS; Guido Mountjoy, 'The Comic Alpenstock', *Dublin University* Magazine, (Oct. 1847); Gaze, *Outline Plan Holland and Belgium*, p 7; William White, quoted in Mark Girouard, *The Victorian Country House* (1979), pp. 252–3.

11   Orville Dewey, *The Old World and the New* . . . (New York, 1836), p 240; Anne Bowman, *The Common Things of Every-day Life* . . . (1857), p 162.

12   G. D. Ruffini, *The Paragreens* . . . (1856), ch. 1.

13   Starke, *Travels in Europe* (1828), p. 441; Robley Dunglison, *Medical Lexicon* . . . (1846), *passim*; Mountjoy, 'The Comic Alpenstock'.

14   William Brockedon, *Journals of Excursions in the Alps* (1833), p. 276; Starke, *Travels in Europe* (1828), p. 440; Baedeker, *Spain and Portugal* . . . (1908), p. xxix; Malmesbury, *Memoirs of an Ex-Minister*, I, pp. 28–9; Baedeker, *Central Italy and Rome* . . . (1909), p. x.

15   'The Roving Englishman', *H.W.*, 13 Nov. 1852; Croft, 'The Nature and Growth . . . 1840–70', p. 262; Lindy Woodhead, *Shopping, Seduction & Mr Selfridge* (2007), p. 3; Norah Waugh, *Corsets and Crinolines* (1954), pp. 127 *ff*; Mary Eyre, *A Lady's Walks* . . . (1865), p. 1.

16   Gaze, *Holland and Belgium* . . ., p. 7.

17   'The Roving Englishman', *H.W.*, 13 Nov. 1852.

18   Joseph Strutt to his father, 26 Aug. 1820, Galton MS, MS 3101/C/E/5/17/9; Granville Lloyd Baker to his mother, 24 Mar. 1864, Lloyd-Baker MS.

19   Oscar Browning, *Memories of Sixty Years* . . . (1910), p. 55; Macmillan, *Guide to Switzerland* (1904), p. lxxxiii.

20   Jerome, *Pilgrimage*, p. 15; Lady Vavasour, *My Last Tour and First Work* . . . (1842), p. 13; Blanchard Jerrold, *The Life* . . . *of Douglas Jerrold*, p. 168.

21   Hillard, *Six Months*, p. 270; Joseph Conrad, *A Personal Record* . . . (2005), p. 40.

22   Richard Doyle, *The Foreign Tour of Messrs Brown, Jones and Robinson* (1855), p. 74; Richard Temple-Nugent-Brydges-Chandos-Grenville, *The Private Diary of Richard, Duke of Buckingham*, 3 vols (1862), I, pp. 135–8; *A Handbook for Travellers* . . . *Holland* . . . *Switzerland* (1853), p. xxvii; *Chambers's Handy Guide to Paris* . . . (1863), p. 178; *Notes and Queries*, 1 Aug. 1891.

23   Hervé, *How to Enjoy Paris* . . . (1818), p.120; Zamoyski, *Rites of Peace* (2007), p. 192; Quoted in Mullen and Munson, *Victoria*, pp. 68–9.

24   Mullen and Munson, *Victoria*, pp. 68–9; 'Aesthetics of Dress', *B.E.M.*, (Feb.

1846); George Augustus Sala, *Dutch Pictures* . . . (1861), p. 262; 'A Righi Day,' *N.M.M.*, (July 1854).

25   Beadles MS, 3439.

26   O. A. Sherrard, d., 30 July 1860, *Two Victorian Girls* (1966), p. 163; John Strang, *Travelling Notes in France* . . . (1863, Glasgow), p. 44.

27   Laura Balfour to A. J. Balfour, n.d. [1890], Balfour MS, GD 433/2/477; Davidson, *Hints to Lady Travellers*, p. 43.

28   *New York Times*, 27 Mar. 1898; Annesley, *My Parisian Year*, pp. 241-2.

29   *H.W.* (1853) p. 270. See advertisement in *Bradshaw's Illustrated Hand-Book to Italy* . . . (1862), p. 280.

30   *The Graphic*, 10 Oct. 1896; Augustus Hare to his mother, 18 July 1853, Augustus J.C. Hare, *The Story of My Life*, 6 vols (1896), I, p. 435; Shand, *Old-Time Travel*, pp. 42-3.

31   Torr, *Small Talk at Wreyland*, I, pp. 74-5.

32   Johann Georg Kohl, *Austria* . . . (1844), p. 2.

33   Gaze, *Switzerland: How To See It* . . ., pp. 22-4; C. W.Chute, d., 10 Sept. 1873, Chute MS; 'Hints from a Swiss Notebook', *Tait's Edinburgh Magazine*, (July 1852).

34   R. S. Charnock, *Guide to the Tyrol* (1857), p. 101; Macmillan, *Guide to Switzerland*, p. xcii.

35   C. D.Warner, *Complete Works of Charles Dudley Warner*. Vol. II. *Saunterings. Alpine Notes: Our English Friends*; <www.gutenberg.org>.

36   *The Graphic*, 24 Oct. 1874; H. W.Cole, *A Lady's Tour Round Monte Rosa* (1859), pp. 7-9; Macmillan, *Guide to Switzerland*, pp. lxxxiii, xcii.

CHAPTER 8 ENGLISH COMFORTS AND ENGLISH SANITATION

1   Lady Holland to Francis Horner, 1 Oct. 1816, Leonard Horner (ed.), *Memoirs and Correspondence of Francis Horner*, 2 vols (1853), II, p. 373; Alfred Elwes' *Dictionnaire Français-Anglais* . . . (1855), p. 211; H. H. Woods, d., 25 June 1827, Curtis (Woods) MS.

2   Cobbett, *Journal*, p. 167; Mr Moncrieff, *M.L.*, 23 Feb. 1839.

3   The Rev Isaac Taylor, *Scenes in Europe* . . . (1821), p. 67.

4   Quoted in Lady Dorothy Nevill, *Under Five Reigns* (1910), p. 40.

5   Charles Lever, *The Confessions of Harry Lorrequer* (1839), IV, p. 25; J. L. Maquay, Snr, d., 17 Oct. 1814, Maquay MS; Antoine-Claude Pasquin dit Valéry, *Voyages historiques et littéraires en Italie* (1843), p. 25; Valéry, *Voyages en Corse* . . ., 2 vols (1837), I, p. 82; 'The East and South of Europe'.

6   'Back Again,' *C.J.*, 10 Jan. 1863; Lady Blessington, d., 1 Sept. 1822, *The Idler*, p. 9; 'Travelling Englishmen', *E.C.J.*, 22 Oct. 1853; *The Times*, 25 Mar. 1853.

7   Anthony Trollope, *Autobiography* (1950 edn), p. 113; Marianne North [Mrs John Addington Symonds, ed.], *Some Further Recollections of a Happy Life* . . . (1893), p. 3; C. R. Weld, *The Pyrenees, West and East* (1859), p. 35.

8   *Bradshaw's Illustrated Travellers' Hand Book in France* (1857), p. 226; Helen Mason, d., 17 Nov. 1859, Wickham MS; Sibella Bonham Carter, d., 19 Oct. 1894, Bonham Carter MS, 94M72/F166.

9   Starke, *Information* (1828), p. 452; *Galignani's New Paris Guide for 1853*, p. 12 and n. 1.

10   *A Handbook for Southern Germany and Austria* (1879), *passim*; Baedeker, *Paris and Its Environs* (1896), pp. 3–5; Baedeker, *Italy from the Alps to Naples* (1909), p. 113. See *Macmillan's Guide to Switzerland* (1904), p. lxxxvii.

11   Viator, *Cautions*, p. 12; Shand, *Old-Time Travel*, p. 369; Lord Clarendon to the Duchess of Manchester, 17 Aug. 1861; A. L. Kennedy (ed.), '*My Dear Duchess*' . . . (1956), p. 167; *The Washington Post*, 22 Oct. 1851.

12   Trollope, *Autobiography*, pp. 114–15; Baedeker, *Italy: Handbook for Travellers* (1903), p. xix; *Macmillan's Guide to Switzerland* (1904), p. lxxxvii.

13   John Blackwood to his parents, n.d. [1834] in Porter, *Annals*, III.9; *A Handbook for Travellers in South Germany and Austria* . . . (1879), p. xviii; 'The Roving Englishman', *H.W.*, 25 Dec. 1852.

14   Charles Matthews and Lady Blessington, quoted in Michael Sadleir, *Blessington-D'Orsay: A Masquerade* (1933), pp. 96–7; Trollope, *Vienna and the Austrians*, I, pp. 240–1.

15   Lady Blessington, d.,1 Sept. 1822, *The Idler*, p. 9; C. W. Cope, *Reminiscences of Charles West Cope* . . . (1891), pp. 56–8; Lord Malmesbury, d., 22 Mar. 1832, *Memoirs of an Ex-Minister*, I, p. 49; Wilson, *Three Weeks Scamper*, pp. 149–50.

16   *A Handbook for Travellers on the Continent* . . . *Holland* . . . *Switzerland* (1854), p. 200; Susan Horner, d., 10 Dec. 1847, Horner MS; Butler, 'Our Tour'; *A Handbook for Travellers on the Continent* . . . *Holland* . . . *Switzerland* (1854), p. 200.

17   J. L. Maquay, Snr, d., 14 Sept. 1815, Maquay MS; Lord Fortescue, d., 27 Sept. 1815, Fortescue MS, 1262 M/FD 20; Starke, *Information* (1828), pp. 440–2; 'Memorandums of a Month's Tour in Sicily', *B.E.M.* (July 1844); Mary Wilson, d., 13 July 1847, Simpson (ed.), *A European Journal*, p. 163; Doyle, *Brown, Jones and Robinson*, p. 31.

18   J. A. Symonds to H. G. Dakyns, 30 Apr. 1873, H. M. Schueller & R.L. Peters [eds.], *The Letters of John Addington Symonds*, 3 vols (Detroit, MI, 1967), II, pp. 295–6; Okey, *A Basketful of Memories*, p. 129.

19   Lord Byron, d., 17 Sept. 1816, in *Alpine Journal*; <www.engphil.astate.edu>; Trollope, *Vienna and the Austrians*, I, p. 179.

20   Gerald Codrington to his mother, n.d. [May 1869], Codrington MS, D1610
     C 112; McManus, *The American Woman Abroad*, p. 308.

21   *A Hand-Book for Travellers in Switzerland* (1838), *passim*; Caius, 'Notes by
     the Road. II', *The American Whig Review* (Nov. 1846); Martha Wilmot to
     her sister, 3 Sep. 1819, *More Letters*, p. 20.

22   G. P. Jervoise, d., 25 July 1826, Jervoise MS, 44M69/E13/12/159(2); 'Some
     Circular Notes', *Punch*, 5 Sept. 1892; *Notes of a Tour*, p. 34, Hill MS.

23   Anthony Trollope, quoted in Mullen, *Anthony Trollope*, p. 602; Doyle,
     Brown, Jones and Robinson, p. 17; Jerome, *Pilgrimage*, p. 86.

24   Cobbett, *Journal*, p. 4; John Ruskin, *Praeterita*, p. 402; Twain, *A Tramp
     Abroad*, Appendix A: 'The Portier'; Henry James, *A Little Tour in France*
     (Oxford, 1984), pp. 83–4.

25   Robert Parker, d., 15 Aug. 1818, Shelley MS, 18M51/559; Susan Horner, d.,
     29 Nov. and 1 Dec. 1847, Horner MS; Arnold Bennett, d., 14 Apr. 1910,
     Florentine Journal 1st April – 25th May 1910 (1967), p. 48.

26   'Back Again', *C.J.*, 10 Jan. 1863; [Hodder], *Old Merry's Travels*, p. 143;
     'Excursion to Brittany 147', Torr MS, 57886.

27   R. L. Stevenson, 'The Amateur Emigrant', in *Essays of Travel*, p. 14;
     Matthews, d., 10 Dec. 1817, *Invalid*, I, p. 71; Edward Horsman, d., 26 Aug.
     1828, Horsman MS, D/RA/A/3E/20; Thomas Best, d., 28 Oct., 22 and 27
     Nov., 1 Dec.1858, 5, 6 and 15 Jan., 1,6 and 23 Feb. 1859; 30 Nov. 1858, Best
     MS; G.V. Poore to Marcus Beck, n.d. [May/June 1870], Poore MS, 39M85/
     PC/F28/7; Thomas Best, d., 23 Feb. 1859, Best MS.

28   Matthew Todd, d., 14 Oct. 1814, *Journal*, pp. 53–4.

29   Jerry White, *London in the Nineteenth Century* ... (2007), pp. 48–55;
     Virginia Smith, *Clean: A History of Personal Hygiene* ... (Oxford, 2007),
     pp. 235, 284–9; Virginia Woolf; [Jeanne Schulkind, ed], *Moments of Being*
     (2002), p. 56.

30   Matthews, 3 Dec. 1818, *Invalid*, II, p. 203; Agassiz, *A Journey*, p. 33; T. K.
     Chambers, *A Manual of Diet in Health and Disease* (1875), pp. 171–2; A. C.
     G. Jobert, *The French Pronouncing Hand-Book* ... (1853), p. 50; Wilson,
     Three Weeks' Scamper, p. 259; John Oglander to his wife, 12 Jan. 1899,
     Oglander MS, OB/CC/2004D.

31   Viator, *Cautions*, pp. 13, 35–9.

32   Chambers, *A Manual of Diet*, pp. 171–2.

33   *A Handbook for Travellers in France. Part I* ... (1882), p. [24].

34   Henry Ponsonby to his wife, n.d. [Aug. – Sept. 1868], quoted in Peter
     Arengo-Jones, *Queen Victoria in Switzerland* (1995), p. 74.

35   Viator, *Cautions*, p. 17; [Kemble], *A Year of Consolation*, I, p. 6; Edward
     Lear, *Illustrated Excursions in Italy* (1846), quoted in Hillard, *Six Months*,
     p. 259 n1.

36 Henry James to his mother, 13 Oct. 1869, Percy Lubbock (ed.), *The Letters of Henry James* (1920), p. 23; Quoted in G. M. Young [G.K. Clark, ed], *Portrait of an Age* . . . (1997), pp. 41–2.

37 Wilson, d., 31 Jan. 1847 in *A European Journal*, p. 28; Jerome, *Pilgrimage*, pp. 77–79.

38 Lord Ernle, *From Whippingham to Westminster* (1938), pp. 79–80; David Bogue, *Paris and Its Environs* (1855), p. 62; G. V. Poore to Marcus Beck, 21 May 1870 Poore MS, 39M85/PC/F28/6; Gerald Codrington to his mother, 29 May 1869, Codrington MS, D1610 C112; McManus, *The American Woman Abroad*, p. 304.

39 *A Handbook for Travellers in France. Part I* . . . (1882), p. [24]; Sir Charles Oman, *Memories of Victorian Oxford* (1941), pp. 180–1.

40 Starke, *Information* (1828), p. 442; Baedeker, *Italy . . . Southern Italy and Sicily* (1880), p. xxiv; Baedeker, *Italy* (1903), pp. xxvi xxviii.

41 Anon., 'Back Again', *C.J.*, 10 Jan. 1863; *A Handbook for Travellers in South Germany and Austria: Part II* (1890), p. [40]; Sir Sidney Lee, *King Edward VII* . . ., 2 vols (1925), II, pp. 687–8.

42 W. H. Fox Talbot to Charles Feilding, 23 Jul. 1833 in Fox Talbot MS, Doc. 02725; Shand, *Old-Time Travel*, pp. 151–2; Barrow, *Tour*, p. 107.

43 'Northern Italy,' *F.M.*, (June 1843); Symonds, *Our Life in the Swiss Highlands*, p. 165; Matilda Betham-Edwards, *East of Paris* . . . (1902), ch. 12.

44 Anthony Trollope, *North America*, pp. 480–2.

45 [Hodder], *Old Merry's Travels*, p. 35.

46 These details were taken from the advertisement sections of *A Handbook for Travellers in France: Part I* . . . (1882), pp. [7–69]; *The Times*, 16 Jan. 1890; *Macmillan's Guide to Switzerland*, pp. xv–lvii; W. P. Fetridge, *Harper's Hand-Book for Travellers in Europe and the East* (New York, 1873), I, p. 98 (advertising section), and *A Handbook of Rome and the Campagna* (1899); website of the Conseil Général des Alpes-Maritimes (<www.cg06.fr>); see anon., *The Hotels of Switzerland* (Basle, 1910), *passim*.

47 T. Francis Bumpus, *Summer Holidays among the Glories of France* . . . (1901), pp. 220–1.

48 Havelock Ellis, d., 31 July 1912, *Impressions and Comments* (1914–24) online; McManus, *The American Woman Abroad*, p. 316; Baedeker, *Italy . . .* (1903), pp. vi, xxvi–xxviii.

49 P. I. Tchaikovsky to Nikolai Tchaikovsky, 22 Feb.–6 Mar. 1890, *Letters*, p. 439; quoted in Nicola Beauman, *Morgan: A Biography of E.M. Forster* (1993), p. 107.

50 Chapman-Huston, *Sir James Reckitt*, pp 132–8.

51 Joan Evans, *Prelude & Fugue* . . . (1964), pp. 60–1.

52 McManus, *The American Woman Abroad*. The material used in this and the following two paragraphs is taken from ch. 12.

CHAPTER 9 MEN OF GARLIC – THE TOURIST AND FOOD

1   E. Ernest Bilbrough, *Twixt France and Spain* (1883), pp. 22–3.

2   Viator, *Cautions*, p. 31; H. H. Woods, d., 10 June 1828, Curtis (Woods) MS; 'Back Again', *C.J.*, 10 Jan 1863.

3   Hervé, *How to Enjoy Paris . . . 1842*, p. 3; Trollope, *Vienna*, I, p. 130; Henry Matthews, d, 3 Dec. 1818, *Invalid*, II, pp. 199–200.

4   *Bradshaw's Illustrated Travellers' Hand Book in France* 1857), p. xxiv. J.E. Pollock, 'Considerations on the Climate of Italy', *London Medical Gazette*, 29 Nov. 1850.

5   [R. K. Philp], *The Dictionary of Daily Wants* (1861), p. 192; *The Times*, 10 Apr. 1914; *The* Times, 11 June 1912; Alan Davidson, *The Oxford Companion to Food* (2006), p. 228; John Mayne, d., 31 Jan. 1815, *Journal*, p. 261.

6   *Notes on a Tour*, p. 34, Hill MS; E. H. Barker, *Wanderings by Southern Waters . . .* (1893), pp. 186–7.

7   Jerrold, *Cockaynes*, ch. 4; *The Times*, 10 Oct. 1887; 'A New Sentimental Journey', *B.E.M.*, (Apr. 1847); H. H. Woods, d., 10 June 1827, Curtis (Woods) MS; *Notes on a Tour . . .*, p. 34, Hill MS; Kemble, *A Year of Consolation*, I, p. 43.

8   Torr Family, d., 12 Aug. 1855, Torr MS, 547874.

9   Kathryn Hughes, *The Short Life and Long Times of Mrs Beeton* (2005), pp. 271–3.

10 Agassiz, *A Journey*, p. 40; Francis Pigou, *Phases of My Life* (1898), pp. 21–2; John Mayne, d., 26 Aug. 1814, *Journal*, p 9; Thomas Best, d., 26 Nov. 1858, Best MS; Clarissa Trant, d., 5 April 1815, C. G. Luard (ed.), *The Journal of Clarissa Trant 1800–1832* (1925), p. 54.

11 'The Calabrian Outlaws', *The North of England Magazine* (July 1843); Newnham-Davis and Bastard, *The Gourmet's Guide*, p. 176; *Murray's Modern Cookery Book . . . by a Lady* (1851), p. 381; Matthews, d., 23 Mar. 1818, *Invalid*, I, p. 257; Baedeker, *Italy Handbook for Travellers . . . Southern Italy and Sicily . . .* (1903), p. xxii.

12 Thomas Best, d., 12 Feb. 1859, Best MS; 'Macaroni-Making', *H.W.*, 30 Jan. 1858; Charles MacFarlane, *Popular Customs . . . in the South of Italy* (1846), pp. 9–13.

13 *A Handbook for Travellers in Southern Italy* (1862), p 71; Baedeker, *Italy . . . Southern Italy and Sicily*, p. xxi; Granville Lloyd-Baker to his mother, 1 Apr. 1864, Lloyd-Baker MS.

14 Beadles MS, 3439; Rebecca L. Spang, *The Invention of the Restaurant* (2000), p. 172; Baedeker, *Southern France* (1914), p. xix.

15 Lord William Pitt Lenox, *Fifty Years' Biographical Reminiscences* (1863), p. 302; inserted in Shelley MS, 18M51/560.

16 William Jesse, *The Life of George Brummell . . .*, 2 vols (1855), II, p. 32; *A Handbook for Travellers in France . . . Part I* (1882), p. 26.

17 *Stanford's Paris Guide* (1862), p. 34; *Gailgnani's New Paris Guide for 1853*, p. 14; Granville Lloyd-Baker to his mother, n.d. [1860], Lloyd-Baker MS.

18 Abraham Hayward, *The Art of Dining* (1852), p. 52; 'France and Paris Forty, Thirty, and Twenty Years Ago', *F.M.* (Sept. 1860); Newnham-Davis and Bastard, *The Gourmet's Guide*, pp. 1, 19, 30.

19 Newnham-Davis and Bastard, *The Gourmet's Guide*, p. 89; Bishop Hynes, d., 1 Jan. 1853, Hynes MS; Matthews, 12 Dec 1817, *Invalid*, I.74; E. B. Browning to Henrietta Barrett, [?] 24–30 Apr. 1847, in Philip Kelley and Scott Lewis (eds), *The Brownings' Correspondence* (1984-), XIV, p. 180; *Stanford's Paris Guide* (1862), p. 36.

20 *Official Descriptive and Illustrated Catalogue of the Great Exhibition . . .* (1851), p. 648; Davidson, *Hints to Lady Travellers*, p. 57; Frederick Chamier, *My Travels . . .*, 3 vols (1855), I, pp. 9–12.

21 Lewald, *The Italian Sketch-Book*, pp. 94, 96; Torr Family, d., ? Sept. 1843, Torr MS 57886; Mary Gladstone, d., 31 Dec. 1897, in Lucy Masterman (ed.), *Mary Gladstone . . . Diaries and Letters* (1930), p. 441; Anon [G. G. Moore], *More Society Recollections . . .* (1908), pp. 218–19.

22 Mary Gladstone, d., 29 Sept. 1866, *Diaries*, pp 27–8; Torr Family, d., 28 July 1834, Torr MS, 57884; O. A. Sherrard, d., 29 July 1860, *Two Victorian Girls*, p. 162; Amice Lee, *Laurels & Rosemary: The Life of William and Mary Howitt.* (1955), p. 143.

23 'The East and South of Europe'; *A Handbook for Travellers in South Germany and Austria . . .* (1879), pp. xviii–xix.

24 Anthony Trollope, *The Bertrams* (1859), ch. 6; Malmesbury, *Memoirs of an Ex-Minister*, I, pp. 20–1; E. M. Forster, *A Room With a View* (1908), ch. 1.

25 The Rev George Brett, d., 7 Aug. 1828, Ward, *A Romance*, pp. 54–5; James, *A Little Tour in France*, pp. 111–12; Granville Lloyd-Baker, Tour in Normandy 1884, Lloyd-Baker MS.

26 For a black and white illustration see *The American in Paris or Heath's Picturesque Annual for 1844*; Bogue, *Paris and Its Environs*, p. 14.

27 Emma Austen-Leigh, slip of paper dated 3 June [?1860], Austen-Leigh MS.

28 The Hon. Lionel Tollemache, *Old and Odd Memories* (1908), pp. 242–5; Lina Duff-Gordon to Madge Symonds, 12 July 1892, Waterfield MS.

CHAPTER 10 TRAVELLING IS A VERY TROUBLESOME BUSINESS

1   'The Roving Englishman', *H.W.*, 13 Nov. 1852.
2   James Munson (ed.), *The Sayings of Mark Twain* (1992), p. 62; Edward Peek to Henry Peek, 12 July 1870, Peek Papers, 1405.M.add.3/F2.
3   *Notes of a Tour*, p. 33, Hill MS.
4   Harriet Campbell, d., 29 July 1817; G. R. de Beer (ed.), *A Journey to Florence in 1817* (1951), p. 28; Matthews, d., 10–20 Oct. 1817, *Invalid*, I, p. 45; Kirkland, *Holidays Abroad*, I, p. 120.
5   J. H. Newman to Frederick Bowles, 15 Sept. 1846, W. P. Ward, *The Life of John Henry Newman*, 2 vols (1913), I, pp. 136–7; A. C. G. Jobert, *The French Pronouncing Hand-Book* . . . (1853), p. 146; 'The Roving Englishman', *H.W.*, 13 Nov. 1852; John Murray, *The Handbook of Travel Talk* (1847), pp. 166–8.
6   M. J. Torr, d., 25 Mar. 1872, Torr MS, 57908; Forster, *Charles Dickens*, p. 335.
7   S. M. Ellis (ed.), *A Mid-Victorian Pepys* . . . (1923), pp. 311–12; Hallam Tennyson, *Alfred Lord Tennyson* . . . (1899), pp. 512–13; Munson, *Mark Twain*, p. 62.
8   The Rev John Watson to Mrs. P., 20 Nov. 1889; W. R. Nicoll, *'Ian Maclaren'* . . . (1908), p. 153.
9   Okey, *A Basketful of Memories*, p. 75; Jerome, *Three Men on the Bummel*, ch. 11.
10 'The Roving Englishman', *H.W.*, 13 Nov. 1852; D. T. Holmes, *A Scot in France and Switzerland* (1910), p. 9; Starke, *Information* (1828), p. 442.
11 *A Handbook for Travellers in Switzerland* (1838) p. viii; Thomas Hodgskin, *Travels in the North of Germany*, 2 vols (Edinburgh, 1820), II, p. 510.
12 'The Roving Englishman', *H.W.*, 13 Nov. 1852; Shand, *Old-Time Travel*, p. 52; J. T. Delane to G. W. Dasent, 19 Aug. [1854], in A. I. Dasent, *John Thadeus Delane* . . . (1908), I, pp. 179–80.
13 *Guide to Switzerland* (1904), p. lxxxv; H. M. Veale, d., 7 May 1887, Veale MS.
14 *The History of the Times*, II, pp. 415–17.
15 'A Banker's Daughter', *Guide to the Unprotected* . . . (1864), pp. 62–3; G. F. Brown, *The Recollections of a Bishop* (1915), p. 235.
16 'A Day at the Baths of Lucca,' *C.J.*, 3 Apr. 1852; 'Northern Italy', *F.M.*, (June 1843); J. L. Maquay, Jnr, d., 27 Dec. 1843, 14 Jan. 1847, 1 Jan. 1855, Maquay MS.
17 Starke, *Information* (1826), p. 239; L. C. Dickinson, *Letters from Italy 1850–1853* [n.d. 1914?], pp. 65–71; Norman Gash, *Sir Robert Peel* (1972), pp. 80–2.

18 Bishop Hynes, d., 6 Jan. 1853, Hynes MS; Susan Horner, d., 20 Dec. 1847 and 23 Mar. 1848, Horner MS.

19 J. L. Maquay, Snr, d., 25 Dec. 1815, Maquay MS; Edward Horsman, d., 27 Sept. 1828, Horsman MS, D/RA/A/3E/20; Charlotte Horsman, d., 29 Oct. 1846, Horsman MS, D/RA/A/3E/26; Anon., d., 17 May 1895, Freiburg Visit MS; Anon., d., 10 Sept. 1842, Curtis (Journal) MS; Frances Elliot, *Diary of an Idle Woman in Italy*, 2 vols (New York, n.d.), I, pp. 308–9.

20 *A Handbook for Travellers in Northern Italy* (1852), p. xv.

21 Lady Trevelyan, quoted in John Batchelor, *Lady Trevelyan and the Pre-Raphaelite Brotherhood* (2006), pp. 18–21; Henry Dwight Sedgwick, *Francis Parkman* (Boston, 1904), pp. 103–4; Quoted in J. G. Snead-Cox, *The Life of Cardinal Vaughan*, 2 vols (1910), I, p. 360; Matilda Lucas to ?, 30 Apr. 1875, *Two Englishwomen*, p. 23.

22 A. G. Burnett, *France and the French* . . . (1868), pp. 87–9; Pamela Neville-Sington, *Robert Browning* . . . (2004), p. 76.

23 Gaze, *Paris and How to See It*, p. 37; Cooper, *The Walking Parson*, pp. 150–1.

24 Anon., d., 26 May 1895, Freiburg Visit MS; Biber, *The English Church*, pp. 1–3.

25 Biber, *The English Church*, p. 1 n1.

26 'Switzerland in 1873', *The Catholic World*, (June 1874).

27 Flier for 'Proposed English Church at Grindelwald', 8 July 1869, Chute MS; See <www.staugustines-wiesbaden.de/history1914>.

28 J. L. Maquay, Jnr, d., 17 Feb. 1845, Maquay MS; Sibella Bonham Carter, d., 4 Nov. 1894, Bonham Carter MS, 94M72/F166; 'Proposals and Objections to . . . a New . . . Church at Pau', Dryham Park MS, D1799/Z19.

29 Aunt Louisa [Laura Valentine], *Harry Brightside or the Young Traveller in Italy* (1852), pp. 184–5.

30 *The Times*, 28 Aug. and 3 Sept. 1891.

CHAPTER 11 HEARING FROM HOME

1 Duchess of Somerset to Lady Georgiana Beaufort, 11 Oct. 1839, Codrington MS, D1610 C 111.

2 John Oglander to his wife, n.d. [May or June 1894], Oglander MS, OG/CC/1826; Emily Birchall, d., 3 Feb. 1873, *Wedding Tour*, p. 8.

3 Gerald Codrington to his mother, 26 May–20 Sept, 1869, Codrington MS, D1610 C112.

4 J. B. Scott., d. 7 Oct. 1814, Ethel Mann (ed.), *An Englishman at Home and Abroad* . . . (1930), p. 130; see David Pennant, Jnr to his parents, Feilding MS; Parliamentary Papers, XXXIV (1868–9), Post Office (Foreign Mails),

passim; *The Times*, 31 Aug 1850 and 2 Apr. 1891, 18 July 1892; *Handbook Advertiser*, (May 1900), pp. 4, 26, 28, 31; T. A. Trollope to Richard Bentley, 17 Mar. 1872, quoted in Robert H. Taylor, *Certain Small Works* (Princeton, NJ, 1980), pp. 133–4.

5   *Galignani's New Paris Guide for 1853*, p. 10; E. B. Browning to Henrietta Barrett, 24?-30 Apr. 1847, *The Brownings' Correspondence*, XIV, pp. 176–80; Thackeray to Bradbury and Evans, 10 Jan. 1845, Edgar F Harden (ed.), *The Letters and Private Papers of William Makepeace Thackeray: A Supplement*, 2 vols (1994), I, p. 154; *A Handbook . . . Rome and the Campagna* (1899), pp. 24–5.

6   E. B. Browning to Henrietta Barrett Cook, 7 July 1850 and 2–4 Mar. 1848; Leonard Huxley (ed.), *Elizabeth Barrett Browning: Letters to Her Sister . . .* (1929), pp. 124–5, 76; John Oglander to his wife, 1 Oct. 1897, Oglander MS, OG/CC/1933; Oscar Wilde to Leonard Smithers, n.d., [?1 & ?3 Oct. 1897], Merlin Holland and Rupert Hart-Davis (eds), *The Complete Letters of Oscar Wilde* (2000), pp. 951–2.

7   Henry Labouchere, d., 15 Nov. 1870, *Diary of a Besieged Resident in Paris* (1872) <www.gutenberg.org>, p. 92; Gerald Codrington to his mother, 22 June 1869, Codrington MS D1610 C112; Quoted in W. F. Monypenny and G. E. Buckle, *The Life of Benjamin Disraeli . . .*, 2 vols (1929), I, p. 206; Disraeli to Sarah Disraeli, 4 Nov. [1839], M.G. Wiebe *et al.* (eds), *Benjamin Disraeli Letters: 1838–1841* (1987), p. 227.

8   H. B. [Henry Bateman], *Belgium and Up and Down the Rhine . . .* (1839), pp. 281, 341; *Galignani's Messenger* (23 July 1819).

9   *St-Jean-de-Luz Gazette and Visitors' List: A Weekly Record of Local Events*, 28 Feb. 1903. Authors' Collection.

10 *The Times*, 23 May 1908.

11 Diana Cooper-Richet and Emily Borgeaud, *Galignani* (Paris, 1999), *passim*; 'France and Paris, Forty Years . . .'.

12 *The Echo*, quoted in *The Times*, 31 Aug. 1877.

13 *The Times*, 16 Aug. 1895; R. L. Stevenson to his mother, 28 July 1872, Ernest Mehew (ed.), *Selected Letters of Robert Louis Stevenson* (2001), p. 23.

14 C. H. E. Brookfield, *Random Reminiscences* (n.d. [1902]), pp. 35–6.

15 'The Sketcher in Rhine-Land', *F.M.*, (June 1852).

16 H. W. Williams, *Travels in Italy . . .*, 2 vols (1820, Edinburgh), I, p. 246.

17 P. O. Hutchinson, d., 19 May 1838, Hutchinson MS; C. R. Weld, *A Vacation in Brittany* (1856), pp. 130–1.

18 Lowe, *Unprotected Females*, pp. 40–1; A. J. C. Hare to Miss Duff Gordon, 16 Mar. 1899, Julian Browning Autograph Catalogue (January 2005), <www.jbautographs.com>.

19 *The Times*, 30 Aug. and 17 Nov. 1852; Lord Malmesbury, d., 30 Oct. 1852, *Memoirs of an Ex-Minister*, I, p. 361.

20 Quoted in Taylor, *Views A-Foot*, p. 72.

21 Calvert Jones to Talbot, 29 May 1841 and 29 Apr. 1846, Fox Talbot MS, Doc. LA41–034 & LA 46–054; Effie Ruskin to her mother, 24 Feb. 1850, *Young Mrs. Ruskin*, p. 146.

22 Tupper, *Paterfamilias's Diary*, p. 11; Prof. W[illiam] Pole, 'Photography for Travellers and Tourists', *Macmillan's Magazine* (1862).

23 G. E. Thompson, *Spring at the Italian Lakes* (1892), pp. 143–6.

24 See <www.florin.ms/alinari> to obtain a CD-ROM of these sepia photographs. Gerald Codrington to his mother, 11 Aug. 1869, Codrington MS.

CHAPTER 12 THE HAPPY DAYS BEFORE THE WAR

1 Richard Monckton Milnes, MP, House of Commons, 1 Apr. 1852, *Hansard*, 3rd ser., cxx, 482–4.

2 W. W. Ivory to Flos. Long, 2 Aug., n.d. [4 Aug.] 1914. Passport issued by Grant Duff; '*Sauf-Conduit*', Ivory MS, *n.f.*

3 Marshall, *A Spring Walk in Provence*, pp. ix, 3, 4, 11, 13, 16–17, 21, 33, 34–5, 47, 101, 172.

Index